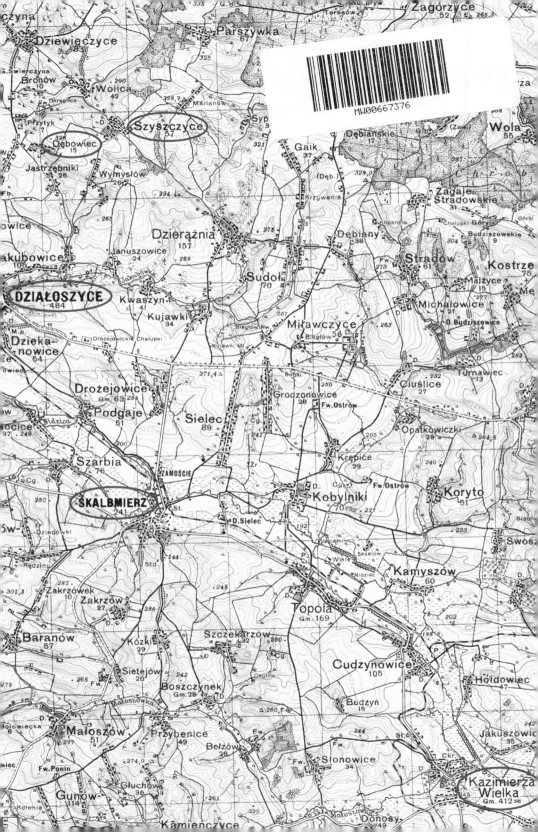

THE UNFINISHED
DIARY
A CHRONICLE OF TEARS

The gripping Holocaust writings of
Chaim Yitzchok Wolgelernter Hy"d

THE UNFINISHED DIARY

A CHRONICLE OF TEARS

ISRAEL BOOKSHOP
Publications

The gripping Holocaust writings of
Chaim Yitzchok Wolgelernter Hy"d

ISBN 978-1-60091-065-4
All Rights Reserved

Library of Congress Control Number: 2015940483

Book & cover design by:

vividesign
SRULY PERL • 845.694.7186
mechelp@gmail.com

Initial translation by Rabbi Avraham Yaakov Finkel
Final translation, editing and research by Mrs. Hindy Mandel
hindymandel@gmail.com

Proofreading by Mrs. E.M. Sonenblick
esonenblick@gmail.com

P. 70-71 map credit: Sir Martin Gilbert/Mrs. Esther Gilbert ©2014

End-leaf 1936/1938 map credit: Wojskowy Instytut Geograficzny-WIG (Polish "Military Institute
of Geography" – 1919-1949), obtained from www.mapywig.org with the help of Marek Zielinski.
Thanks to the Library of Congress, Geography and Map Division: Cynthia Smith, Reference
Specialist; and the United States Holocaust Memorial Museum, Washington, D.C.: Dr. William
F. Meinecke, Jr., Historian; Dr. Pavel Ilyin, Geography Consultant, Registry of Holocaust
Survivors; and Martin Dean, Research Scholar, Center for Advanced Holocaust Studies.

Distributed by:

Israel Bookshop Publications
501 Prospect Street
Lakewood, NJ 08701
Tel: (732) 901-3009
Fax: (732) 901-4012
www.israelbookshoppublications.com
info@israelbookshoppublications.com

Printed in Canada

Distributed in Israel by:
Shanky's
Petach Tikva 16, Jerusalem
972-2-538-6936

Distributed in Europe by:
Lehmanns
Unit E Viking Industrial Park
Rolling Mill Road, Jarrow, Tyne & Wear NE32 3DP
44-191-406-0842

Distributed in Australia by:
Gold's Book and Gift Company
3-13 William Street, Balaclava 3183
613-9527-8775

Distributed in South Africa by:
Kollel Bookshop
Ivy Common, 107 William Road, Norwood
Johannesburg 2192
27-11-728-1822

Alone in the loft of a cowshed I sit,

Enveloped in my double mourning;

Concealed in this hideaway, my soul cries out

And accepts G-d's awesome judgment,

Yisgadal v'yiskadash Shemei rabba — May His great Name be exalted.

Part of a *kinah* (elegy) composed by Chaim Yitzchok Wolgelernter
upon learning of the murder of his parents

בס״ד ד׳ כי תספר באזני בנך כתר״ד לפ״ק

לכב׳ ר׳ פייוועל וואלגעלערנטער שליט״א

ראיתי את העלים ממן על ספר הזכרונות שרשם אביו זצוק״ל בהיות עליו
ימי חרון אף דאזלר וחתם עברו עלינו. הדברים מעוררים את
ואת הרגש ביום גם ואם כי דבר אחד בקום של זכר את
הרשעים אשר התורה צוה אני זכור את אשר עשה לך עמלק,
וגם עם הדברים כלום מאהבת ה׳ ואמונה ה׳.

מה נעים הדברים שוכתבו ספר לדורות ויען
זיין לא ישכחו הדברים בימים הבאים הן הנגלות וכן הנסתרות
וכל זכות עצומה,

דבר זה יהי׳ לזכות ג׳ במשפחה להמשיך בדרך הקדש
לקדש את שם שמים בכל אשר פי עושים ובחייהם
היום יום.

בברכת הצלחה והרבה נחת מכל בני המשפחה

בידידות נאמנה

שמואל קמנצקי

BS"D Wednesday of the Torah portion "...so that you may tell your children," 5774

To the honorable R' Feivel Wolgelernter, *shlit"a*

I have seen the diary pages that [your] father *ztvk"l* recorded as he lived through the years of wrath that passed over us. The work inspires many varied emotions. On the one hand, it is a fulfillment of [the requirement to] remember the actions of the evildoers, as the Torah commanded, "Remember what Amalek did to you...." At the same time, the words are full of love for Hashem and belief in Him.

How vital it is, indeed, that these words be transcribed for posterity so that they not be forgotten – the revealed miracles as well as the hidden ones – by future generations.

This will especially be a *zechus* for the whole family to continue in their holy work, doing all that is in their power to be *mekadesh Shem Shamayim* (sanctify G-d's Name) in their spiritual endeavors and in their daily lives.

With blessings for success and much *nachas* from all members of the family,

In faithful friendship,

[Rabbi] Shmuel Kamenetsky

ISRAEL MEIR LAU
CHIEF RABBI
TEL-AVIV-JAFFA, ISRAEL

ישראל מאיר לאו
הרב הראשי
תל-אביב-יפו, ישראל

בס"ד, ב' באייר תשע"ה
21 באפריל 2015

שלום וברכה,

קבלתי בתודה עותק מהספר "היומן שלא הסתיים – כרוניקה של דמעות", שנכתב ע"י הקדוש חיים יצחק וולגלרנטר הי"ד בשנות השואה האיומות.

מפאת צוק העיתים והשפה הזרה לא עלה בידי לקרוא את הספר, אולם מהמעט שראיתי התרשמתי שמדובר ביומן בעל ערך רב, אשר נכתב בזמן אמת, ומתעד את הזוועות כמות שהם ללא כחל וסרק.

ספר זה חשוב הוא מאין כמותו, לקיים בו מצוות "זכור את אשר עשה לך עמלק ... לא תשכח", לזכור ולא לשכוח את אשר עוללו הרשעים לבני עמנו, מלבד זאת שיש בו משום קיום צוואת הקדושים הי"ד לזכור ולהזכיר לעולם קבל עם ועולם.

ככל שנוקפות השנים ומתמעטים אותם אודים מוצלי אש החיים עדיין בינינו, אשר לעולם לא ישכחו את אירועי אותם הימים, עולה וגוברת חשיבות הוצאת ספר זה ושכמותו.

אני שב ומודה לך על הספר, חזק ואמץ.

בכבוד רב,

הרב ישראל מאיר לאו

לשכה: רח' אורי, 1, ת.ד. 9, תל-אביב-יפו 61000 - טל' 03-6938911 פקס: 03-6938912
OFFICE: 1, URI ST., P.O.B. 9, TEL-AVIV-JAFFA, 61000, ISRAEL - TEL: +972-3-6938911, FAX: +972-3-6938912
דוא"ל: e-mail: lau@rabanut.co.il

BS"D
2 Iyar 5775
April 21, 2015

Shalom u'vrachah,

I received, with thanks, a copy of the book *The Unfinished Diary: A Chronicle of Tears* authored by the *kadosh* Chaim Yitzchok Wolgelernter *Hy"d* during the frightful years of the Holocaust.

Due to time constraints and the foreign language, I was unable to read the book. However, from the little that I was able to see, I realized that we are speaking about a very valuable diary, written at a time of truth, and depicting the tragedy "as is," without exaggerating or deviating from the facts.

This book is unparalleled in its importance, to fulfill by it the commandment of "Remember what Amalek did to you.... Do not forget!" To remember, and never forget, what the *resha'im* did to our nation. Besides for this, it is a fulfillment of the last will and testimony of the *kedoshim Hy"d*, to remember and to remind the world [of what occurred].

As the years pass and the number of survivors saved from the fire – who will never forget the events of those days – dwindles among us, it is all the more important to publish a book like this, and similar volumes.

I thank you again for the book, *chazak v'ematz.*

Rabbi Israel Meir Lau
Chief Rabbi, Tel Aviv-Jaffa

Praise for The Unfinished Diary[1]

True to its name, *The Unfinished Diary: A Chronicle of Tears, The Gripping Holocaust Writings of Chaim Yitzchok Wolgelernter Hy"d* is indeed a chronicle of tears depicting the struggle of a religious Jew and his family to survive the bitter years of the war. We read of the nobility of men and women who offer shelter and a haven, and of the resourcefulness of Jews who survive day by day, event by event, miracle by miracle. We read of the cruelty of other men and women: German oppressors, unrelenting in their pursuit of Jews to the very last one, are joined by Poles – neighbors and fellow countrymen – who exploit the desperation of Jews and empower the oppressor by their indifference, even when they do not directly assist him in his mission. Danger lurks at every moment, with every knock at the door, with every request for food and shelter, with every encounter with a stranger.

One is moved time and again by the strength of faith displayed throughout, the fidelity to Hashem and His commandments but also righteous anger and anguish. Such were the struggles of the believer; such was the anguish of that time and of that world.

One witnesses everything in the extreme in this important diary: cruelty and compassion, the faith of the believer and even the intense fanaticism of the oppressor that enabled him to be so evil. *The Unfinished Diary* is a powerful, painful work to read, one that will stay with the reader long after the last page is turned.

— Dr. Michael Berenbaum
Holocaust scholar
Author, co-author, and editor of twenty books
Project director of the United States Holocaust Memorial Museum (1988-1993)
and director of its Holocaust Research Institute (1993-1997)
Senior Consultant, Kleinman Family Holocaust Education Center

A memoir written while the tragedy of the Holocaust was actually taking place…one of very few such memoirs written by an Orthodox Jew. Its remarkable author maintained his sense of Divine purpose and self-worth through courageous acts of kindness and continued religious observance. He repeatedly put himself at great risk to help family and friends who were hiding with him in an unimaginably hostile environment. He was sustained by his great love for others, as well as his abiding faith in G-d…. The memoir is further enriched by the author's unflinching integrity and his willingness to see the events he was living through in all their historical complexity.

— Menachem Daum, PhD
Creator of Award-winning Documentary Film on Dzialoszyce
Project coordinator for Dzialoszyce Yizkor book translation

---

1. In alphabetical order

This diary is one-of-a-kind. It is the story of a young *talmid chacham*, suffused with Torah, who wrote with rare literary skill, bringing to life vivid imagery and raw emotion from two years of suffering that failed to extinguish the fire in his soul. Moreover, this is the story of a family, one of many like it, that carried with it upon its difficult journey a core of Jewish values, faith, *mesirus nefesh*, and trust in Hashem.

From the story of the individual emerges the story of the many — the family, the community, the Jewish nation as a whole.

It would be worthy that the *kinos* written by the author be included in the Book of Kinos, so that generations to come should know how great was the suffering — and how great was the *emunah*.

— Rebbetzin Esther Farbstein
Director, Holocaust Research Center, Michlalah-Jerusalem College
Author of *Hidden in Thunder*, *The Forgotten Memoirs*, and *Hidden in the Heights*

This is a riveting and deeply moving journal that brings the reader directly into the lives of those brave Jews who lived and died during the Shoah. Vivid, insightful, graphic, and perceptive, *The Unfinished Diary* should be required reading for everyone.

— Rabbi Emanuel Feldman
Rabbi Emeritus, Cong. Beth Jacob, Atlanta, GA
Former editor-in-chief of *Tradition Magazine*
Author of ten books

It is imperative that we convey the lessons of the Holocaust to future generations. *The Unfinished Diary: A Chronicle of Tears*, by Chaim Yitzchok Wolgelernter, vividly describes a world that was lost, as well as how its embers reignited and built the world we merit to know today.

I look forward to this book's publication and am confident of its positive impact on students and adults alike.

— Rabbi Sholom Friedmann
Director, Kleinman Family Holocaust Education Center (KFHEC)

It is truly astounding that seventy years after the war new voices of Holocaust victims can still reach and stir us deeply, as if we heard the story for the first time. The diary of Rabbi Chaim Wolgelernter — beautifully written and deliberately crafted by the author himself as a testimony that the world must hear — promises to become an instant classic of the genre. A deeply religious man with a prodigious memory, Wolgelernter left a manuscript in Yiddish that his surviving son and other family members considered a legacy that must be brought into public domain, for all to know what happened to the Jewish community

of Dzialoszyce – a small town, like many others in wartime Eastern Europe. We owe the author and the dedicated editors a deep debt of gratitude.

— Jan Gross
Professor of History, Princeton University
Author of several books on the Holocaust in Poland including
Neighbors (2001), *Fear* (2006) and *Golden Harvest* (2011)

I have read the book…and found it very powerful…how people in their last few hours… expressed their thoughts…of *emunah* and *kedushah*. [And] how survival was almost impossible even when a person had escaped the initial net which the Nazis had drawn around the towns and *shtetlech*…

— Rabbi Aubrey Hersh
Historian, Senior Lecturer at JLE (Jewish Learning Exchange) – London

…The impact of this monumental diary being written as a current chronicle – bringing the events to life – is immense. We…hold such resources at a premium. Best wishes for success in bringing the vital messages of endurance and *emunah* to Jewish readers.

— Rabbi Shmuel Yaakov Klein
Director, Zechor Yemos Olam, Torah Umesorah

This book is important because it presents a vivid human face to the Holocaust, focusing on the response of an Orthodox family to their challenges during that time.

Audiences of different age and reading levels will relate to and be inspired by the various members of the family who serve as the vehicle to relate events of the Holocaust.

— Ruth Lichtenstein
Publisher, *Hamodia*
Director, Project Witness

Read this book and feel the pain, appreciate the faith, and understand why we refer to victims of the Nazi Holocaust as *kedoshim*. So heartrendingly sad you want to stop reading, so gripping that you can't. The words jump off the page, infused with spirit, blood and tears. The sadness overwhelms you, along with the majesty of the Jewish people; from [the author's] writing, you perceive the tragedy of the entire Jewish exile and specifically the Holocaust, but at the same time the greatness of the eternal people is evident as well.

— Rabbi Pinchos Lipschutz
Yated Ne'eman

The Unfinished Diary is an extraordinary document in the annals of Holocaust literature, an Orthodox rabbi's unique eyewitness account of the *churban* as it was actually unfolding…

[it] reveals shocking new details about Poles and the Holocaust.

— **Dr. Rafael Medoff**
Ami Magazine, May 2015

[*The Unfinished Diary*] is fascinating and unbelievable; a real treasure. I had a hard time putting it down. This is a MUST READ for everybody and a real lesson in *emunah* for all!!!

— **Peter (Avrohom) Rebenwurzel**
Chairman, Raoul Wallenberg Centennial Celebration Commission

I have read the book manuscript with great appreciation. The translation of R. Chaim Yitzhak Wolgelernter's diary promises to make a special, distinguished contribution to the literature of the Holocaust. Written with breathtaking sensitivity by a chassidic Polish Jew, there is almost nothing like it. By means of the author's powerful, careful prose, we are privileged to see from an insider's view the terrible events he and his family experienced.

I will recommend the diary as necessary reading for any Jew – indeed, for any student of this tragic period.

— **Dr. Avraham (Alan) Rosen**
Scholar of Holocaust literature

Three-quarters of a century after the cataclysm of the Holocaust, a captivating voice emerges in the eloquent, heart-wrenching Yiddish diary of Rabbi Chaim Yitzchok Wolgelernter, painstakingly translated from its original.

Rabbi Chaim Yitzchok Wolgelernter did not survive the war. But his son has rescued his father's words from the devastation, ensuring that this legacy from the past will remain a treasure for the future.

— **Rabbi Avi Shafran**
Noted author and Director of Public Affairs, Agudath Israel of America

The Unfinished Diary occupies an important position among the proliferation of Holocaust literature that has been published, for three reasons: A) Its author was a *talmid chacham* of note and a *yerei Shamayim*. His outlook is one of pure *emunah*. B) The diary was penned as the events occurred, at the height of the years 1942-1944, thus expressing the immediacy of the suffering. C) [It includes] the amazing narrative of how the diary was saved, and eventually translated, as well as the discovery of the unmarked family grave and the reburial in Jerusalem.

— **Rabbi Meir Wunder**
Historian and author of *Encyclopedia of Chachmei Galicia*

Table of Contents

BOOK TWO:

Publisher's Note

WITHIN THE GENRE OF HOLOCAUST LITERATURE, a wartime diary is in a class of its own: a voice calling out to us with immediacy and urgency from the midst of the inferno.

Recorded in Yiddish seven decades ago, the diary of Rabbi Chaim Yitzchok Wolgelernter is the work of an Orthodox, chassidic Jew, a brilliant Torah scholar who was a rare recipient of a *heter horaah* (rabbinical ordination) from the legendary Ostrovtzer Rebbe.

Descended from several illustrious authors of commentaries on the Torah, Chaim Yitzchok demonstrated a propensity for the written word from his early youth. As a young yeshivah student, he was the editor of *Beis Meir*, the monthly Torah journal of the Ostrovtze Yeshivah. Fluent in Yiddish, Lashon Kodesh, and Polish, it was only natural that he later turned to his pen as a means of endurance. In a letter to his wife in the winter of 1944 just months before he was slain, Chaim Yitzchok Wolgelernter wrote, *If G-d helps us and we survive, I aspire to take a place in the literary world. This is only thanks to the war. I would have gladly given up this career and kept my old one...*

Comprising some 140 pages of tiny, penciled handwriting, this diary is not only a writer's chronicle of suffering and tragedy but also a philosophical masterpiece replete with Talmudical references and Scriptural verses.[1] It is a portrait of a Jew grappling with the

---

1. Referring to the Ostrovtze chapters [see Appendix C] submitted by Dovid Wolgelernter to the Jewish Historical Institute shortly after the war, Professor Daniel Grinberg, former

incomprehensible, cataclysmic events engulfing him and his people, yet clinging to G-d and finding solace in the Torah. The author's often-witty style reveals the characteristically Jewish ability to discern the comical and the humorous even within misery itself. "Under duress and deprivation, Chaim Yitzchok's sharp mind did not deteriorate but continued to flow like a spring of fresh water," remembered his brother Dovid Wolgelernter.

An unusual aspect of this diary is its structure as a memoir rather than a daily log. The diarist used his time in hiding between September 1942 and June 1944 to fashion and edit over fifty chapters, each with a carefully designed title listed in his handwritten table of contents.

Predominantly in present tense, the manuscript is written from an eyewitness perspective, even when the author himself was clearly not present. A spirited man of courage, Chaim Yitzchok took great risks, leaving his hideout and traveling under extreme duress and danger to determine the whereabouts and come to the aid of various family members. During these ventures, he gleaned information from other Jews or from Polish acquaintances, which, along with his keen psychological insight, enabled him to reconstruct prior and concurrent scenes with precise detail. It is evident that he intended to preserve these events for posterity.[2] Indeed, the author's documentation of the extinction of his hometown, just one of the

---

director of the Institute (1990-1995), writes: "The authors [of the many unpublished personal accounts submitted to the JHI in the first years after the war] represent a wide array of professions and livelihoods... Numerous memoirs were, however, written by simple men of limited outlook and comprehension. All of them fought the day-by-day struggle amid inhuman conditions to survive for a little while longer. Izak Wolgelernter, hidden for over two years in a barn by Polish peasants, was a learned rabbi from Ostrowiec...who left a sublime philosophical treatise in Yiddish..." [*Holocaust Chronicles: Individualizing the Holocaust through Diaries and Other Contemporaneous Personal Accounts*, KTAV Publishing House, 1999].

2. See author's letters, p. 404 and p. 467, in which he refers to the diary as "my Book of Tears."

many flourishing Jewish communities that were destroyed, serves as a formidable response to the propagators of Holocaust denial in our time.

Another distinctive feature is the poignant collection of Hebrew-language acrostic elegies composed by the author each time he learned of the tragic deaths of those who were dear to him, most noteworthy of which is his now famous *kinah* on the Ostrovtzer Rebbe, Rabbi Yechezkel Halstuk *Hy"d*.

The diary of Chaim Yitzchok Wolgelernter powerfully depicts the daunting challenges of those individuals and families who tried desperately to escape the collective fate of European Jewry. It is a compelling record of selflessness and family loyalty, of relentless perseverance and faith, of the remarkable heroism and spiritual resistance exhibited by the victims of the Holocaust.

Mrs. Hindy Mandel
ISRAEL BOOKSHOP PUBLICATIONS

I wish to praise and thank the *Ribono shel Olam* for sending R' Feivel Wolgelernter to me in the spring of 2008 with the diary of his father *Hy"d*. It is a rare privilege and duty to bring a book like this to light and to preserve it for posterity.

Our entire staff dedicated themselves to this important project wholeheartedly. I would like to point out the single-minded determination and dedication of Mrs. Hindy Mandel, Editor-in-Chief of this volume. Originally tasked with performing a simple edit of the manuscript, she recognized the need to go back to the sources and ascertain the sometimes unclear meaning of words, places, or events. The spectacular result was *over six years* of intense effort and meticulous, expert research, together with Mr. Wolgelernter and his son Nafti (who began this work decades ago). This labor of love and beyond-the-call devotion to truth and historical accuracy has brought forth the literary masterpiece that you now hold in your hands.

Moshe Kaufman
ISRAEL BOOKSHOP PUBLICATIONS

Foreword

By Feivel Wolgelernter

IT WAS NOTHING SHORT OF A MIRACLE that I lived through the war years. Born in Poland in 1941, I am a member of the relatively rare class of child survivors of the Holocaust. Despite suffering lifelong effects, most of us cannot fully recall or formulate our experiences.

For me, who was separated from my father when I was twenty-one months old and orphaned at the age of three, the diary is a bridge to his heart and soul — which I bequeath herewith as an eternal legacy to my children and their descendants, linking them to a grandfather they never knew.

Through his heartrending chronicle, they will learn of the large, blossoming Wolgelernter/Platkiewicz family tree that was nearly uprooted, leaving a gaping void of grandparents, aunts, uncles, and cousins on my side. They, and I myself, will emerge with renewed appreciation for the revival and continuity of our family — and the Jewish nation as a whole.

They will hear of the enduring faith of their forebears, who triumphed over incomprehensible suffering as they maintained a constant connection to the *Ribono shel Olam*, calling out to Him in prayer and supplication; studying whatever Torah volumes they found in hiding; keeping kashrus despite a meager supply of food; noting the dates so they could commemorate the Yamim Tovim; weighing difficult decisions through a halachic perspective; and risking their lives to help one another.

The publication of this diary also fulfills a longstanding debt.

I owe it to my many relatives, friends and acquaintances who over the years expressed an avid interest in the history of my family and urged me to publish my father's manuscript.

I owe it to those who themselves experienced — and survived — the events recorded in the diary but unfortunately passed on before they could see it in print. To my Uncle Dovid Wolgelernter *z"l* and my cousin Feivel Erlich *z"l*, who set out to prepare a new refuge for the group, only to discover that the two of them had become lone remnants. To my cousin Helenka (Chayele Erlich) Dresner *a"h*, who, while living in Warsaw with Aryan papers, arranged for the family's gold coins to be exchanged for currency, which she or her younger sister Esther'l *Hy"d* delivered to the group. To Avraham Fuhrman *z"l*, the partisan who visited my father in his Debowiec hideout and was instrumental decades later in the discovery of the burial place of our slain family members. And finally, to our dear friends, Dzialoszycers Chaim Pomeranz *z"l*, his sister Lola Kiven *a"h*, and Kalmish Epstein *z"l*, son of Rav Eliezer Epstein *Hy"d*.

Above all, I owe this book to my parents.

To my dear stepfather, R' Yisroel Mordechai Finkelstein *z"l*, who felt humbled and privileged to take care of my mother and myself.

To my dear mother *a"h*, who parted from her husband and all her loved ones and traveled with me, in the guise of gentiles, into the unknown so that I might live.

And lastly, with the publication of this diary, I fulfill the will of my father, may Hashem avenge his blood, who desired to disseminate his writings to the world so that the millions of *kedoshim* would not be forgotten.

Feivel Wolgelernter
Zurich, Switzerland

Seventy Years: The Journey of My Father's Diary

By Feivel Wolgelernter

GROWING UP, I CAME TO KNOW my father through my mother's reminiscences: A brilliant *talmid chacham* descended from illustrious lineage ... a noted disciple of the Ostrovtzer Rebbe *Hy"d* ... a worldly and wise, warm and kindhearted man, distinguished both in his physical stature and by his standing in the community.

As a child, looking through my mother's box of pictures one day, I came upon a photo of a heap of papers atop an old chair. It was my first encounter with my father's diary.

How the diary outlived its author was never established with certainty,

Diary pages on a chair in Gleiwitz, 1946

but in all probability, my uncle Dovid Wolgelernter carried the pages in his rucksack when he set out in advance of the group's planned transfer to a new refuge in June of 1944.

After liberation, Dovid Wolgelernter guarded his slain brother's written legacy with his heart and soul, taking it with him when he left Europe for Canada in 1947.[3] The diary remained in his possession and continued to be a focal point in his life: he attempted to assuage his grief by reading it and rereading it, even rewriting parts of it in his own hand. In an attempt to have it published, he sent the original Yiddish manuscript to the well-known author and journalist Menashe Unger in New York. Unfortunately, it was lost,[4] and my uncle despaired of putting in further effort.

He did succeed, however, in publicizing the existence of the diary, submitting parts of it, along with several articles about the group's experiences, to the Yiddish-language newspapers and journals of the postwar period — the *Daily Hebrew Journal* of Toronto, *Der Tag Morgen Journal*, *Unzer Veg*, and *The Forward*. He also contributed two diary chapters and a chapter of his own authorship to the *Sefer Yizkor shel Kehillat Dzialoszyce V'hasevivah*, published in Israel in 1973. As early as 1950, the *kinah* of Chaim Yitzchok Wolgelernter on the Ostrovtzer Rebbe *Hy"d* gained renown when it was printed in *Meir Einei Chachamim*, a *sefer* preserving the Ostrovtze legacy, and thereafter in several other *sefarim*.[5]

---

3. Shortly after the war, while still in Poland, Dovid Wolgelernter submitted the Ostrovtze chapters [see Appendix C] as well as a notebook containing a Hebrew-language synopsis of the diary [see Introduction] to the Jewish Historical Institute of Warsaw. A copy of these materials may be found in the Institute archives [sign. 302\46].

4. Ed. Note: Whether the lost manuscript was a copy rewritten in Dovid Wolgelernter's hand or a second, edited version written by the diarist himself remains unclear.

5. See Appendix C

▶ *Daily Hebrew Journal* of Toronto, December 1, 1948

▲

Der Tag Morgen Journal, October 13, 1963

▶ *Unzer Veg,* 1963

It wasn't until I was twenty-three years old — a full two decades after its final chapter was penned — that I took possession of my father's diary. Uncle Dovid bequeathed it to me in 1964 on the occasion of my wedding, with the hope that I would publish the work.

Minuscule Yiddish writing filled both sides of some seventy pages of various types of paper, mostly 14x20 cm (5.5x8 in.), beginning to yellow and disintegrate with age.

Cover of notebook

In addition, a bound notebook, addressed to Uncle Avraham in Toronto, contained an eight-page Hebrew-language chronicle and a collection of acrostic *kinos.*

Thankfully, I treated the pages with a protective spray to prevent further deterioration. But unfortunately, I tucked the diary into a drawer, where it lay untouched for the next twenty-four years. I could not read the cramped, penciled handwriting, and disappointed my uncle by failing to fulfill his wish.

As I raised my children, I would occasionally share my childhood recollections and point to the diary in the drawer. From an early

age, my son Nafti was most passionately interested in knowing his roots and understanding the sad saga of our family during the Holocaust.

In 1988, as an eighteen-year-old student in the Philadelphia Yeshivah, Nafti resolved to do what I should have done myself: to prepare the manuscript for publication. I carefully photocopied all the pages for him — I never let anyone handle the originals — and, notwithstanding the diminished quality of the copies, he began to read.

Two obstacles immediately became apparent. The text, crowded onto the page and written in a Polish-Yiddish dialect, was difficult to make out. What's more, the unbound pages were neither numbered nor dated. And although there was a table of contents listing fifty chapter titles, these titles were not recorded on the corresponding diary pages. Thus, the diary was a hodgepodge of written material.

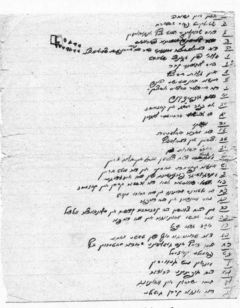

Original, handwritten table of contents

Upon the suggestion of his *rebbi* Rav Yitzchok Perman, himself a Wolgelernter descendant, Nafti sent the photocopies to three Yiddish handwriting experts in New York, who laboriously transcribed the sentences and paragraphs in their own hand.

The transcription, including a number of difficult pages that Nafti rewrote himself, was later typed on a borrowed PC and stored on a

diskette. Still, each page remained a disconnected entity, rife with errors and omissions.

During *bein hazmanim* of 1990, Nafti flew to Toronto to work with Uncle Dovid. The trip yielded a rudimentary understanding of the diary, with large sections rewritten in Uncle Dovid's hand.

In 1991, after Nafti married and settled in Eretz Yisrael, he redoubled his efforts, enlisting the aid of his wife's cousin Ephraim Wolodarsky. Together they compared the photocopied originals to the typed text and to Uncle Dovid's version, line by line. Consequently, Nafti became thoroughly versed in his grandfather's handwriting and diction.

My cousin Feivel Erlich shared his personal memories, and native Dzialoszycer Chaim Pomeranz visited every few weeks, defining old Yiddish terms and Polish words. Nafti contacted and questioned other Dzialoszyce survivors and attended their yearly gatherings. Naturally, he turned to my mother for help as well, showing her portions of the diary, but this proved too painful for her.

Despite these painstaking efforts, the chronology of events and corresponding allocation of the fifty-some chapters remained unclear.

In 1992, Nafti traveled to Toronto again. For two intense weeks, my elderly uncle poured out his anguished memories to his young great-nephew. He deciphered unclear words and passages in the diary, and finalized his handwritten, Yiddish-language Epilogue. Combing through his memorabilia, Uncle Dovid found several additional diary chapters. At last, the pages were pieced together in their proper progression!

After Nafti returned home, he continued to perfect the transcription with a newfound grasp of the diary. His labor of love reached a climax when his research culminated in the discovery that

the burial place of our murdered family members was known, resulting in our expedition to Poland shortly after Pesach of 1993.[6]

This monumental event opened the floodgates of my mother's memories. My eldest son Chaim Yitzchok encouraged her to share her experiences, which he recorded on several cassettes. These form the basis of the *Survival and Renewal* section in Book Two.

Listening to the tapes broadened my appreciation of my family history and my parents' sacrifices and suffering during the war, which further spurred me to proceed with the goal of publishing my father's diary.

Only after I sold my business and retired, however, did I begin to devote serious attention to that which Nafti had dedicated most of his spare time for a full decade.

The next stage in the preparation of this book involved the cumulative efforts of a number of people.

In 2005, I engaged the services of the noted translator Rabbi Avraham Yaakov Finkel, a Holocaust survivor whose fluency in four languages enabled him to translate the Yiddish text, Hebrew poems, and parts of the book that Nafti and I authored in German. It took two years to produce the initial English-language draft.

At that time, I brought the original diary pages with me from Switzerland to Israel, where Rabbi Avraham Krieger, founder of the Shem Olam Institute of Holocaust Studies, scanned each one on high-quality equipment in his Kfar Haroeh office. This allowed the diary to be read in its original form, preserving it for posterity.

I then approached various publishing companies. R' Moshe Kaufman, director of Israel Bookshop Publications, perceived the historic value and uniqueness of this manuscript and undertook the

---

6. See Postscript: *Finding the Family Grave*

multi-faceted responsibilities involved in presenting this work to the public.

Mrs. Hindy Mandel was engaged as the project editor. The eldest grandchild of Holocaust survivors, she was passionate in her aim to preserve the authentic voice of the diarist. Poring over the computer scans of the handwritten diary pages, she immersed herself in the nuances and tone of my father's writing, ensuring that the English-language text captured the poignancy and wit of the Yiddish original as accurately as possible. Due to the nature of this diary as an eyewitness testimony, all of the myriad historical facts and terminology recorded in Yiddish required impeccable research, which was footnoted as necessary. The names of the nearly sixty towns and villages and the numerous people mentioned in the diary were properly transliterated from the Yiddish, using maps of Poland, Holocaust databases and genealogical sources.[7] All Torah citations were verified. Hundreds of hours of phone conversations between us, in consultation with Nafti, illuminated hitherto misinterpreted portions of the narrative.

It is only due to these collaborative, herculean efforts that this diary, written seven decades ago, has finally seen the light of day.

⁜

Mention must be made of my longtime former colleague Marek Schmidt, a native of Poland, for his help in all matters Polish-language related. He obtained and translated family documents from the Polish Bureau of Records, and wrote for official permission

---

7. The 1929 Dzialoszyce Business Directory, Kielce-Radom SIG Journal at www.jri-poland.org; the Central Database of Shoah Victims' Names at www.yadvashem.org; the Holocaust Survivors and Victims Database at www.ushmm.org; The JewishGen Gazetteer at www.jewishgen.org; the Virtual Shtetl at www.sztetl.org.pl/en; the Yivo Institute for Jewish Research at www.yivoinstitute.org; *Where Once We Walked: A Guide to the Jewish Communities Destroyed in the Holocaust*, Gary Mokotoff and Sallyann Amdur Sack with Alexander Sharon, Avotaynu, 2002.

to exhume the grave of my family. It should be noted that during the war, his aunt Jaroslawa Wolosianska saved the lives of dozens of Jews, for which she was later recognized as a Righteous Gentile by Yad Vashem.

My thanks to Klara Carmely, daughter of our dear family friend Chaim Pomeranz, who reviewed the initial English-language draft and offered many constructive suggestions.

Credit is due to my son-in-law Rabbi Ezra Bloch, a noted *talmid chacham* and editor, who assisted with the research and translation of Torah sources.

Mrs. Esther Gilbert, widow of the late Sir Martin Gilbert, took an interest in this project and used her experience in cartography and Holocaust history to draw the maps found in the prologue section.

Hagaon Rav Shmuel Kamenetsky, Rosh Yeshivah of the Philadelphia Yeshivah, where my sons studied, graciously agreed to read the manuscript, especially as his father, Hagaon Rav Yaakov Kamenetsky *zt"l*, had a close relationship with two of my father's cousins, Rav Sholom Pinchas and Rav Yaakov Yitzchok Wohlgelernter.

I extend my appreciation to Israel Bookshop Publications for shepherding this project from beginning to end. Mrs. Malkie Gendelman served as editorial consultant, offering ongoing, indispensable advice. Mrs. Elky Langer reviewed the manuscript and submitted helpful input. Mrs. Esther Malky Sonenblick meticulously proofread the final text, efficiently tied up the manifold, longstanding loose ends, and readied the manuscript for layout. Mrs. Liron Delmar oversaw the entire publication process, lending her considerable technical expertise. Under the artistic eye of graphics designer Mr. Sruly Perl, the book has been transformed into a masterful creation.

I am deeply indebted to my wife Rachel for encouraging me and our son Nafti to undertake the enormous task of bringing this work to publication, and for creating the atmosphere at home that made it possible all these years. Above all, I offer my humble gratitude to the *Ribono shel Olam* — *Who has kept us alive and sustained us and brought us to this time* — for granting me the merit of seeing my children and grandchildren walk in my father's footsteps.

BOOK ONE

Prologue

By Nafti Wolgelernter

LOST IN THOUGHT, WE STROLL through the streets, passing many abandoned houses, overgrown backyards, men loitering in front of closed shops. There are only 1700 inhabitants in this town. The place gives a run-down, depressed, almost lifeless impression.

Dzialoszyce, April 1993 — *Judenrein* by the Nazis since 1942; cleansed forever by its own Polish inhabitants through the pogrom of 1945.

Rising starkly before us is a large, once magnificent shul building in ruins. A deteriorating *beis medrash* stands next to it. Mute witnesses of truth.

We continue past the deserted market square, and arrive at the Platkiewicz family home.

Standing there, I am overcome with emotion.

So this is where my great-grandmother Yachet'l Platkiewicz conducted her chessed empire. Here is where my Oma Chayele was born and raised. Here my grandparents spent their few happy years together. This is where my father was born.

Adas Yisroel synagogue, Dzialoszyce, Poland, 1993

Beis medrash adjacent to shul, 1993

Oma's thoughts never left this place. It was the focal point of the many tales she and Chaim Pomeranz, our dear family friend, told me over the years.

I never knew my grandfather; my father himself could not remember him. But his picture hangs on my wall. Tears spring to my eyes whenever I look at it. Grandfather, Grandmother, and their sweet little daughter. Proud young parents, radiating pure family happiness.

Nafti Wolgelernter in front of the Platkiewicz family apartments and shop, Dzialoszyce, 1993

From time to time, my father would show me his father's white *kittel*; the gold pocket watch his father received as a *chassan*; and a stack of yellowed pages, filled with tiny handwriting. His father's diary of the war years.

What do those pages tell us?

What happened to Grandfather?

Where is his grave?

I had so many questions. No one seemed to be able to give me precise answers. Oma could not speak; she always began to cry. I was missing a part of my roots, a piece of my identity.

As far back as I can remember, I was determined to do everything possible to lift the shroud of secrecy and resolve my questions.

And now I stood, together with my father and brother, in front of the family home in Dzialoszyce, stunned, frozen in place.

History became reality.

Dzialoszyce in the Interwar Period[1]

Less than fifty kilometers (thirty miles) northeast of Krakow, among the hamlets and villages that dot the Polish countryside, there once was a vibrant town of close to nine thousand inhabitants. In simple but charming two-story, attached houses, amidst colorful gardens, trees, and grassy fields, lived some seven thousand Jews — 80 percent of the populace — and two thousand Poles.[2]

Dzialoszyce (pron. *Dzialoshitz*), the governing seat of its *gmina* (administrative district), was a bustling center of commerce, the hub of the region. Hundreds of farmers, merchants, and peasants from the surrounding area regularly rode into town on horse-drawn carts or by *kolejka*, the narrow-gauge railroad that wound its way through the countryside.

---

1. Based primarily on the recollections of my grandmother Chayele [Wolgelernter] Finkelstein, my great-uncle Dovid Wolgelernter, cousin Feivel Erlich, Chaim Pomeranz and other former Dzialoszycers.

2. Individual Jews began to arrive in Dzialoszyce, then a tiny, fledgling village, during the sixteenth century (possibly even as early as the fourteenth century during the reign of Casimir the Great when a wave of Jews migrated to Poland). Increasing numbers of Jews began to settle there after the landowner granted rights to Jews in 1707. By the mid-eighteenth century, Jews constituted a majority of the population, and thereafter Dzialoszyce rapidly grew to become a large, overwhelmingly Jewish town and a center of trade and manufacturing. Construction of a large, magnificent synagogue building was completed in 1856. The latter half of the nineteenth century also saw construction of a Jewish hospital, a Jewish cemetery at the juncture leading to Skalbmierz, and a Talmud Torah. In spite of many obstacles, such as a cholera outbreak and huge fire at the turn of the twentieth century, as well as the primitive conditions of the town that prompted emigration to larger, more developed cities, the Jewish community of Dzialoszyce continued to expand.

Here they found a multitude of mostly Jewish-owned industries, such as chicory factories, tanneries, brickyards, water and oil mills, and Jewish-owned shops selling everything from housewares to haberdashery, textiles and leather goods. There were dozens of groceries and several bakeries, teashops and restaurants. Carpenters, tailors, shoemakers, and watchmakers were among the many Jewish craftsmen who provided every possible service. There were two Jewish doctors, a Jewish dentist, and a Jewish pharmacist. Loans could be arranged through Jewish-owned banks. On Tuesdays and Fridays, stalls featuring an assortment of wares filled the market square. Yiddish was the main language in the streets and in the marketplace. Most of the Poles in the area understood it; some even spoke it.

Despite the strict enforcement of the Sunday Closing Law in Poland, Jewish merchants could not resist opening their shops to the hundreds of Catholic Poles who flocked to Dzialoszyce to attend Sunday services at the district's main church. One by one, shutters were raised, and over time, Sunday became an unofficial market day. Shopkeepers posted a lookout, who would quickly bolt the door and let the customers out the back as soon as he spotted the town constable; regardless, the officer would often look the other way, happy to accept a fat tip to augment his meager salary.

The local Polish authorities did not hide their antipathy towards the Jewish majority. They realized that non-Jews would not stand a chance against Jewish candidates in the town council elections. Consequently, they passed legislation allowing the mayor and the most important officials to be appointed by the government, leaving elections for lesser positions only.[3] In this way, the Polish minority retained political control over the town.

---

3. In 1924, Icek Rubin, a Gerrer chassid, was elected to the position of deputy mayor. Pesach Szternberg, a Zionist who headed the Jewish community council for many years, served as deputy mayor of Dzialoszyce in the years prior to WWII.

Anti-Semitic slurs could occasionally be heard in Dzialoszyce. But in the event a non-Jew perpetrated a hateful act, be he a porter or the all-important Catholic priest, the swift and punitive reaction by the Jewish townspeople served as a long-lasting deterrent.

Once, while traveling on the *kolejka*, Uncle Yisroel Platkiewicz overheard a gentile insurance agent denigrating the Jews of Dzialoszyce. After Yisroel publicized these remarks, the Pole gradually lost his customers. When he became aware of the reason for his business decline, he challenged Yisroel at the *beis din* of the *rav*, accusing him of libel. Yisroel maintained that he had personally heard the anti-Semitic comment. Afraid that the *rav* would favor Yisroel, the agent shouted, "By the life of my daughters, I did not say it!" Within the year, both of his daughters died.

As in other cities and towns in Poland, the Jewish community's religious and internal affairs were governed by its own administrative board, known as the Kehillah,[4] which headed and funded various *tzedakah* and *chessed* committees and appointed a communal *rav*,

Rav Mordechai Yitzchok Staszewski (r) with his *shamash*
Photo credit: *Sefer Yizkor shel Kehillat Dzialoszyce V'hasevivah*

chazzan, *shochet*, and other functionaries. The official rabbi of Dzialoszyce in the interwar period was Rav Mordechai Yitzchok Staszewski, who succeeded his father and grandfather.

---

4. *Judenrat* officials were later chosen from this pool of communal leaders.

In the center of Dzialoszyce stood the Adas Yisroel synagogue, an imposing edifice of remarkable artistry and architecture, which could accommodate hundreds of congregants. Next to it was a large *beis medrash* where the sound of Torah and *tefillah* never ceased; a *minyan* could be joined there from morning to night. Yeshivah students pored over their Gemara volumes. Artisans and stallkeepers left the market before evening and headed to the *beis medrash* to *daven* Minchah and Maariv, or to hear a sermon from a visiting *baal darshan*. Adjacent to the *beis medrash* was a bathhouse with a *mikveh* and *shvitz*, run by Antek the caretaker, who could hardly refill the hot water fast enough on Erev Shabbos.

There were numerous *shtieblech* as well, frequented by chassidim of the Gerrer, Chentshiner, Czernobyler, and Aleksander Rebbes, whose centers were in other parts of Poland. Rav Eliezer Epstein, grandson of the Rebbe Reb Kalmish of Neustadt, was the resident rebbe of Dzialoszyce with his own *shtiebel* and followers.

Religious life was celebrated with irrepressible exuberance. On Simchas Torah, a large group of worshippers would meet the *rav* at his house and accompany him all the way to the shul with lively singing. Weddings and other festivities were held in the open with the *chassan* and *kallah* escorted from their

Rav Eliezer Epstein (c) with his son Yonasan (l) and a chassid

homes to the outdoor *chuppah* set up in front of the main shul. A long procession of relatives, friends, and well-wishers followed the *chassan*, singing and dancing to the spirited music of the local *klezmer* band. (Poor townspeople often married on Erev Shabbos, in which case a Friday afternoon *chuppah* was followed by a Shabbos *seudah* for immediate family, with additional guests for dessert.)

The *Haskalah*[5] movement that swept through Europe in the nineteenth century did not infiltrate the remote town of Dzialoszyce until shortly before World War I. At that time, a group of young Torah students who took an interest in the proliferation of modern Hebrew and Yiddish literature formed youth clubs and established a library in Dzialoszyce. After the Balfour Declaration in 1917, the Zionist movement spreading rapidly throughout Poland became active locally, captivating a large percentage of the town's population. It was thus that the interwar *kehillah* of Dzialoszyce spanned a colorful spectrum of old-time chassidim,[6] *maskilim*, and Zionists of all persuasions.

Although a great many Jews abandoned their religious observance, there was no public desecration of Shabbos. Jewish peddlers who left home on Sunday returned to town on Friday. And should the sun begin to set while they were still on the road, they would whip their horses into a gallop so as to arrive before the onset of Shabbos.

Deep-rooted traditions and rituals, such as those that accompanied the approach of the new year, remained sacrosanct, as evidenced by this excerpt of an unnumbered, whimsical chapter by Chaim Yitzchok Wolgelernter.[7]

---

5. Jewish "Enlightenment"

6. There were few, if any, Jews of Lithuanian or German background.

7. This chapter is one of several that were not included by the author in the diary's handwritten table of contents; see Appendices.

In our shtetl Dzialoszyce, you could tell when Rosh Chodesh Elul arrived; you had your first taste of the significance of the upcoming Yamim Nora'im.

Already on Erev Rosh Chodesh, the atmosphere underwent a distinct change. An air of awe permeated the town as people began to gather, even before noon, for the Yom Kippur Katan service in the big shul. Many new faces appeared in the shul, including the rav, the rebbe, and other distinguished personalities who ordinarily preferred to daven in the local chassidic shtieblech. And while some townspeople maintained the Yom Kippur Katan custom every month — albeit hurriedly and without ceremony — and others did not, there was a yearly tradition that on Erev Rosh Chodesh Elul everyone recited it together in the big shul.

Even Jews who generally did not attend a weekday minyan except on a yahrzeit, closed their shops and came to the shul. The regular members — simple people, laborers, porters, and the like — took advantage of their fixed seats up front to sit as close as possible to the rav and the rebbe.

Reb Heshele Melamed marches in, leading his class of little boys. They are our first line of defense, pure and without sin. Just the breath emanating from the mouths of these little cheder children could topple the walls of Yericho! After washing their hands at the basin, they line up on the benches around the bimah.

Wolf the shamash stands on the bimah and gazes with satisfaction at the multitude coming to his shul. Even the trilling of the birds that have flown in through the open windows adds to the unique Elul atmosphere.

A nervous old Yid'l, thinking he is late, comes hurrying into the shul. In his haste, he has forgotten his gartel. He borrows his neighbor's handkerchief and ties it together with his own, creating a makeshift gartel. He is ready to daven.

Up in the gallery, there is much commotion as the devout women of the town arrive, each carrying a thick Korban Minchah siddur and a tearstained book of techinos with a fresh handkerchief inside. The usual chatter is absent. Feeling the gravity of the upcoming Yom Hadin, everyone is subdued.

The shul is almost full. The rebbe is already standing in his place, the elderly rav sitting up front to the left of the aron hakodesh, facing the congregation as he peruses a sefer. Reb Avraham Yitzchok Zions, who sits in shul every day all summer long, davening and learning in his tallis and tefillin from early morning until one o'clock in the afternoon, is still finishing his daily program.

"What are we waiting for?" people ask one another. "It's almost one o'clock!"

It seems Reb Chaim Yeshayah [Kac], the shliach tzibbur, is not here yet. He is not back from the mikveh… But as always, he is punctual. He hurries along, the corners of a towel sticking out from underneath his unbuttoned chalat, his white beard and peyos dripping with mikveh water. Two bushy eyebrows visible beneath the brim of his round hat lend him a fearsome appearance.

The Yom Kippur Katan service begins, with Kaddish intoned to the ancient niggun of the Yamim Nora'im. Lifting his rod like a choirmaster's baton, Reb Heshele signals to the children when it is time to respond. The accompaniment of the one hundred lilting voices of the boys' choir rouses the congregation and triggers a storm of emotion in the women's section; the sound of weeping is heard from all sides.

People wish each other a fervent "gut yahr." The merchants are more scrupulous in their dealings and do not have to be reminded to give honest weight. The produce peddlers on the market square, who might take a few cucumbers out of the sacks they purchased from the peasants, are more restrained now. Their consciences do not allow them to shortchange their customers.

On the following day, Rosh Chodesh Elul, the first blasts of the shofar stir everyone's hearts, even the non-observant Jews. Little cheder boys learn how to blow the shofar. The chazzanim begin practicing the nussach of the Yamim Nora'im davening. Koppel Miodownik, the baal Mussaf in the rebbe's shtiebel, avoids immersing himself in a cold mikveh all month for fear of catching cold; Kalman Paczes wears a warm scarf around his neck.

The cemetery is as crowded as an annual trade fair, with everyone visiting the graves of their ancestors. Icek'l the gravedigger is there, too. His two goats, which usually graze freely on the grass growing between the graves, are now tied to the fence. They stare at their master, wondering why they cannot amble around the cemetery as on other days. You would think that this simple man knows nothing more than how to dig a grave. But in his kingdom of the dead, Icek'l is an expert. He can clearly articulate when your mother-in-law's ancestors passed away and where they lie buried.

Alter Kalimacher, a self-taught master of all trades, is in the cemetery, too. Besmeared with lime and cement, he patches cracked foundations and paints faded inscriptions; people who have put off repairing damaged tombstones all year want the repairs done now that everyone is visiting the cemetery.

It is Elul in Dzialoszyce.

Platkiewicz Family

Highly regarded in Dzialoszyce, the Platkiewicz family was descended from Rabbi Shabsai Hakohen, the renowned *Shach*.

Reb Shraga Feivel Platkiewicz [c.1878–1918] was a prominent chassid of the Chentshiner Rebbe.

His wife, Yachet, née Lis, became known for her unstinting generosity. In her early years of marriage, she gave her wedding diamond to her brother Yochanan who was in dire financial straits, never telling her husband that she had had her ring fitted with an imitation stone.

On one occasion, when her husband consulted with her regarding granting a loan, she responded, "Why didn't you lend the money on the spot? Now that you delayed, you should give double the amount!"

The couple had seven children. Two died in early childhood.

When Tzinne, the eldest daughter, was sixteen years old, her father arranged a match for her with Hershel (Mordechai Tzvi) Erlich, an outstanding *talmid* of the Sochatchover Rebbe.

Soon afterwards, in 1918, forty-year-old Shraga Feivel Platkiewicz was among more than two hundred elite young men of Dzialoszyce whose lives were claimed by a typhoid epidemic that erupted at the end of World War I. The collective tragedy left a devastating impact on the townspeople, who spoke about it for years to come. Like most of the other widows, Yachet did not remarry, as men of comparable religious caliber were rare at the time.

Hershel Erlich asked the Sochatchover Rebbe whether he should proceed with the *shidduch*. Answered the rebbe: "Is it the fault of the girl that her father died?" The couple married and settled in the city of Sosnowiec, where young Hershel's noble character traits and exceptional *yiras Shamayim* earned him a reputation as a tzaddik.

Tzinne Erlich

The Platkiewicz family was left destitute as a result of the dissolution of Reb Shraga Feivel's business partnership following his death. Forced to fend for herself financially, Yachet courageously opened a textile shop. Her engaging personality, combined with her integrity and business acumen, enabled her to become the leading dry-goods dealer in a town that boasted a sizeable number of textile firms.

She could now continue to be a source of succor to others. Her very name — "Yachet'l Platkiewicz" — became synonymous with charity and hospitality. She set a beautiful example for her children, singlehandedly raising them to become righteous, Torah-observant Jews.

Yisroel, as the eldest son, helped his mother in the business, gradually taking over an increasing share of the daily burden. A devout and G-d-fearing Jew, he was noted for his honesty in commercial dealings.

With the stiff competition in the textile trade, merchants continuously slashed their prices, even selling goods below cost. Consequently, many could not pay their suppliers and declared bankruptcy every few years, settling with their creditors for fifty groschen on the zloty. The Platkiewicz textile shop, however, stayed clear of such corrupt practices.

A friend of the family once challenged Yisroel: "How can you succeed in business when other shopkeepers sell their merchandise at cut-rate prices?"

Unruffled, Yisroel replied, "Do you really think these merchants benefit from their deceitful dealings? When I go to Lodz on a buying trip, the large textile manufacturers treat me royally. They offer me quality merchandise at the lowest prices since they know that I pay my bills on time. That's how I am able to stay ahead of the competition."

Yisroel married Feigele, née Isserowsky. He and his young wife settled in Dzialoszyce and had two children, Feivele and Mordche'le.

Chayele Platkiewicz

Compulsory education for girls required Chayele to attend the local government-sponsored school, where she learned to speak Polish flawlessly. (This skill would later enable her to pose as a non-Jew.)

Sarah Schenirer came to town when Chayele was in her teens. Her wisdom and vivacious personality left a deep impression on the people of Dzialoszyce. During her stay she gave lectures and established a Jewish school for girls, so that Reizele, five years Chayele's junior, was able to attend Bais Yaakov.

Chayele Platkiewicz, just before her wedding in 1936

Reizele Platkiewicz, 1939

Great jubilation marked the announcement of Chayele's engagement in late 1934 to Chaim Yitzchok Wolgelernter of nearby Kazimierza Wielka. An outstanding Ostrovtzer *talmid* who often came to town to tutor the sons of Rav Eliezer Epstein, Chaim Yitzchok was well known in Dzialoszyce.

Wolgelernter Family/Kazimierza Wielka

Born in 1911 in the town of Ozarow, Chaim Yitzchok, or Chaim'l, as he was fondly called, was the fourth of eight children — two died in early childhood — of Rav Yeshayah Wolgelernter and his wife Hendel Rivkah, née Selzer.

Rav Yeshayah and Hendel Rivkah Wolgelernter

Some time after 1913, the family relocated to Kazimierza Wielka, where Rav Yeshayah had accepted the position of communal *shochet*. Sixteen kilometers (ten miles) from Dzialoszyce, Kazimierza Wielka, often referred to simply as Kazimierz,[8] was a large village designated as the administrative seat of its *gmina*. The district courthouse and offices were located on the village square. Several flour mills and sugar refineries employed Jews from the area. Since the Jewish community consisted of only eighty families, comprising a small minority of the general population, it was considered a branch of the larger *kehillah* of Koszyce and was not afforded its

---

8. Now a bustling town, Kazimierza Wielka, 45 km (twenty-eight miles) northeast of Krakow, should not be confused with the better-known Kazimierz, Krakow's historic Jewish quarter.

own rabbi. Thus, aside from his duties as the *shochet*, Rav Yeshayah also served as the unofficial *rav* of Kazimierza Wielka and the *shliach tzibbur* for the Yamim Nora'im.

Born in 1879 in the city of Ostrowiec (*Ostrovtze*) to his parents Rav Yechiel Issamar and Leah, Rav Yeshayah descended from illustrious lineage. A great-grandson of the saintly Rav Issamar of Konskowola, Rav Yeshayah followed scrupulously in his ancestors' ways. As a devout and exalted chassid, he spent his days engrossed in *davening* and learning, fasting every Monday and Thursday and taking great pains to immerse in a *mikveh* even in the most frigid weather. The Chentshiner Rebbe regarded Rav Yeshayah highly and engaged him as his personal *shochet* during his vacations in Marienbad.

Rav Yeshayah Wolgelernter (r) in Marienbad with the
Chentshiner Rebbe (second from left)

Wolgelernter Family History

Rav Issamar of Konskowola [d.1831]

The first to assume the family surname was Rav Issamar of Konskowola, one of the primary disciples of the Chozeh of Lublin, the Yehudi Hakadosh of Pshischa, and the Maggid of Kozhnitz, with whom he was also a *mechutan*. He was famed as a *gaon* in both the revealed and hidden parts of Torah.

Family lore has it that at the turn of the nineteenth century, when Austrian officials arrived in Polish villages and towns after new legislation required Jews to choose permanent surnames, Rav Issamar was engaged in his Torah studies and would not be interrupted. Bystanders described Rav Issamar's characteristics and occupation as a "well-learned man." Hence, the name "*Wohl Gelernter*" was assigned by the official and became the family surname. Great-grandson Rav Yeshayah later adopted the variant spelling Wolgelernter.

Referred to as the "Seraph of Konskowola" for his ability to effect Heavenly miracles on behalf of his supplicants, Rav Issamar also came to be known posthumously as the *Mishmeres Issamar*, the title of his profound commentary on the weekly *parshah*, which he did not publish in his lifetime due to his modesty. The *sefer* was published in 1870 by his son Rav Chaim Moshe Yitzchok and was reprinted in a revised, two-volume edition by fifth-generation descendant Feivel Wolgelernter in 2007. Additional, unpublished manuscripts written by Rav Issamar, including his *Sefer Hachalomos* in which he recorded *chiddushim* revealed to him in dreams, are not extant.

In his early years, Rav Issamar was well off, having inherited a substantial sum from his father Rav Yisroel. However, he immersed himself in Torah learning and distributed his fortune to the poor.

Years later, in a *hesped* for his father Rav Yechiel Issamar, printed in *Habe'er*, Rav Yeshayah Wolgelernter wrote: *My grandfather* [Rav Chaim Moshe Yitzchok] *zt"l related to me that his father, the Mishmeres Issamar, knew how to play all sorts of musical instruments. His talmidim would join him every night at chatzos with instruments in their hands. Said Hakadosh Baruch Hu to His Heavenly retinue: "Come, let us descend to hear the music of chatzos, played before Me by Rav Issamar of Konskowola."*

Rav Chaim Moshe Yitzchok [b.1816]

Rav Chaim Moshe Yitzchok and his sister, children of Rav Issamar of Konskowola, married siblings Matil and Dovid of the illustrious Horowitz family, paternal great-grandchildren of Rav Yaakov Yitzchok Horowitz, the Chozeh of Lublin, and maternal great-grandchildren of Rav Shmuel Shmaryahu of Ostrovtze, author of *Zichron Shmuel*, who was a disciple of the Chozeh, the Maggid of Kozhnitz, and the Yehudi Hakadosh of Pshischa.

Rav Chaim Moshe Yitzchok chose not to succeed his father as a *rav* and leader; he feared his *brachos* would not be assured of success as were his father's. When Rav Yeshayah Wolgelernter later lamented the cessation of *rabbanus* in the family, his father Rav Yechiel Issamar explained [*ibid.*]: *My father Rav Chaim Moshe Yitzchok maintained: "Sonei matanos yichyeh — One who hates gifts will live"* [see interpretation of the Maggid of Mezritch quoted in *Habe'er*]. *Every leader will have to give a din v'cheshbon for the gifts he received from people for whom he was unable to effect a yeshuah.*

Rav Yechiel Issamar [1844-1933]

Rav Yechiel Issamar, son of Rav Chaim Moshe Yitzchok, married Leah, née Horowitz-Sternfeld, daughter of Dovid Horowitz [see above]; hence, they were first cousins twice over.

Rav Yechiel Issamar spent his life immersed in Torah, attaching himself to the great chassidic rebbes of his day. He was a paragon of *simchah* and pleasantness in his interactions with others. Those who heard him play *Hamavdil* and *Eliyahu* on his fiddle on Motza'ei Shabbos were inspired with thoughts of *teshuvah*.

Rav Yechiel Issamar lived in Ostrowiec until his passing at a ripe old age. He maintained a close connection with the legendary first Ostrovtzer Rebbe, Rav Meir Yechiel Halstuk, singing *zemiros* for the rebbe on Shabbos and Yom Tov.

The children of Rav Yechiel Issamar and Leah Wohlgelernter were Shmuel Yaakov, Reizel, Yisroel Elazar, Yeshayah — father of Chaim Yitzchok — and Kalmen.

Title page of *Mishmeres Issamar* by Rav Issamar of Konskowola; printed in Poland in 1870

Sitting: Rav Yechiel Issamar and Leah Wohlgelernter; standing: son Rav Yeshayah and grandson Avraham

A well-known branch of the family descends from Rav Yisroel Elazar [1872–1927], who immigrated to Canada in 1920. He was a reputable *shochet* and a *baal tefillah* at Beth Hakenesseth Hagadol Anshei Ostrowce of Toronto. Three of his sons held prominent positions: Rabbi Yaakov Yitzchok Wohlgelernter [1899–1966], principal of the Eitz Chaim school in Toronto; Rabbi Sholom Pinchas Wohlgelernter [1901–1976], *rav* of Congregation Bikur Cholim in Seattle; Rabbi Yerachmiel Elimelech [Itamar] Wohlgelernter [1910–1994], *rav* in Detroit who later immigrated to Israel and served as the secretary of the Chief Rabbinate under Rabbi Yitzchok Isaac Halevi Herzog. Rav Yisroel Elazar's oldest daughter Matil was married to Rabbi Yochanan Spiegel, *rav* of a shul in the Bronx.

(l-r) Meir, Matil [Mandel], R' Yeshayah, Hendel Rivkah, and Yitta Wolgelernter, summer 1930

(l-r) Chaim Yitzchok and Dovid, 1920s　　(l-r) Meir, Yitta, Chaim Yitzchok

(l-r) Chaim Yitzchok, Dovid, Yitta, Meir, child presumed to be Matil's son Meir
Avigdor, on a family outing in 1935

With complete selflessness, Rav Yeshayah assisted anyone in need, including *Yidden* from neighboring villages and towns who were summoned to the Kazimierz courthouse. He would plead with the judge to drop the charges and release the Jew from jail before Shabbos. "This crime certainly doesn't warrant the anguish that a Jew experiences when he is forced to spend Shabbos in jail!" argued Rav Yeshayah. Despite limited understanding of the rabbi's medley of Yiddish and broken Polish, the judge respected his sincerity and uprightness and generally granted his request. When the judge stood firm, Rav Yeshayah did not hesitate to turn to the local Catholic priest. Drawing on the latter's familiarity with the Hebrew tongue, Rav Yeshayah would say: "Look, I am a *kadosh* and you are a *kadosh*, so let's join forces and get the poor fellow out of jail."

At great financial sacrifice, Rav Yeshayah sent his four sons — Avramele, Chaim'l, Dovid'l, and Meir'l — to learn in the *yeshivos* of Krakow. After a few years, only Chaim Yitzchok remained away from home. His brothers could not endure the privations of a yeshivah student in those days and returned to Kazimierz to continue their studies in the local *beis medrash*, as was customary at the time. All of the Wolgelernter sons studied *shechitah*, which enabled them to help their father. Meir was a gifted *sofer* as well.

(l-r) Chaim Yitzchok, Meir, Dovid

Avraham, the eldest of the boys, left for Canada in the late 1920s to escape army service and the grinding poverty in Poland. He

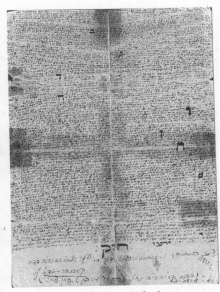

Megillas Esther written in microscopic letters by ten–year–old Meir Wolgelernter on a postcard sent to his brother Avraham in Hamilton, Ontario, December 1930 [previously published in the Yiddish-language *Forward*, March 12, 1976]

planned to earn a livelihood by joining his uncle Rav Yisroel Elazar Wohlgelernter, who was a *shochet* in Toronto. Letters from his parents reveal their great angst over his departure, as they feared the influence of the American culture on their son. Avraham married in Toronto in 1935 and settled there.

Matil, the eldest of the Wolgelernter children, married Chaim Yosef Mandel. The couple settled in the town of

Matil and Chaim Yosef Mandel

Letter sent by Rav Yeshayah Wolgelernter to son Avraham in Canada

Zawichost. They had two children, Meir Avigdor and Yechiel Issamar.

Chaim Yitzchok Wolgelernter

From his earliest years, it was evident that Chaim Yitzchok was no ordinary youngster. Gifted with an insatiable thirst for knowledge, he took an interest in the world around him, but devoted himself with passionate intensity to his Torah studies.

After his bar mitzvah, he went to Krakow to benefit from the city's many *yeshivos*. Under the tutelage of Rav Nechemya Rosenfeld at the Krakow branch of the newly established Kesser Torah-Radomsk network, Chaim Yitzchok became a budding *talmid chacham*. At the yeshivah of Rav Yehuda Meir Levin, known as Rav Yudel Ostrovtzer, Chaim Yitzchok was introduced to the Ostrovtze *derech halimud*.

Seeking solutions to complex Talmudical and halachic questions, the precocious teenager corresponded with *gedolim* of his day, most notably the Rogatchover Gaon.[9]

In 1928, to further his level of learning, Chaim Yitzchok traveled to the city of Ostrowiec — where his elderly grandfather Rav Yechiel Issamar lived — to seek admission to Beis Meir, the renowned yeshivah established by the second Ostrovtzer Rebbe, Rav Yechezkel Halstuk. After passing the rigorous exam that allowed only the most brilliant students to be admitted, Chaim Yitzchok immersed himself in his life's goal: scaling the heights of Torah. Before long, he was counted among the outstanding Ostrovtzer disciples.

His gift of writing was soon acknowledged. After Shabbos and Yom Tov, a group of *bachurim* would gather to review the rebbe's

---

9. Responsa to R' Chaim Yitzchok Wolgelernter may be found in *Meishiv Shalom* by Rav Shalom Yosef Feigenbaum, Rav of Lokacze, and in *Tzafnas Paneach* by Rav Yosef Rosen, the Rogatchover Gaon; see Addendum.

shiurim and *drashos*. Chaim Yitzchok was elected to be the "recording secretary." The contents of his lucid and thorough notes came alive; reading them, you felt as if you had seen and heard the rebbe in person. Remarkably, when the rebbe himself recognized his young disciple's talented pen, he encouraged him to record the daily *shiurim*, something which had never before been done in Ostrovtze.[10]

Rav Yechezkel Halevi Halstuk,
second Ostrovtzer Rebbe

In addition, Chaim Yitzchok was appointed editor of the yeshivah's monthly Torah journal *Beis Meir*. He also contributed to various Torah journals in Poland, such as *Darkeinu* and *Habe'er*.[11]

When he was just shy of eighteen, Chaim Yitzchok and his *chavrusa* Aharon Rappaport approached the rebbe and asked to be tested for *heter horaah*. Although it was often bestowed in Poland in order to encourage the study of Halachah, it was rarely conferred by the Ostrovtzer Rebbe, and then only after an unusually comprehensive oral exam. The rebbe cross-examined his two young disciples, finally consenting. "You truly know the subject

---

10. See the author's own, more detailed account in Appendix C: *Memories of Ostrovtze*.

11. *Meorei Galicia: Encyclopedia L'chachmei Galicia*, by Rabbi Meir Wunder, lists R' Chaim Yitzchok Wolgelernter as a student in Krakow whose *divrei Torah* may be found in various Torah journals; see Addendum.

matter; therefore, I will grant you *heter horaah*. However, since I value you as my own children, I beg you not to take on a position as a communal *rav*, as it is a difficult and thankless task."

Chaim Yitzchok continued learning with great diligence, toiling ceaselessly in Torah. At the age of twenty-three, he became engaged to Chayele, the daughter of Yachet Platkiewicz of Dzialoszyce. He remained in the Ostrovtze Yeshivah until his marriage a year and a half later.

Cover of 1936 issue of *Beis Meir*, edited by Chaim Yitzchok Wolgelernter

---

The wedding of Chaim Yitzchok Wolgelernter and Chayele Platkiewicz was celebrated in Dzialoszyce on 10 Adar/March 4, 1936. On that day, the poor people of Dzialoszyce and its surroundings were invited to a sumptuous banquet. Subsequently, a *seudah* was held at night for family and friends.

The young couple settled in Dzialoszyce, living next to Chayele's mother Yachet in an apartment behind the textile

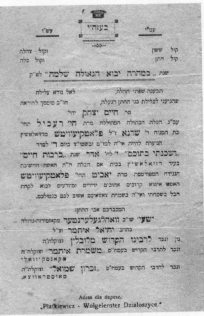

Wedding announcement of Chaim Yitzchok and Chayele Wolgelernter

shop. Chaim Yitzchok continued his Torah studies, delivered *shiurim*, and helped in the family business. He regularly visited Ostrowiec, maintaining a close connection to the rebbe.

Chaim Yitzchok remained a devoted son and brother, assisting his parents and siblings, who were enduring hard times. His younger, unmarried sister Yitta had assumed most of the household responsibilities, as their

Chaim Yitzchok and Chayele Wolgelernter in Krakow, late 1930s

mother Hendel Rivkah's health was deteriorating. In addition, Rav Yeshayah suffered intense emotional anguish due to an

Yitta Wolgelernter, Kazimierza Wielka, late 1930s

inter-communal conflict, as well as the loss of his salary as a *shochet* following the ban on ritual slaughter in Poland. His livelihood now depended on private requests for *shechitah*, which declined considerably with the rising price of fowl. The family became destitute, unable to put food on the table.

On top of all this, as war loomed on the horizon, nineteen-year-old Meir received a draft notice for Polish army service to begin after Sukkos of 1939. In a letter dated June 1939, addressed to his brother Avraham in Canada, Meir wrote:

> *The situation at home is catastrophic. Moreover, a tzarah has befallen me personally. I was called down before the military this week … I did the same thing you did … but the strict*

Identity photo of Meir Wolgelernter

> *committee ignored the fact that I had lost ten kilos and accepted me anyway because of the war atmosphere hovering over the world. I'm sure it is needless for me to point out what took place at home from the moment this grievous news was received … Mother cries day and night, which obviously doesn't affect her health in the best way. We did whatever we could to prevent this misfortune from materializing … But it turned out that there was nothing to be done.*

> *Father and Mother bade me to write and ask that you try with all your might to bring me to Canada … Write back very soon with specific instructions as to what documents I must send you and what steps you have taken … Maybe once I am in America, I will be able to do something to help our home so that our family will not live dark, bitter years of poverty and illness.*

We impatiently look forward to your quick response,
Your brother who wishes you all the best and awaits Hashem's help,
Meir

After nearly three years of marriage, when Chaim Yitzchok and Chayele were not blessed with a child, they became concerned. "You will have children when hair grows on the palm of my hand," was the doctor's grim prognosis.

On Purim 5699/1939, during one of his frequent visits to the Ostrovtzer Rebbe, Chaim Yitzchok poured out his troubled heart. "Travel home by way of Lizhensk (Pol. *Lezajsk*) and *daven* at the *kever* of the Noam Elimelech," advised the rebbe. "When you come back to me for Shavuos, I trust you will have good tidings."

Indeed, nine months later, at the end of November 1939, Chayele gave birth to a baby girl, named Sarah Leah. The birth of a son, Shraga Feivel, followed in February 1941.

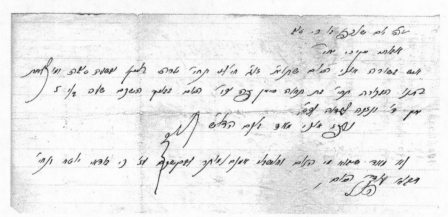

Note sent by Chaim Yitzchok to his parents informing them of his daughter's birth

Unfortunately, the young couple's bliss was overshadowed by the German invasion of Poland and the ever-worsening conditions of the Jews.

Chaim Yitzchok and Chayele with their firstborn child, autumn 1940;
note white armband on sleeve

Dzialoszyce: September 1939–September 1942

The outbreak of war found all of Yachet Platkiewicz's children in Dzialoszyce. Hershel and Tzinne'le had joined a wave of Jews fleeing the border city of Sosnowiec in advance of the German invasion. On September 8, soon after they arrived in town with their five children and rented an apartment near Yachet, Dzialoszyce was occupied by German troops.

The soldiers proceeded to seal all Jewish-owned businesses. The successful Platkiewicz textile shop, which faced the main street, was one of the first to be affected.

Chayele Erlich, eldest daughter of
Hershel and Tzinne'le

Esther Erlich, second daughter of
Hershel and Tzinne'le

The family responded by moving substantial quantities of silk, wool and other fabrics into Yachet's apartment through a small window in the shared wall between her apartment and the shop. Arrangements were then made to transport the textiles to gentile friends in Dzialoszyce and the surrounding area who agreed to store the goods for a fee.

Business continued uninterrupted. The customers came to Yachet's apartment to place their orders, and a young Dzialoszycer by the name of Mechel Kamelgard was employed to pick up the merchandise and deliver it to the clients.

Soon, a series of anti-Jewish decrees followed. Jews were required to wear identifying armbands and were prohibited from leaving their homes after dark, traveling by train, or stepping out of town limits.

Well-to-do Jews were targeted by the Germans for hostage-taking. The ransom money covered the salaries of the district

security force. Yachet Platkiewicz was one of several Jews who were hauled off and imprisoned in Kazimierza Wielka. Fortunately, after an exorbitant sum was extracted from the families, the victims were released unharmed.

As in other large Jewish communities, a *Judenrat* (Jewish council) was established in Dzialoszyce to serve as the intermediary between the Germans and the local Jews. Drawn from the pool of existing Kehillah leaders, its members had the distasteful task of proclaiming and implementing German orders, which were enforced by a newly formed entity — the *Ordnungsdienst*, or Jewish police.

Hoping to be exempt from anti-Jewish decrees and, later, the impending deportations, *Judenrat* officials often ingratiated themselves with the Germans, at the expense of their fellow Jews. When German officers issued an order for a large quantity of piece goods for women's dresses, the *Judenrat* directed them to the Platkiewicz textile shop. On several occasions, the family was forced to pay heavy sums in currency or goods, largely as a result of the underhanded behavior of the *Judenrat*. Once, when Yisroel did not immediately deliver the requested money, he was arrested and imprisoned in the regional German headquarters in Miechow. The members of the Dzialoszyce *Judenrat* naively believed the promise of protection extended by Beyerlein, chief of the Miechow SD (*Sicherheitsdienst*/Security Service)[12] and failed to realize, until it was too late, that they were simply being exploited.[13]

With no source of income, more and more families began to feel hunger pangs. As a remedy, the government issued ration cards that could be exchanged for coarse black bread. The Jewish community organized a soup kitchen, which doled out hundreds of hot meals to the poor.

---

12. SS intelligence agency operating in conjunction with the Gestapo

13. See Appendix A for the diarist's account of the *Judenrat* in Dzialoszyce.

Being well off, the Platkiewicz family did not suffer deprivation; for the right price, one could obtain food. The family debated the proper way to conduct themselves in these difficult times.

"How can we live in comfort when other people are starving?" argued Yisroel. "Let's use the ration cards and eat black bread."

"In theory you are right," countered Chaim Yitzchok. "However, I believe that if we take part in the misery of the poor and suffer along with them, we will become callous to their needs, whereas if we continue to live according to our means, we will feel compassion for those who have less than us, and we will be driven to help them."

Chaim Yitzchok's argument prevailed and was borne out in full. The Platkiewicz family continued to maintain a relatively higher standard. On the occasion of little Feivele's *bris* in 1941, turkey, which was quite costly to obtain, was served at the *seudah*. The family distributed its ration cards to needy families, and Yachet's kitchen turned out hundreds of daily meals, cooked in large pots purchased by Chaim Yitzchok. Everyone was welcome without question. But were a family member to help himself to a plate of

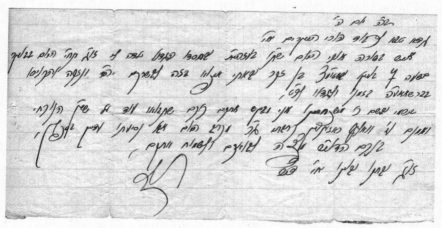

Note sent by Chaim Yitzchok to his parents informing them of his son's birth

the tasty food, Yachet would scold him: "This food is meant for the needy. We have enough to eat from the food which Malka [the maid] prepares for us."

Although the Jews of Dzialoszyce were forbidden to leave town limits, they were not surrounded by ghetto walls or barbed-wire fences. Nor were they under constant heavy guard — the local German authorities were headquartered in Miechow, twenty-three kilometers (fourteen miles) to the west. Consequently, several thousand refugees came to Dzialoszyce from ghettos in larger cities, swelling the Jewish population to well over ten thousand.[14] Hundreds of people were housed in public buildings, such as the *beis medrash* and shul.

Feivele Wolgelernter, about one year old, beginning of 1942

When Jewish refugees escaped their homes in the burning towns of Pinczow and Szczekociny, arriving in Dzialoszyce on Erev Rosh Hashanah of 1940, Chaim Yitzchok bought a large quantity of challah and the Platkiewicz family prepared for a throng of new guests.

Yachet begged her youngest brother, Uncle Yosef Shaul Lis, and his wife, who were living in terrible conditions in the Lodz ghetto, to come to Dzialoszyce. After they moved in with Yachet, *Miema* (Auntie) joined in her sister-in-law's *chessed* activities, spending her days cooking meals for the poor.

---

14. Some sources cite estimates of twelve thousand or more.

In late 1941, Chaim Yitzchok and Chayele's long-awaited firstborn daughter, two-year-old Sarah Leah, contracted pneumonia, which was potentially fatal for a child so young. The local doctor did his best, but as her condition grew worse by the day, he gave her no chance of recovery. In light of this, the little girl was given the added name Alte as an omen that she merit to live a long life and grow old in good health. She was called Alte'le from then on.

Despite the prohibition of leaving town and using any means of transportation, Chayele's resourceful younger sister Reizele traveled to Krakow to fetch a famous lung specialist. The doctor advised that Alte'le be admitted to the Krakow hospital.

For three long months, Chaim Yitzchok remained in the Krakow hospital with the gravely ill Alte'le, accompanied by Reizele, who dedicated herself to her young niece's welfare. As the child miraculously recovered, the doctor declared in amazement, "When the war ends, you should build a synagogue to thank G-d!"

Life for the Jews went from bad to worse. Dozens of young men from Dzialoszyce were rounded up daily and taken away. At first no one knew their fate, but after a while it became clear that they had been consigned to labor camps in the Krakow suburbs of Kostrze or Podgorze, and later in Prokocim. When news reached the community of the unbearable conditions in these camps, the townspeople organized committees to send packages of food and clothing to the inmates.

In the face of increasing oppression and danger, the Jews of Dzialoszyce displayed great faith and courage. Although public prayer was forbidden and the big shul and all the *shtieblech* were closed, *Yidden* gathered to *daven* wherever they could squeeze a *minyan*. And although *shechitah* was banned, any meat that was available for sale was always kosher. The decree against wearing a

beard caused great anguish. A number of chassidim disobeyed the order and did not go out in public to avoid being caught.

Characteristically, Jews clung to every shred of hope, and despite the ever-worsening situation, most Polish Jews did not see the writing on the wall. The Nazis cleverly concealed their intentions and used various ploys to allay fear and suspicion among the Jews. Rumors abounded, many of which lifted the morale of the Jews and fed their belief in a possible German defeat, especially once Germany began to suffer losses on the Russian front.

Distressed by the apathy of many Jewish leaders, Chaim Yitzchok dreamed of taking his wife and children to Eretz Yisrael but would not abandon his close-knit extended family.

By July 1942, refugees from other parts of the country were bringing reports of atrocities they had witnessed and of so-called *Aussiedlungen* — "resettlement" actions — in which entire communities of Jews were rounded up and deported to unknown destinations.

As the Jews of Dzialoszyce became aware of the gravity of their situation, hope faded and was replaced by a creeping sense of dread and despair. Even the greatest optimists fell silent. Still, no one could have imagined in his wildest dreams that Jewish life in Dzialoszyce was about to come to an end.

[Historical details have been drawn from the following sources, to which the reader is referred for further research: *Pinkas Hakehillot, Polen*, Vol. VII, Yad Vashem, 1999, translated in the Kielce-Radom SIG Journal at www.jewishgen.org; the Virtual Shtetl portal of the Museum of the History of Polish Jews at www.sztetl.org.pl; and *Sefer Yizkor shel Kehillat Dzialoszyce V'hasevivah*, Tel Aviv, 1973, translated at www.jewishgen.org and in the *Dzialoszyce Memorial Book*, JewishGen, 2012.]

Platkiewicz Family

Yachet (*née Lis*)   [1879–1944]
widow of **Shraga Feivel Platkiewicz**   [c.1878–1918]

1. **Tzinne**   [1901–1944]
    m. **Mordechai Tzvi** (Hershel) **Erlich**   [1898–1944]
        Children:
        Chaya (Chayele)   [1922–2012]
        Shraga Feivel (Feivel)   [1923–2011]
        Esther   [1928–1944]
        Avraham Reuven (Reuven)   [1929–1944]
        Gittel   [1932–1942]

2. **Yisroel Tzvi** (Yisroel)   [1903–1943]
    m. **Feige** (*née Isserovski*)   [1907–1943]
        Children:
        Shraga Feivel (Feivel)   [1933–1943]
        Mordechai   [1935–1943]

3. **Chana Mariam**   [1909–c.1913]

4. **Chaya Rechel** (Chayele)   [1912–2006]
    m. **Chaim Yitzchok Wolgelernter** (*author*)   [1911–1944]
        Children:
        Alte Sarah Leah (Alte'le)   [1939–1942]
        Shraga Feivel (Feivel)   [b.1941]

5. **Dovid Zalmen**   [1914–1942]

6. **Fradel**   (*died in infancy*)

7. **Reizel**   [c.1917–1942]

Wolgelernter Family

Yeshayah Wolgelernter   [1879-1942]
and **Hendel Rivkah** (*née Selzer*)   [1882-1942]

1. **Matil Dobra** (Matil)   [1906-1942]
   m. **Chaim Yosef Mandel**   [? -1942]
       Children:
       Meir Avigdor   [c.1930-1942]
       Yechiel Issamar   [1935-1942]

2. **Avraham Moshe** (Avramele)   [1907-1972]
   m. **Rivka Goldschlager**   [1906-1970]
       Children:
       Yaakov Yitzchok   [1937-1949]
       Yechiel Meir   [b.1939]
       Esther   [1944-2014]

3. **Chaya Sarah**   (*died age 2*)

4. **Chaim Yitzchok** (Chaim'l) (*author*)   [1911-1944]
   m. **Chaya Rechel** (Chayele) (*née Platkiewicz*)   [1912-2006]
       Children:
       Alte Sarah Leah (Alte'le)   [1939-1942]
       Shraga Feivel (Feivel)   [b.1941]

5. **Dovid Yaakov** (Dovid'l)   [1913-1996]
   m. **Mindel Zilberstein**   [1925-2012]
       Children:
       Yeshayah Boruch   [b.1952]
       Chava Hendel   [b.1955]

6. **Yitta Reizel** (Yitta'le)   [1918-1942]

7. **Leib**   (*died age 1*)

8. **Meir Shmuel Eliyahu** (Meir'l)   [1920-1944]

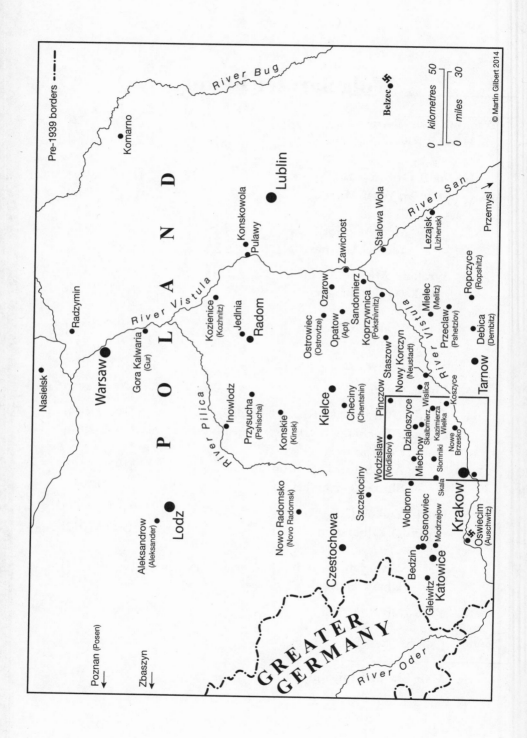

Pre-1939 borders ▪━▪━

© Martin Gilbert 2014

River Bug

River San

River Vistula

River Pilica

River Vistula

River Oder

POLAND

GREATER GERMANY

Belzec ⚡

Komarno

Lublin

Konskowola

Konskowola
Pulawy

Zawichost

Stalowa Wola

Lezajsk
(Lizhensk)

Przemysl →

Radzymin

Nasielsk

Warsaw

Gora Kalwaria
(Gur)

Kozienice
(Kozhnitz)

Jedlnia

Radom

Ostrowiec
(Ostrovtze)

Ozarow

Opatow
(Apt)

Sandomierz

Koprzywnica
(Pokshivnitz)

Mielec
(Melitz)

Przeclaw
(Pshetzlov)

Debica
(Dembitz)

Ropczyce
(Ropshitz)

Inowlodz

Przysucha
(Pshischa)

Kielce

Checiny
(Chentshin)

Pinczow

Staszow

Nowy Korczyn
(Neustadt)

Wislica

Koszyce

Tarnow

Konskie
(Kinsk)

Wodzislaw
(Voidislov)

Dzialoszyce

Miechow

Skalbmierz

Kazimierza
Wielka

Slomniki

Nowe
Brzesko

Szczekociny

Wolbrom

Skala

Modrzejow

Krakow

Aleksandrow
(Aleksander)

Lodz

Nowo Radomsko
(Novo Radomsk)

Szczekociny

Sosnowiec

Bedzin

Oswiecim
(Auschwitz) ⚡

Czestochowa

Gleiwitz

Katowice

Poznan (Posen) →

Zbaszyn →

0 ____ 50
kilometres

0 ____ 30
miles

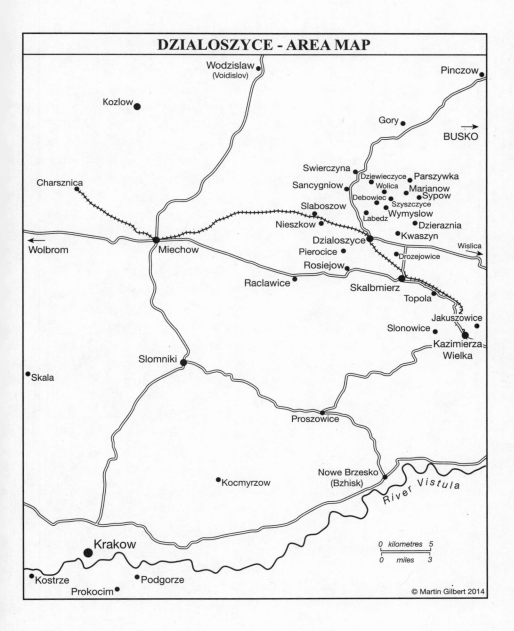

DZIALOSZYCE - AREA MAP

Wodzislaw
(Voidislov)

Pinczow

Kozlow

Gory

BUSKO

Swierczyna

Dziewieczyce   Parszywka
Sancygniow   Wolica   Marianow
Debowiec   Sypow
Szyszczyce
Slaboszow   Labedz   Wymyslow
Charsznica
Nieszkow   Dzieraznia
Wolbrom
Kwaszyn
Miechow   Dzialoszyce   Wislica
Pierocice   Drozejowice
Rosiejow
Raclawice   Skalbmierz   Topola
Jakuszowice
Slonowice
Kazimierza
Wielka
Slomniki

Skala

Proszowice

Nowe Brzesko
(Bzhisk)   River Vistula
Kocmyrzow

0   kilometres   5
Krakow
0   miles   3

Kostrze   Podgorze
Prokocim

© Martin Gilbert 2014

THE DIARY
Sefer Hadma'os:
A Chronicle
of Tears

Introduction

Shivah Asar B'Tammuz 5703/July 20, 1943 — in the loft[1]

Cooped up in my hideout in the loft of a cow barn, I thought of writing down some of the trials that befell me during the first expulsion raid, which took place in my hometown Dzialoszyce on 22 Elul 5702, and during the second, regional raid on 29 Mar Cheshvan 5703, which also included my native Kazimierza Wielka where my parents lived.

I do not intend to give a detailed report of the events in my personal life. The time is not right for it and I do not have the strength to focus my thoughts. My goal is only to highlight several main themes, so that if, chalilah, it is a Heavenly decree that there not be a remnant of the House of Israel in Europe after this dreadful war, I must accept the justice of the Divine judgment and I shall leave these lines as a memorial.

Perhaps it will reach the hands of my brother, Avraham Moshe Wolgelernter, 35 Kensington Avenue, in Toronto, Canada, and he will learn the fate of his relatives in Europe. If a spark still glows in his heart

---

1. Translated from an eight-page Hebrew-language chronicle, recorded by Chaim Yitzchok Wolgelernter in a bound notebook that was addressed but not mailed to his brother Avraham in Canada; the Jewish Historical Institute of Warsaw sent it to Avraham in 1948. In it the author documented the fate of the family and included meticulously rewritten copies of the acrostic *kinos* he had composed in memory of those who had recently perished. It serves here as an introduction to the full Yiddish diary.

towards his martyred parents and sister, may Hashem avenge their blood, and towards his brothers, who are still alive as I write these lines, and his tears upon reading these lines will blend with ours on the fresh grave of our saintly parents, that will be my reward. I thank the Almighty, Who has not abandoned the house of my forefathers and has left a remnant of our family in Canada so that our name will not be erased from Klal Yisrael.

The year 5696 marked the dawning of a new era in my life, a time of happiness in the full sense of the word. After studying in various yeshivos in Krakow and subsequently in Ostrowiec — where I learned by the holy Ostrovtzer Rebbe and received heter horaah as well as kabbalah in shechitah — I married my wife Chaya Rechel, daughter of the late Reb Shraga Feivel Platkiewicz a"h of Dzialoszyce, on Wednesday, 10 Adar 5696/March 4, 1936.

Upon stepping over the threshold of the home of my mother-in-law, Mrs. Yachet Platkiewicz, I found a fitting fusion of Torah and worldly grandeur. Her oldest son, my brother-in-law Yisroel, who managed the business, was like a father to me. He introduced me to the world of commerce and saw to it that all my needs were met. My wife Chayele was an intelligent, refined, and giving person. My mother-in-law was a tzaddekes crowned with noble character traits, and my young sister-in-law, Reizele — indeed the entire family — treated me with much warmth. It was in this loving familial atmosphere that my life before the churban proceeded in a calm, peaceful rhythm.

In the first year of the war, on Tuesday, 16 Kislev 5700/November 28, 1939, almost four years after our wedding, our daughter Alte Sarah Leah was born. Our joy was boundless. The sweet little child was the mortar that reinforced our loving relationship. She was truly an adorable child, and my parents derived much joy from her during their visits to us.

In the second year of the war, on Thursday, 9 Shevat 5701/February 6, 1941, our dear son was born. We named him Shraga Feivel after my father-in-law z"l. The bris was celebrated on the eighth day with a magnificent

seudah, with the participation of the leading members of the kehillah. In spite of the difficulty of traveling by train, which was prohibited to Jews, my parents came from Kazimierza Wielka to take part in our simchah. My father was the sandek and the rebbe, Rav Eliezer Epstein, was the mohel.

Life by my parents in Kazimierz continued as before, except that my father no longer received a communal salary as a shochet and the family was in dire financial straits. I helped as much as I could. My brothers, Dovid'l and Meir'l, lived with my parents. Dovid was learning shechitah and helped Father in his work.

My sister Yitta was a lovely rose in the garden of our family, a beautiful girl with outstanding character traits, intelligent, sensitive and kind. It was no wonder that suitable matches were suggested from all sides. My parents decided on Mottel, the son of Alter the shochet [of Skalbmierz]. However, the shidduch never came to fruition, as war had begun. At first, no one believed it would last long, so why rush into such a crucial decision. Later, when it became clear that the end of the war was not in sight, the time was not right, as every day brought new decrees, one harsher than the other, and everyone was absorbed with his own troubles. On top of all that, Mottel lost his father a year before the expulsion. Could anyone have imagined that my sister Yitta, may Hashem avenge her blood, was to fall victim herself?

My sister Matil and her husband Chaim Yosef lived in Zawichost with their two children, Meir Avigdor and Yechiel Issamar. Beset by trouble too, they were hoping for better times. They spent the Yamim Nora'im and Sukkos 5702/1942 with my parents in Kazimierz.

Soon after, dark clouds began to cover the horizon. Anti-Jewish measures came in quick succession, culminating this past year in a systematic round of expulsions, first in the large cities, then in the small towns, and finally on the fateful day, Wednesday, 20 Elul, when calamity struck Dzialoszyce.

[The description of events are omitted here, since they are described in greater detail in the diary.]

As I write these concluding lines, we are in the barn loft on 21 Elul 5703/1943, the yahrzeit of the first expulsion raid in Dzialoszyce.

As for the remainder of our memoirs and the details of what we experienced during this time, they are written in Yiddish in a special journal that I recorded as a memorial while confined to my hideout.

May Hashem grant me the merit to be freed from here and to see vengeance for the lives of our dear relatives who fell during this season of blood.

Chaim Yitzchok Wolgelernter,
son of Yeshayah and Hendel Rivkah
21 Elul 5703

First page of Yiddish diary

Note to the Reader:

•Although the diary opens with the date Tuesday, 19 Elul 5702/September 1, 1942, it is not known when the chapters were actually recorded. There are no daily, dated entries and little mention of specific dates. However, it is possible to deduce the dates of most events by following the progression of days, Yamim Tovim, months, and seasons. These dates have been included in brackets for the benefit of the reader.

•In an effort to preserve the authenticity of the author's writing style, grammatical inconsistencies in the usage of tenses in the original Yiddish have been retained in the English translation.

CHAPTER 1

Jews Repent

TUESDAY, 19 ELUL/SEPTEMBER 1 [1942]

The town of Dzialoszyce is greatly distressed. The tragic happenings in Proszowice, Nowe Brzesko (*Bzhisk*), Skala, and Slomniki, which occurred on Friday and Shabbos, have shaken everyone.

True, the assembled Jews are still standing in the fields of Slomniki. They hope for a miracle. Rumors abound; some people claim that foreign powers have intervened to forestall the deportation. Meanwhile, although they are under heavy guard, a few individuals risk their lives and slip out. They tell us dreadful things. Listening to their accounts grips us with horror. We cannot bear the tension any longer, as we ponder how to escape the danger lurking just behind our backs.

For the second time, several wagons loaded with bread set out quickly to Slomniki. A few sacks of apples are sent along to lift the people's spirits. It is the last *chessed* we can perform for our brethren.

As an act of *pidyon nefesh*,[1] women go around town collecting clothing for the poor. Everyone gives openhandedly.

We go to the *beis olam* again. It is the third day of a public fast proclaimed by the *rav*, Rabbi Mordechai Staszewski. Today the shofar will be blown in the cemetery. There is also talk of setting up a *chuppah* there to marry off needy orphans.

The *ohel* of the Rebbe Reb Yoske'le[2] is filled with *kvitlech*. All the gravestones are besieged by people pouring out their heavy hearts. Mothers have come with infants in their arms. Elderly and frail people were carried to the cemetery. They have no desire to return home, for who will remain to carry them back...?

The semi-paralyzed *rav*, aided by his two grandsons, enters the cemetery and makes his way to the *kever* of his father, the previous *rav* of Dzialoszyce.[3] His words, fiery as glowing-hot coals, pierce our hearts.

"*Tatte!*" he cries out. "For this you left me as your successor over forty years ago — that in my old age I should see a dreadful calamity befall my *kehillah*? Why don't you ask our ancestor Reb Mordche'le Staszower to go with his saintly brother Reb Meir'l Apter and split open the Gates of Mercy that have been hammered shut! *Tatte*, what are you waiting for? Don't say that Jews have sinned. Repentance can always help.

"*Yidden!* Everyone answer! Will you do *teshuvah?*"

The roaring "Yes!" of a thousand voices reverberated.

"I will not leave from here, Father. I have a burial plot right next to you, which was prepared for me shortly after you passed away. What pleasure have I had in my life? Lying near you is my gifted son Ber'ke, who died a death of *kareis*, torn away in the prime of his

---

1. Charitable deed performed to redeem one from calamity

2. Rabbi Yosef Dovid Frydman, *rav* of Dzialoszyce in the latter half of the nineteenth century

3. Rabbi Moshe Yechiel Staszewski, *rav* of Dzialoszyce at the turn of the twentieth century

life during the previous war. Shall I now, in my later years, endure another act of *kareis* through war, this time of my entire town? Why must I see the destruction of my *kehillah*, the annihilation of a large Jewish community?

"And my second son, the *rav* of Skalbmierz, who died just recently — was he a minor sacrifice? What more is demanded of us? Is a *korban* our only means of atonement?

"*Yidden*, I will be a *kapparah* for the town of Dzialoszyce! I offer myself as a *Korban Chatas* on your behalf..."

With that, the *rav* fell into a faint. The very earth trembled from the wailing and sobbing that ensued.

When the *rav* came to, he blew the shofar. The exalted atmosphere of *Ne'ilah* enveloped us.

We left the cemetery with a feeling of relief, as if a heavy stone was lifted from our hearts. But as we walked home, we heard the bitter news: The wagons of food we had sent to Slomniki had turned back midway. It was all over. The assemblage of Jews had been taken away, deported by train.

All hope burst like a soap bubble as a threatening black cloud descended over the Jewish horizon of Dzialoszyce.

CHAPTER 2

Calm Before the Storm

TUESDAY NIGHT, 11:00 P.M. My sister-in-law Reizele and I are visiting my gravely ill brother-in-law Yisroel. The doctor has just stepped away from the sickbed after diagnosing Yisroel with a bleeding ulcer and administering two strong injections. His temperature is nearly 40 degrees (104°F). He is not allowed to move at all, not even to stir his hands, and ice-cold compresses must be applied without stop.

"*Panie Doktorze*, what do we do with him?" I ask. "You know the situation in Dzialoszyce."

"Yes, I know..." The doctor hesitates. "But the patient is in critical condition. It'll be a good while until he'll be able to move about."

Perhaps we should admit him to the hospital? Also impossible. What are we to do? How can we forsake Yisroel, the head of our family, who did so much for us, who simply sacrificed himself for his siblings? Now that he is in such a state, how can we abandon him?

Forgetting everything else, our minds concentrate on one goal: saving Yisroel. But how?

I decided to go to the *Judenrat* again and put up a fight. "How could you?!" I confronted the Council members. "You promised to give Yisroel a special armband for his work in the provisions department of the *Arbeitsamt* (Labor Office). For this you charged us thousands of zlotys. Assign him any position, as long as he gets a stamped identity card from Beyerlein exempting him from deportation. What do we do with such a critically ill person? You know full well that we never asked the Council for anything before. But this is a question of life and death!"

I did not, however, achieve any positive results. All our good friends turned their backs on me. Lewkowicz, who used to take loans from our family before the war — which he often forgot to repay — turned a deaf ear when I appealed to his conscience. He was too busy arranging his brother-in-law Smolarczyk's last-minute acceptance into the *Ordnungsdienst*. Things did not look good.

I head back to Yisroel. I try Pesach Szternberg, Yisroel's neighbor, who has a great deal of influence in the *Judenrat*. The sort of old-style *maskil* who is also a Torah scholar, he assures me he will intervene on our behalf. "But," he adds, "with G-d's help, this situation will pass." Sitting unperturbedly before his open Gemara, he shows me a letter he received today from his father, citing a reference from the Vilna Gaon that seems to indicate that Mashiach will arrive at the end of the war.

Szternberg comes along with me to visit Yisroel. He offers glib words of consolation. I, however, cannot be pacified. Yisroel's sweat-soaked, feverish face spurs me to think of a solution to this unfortunate situation.

Reizele and I return home. Everyone is asleep. My sweet little daughter Alte'le lies on my bed so serenely. My dear little son Feivele sucks rhythmically on his pacifier. I can hear their young hearts beating. *Merciful Father in Heaven, what sin have these innocent*

babies committed? How peacefully they sleep before the gathering storm. How can I save them all? And Yisroel?

Reizele, usually bursting with clever ideas, now lies down wearily on the couch and dozes off. She is broken, powerless. Tomorrow, with Hashem's help, we will yet come up with something.

I do not retire for the night but lie down near my dear little daughter. I embrace her precious little form. *Ach, poor child, how I suffered along with you just a short while ago when you were so gravely ill. But Hashem helped and you came back to us. So will He continue to help us now.*

It is a quiet, calm night. Too calm. The calm before a storm.

I make plans:

Chayele will take little Feivele with her to Debowiec (*Dembovitz*) where a certain Mrs. Winiarski promised to take them in for a few days — or to our friend Latosz in Kwaszyn.

Reizele will take Alte'le with her to Mrs. Dzieszyce's daughter in Pierocice, who just today agreed to shelter them, "because they do not look Jewish at all." Then again, Reizele might even succeed in getting a factory worker's certificate. Her (Jewish) English-language teacher promised to arrange it, using his brother's connections at the factory.

Hershel and Tzinne'le and their children will join their neighbor Shmuel Yossel who promised to accompany them to a Polish village he is familiar with.

My mother-in-law will go along with one of her children.

As for myself, I am not too worried. I will find somewhere to go. If things work out with the car that is supposed to come from the Kostrze labor camp to pick up Itche Mayer Shochet,[1] I will go along with him. That might be the best solution for me. They say

---

1. Appellation for Itche Mayer Frydberg, a communal *shochet* (ritual slaughterer) in Dzialoszyce; occupations were often used as if they were surnames.

the conditions in Kostrze are quite decent and there is no fear of deportation, since the Germans need the services of the laborers. *Im yirtzeh Hashem*, I will phone again tomorrow.

Yisroel, on the other hand, presents a serious predicament. Perhaps at the last minute the *Judenrat* people will take pity on him after all and insert his name on the new list of officials they will be receiving tomorrow. Or we may have no choice but to admit him to the hospital, even though he mustn't be moved.

With all these plans, the night passes.

Morning dawns [Wednesday, September 2]. It is a very hot day. Outside, the streets are filled with people rushing about in confusion. A Tishah B'Av atmosphere prevails in my household. No one knows what to attend to first.

I go over to Yisroel's house. He spent a sleepless night. His temperature did not drop; he needs more injections. Finally, he dozes off. His sickly pallor frightens me, but there is no time to think. I hurry home in a daze.

With tear-streaked faces, the Jews appeal to the Polish farmers who have come into Dzialoszyce. Having sensed with a peasant's sense of smell what is about to happen, they hastened into town, ostensibly to save their Jewish friends. In the meantime, they acquire whatever they can for next to nothing. They will buy anything and are not ashamed to make any offer, down to the pants you are wearing. "If you are deported or killed," they point out, "what will you gain by leaving your possessions behind? You want us to save you? Hide you? By all means! Why not! Sure! You can come to us." We give them all our possessions, practically for free.

There stands Mrs. Wrablowski, a wealthy Polish woman from Labedz, feigning tears. Her husband is the mayor of their village; her sister is a schoolteacher. With a red kerchief knotted at the side of her head, she, too, tries to look like an intellectual.

"She really is a good old friend," Chayele observes, as she packs up a few items to leave with Mrs. Wrablowski for safekeeping: her green wedding suit, her black woolen dress, and other valuables. "With whom shall we hide our things if not with her? She says if her husband weren't the mayor, whose activities will be more closely watched, she would offer to shelter some of us."

We had to believe her. What choice did we have?

In the midst of all this, we realize we have no currency left. We had given our last few thousand zlotys to the *Judenrat* to procure an official position for Yisroel. Reizele dashes out to obtain some money. She will arrange it somehow. She can always be relied upon.

No one is available to look after the children now. Glumly, they try to spoon up the burnt semolina-and-milk that Malka the maid had hurriedly cooked for them. Apparently, my bright children sense instinctively that there are more important things for everyone to do than attend to them. My sweet little daughter, her own face smeared with food, offers spoonfuls of cereal into her little brother's mouth. "Eat, Feiveshe. *Mamusia* doesn't have time."

The hours race by wildly. It is already noontime. A taxi of German officers arrives. We can see them sealing the Jewish workshops. It is not a good sign. That's how it all began in Slomniki.

Reizele returns with a small sum of zlotys.

Uncle Yosef Shaul is still sitting by his Mishnayos, determined to finish the *seder* of Mishnah he is learning. He is a great and devout *talmid chacham* and a wise, worldly person, who, from the start of the war, harbored no illusions. Ever since he came to live with us after he and his wife were expelled from their home in Lodz, he kept saying, "The Jewish situation is hopeless." No argument could convince him otherwise. Finding no purpose in refuting his opponents, he wouldn't say more than: "You'll see... Back in Lodz I saw and heard it all," and he would resume his studies.

Now, even he feels a bit uneasy and the sclerosis he suffers from is affecting him more than usual. Nevertheless, he must conduct the *siyum*, for who knows what tomorrow will bring. In this world one must not abandon an unfinished task.

Miema, his wife, is a devoted communal worker. As an act of *pidyon nefesh*, she and other pious women collected basketfuls of clothes to distribute to the poor. She is hoarse now, after delivering a fiery lecture at the cemetery, which inspired all the women in unison to make a pledge to improve in their religious practice.

"I have faith that this is a Heavenly test," she declares. "Hashem wants the Jewish people to do *teshuvah*. And indeed we are! Just look at what took place in the cemetery, where observant and non-observant Jews alike gathered to *daven* to Hashem."

"If only it were so..." Uncle says, swaying sadly. "I envy her *emunah* and *bitachon*."

By now it is 4:00 p.m.

Our Polish friend Wrubel, a restaurant owner, tells us in confidence that the Germans ordered several hundred meals for 7:00 p.m. this evening — which means that their arrival is definite. We have got to do something before the 6:00 p.m. Miechow train pulls in!

Reizele rushes out to pick up her identity card, which she had given to her teacher to stamp at the factory.

Suddenly, Yisroel walks in. Leaning heavily on a cane, he continually wipes sweat off his face.

"I could not sit still," he explains. "I went to the *Judenrat* office myself to beg them for an armband but no one was willing to talk to me. Something tells me not to check into the hospital. So I have decided, sick as I am, to leave Dzialoszyce. If I don't make it, I'd rather die on the road in the hands of G-d than perish at the hands of those murderers."

Sobbing bitterly, Yisroel takes leave of us.

Hershel comes running in breathlessly to say goodbye. "I have decided to leave Dzialoszyce with my neighbor Shmuel Yossel," he says. "I'm hurrying to the barber[2] and will stop by again on my way back."

Chayele readies the children and my mother-in-law packs some more food into the prepared rucksacks. My uncle and aunt do not have plans to leave. Because of his sclerosis, Uncle Yosef Shaul is incapable of walking even ten meters and *Miema* does not want to abandon him. They decide to remain here.

I am very agitated and cannot think clearly. Instinctively, I embrace my sweet little children.

Hershel is back from the barber. "I'm going," he announces.

"Maybe I can join you?" I ask, without thinking it through.

"Why not!" he replies.

I go; I fly out the door, not even remembering to take my rucksack with me.

Reizele returns at the last minute. She could not wait any longer for her identity card.

"It's late, Chayele," she says. "I'm leaving. May we live to see each other again!" She grabs Alte'le in one hand and her rucksack in the other. A quick kiss to the *mezuzah*, and she is gone.

Chayele, my mother-in-law and Feivele were the last ones to leave the harmonious and idyllic house of Yachet Platkiewicz.

---

2. Jews going into hiding would shave off their beards and *peyos*.

CHAPTER 3

The Millenia-Old "Why"

THE WORST OF THE WORST came to pass.

On Wednesday, 20 Elul/September 2 [1942], at 6:00 p.m., the "saviors of European civilization" in the garb of Gestapo executioners arrived with the Miechow train.[1]

They were accompanied by the *Junacy*,[2] the cream of Poland's youth, who, now that they had lost their homeland, put themselves at the disposal of their erstwhile enemy. For a shot of liquor, a *Junak* was willing to implement Germany's ruthless campaign against the defenseless, perpetually persecuted Jew — the very Jew who had just recently shed his own blood alongside him on the battlefield in the struggle for Poland's freedom, perhaps fighting even more valiantly than these shameless beasts.

The town was blockaded by *Junacy* holding sharp spades. Panic and turmoil ensued. Carrying their children, frightened, bewildered

---

1. According to the diarist's Hebrew-language chronicle, approximately two hundred Gestapo agents and three hundred *Junacy* arrived in Dzialoszyce.

2. *Pl.* of *Junak*; members of Polish young men's labor brigades (*Baudienst*)

Jews ran through the streets, searching for a way to break through the chain of drunken Polish youths.

After leaving the house, Reizele met her teacher, who handed her the stamped identity card from the factory. "Now it is unnecessary for you to escape," he advised. "To be on the safe side, you can stay in my apartment on the outskirts of town until things blow over. I have decided to do the same. Surely they won't search for Jews there, since they wouldn't know that Jews live in that area. Besides, no one could tell that you and your young niece are Jewish."

The usually strong-minded Reizele allowed herself to be persuaded and went along to her teacher's house. Feeling somewhat reassured, she put Alte'le to sleep. Not long after, looking out the window, she saw the brash *Junacy* youth. They were sealing off this area, too.

A moment later, a tall, despicable German, accompanied by a Jewish policeman, entered. "Why aren't you in the market square together with all the *verfluchte Juden?*" he bellowed in his bass voice. Brandishing a revolver, he threatened to shoot.

Overcome with terror, Reizele grabbed the sleeping Alte'le, who stirred in her arms and awakened in confusion.

Moments later, they stand with all the Jews in the market square. Tears choking her throat, Reizele weeps quietly, then begins to cry.

"Why are you crying, Auntie?" asks the child.

Why? You ask why, my darling daughter? It is a question of two thousand years of hot, bubbling blood dripping until this very day, which remains unanswered. Shall your Aunt Reizele know why?

You ask why, my precious G-d-given child? When you were ill, my world turned dark. My heart broke, looking at your sparkling, intelligent little eyes that pleaded, "Please save me!" Hashem accepted our prayers and granted you back your young life, and you returned home in good health to your father and mother. Why then, innocent little soul, should you now

suffer the brutal fate of being torn away from your parents and deported to an unknown destination?

And why has your Aunt Reizele — a pure and virtuous person, a proud, true Jewish daughter with a thirst for life, for a spiritual life which she wove in her vivid imagination; Reizele, the budding rose of our family, who selflessly extended herself during this war to save people from becoming sacrifices of the modern-day, twentieth-century Molech[3] — become a korban herself? Possessing the essence of a spiritual giant, this quiet, modest Jewish girl perpetually fought not to let her soul be swept along with the tides of laxity and immorality. Now, while trying to save you, my dear child, she has been physically swept away along with you. Why should such a fertile young tree be chopped down in the midst of blossoming? Why...?

Thousands, nay millions, of whys hover over our nearly decimated Jewish nation. And why was this eternally persecuted nation created in the first place?

The drunken singing and carousing of the *Junacy* can be heard from afar. The Blue Police[4] is at work, too, beating, kicking, and cursing the frightened Jews, whose screams pierce the air.

Our local police are not to be left out either. Ordaszinski, the easygoing town constable who made himself at home with every Dzialoszycer — there wasn't a Jewish household where he didn't indulge his drunken gluttony and accept all sorts of bribes — now struts through the streets, prodding his big dog upon the hapless, wretched Jews.

"Accursed Jews, your time has come!" he snarls at his good old Jewish friends. "Who, if not Hitler, knows how to resolve the Jewish Question? Certainly not our corrupt Polish government who continually conducted discussions in the *Sejm* (Polish

---

3.   Ancient form of idol worship in which children were passed between two bonfires and consumed as sacrifices

4.   Popular name for the paramilitary Polish police force created by Nazi Germany to keep law and order in occupied Poland

Parliament) about you Jews but never did anything substantial about it! Now and then, Jewish businesses were confiscated or boycotted and Jewish students were beaten on the trains. That was worthless. What did we gain from that?"

Ah…things will be altogether different now, muses Ordaszinski, thinking of the substantial amount of merchandise that several of his Jewish friends in the shoe and textile industries had entrusted with him for safekeeping a few days ago. *Now I will really live it up!*

But I better watch out because this expulsion is not the end of them all. Granted, most of the Jews will be deported from Dzialoszyce. But we must keep our eyes open for the escapees who will be hiding in the villages with those boorish farmers. How many Jews have I myself seen today, running through the fields towards the countryside! No harm done — we'll figure out a way to deal with them.

Although the Germans are now implementing their agenda, they are not going to search for these Jews. First of all, the Germans do not know the ins and outs of the villages. Besides, they are afraid of the Polish partisans circulating in the area, and they do not have enough troops for full-scale expeditions. We — the Polish police — will have to take over. We know every nook and cranny in the villages. Thinking that we won't harm them, the Jews will not be so quick to take cover when they see us. Yes, we'll take care of it, and how!

We must do this. If not, some Jews may survive and we will pay for it dearly after the war. In addition, the Jews abroad will take revenge on us. But if there are no surviving witnesses, we'll be able to blame it all on the Germans.

Who knows if some of the children of those who gave me their merchandise aren't hiding in one of the villages? Their parents are now standing in the market square with their rucksacks, glancing in my direction to see if I notice them. They want me to help them somehow. I had better not show that I see them. What if their children come back to me later for the merchandise? True, I wouldn't have to give them anything — they couldn't force me. But

I know those Jews very well. They would be determined enough to take me to court even if they knew they would lose.

I'm sure many of us Poles are thinking along the same lines, for which Pole isn't holding Jewish belongings, some more, some less? We'll find the means to deal with those who rescue and give shelter to Jews. Once we rough up one of those peasant boors, he'll inform on the next one. After all, can a peasant keep a secret?

What can I expect for the future? After the war, when Poland will be an independent country again, I'll really need this merchandise. I didn't have much from Poland. How much did I earn as a policeman? I could barely make ends meet. It was just enough to pay for a few meals at Kulzynski's and nothing more. Since the war, it's been totally different. Raid a Jewish store, confiscate the goods, and give the Germans ten percent. Now add to that the merchandise I was given for safekeeping and I'll have more than enough. The Jews had such trust in me they wanted to give me even more. And why not? I played the role quite well!

I did a good job walling off my cellar! Even that dastardly Madejski[5] won't be able to find anything there.

At that, Ordaszinski smacks his fat lips together with pleasure. "Fetch him!" he roars, goading his dog upon an old Jewish man. Instantly, the hem of the Jew's coat is in the dog's mouth.

Yes, Ordaszinski concludes, *for us, this is Poland's revival!*

---

5. Dzialoszyce police officer who became an undercover agent in Miechow; see Chapter 7

CHAPTER 4

The Catastrophe
Has Begun

THE WHEEL OF HISTORY has gone into reverse. A most original scene
unfolds before the eye: a novel version of the Exodus. In haste, staffs
in their hands and bundles on their shoulders, but, unfortunately,
going in the opposite direction. Our possessions, acquired through
generations of backbreaking toil, we leave for our neighbors, today's
Egyptians. As for the Plagues — we take them along with us!

One by one the Jews arrive, even before the designated deadline,
filling the big Dzialoszyce market square with long rows of
frightened faces. Their minds work at a feverish pace, jumbled
thoughts punctuated by flashes of hope — *Hashem will yet help.*

Now and then a cry erupts from a child demanding food. An old
woman sitting on the ground whispers a prayer: "*Derbaremdiger
Bashefer*, Merciful Creator, display a miracle! Have pity on the
innocent little babies!"

Leaning against the lamppost in the center of the square is the
rebbe of our town, Rav Eliezer Epstein. He is a fourth-generation

descendant of the holy Maor Vashemesh;[1] great-grandson of the *Guter Yid*;[2] grandson of the Rebbe Reb Kalmish of Neustadt; and son-in-law of the renowned Komarner Rebbe. This great tzaddik continued to braid the chain of his holy dynasty, sitting for many years in his small *beis medrash*, immersed in wholehearted, uninterrupted prayer until the German murderers tore him away from his open Tehillim. He stands here completing his unfinished psalms, tears streaming from his eyes.

The only belongings he brought along are his *tallis* and the *tefillin* he inherited from his saintly great-grandfather, the *Guter Yid*. These *tefillin* he must keep with him; according to family tradition, they are a safeguard against all evil. Alas, he could not take along his five Torah scrolls, each of which had been owned by a long line of distinguished ancestors.

"How can we allow our holiest articles to fall into those impure hands?" the rebbe laments. "Perhaps *Hashem Yisbarach* will help and the merits of my ancestors will protect us, so that we will yet return to *daven* and praise our Creator for the kindness He will have bestowed upon us. After all, do we have enough *zechusim* of our own? In today's time of *hester panim*, when our minds are incapable of absorbing lofty insights, how could we possibly rise to the spiritual level of my illustrious predecessors, to their fiery service of the Creator? Hence, we are unable to be in the realm of '*Tzaddik gozer*'[3] and must await Hashem's benevolence, just as when our people stood at the Yam Suf.

---

1. Rav Kalonymus Kalman Epstein, disciple of Reb Elimelech of Lizhensk and the Chozeh of Lublin

2. Rav Yosef Baruch of Neustadt, son of the Maor Vashemesh

3. *Tzaddik gozer v'Hakadosh Baruch Hu mekayem* — "A righteous person decrees and the Holy One fulfills."

"But where can we find a leader like Moshe Rabbeinu to inspire us? All the great tzaddikim of our time are reportedly not with us anymore. Still, our Sages taught: 'Gedolim tzaddikim b'misasam.' Righteous people achieve greater things after their demise than during their lifetime. May they arouse Heavenly mercy for us from above."

Standing by the rebbe's side is the rebbetzin, a woman of boundless piety and kindness. She conducted her household in the openhanded style she inherited from the royal home of her father, the Komarner Rebbe.

Everyone was on her mind.

"What's the name of that poor peddler whose feet can no longer carry him in his old age? We must send him a meal. Who will think of him as he lies in bed unable to move? He could starve to death!" Day after day she sent him meals, being vigilant that no one should know about it. *Publicizing your tzedakah activities takes the soul out of the mitzvah*, she learned from her great-grandfather Reb Eizik'l Komarner.

"And what about the meshulach for the yeshivah? It's nine o'clock already. Surely he hasn't had breakfast yet!" Not waiting for anyone, she herself prepared food for him.

"I just saw a stranger in town. Go ahead, Yuntche, invite him in!" The rebbetzin herself set the table for him, not in the kitchen but in the main room. The Yid, a simple guest, did not understand what it was all about. And what a meal! Not even on Yom Tov did he eat like this. As he was leaving, the rebbetzin gave him a nice sum of money and a small parcel. Once outside, he saw that it was a shirt. Yes, in the midst of all the bustle, the rebbetzin had noticed that the Yid was wearing a torn shirt.

This hardworking woman, who was in poor health herself, even found time to go around town collecting money for the sick and the needy. And staying up at night with an ill person, or doing a

taharah that no one else was willing to undertake, was a matter of course for her. She took no notice of the fact that her own household was pressed for money. Without telling anyone, she sold some of the valuables and expensive clothes that she had brought with her from her wealthy childhood home. She felt that *tzedakah* must not be restricted.

When it came to *shidduchim* for the children, the *rebbetzin* set the standard: she would consider only a match from the court of a rebbe of distinguished ancestry. Their oldest son Yosef, already a rebbe in his own right, is a son-in-law of the Pshetzlover Rebbe, a descendant of the great Ropshitzer Rebbe. Their daughter Dina'le's husband Leibish is an accomplished Torah scholar of sterling character, admired by all. The couple established a prominent chassidic home in Eretz Yisrael; reports of their two children filled the *rebbetzin's* heart with joy. Yisroel'ke, the Kinsker Rebbe's son-in-law, has also become a rebbe himself. Eizik, son-in-law of the Pokshivnitzer Rebbe, has already, during the short span of time that he has lived in Lodz, made a name for himself as a communal activist and *mohel*.

The younger, unmarried children, all of noble character, were forced to go into business to sustain the family after this bitter war broke out suddenly. Nonetheless, with Hashem's help, when the war ends they will marry and continue in the exalted path of their parents.

Even now, the *rebbetzin* does not stand idle but hurries about, attending to anyone who is weak, handing something to one person, to another a few drops of the medicine she always carries for her heart condition. She soothes crying children, and encourages everyone.

The *rebbetzin's* sister, widow of the Radzyminer Rebbe, had come to Dzialoszyce with her oldest son and daughter in order to save her family from the terrible conditions in Warsaw. She, too,

stands in the market square. Wringing her hands, she bemoans her fate. "For this I had to come all the way from Warsaw? Would I not have been better off being buried in the Warsaw cemetery next to my husband and my son Mendel, son-in-law of the Aleksander Rebbe, who was torn away from me by typhus?"

My little Alte'le plays with the *rebbetzin's* grandchildren — Yisroel'ke's children and Eizik's only daughter; Eizik's wife had already been deported from Tarnow together with her father, the Pokshivnitzer Rebbe.

"Time to *daven* Maariv!" a devout chassidic Yid calls out. "And why not with a *minyan!*"

Within moments, *"V'Hu Rachum"* begins, intoned in the Skarbover melody. "He, the Merciful One, is forgiving of iniquity and does not destroy!" A chorus of a thousand voices erupts in a bitter outcry: *"V'lo yashchis* — and does not destroy! *Heiliger Tatte, v'lo yashchis…!"*

My precious little daughter rests in her aunt Reizele's lap, shivering in the chilly Elul night. "Auntie, let's go home to *Tatteshe, Mammeshe* and Feivele," she whimpers pleadingly. "It's so cold…"

My poor child, what home is there to return to? To your father who lies hidden in the wheat fields of Szyszczyce? Or to your mother and little brother, drenched with dew somewhere in Sypow among the peasant bandits who robbed them of everything down to your little brother's last shirt and broke your gentle, frail Babbeshe's hand, the right hand which gave so much tzedakah — is that where you want to go?

Alas, bright child, a boundary, a great dividing line, has been drawn just over an hour ago by that Junak, brother of your little friend Zasia who played with you earlier today in the yard, the friend with whom you shared the apple out of your mouth.

And you, heartbroken dear Reizele — is it possible to penetrate your noble heart to plumb the depths of your anguish in these awful moments?

CHAPTER 5

The Dzialoszyce
Monument to the New
European Civilization[1]

THE TENSION IN THE CROWDED Dzialoszyce market square mounts.
Everyone waits, not knowing what will happen next but certain it
is not something good.

Children, formerly pampered and protected, wander about with
frightened eyes. Lost in the throng, they search desperately for their
mothers.

Young Mrs. Granetman, an expectant mother, lies on the ground.
She has tried to commit suicide and is in the throes of a struggle
with the merciless Angel of Death, who will not so quickly indulge
her wish.

---

1. Ed. Note: Chapter 5, listed in the diarist's handwritten table of contents, is the only chapter
that is no longer extant in its original form. The translation of this chapter was done from a
postwar transcription by the author's brother Dovid Wolgelernter.

Young women holding nursing babies in their arms attempt to soothe their older children to sleep. In hoarse, choked voices, they offer words of comfort. "We are traveling to *Tatte*." Yes, they were going to their Father in Heaven, Who had granted them life and now willed its return.

Absorbed in reverie, people reflect, *Just last night we were home together with our families and now... How long ago it seems... What has happened to us?* Their thoughts are interrupted by piercing screams and gunshots.

They are lined up in rows. With the specter of deportation hovering over them, they strain to whisper final parting words to one another, preparing to take leave of the place where they and their ancestors lived for generations.

Gunshots continue to resound through the air. The German killers are roaming the streets, searching the houses for the sick and elderly who were not able to leave their apartments; they receive their sentence on the spot, saving them the trouble of reporting to the market square. Word spreads that the ninety-six-year-old, partially paralyzed Rav Mordechai Staszewski has been murdered in his home.

Neither do the *Junacy* stand by empty-handed. With spades, pitchforks, and axes, they attack the weakened, tormented Jews. Many fall victim to these depraved murderers. Within a short time, the streets are strewn with the dead and wounded.

Some pious *Yidden* are still *davening*, silently beseeching the Master of the World to have mercy. Others accept the terrible Divine decree with equanimity. *This must be the chevlei Mashiach that our great tzaddikim prayed they would not live to see.*

Suddenly, a raucous shout is heard. "*Achtung...!*"

The tumultuous noise ceases at once, as a long line of previously prepared farm wagons moves into the middle of the square.

With feigned civility, the Germans begin to seat the elderly and anyone who wishes to be first to relocate to the special place designated for the "resettlement of the Jews." The throng presses forward as people hurry to take a seat. Fifty-some wagons are soon filled with 1500 Jews. The Germans reassure those who did not make it into the wagons. "Don't worry. If you'd like, the wagons will come back to get you."

Perhaps we will be spared, some think, *for if, Heaven forbid, they intend to kill us, they would shoot us here on the spot. Why would they go to the trouble of bringing the wagons back for us?*

The people in the wagons are complacent. They cast their last looks at the town they are leaving behind. They can still see the roof of the shul, its white metallic shingles gleaming in the distance. "May we live to return to our holy shul to *daven* and thank *Hashem Yisbarach!*" they exclaim.

What an exalted nation Klal Yisrael is. At a time of great tragedy, on their last breath, our people forget their earthly needs and the danger threatening their existence. Their only request is to be able to *daven*, to connect to the higher, loftier realms. Perhaps that is why we are persecuted and afflicted with physical suffering. For a Jew's world is not the physical one but the spiritual: this world is only an antechamber to the world that awaits him.

Barely ten minutes later, the wagons stop in an area of pitted terrain near the Jewish cemetery at the outskirts of town, where diseased horses and mad dogs are put to sleep. A horrific, bloodcurdling scene is revealed, a scene so ghastly it could not have been conceived by the keenest power of fantasy: Next to a deep, wide pit, which the *Junacy* and peasants had dug expressly for this purpose, stood a row of German Inquisitors, armed with machine guns.

The command was issued before anyone could think. In a moment's time, every Jew was to remove his clothes, place them

along with all his possessions on the ground nearby, and stand at the edge of the pit.

Standing naked before the pit, each person gazed disbelievingly into his own grave, waiting, imploring the *Ribono shel Olam* to deliver him from these terrible moments.

"Move as close as possible to the edge!" The genteel Germans wanted the people to drop into the pit on their own so they would not have to dirty their hands touching the corpses.

Immediately, the beasts began to fire into the mass of people. The sound of gunshots and the screams of Shema Yisrael of the *kedoshim* of Dzialoszyce reverberated through the night. Bodies rained into the pit. No one bothered to check if the victims were dead. Some were only wounded. Others fell into their grave from terror alone. There were those who threw themselves into the pit, intending to find a way to climb out later and save themselves. Within a few hours, the mass grave was filled with more than 1500 victims.

Local Poles stood before the open grave, some saddened, others pleased. Recognizing Jewish acquaintances lying in the pit, they shook their heads sorrowfully, or smiled.

On one end of the pit lay Mrs. Wajnsztajn, her one-year-old daughter in her arms. Because she had a young child, she had climbed onto one of the wagons without knowing where it would take her. She met her death with a bullet through her head and fell into the pit, clutching her baby. The bullet did not hit the baby girl; she was still alive. Hungry and not finding anything to eat, the unfortunate soul cupped the warm marrow spurting from the gaping wound on her mother's head into her little hands. The polite German beasts, not wanting to disturb the child while eating, allowed her to live.

On another side of the pit lay the body of Reb Moshe Dovid Pomeranz, the aged *gabbai* of the *chevra kaddisha*. How much effort

he had expended, hurrying in the middle of the night to stay with the deceased and performing the *taharah*. As for his own *taharah* — it was performed with the blood that flowed on him from his fellow victims.

"Brrr..." The town dogcatcher, present at the site, shuddered with horror. "I would not even dispose of rabid dogs with such sadism!"

One by one, the Jews who were killed in their homes were brought to the pit. Along came Wojtek Gracal, the town drunkard, carrying the body of the ninety-six-year-old *rav*, wrapped in his Shabbos *tallis* with the silver *atarah*. Wojtek's drunken conscience had prompted him to bury the rabbi.

Boisterous, shameless laughter greeted the *rav's* remains. "Ah, the *rabbiner* with the beard! Hurry up and get rid of that rubbish." The dignified beard, so vigilantly guarded by the *rav* during the three years of the war, was disheveled now.

"Phooey!" exclaimed Wojtek.

That was the eulogy and the Kaddish for the *rav* of Dzialoszyce, Hagaon Rav Mordechai Staszewski. The *kever* he had prepared forty years earlier next to his father remained bereft.

The people in town heard the sound of shooting like a distant rumble of thunder. They understood at once what had happened to the transport of 1500 *kedoshim*. That very night they said Kaddish for their friends and relatives — and perhaps for themselves as well.

In the middle of the night, the *Junacy* and the local peasants took the freshly dug earth and covered up the stain of disgrace of the new European civilization.

They say that a day later the earth was still moving from the live victims who were trying desperately to crawl out of their grave.

CHAPTER 6

Funeral of an Entire Town

THE EMPTY SPACES AMONG THE ROWS in the market square, left by the 1500 *kedoshim* who were taken away, are replenished by new arrivals: Jews who had entrusted or gifted their possessions to Polish landlords and friends in exchange for a hiding place, only to be betrayed at the last minute.

There were Poles who simply handed the Jews over to the Germans, who killed them on the spot. Then there were the more decent Poles who did not inform on the Jews, but brought to their attention that their place of hiding was known and that it would therefore be advisable for them to report to the market square rather than perish by a bullet.

And so, the tenants of the wealthy Polish landlord Karol Smaczny, led by the Richter family, arrive in the market square. They had given all their possessions to Smaczny, for which he did construct a special hideout where they could stay for a while. But at the last minute, having safely stored everything away, he politely explained: "The word is out that I am hiding Jews. So I must ask you to have compassion on me and please leave. You see, I want to stay alive. You people are condemned to death anyway, so what difference

does it make if you die today or tomorrow?" Thereupon, his tenants, numbering more than twenty people, had no choice but to present themselves at the market square.

Also approaching the square is Fishel Skopicki, hanging his head in shame. He considered himself a shrewd operator and prided himself on having visited America. Yet he let himself be convinced by his Polish landlord's sons Kozek and Witek Zwolinski to hand over eight bundles of expensive furs, which his wealthy furrier son from Sosnowiec had stored with him at the beginning of the war. In exchange, they promised to hide him and his wife. "A large group would be too difficult," they explained, "but you are just two people!" At the last minute, they, too, came up with the same refrain. He, Fishel Skopicki, was fooled!

Dozens of such people, heads bowed, fill the rows. But there were cases more tragic than these.

On the sidewalk lie the bodies of Yosef Yudel Mandelbaum and his family. His Polish manager Aleksik had taken possession of Mandelbaum's large leather enterprise and, ultimately, all his assets. With no regard for all this, Aleksik himself led the Germans into the concealed room in which the family was hiding, and stood by while the murderers shot them all outside.

Then there was the case of Adamczyk, the Polish town hall official and former army officer, to whom Szydlowski had left all his belongings in exchange for the safekeeping of his two-year-old child whom he could not take with him when he fled Dzialoszyce. Adamczyk now brought the little boy over to a German. "I found this child in an abandoned Jewish house," he declared. Without further ado, the German crushed the child's head with the barrel of his rifle, leaving his body lying on the street in a pool of blood.

The wealthy, aristocratic Tuvia Meryn arrives in the market square. Elderly and frail, he had decided to remain at home, where he impatiently awaited a dreaded death. Having received an order

to stop shooting, the Germans bring him to the square in his pajamas.

With Moszenberg in the lead, all the hospital personnel, including the doctors, are brought to the market square, too; the patients had already been murdered.

The sun blazes down. The heat is unbearable. Tormented by thirst, people beg passing Polish acquaintances for something to drink. Several Poles take pity and furtively bring bottles of water — for which they take fifty-zloty notes or other valuables.

People envy those who have already perished, and cast hateful glances at the members of the *Judenrat* and Jewish police and the other Kehillah officials who will be staying on in Dzialoszyce and are busily making the rounds. *Why? What good deeds have they performed to deserve this? No use asking questions!*

Before long, an extraordinary tumult ensues. The Jewish policemen swing their clubs left and right upon the packed multitude. "Make way!" they shout.

An important personage had arrived from Krakow.

Nobody knows yet just who he is, but everyone begins to breathe easier. Perhaps there will be a last-minute reprieve. After all, the town had offered enough sacrifices already.

The Jewish police keep order. The German executioners stand at attention and salute the passing limousine in which sits a gaunt German officer in high-ranking uniform. Word spreads quickly through the crowd. "It's Kunde,[1] the Gestapo chief of the entire Krakow district!"

As the officer enters the *Judenrat* building, the atmosphere in the market square is very tense; every minute feels like a year. *What new orders did he bring that couldn't have been relayed by his loyal*

---

1. Hauptscharführer Wilhelm Kunde was prosecuted in 1967 and sentenced to seven years in prison. Yisroel Mordechai Finkelstein (Chayele Wolgelernter's second husband), a former labor camp inmate, was summoned to testify against him.

henchmen? Surely, it must be something positive, at least an easing of our situation if not a complete turnaround...

After a time, beer bottles and food items wrapped in paper from Epsztajn's Restaurant are delivered to the *Judenrat* office. "If they are eating and drinking together, it's a good sign," people whisper to each other.

Suddenly, like a thunderbolt, the news carries from one person to the next: "Kunde has ordered everyone, without exception — *Judenrat, Ordnungsdienst, Sanitärdienst* (Medical Service), and anyone else with a red-lettered official armband, wives and children included — to report to the market square. He will not acknowledge the identity cards recently stamped by Beyerlein. They have ten minutes to assemble. Anyone who shows up a minute late will be shot!"

The *Judenrat* officials went into a stupor. They were still intoxicated from the drinking party they had thrown just an hour earlier to celebrate their great, last-minute victory in getting their documents stamped by Beyerlein, in exchange for vast amounts of assets collected from the Jews of Dzialoszyce. The power elite, who were so condescending towards the common Jew who came to their office for a favor or a tax reduction, had now become weaklings. They were helpless as children, not knowing where to turn first.

The time raced by. The allotted ten minutes were almost over. Without time to prepare a knapsack, all they could manage to do was fill their pockets with some gold coins and other valuables from the cashbox. Dazed, their faces deathly pale, they joined the lineup of Jews in the market square, four abreast, ready to march.

It is obvious that Chairman Kruk has lost his mind. Breathing heavily, his head hanging down, he cannot stand still. Each time he darts in and out of his place on line, he receives a rifle blow to his head or a kick from a German boot. In response, his bulging eyes look at his attacker so queerly that the latter turns his head to avoid

Kruk's gaze. His intermittent fits of hysterical laughter serve to convince everyone that he is seriously deranged. At this, even the staunchest optimists who had faith until the last minute throw up their hands in despair and resignation.

The funeral procession of Dzialoszyce Jewry commences. Encircled on all sides by German officers, Blue Police, local Polish police, and *Junacy,* the Jews begin to march, bundles in hand. The more decent Polish neighbors stay out of sight, unable to watch the scene. Some shed tears. The intelligent young Wozniak of the ironware shop closes his business as a sign of grief. Some Poles hurriedly hand bottles of water or slices of bread to the Dzialoszyce police to give to their Jewish friends. The policemen take the items but soon toss them away.

The market square is cleared of people, but the ground is wet from the tears the Jews have shed there.

At the railroad station, the entire platform is surrounded by police, guns in hand, keeping a tight watch to prevent anyone from escaping. Several *kolejka* trains with open wagons stand ready.

The throng pushes forward; the crowding is indescribable. Awful screams and howls erupt, as rifle butts club people on the head. Trampled victims, children lying under the wagons; blood flows. From afar, the sound of singing! A Jew stands, wrapped in *tallis* and *tefillin,* reciting Hallel.

A woman cannot lift herself up onto the train with both of her young children. She abandons them. The guards shoot into the masses that do not fit into the already full wagons; the people inside stand packed together like sardines. They shove in a few more people, one on top of another, until some fall out.

The order to depart rings out.

"*Abfahren…!*"

But the stationmaster is not on the platform.

The order is given to pull out without his authorization.

The first train begins to move ... then the second ... the third ... the fourth... The dreadful screams and wails linger in the air. And on the ground, there is blood everywhere.

In his office, the stationmaster lies unconscious. As his wife and children apply cold compresses to his head, he is heard mumbling some incomprehensible words: "*Shema ... Yis...*"

Unable to watch the cruel scene, he had passed out.

CHAPTER 7

Grave of the Living

THE TOWN OF MIECHOW gained significance in the wake of the war, when the bulk of the burned-down Pinczow district was added to the Miechow zone. The *Landrat* (German district administrator) appointed a Jewish director over all the *kehillos* in the newly enlarged county, so that Miechow now became the metropolis of the entire region.

The director, a fellow by the name of Appelbaum, was a native of Modrzejow who lived in Katowice before the war. A chance acquaintanceship with a German officer in Katowice and a good command of the German language enabled Appelbaum to rise to prominence. His task was clear: he was to be the liaison between the Jewish communities in his domain and the German authorities, who expected him to implement their orders for slave laborers, money and other items. Whether he helped any of those communities cannot be substantiated. Suffice it to say that he drew a comfortable salary, in addition to regularly taking sizeable amounts of money for providing Jews with permits to leave town or use the railroad.

For his residence of Miechow, he did accomplish a lot. All undesirable elements, namely, the poor, were transferred to neighboring Dzialoszyce under the pretext that Miechow, as the seat of county government, could only establish a small ghetto, which could not absorb the entire Jewish population. Therefore, the surplus had to be sent to Dzialoszyce, with its eight thousand Jewish inhabitants. Why he chose the poor was a secret to which only Herr Appelbaum was privy.

Appelbaum put his full influence to use when he persuaded the Germans to expel a contingent of Miechow's Jews, rather than conduct a full-scale *Aussiedlung*. And so, a week ago, when Proszowice, Skala, and Slomniki were deported, only three hundred Jews were taken from Miechow, all of them old people. More than double remained in town.

The heartrending scene of elderly parents parting from their children was tragic enough. Some children, unable to bear watching their parents taken away by force, stayed out of sight. And who carried it out? The Jewish police. Fellow Jews! In fact, it was with this stipulation that the German authorities had consented to a partial deportation — if the Jews did it to themselves.

The wound is still open, still bleeding. People attempt to appease themselves: *Had all of us been deported, would it have been any easier for our parents?*

It was these remaining Jews of Miechow who now came forward in an extraordinary manner to help the newly arrived transport of Dzialoszyce Jews standing knee-deep in the marshes around town.[1] They received permission to bring water and food out of the ghetto for their unfortunate brethren. A special committee was formed. Men and women, old and young, even little children, all with

---

1. The Jews of Dzialoszyce were transferred by *kolejka* trains to Miechow, where they now awaited their fate. As the rail hub linking the narrow-gauge train lines to the larger railroads, Miechow had become the region's headquarters for cattle-car deportations.

yellow armbands, collected a variety of delicacies to bring to the marshes — bread, butter, fruit, jelly and, most importantly, water, lemonade and milk for the children of Dzialoszyce, who were on the verge of passing out from thirst.

With tearstained faces, the Jews of Miechow tried to offer comfort. "At least you Dzialoszycers still have someone who can help you! Who will be left to bring something for us...?"

It was small consolation, but no one could come up with anything better to say. Besides, the Jews of Dzialoszyce could not concentrate on small talk. All they could do was pray for this dreadful situation to end. They had tasted the feeling of people who are lined up to be shot when, unexpectedly, the executioner's rifle misfires. Oh, but that painful moment...!

In the meantime, the Blue Police and the Polish secret agents on guard had their own agenda. Madejski, a former Dzialoszyce police officer who was now an undercover agent in Miechow, selected the well-to-do Dzialoszyce Jews and, along with his colleagues, led them down to the Chabubker forest. There the agents confiscated their possessions and escorted the Jews back with a beating, warning them not to tell the authorities.

No one even considers rescue. It is no longer possible. They cannot shed another tear; the wellsprings have dried up. There is but one thing they fail to understand: when they so carefully prepared their rucksacks, how did they forget to include the most important thing? A certain small bottle of powder. With a quick swallow, it would all be over.

The day wears on. The sun beats down mercilessly. My frail little daughter, who is prone to catching cold, has developed a high fever. She lies on two neighboring bundles, which Reizele has fashioned into a bed. With her parched little lips and flashing eyes, she pleads in a feeble voice, "I want to go home..."

Reizele stands there, wringing her hands, tearing her hair out in despair. What could she do? Who could help her? People's hearts had turned to stone. Their shoes smeared with blood, they stepped indifferently over the bodies of the dying and the dead. The marshes were fuller with blood than water.

As night falls, it turns freezing cold. Shivering, their teeth chattering, somehow they survive the night.

In the morning [Friday, September 4], the good-hearted Jews of Miechow again bring warm milk, fresh bread, and other treats. This is the last time before they part. But with minds weighed down and hearts torn, who can eat or drink?

Every few minutes, vicious shouting is heard from the police on duty. Then, for the second time, a message travels from one person to the next.

"Miechow is being deported along with us…!"

The news does not wait long for confirmation. A column of German soldiers comes into view, behind which marches the Jewish population of Miechow. At the head of the line walks the *rav* of Miechow, Rabbi Henoch Szajnfrucht, slowly, proudly, a majestic figure wearing a silk *bekeshe* with a *gartel*, holding a silver-handled cane in one hand, carrying his *tallis* and *tefillin* in the other. And his eyes, those otherworldly eyes — flashing from them was the semblance of Rabbi Akiva and his fellow *Asarah Harugei Malchus*.[2] If the opportunity arose for him to fulfill the commandment of accepting G-d's sovereignty with all one's soul — "even when He takes your soul"[3] — shall he not accept it upon himself willingly? He is proud that he will imminently enter the palace of those heroes

---

2. Ten Martyrs murdered by the Romans in the period after the destruction of the second Temple

3. *"You shall love Hashem, your G-d … with all your soul"* [*Devarim* 6:5]. *"With all your soul"* denotes serving G-d while forfeiting your life [*Brachos* 61b]. All his life Rabbi Akiva wondered if he would have the privilege of serving G-d to such a degree.

who die in sanctification of the Name of Hashem. His gaze, piercing as a spear, falls upon a vile German standing directly in his path. The latter shivers instinctively and moves out of the way.

After the *rav* walks Avram'che Frydrych, a *kehillah* activist with a warm Jewish heart; Yehoshua Koppel; Avraham Sercerz; Ezriel Koplewicz; Chairman Edelis along with all the *Judenrat* officials and their wives and children, even the Jewish policemen. Eyes scan the line, searching for Appelbaum. It seems he escaped to Krakow at the last minute.

The Jews are lined up once again. Müller, the director of the Krakow *Arbeitsamt*, has arrived in Miechow, seeking laborers for the Krakow-area work sites. Young, healthy men are selected and ordered to stand in the rear.

Some time elapses as the German officials confer with each other. The two groups of Jews face each other. They do not know who is better off. The young men selected for labor, including the Jewish policemen, stand there gnashing their teeth and clenching their fists. In the years before the war, they had been active in various political parties, conducting meetings and founding untold factions and sub-factions; you would need to complete a special course just to remember all those names. Perhaps even the leaders themselves could not distinguish between one platform and the next. It was mostly propaganda, rousing youthful temperaments to engage in their party's struggle by disrupting an opposing party's meeting with rotten eggs, sometimes even with tear gas.

When the visionary idea of a mass emigration of Polish Jewry to Palestine was suggested, its proponents were decried as traitors and their message was hushed up in the press by some of the secular parties that placed no importance on a Jewish land or language. On the contrary, they were afraid of losing their power should the masses leave. The religious parties and their leaders could not agree on a common policy regarding Eretz Yisrael, and alignment with

the non-religious was out of the question. Zionists, Bundists, Communists, Agudists, Orthodox and secular — they could not be united by the ray of hope shining from afar, from a small, blossoming land.

They all stand here together now, united by the catastrophe. But unfortunately, it is too late.

There is no time for soul-searching. The Jews are marching again, this time in their final funeral procession.

As they line up on the platform at the Miechow rail station, a train pulls in with a column of wagons so long, it blinds the eye.

If they ever harbored any illusions about the reports of sealed boxcars transporting hundreds of people to unknown destinations, left on a rail siding until it was certain the occupants were no longer alive, now, standing face to face with reality, they became convinced it was even worse than what they had heard. As the railcars were thrown open, the smell of disinfectant mingling with the stench of congealed body fluids overcame their senses and elicited a wave of nausea.

The young men selected for labor were placed in the open wagons at the rear of the train and ordered to crouch down. Expressing farewell, even with a last glance at their family members, who were being shoved into the sealed cars at the front, was denied them. Only their desperate cries could be heard: the death elegy of an entire nation.

A resounding whistle from the locomotive...and the six-thousandfold grave of the living disappeared.

CHAPTER 8

Exile in Szyszczyce

WENDING ITS WAY THROUGH partially plowed fields is a long caravan of Jews who escaped the besieged town of Dzialoszyce, carrying rucksacks on their shoulders in which they had packed only the barest necessities — some food and clothes to last until the storm blew over, when those who managed to save themselves would return home.

People still think this is a passing phenomenon. It defies belief that a 90 percent Jewish town will be emptied of over eight thousand Jews with none remaining. Surely the *Judenrat*, *Ordnungsdienst*, and other Kehillah officials will be allowed to stay in town, and those who escaped will be able to join them once the danger is over.

The stories we had heard about Lublin and other cities where deportations had taken place earlier had seemed like myths. Today we face reality. Carrying their bewildered children, delicate women who had never walked through rough country terrain stumble over the furrowed earth, losing their fine summer shoes. They trudge on in an effort to get as far away from Dzialoszyce as possible, occasionally taking a sip of water to quicken their lagging spirits.

As nightfall approaches [Wednesday, September 2], we do not dwell on what will be. Surely the peasants will take us in. Some of us had arranged shelter with Polish acquaintances. In the worst case, we'll pay a few zlotys. We can tell that the Poles empathize with our distress. They shake their heads sadly and give us directions. Some bring us bread, water, even milk for the children.

Our friend Shmuel Yossel devotes himself fully to us. Holding their three-month-old baby, his wife walks alongside unassisted. "My wife does not need a guide," he explains. "She was born in the countryside and is familiar with these parts. All the farmers know her and will offer to take her in. As for your brother-in-law Hershel and his wife, his sons Feivel and Reuven, and his young daughter Gittele — they lived in Sosnowiec before the war. They are city people who are not used to carrying heavy bundles and walking these country paths." He helps them carry their rucksacks, and makes sure they rest from time to time.

It is only now that I realize that I did not even bring along my own rucksack, so distraught had I been.

What happened to me? How did I leave Chayele and the children behind? Granted, we had agreed that she was going to take our little Feivele with her. And Reizele had insisted she would take Alte'le. Having helped Alte'le a year ago when she was so gravely ill, she wanted to rescue her from this danger, too. Nevertheless, they are women, and the children are young and need to be carried. What can I do now? It was the last minute when I got out of Dzialoszyce — and they were still home! If only they managed to leave in time…

I am miserable. I take no notice of the hours passing by. It is already early evening and will soon turn dark.

"We've covered six kilometers," Shmuel Yossel tells us. "Another stretch and we'll be in Szyszczyce, the village where I know many decent Poles."

By now we are tired. My brother-in-law Hershel's lovely ten-year-old daughter Gittele does not want to give over her rucksack to her mother. "I'm not tired, *Mammeshe*. I can carry it just like everyone else."

Yes, this proud little child knows all. She already bears the weight of the Jewish people's two-thousand-year journey on her young shoulders.

We sit down under a tree to rest a bit and Shmuel Yossel brings us fresh cold water from a well. "Let's wait here," he says. "As soon as it gets very dark, we'll go into the village. I trust that from all my acquaintances someone will let us in. But, G-d forbid, if not — you never know these days — I arranged shelter with Ludwik Juszcyk, who lives at the edge of the forest, about one kilometer outside the village. Ludwik is a lawless peasant who needs all the money he can get for drinking. He is capable of robbing and stealing, too, but he would not betray us.

"I'm beginning to think it might even be the best place for us. Since it's outside the village and near a forest, years could go by without anyone passing there — you can only get there by crossing hilly terrain. Still, he is the sort of person the whole area trembles from. Hopefully, he won't rob us since he knows me well and would be ashamed to do so in my presence. Besides, what alternative do we have? Any decent, law-abiding peasant who isn't greedy for money will be too afraid to harbor Jews. Ludwik has no fear. That is one thing we can depend on."

The grass becomes wet with the evening dew. We *daven* Minchah as if it were Erev Yom Kippur, feeling the lowliness of being worthless creatures, people without a home.

After it turns dark, I make out the daughter of Zimak the *poritz* passing by. On her frequent trips to our store, she had always been attentive to my children.

I approach her. "Would you let us in to spend the night, if only in a barn?"

She does not recognize me at first. Then: "Ah, I know you!"

With utmost politeness, she proceeds to explain that it is prohibited under penalty of death for Poles to shelter Jews.

We tiptoe through the village. Shmuel Yossel leaves us on our own while he goes to meet his acquaintances. Every minute of his absence seems like a year. We begin to ponder whether he has abandoned us. *Maybe our group is too much trouble. What will we do without him? We do not know where to turn in this strange, dark place.*

But Shmuel Yossel soon returns. "I met up with the manager of the Zimak estate and promised him whatever he wants if he would just allow us to stay in any of the numerous stables or storage chambers on the estate," he explains. "The *poritz* wouldn't even have to know about it."

The manager, an intelligent young man, himself a refugee of a German-occupied city, is moved by our plight. Quietly, he opens a barn and lets us in. "But you've all got to leave before daybreak," he declares. "I'm afraid Zimak will find out. This is a serious offense, punishable by death."

Exhausted and frightened, we bed down on the straw. The manager brings us water. "Keep quiet and do not talk," he cautions. "I will stay up all night and stand guard."

With pounding hearts, we lie there shivering. It is a cold night and we had left town in summer clothes. *Where is my Chayele...?* I wonder. *Where are my children...? And Yisroel...?* I dread to think of Yisroel. How could he possibly endure such wandering, sick as he was when we left him? *O Hashem, show us miracles!*

Hardly had we dozed off when the manager came in, his entire body trembling. "You must go! I hear them shooting not far from here. In fact, it sounds quite close. Who knows if they aren't in the next village over? Escape! Save yourselves!"

"Where can we run at this hour?" we plead. "It's past one o'clock in the morning!"

"Just get going...! Go...!" he cries.

Shmuel Yossel hurries to get his wife and child and his elderly mother and sister, who had all taken refuge with an acquaintance. In the meantime, the manager leads us to the estate's potato patch. He refuses the reward we offer him for his kindness and stations himself on the road to wait for Shmuel Yossel in order to tell him where we are. As we lie stretched out among the wet potatoes, we do not even feel the cold.

Shmuel Yossel arrives with his family members. "Come, let's go to Ludwik," he says. "We cannot stay here in the village. I heard the gunshots, too. It's possible that in the quiet of night, it seems closer than it is. Still, remaining here is dangerous."

We move on, dragging our feet across the hills until we reach Ludwik's house. Welcoming us cordially, he puts out bread and water, awakens his daughter and prepares her room for us, bringing in fresh straw for bedding.

"Have no fear," he drawls, not entirely sober yet from the day's drinking, having used the advance that Shmuel Yossel had given him earlier today. "You are with me — Ludwik!

"The dogs won't come here to search, but in the worst case, I have even prepared a *skrytka*[1] under the straw of the barn floor. Make yourselves comfortable and give me your bundles — I'll lock them in the closet. Don't be afraid. Jozek, tell them who I am. They don't know me."

He rambles on and on, but we do not hear anything more. After all the walking, and the terror we had experienced, we are worn out and very hungry. The hearty black bread and water that Ludwik set out is very enticing. We eat, having in mind to thank *Hashem*

---

1. Concealed place, often a pit dug under a stable as a makeshift bunker

Yisbarach that we had found such a decent person to take us in. Ludwik is not at all the way Shmuel Yossel portrayed him. Shmuel Yossel apparently wanted to give us a pleasant surprise.

We lie awake for a long time; our host went to sleep in his room. As I converse with Shmuel Yossel, whom I barely knew back home, I see before me a simple, unpretentious, virtuous person, a man with a pure Jewish heart who is ready to extend himself, without any ulterior motives, for the simplest Jew.

He bemoans the fate of the *rav* of Dzialoszyce, albeit the *rav* was in his nineties and partially paralyzed. "I should have carried him on my shoulders and rescued him! Also the Pinchever Rebbe, Itche Mayer Shochet and others. I could have found places to hide them — I have many Polish acquaintances. Rescuing yourself alone is no great feat!"

Dear G-d, Master of the Universe, I think, *who would have imagined that in such a seemingly unremarkable young man there could flow so much ahavas Yisrael?*

I believe that with Hashem's help we will be saved under the guidance of this young man. What a pity that Chayele and the children, Reizele, my mother-in-law, and Yisroel are not here with us. Who could have known? What a pity...

CHAPTER 9

In the Hands of Bandits

OUR HOST LUDWIK HAD RISEN long before us on Thursday morning [September 3]. Smiling broadly, he greets us with a hearty good morning and asks what we would like for breakfast. With that, he expects another advance; he is already sober from yesterday's drinking and needs a refresher. We give him a nice sum. Though he promises to bring bread, milk and whatever else we want, he does not bring us anything and we eat the food we have with us from home.

Ludwik heads into the village to find out the latest news. After a while, he returns, dazed and trembling with fright. The man who fears no one and whose very name strikes terror in others is not his usual self. With the talent of an actor, he presents to us what took place in Szyszczyce.

"The Germans and the *Junacy* arrived last night and conducted a search raid for Jews. On the south side of Szyszczyce, near Dzieraznia, they killed over forty people! The *Junacy* happened upon Abrams and his wife and two daughters just as they were coming out of the mayor's barn. When one daughter tried to escape, they cracked her

skull open with their spades. They led Abrams' wife and other daughter to the Germans, who promptly shot them dead. When the mayor pleaded with the *Junacy* to release them, they threatened to take him along to the Germans, too. Only Abrams himself got away.

"Things are bad. They are searching everywhere and will certainly come here, too. You must leave! I will lead you to the forest, and when things quiet down you can come back."

Moments later Ludwik's wife and daughter come dashing in, on the verge of collapse. "We hear shooting! Run!" they wail.

We pack our bags in a hurry and follow Ludwik into the forest. "I'll stand guard and give you a signal if anything happens," he says.

Ludwik heads out of the forest. Sitting there on the alert, fearful of the slightest rustle, we truly begin to feel the bitter taste of exile. Suddenly, three unfamiliar faces with cold, devious eyes rise before us, as if from under the earth. With sharp axes in their hands, they appear to be woodsmen. Immediately recognizing the men as infamous bandits from the village of Parszywka, Shmuel Yossel turns pale. We huddle together.

"Hands up!" comes the command. "Leave go of your bundles!" They search us, looking for hidden zlotys.

"Can't you see how wretched we are?" we plead desperately. "If you let us live, we'll give you whatever you want!"

Shmuel Yossel, visibly overwrought, addresses the men by name. "You, Jozef, Staszek — I know you all! How can you Parszywka landowners even think of doing such a thing?"

If Shmuel Yossel, who grew up among the peasants and knows their mannerisms and character, is so affected, it is an indication that our situation is dire.

The fellows say no more but move off to the side to confer with each other. Apparently, Shmuel Yossel's words have made an impact.

"Jozek knows us," they murmur. "He knows we are estate owners in Parszywka. If he tells people what we have done here, we are doomed! Granted, the other Parszywka villagers are bandits, too, who do not consider it a disgrace to rob people. That is, if they do it themselves. When someone else commits an offense, they will not forgive him, and by the next day his barn and stable will be up in smoke.

"If Jozek wouldn't be here, it would be a different story. Not a soul would know what we are up to. We must think of a way to get rid of him — but not in broad daylight. They won't escape that quickly. Maybe we can accomplish the job tonight. In the meantime, let's take some of their possessions, so they'll think we're done with them. Once they feel safe, we can fix things. Or perhaps, if we offer them a good hideout, we can even persuade them to come with us. Let's bring them food in order to gain their trust."

They return to our group. With feigned sympathy, they claim it was all a joke. "We did not intend to rob you, G–d forbid! We are human, too. Do we know what fate has in store for *us*? Of course, if you want to honor us with a couple of zlotys, we might take it. For how much can we earn nowadays from our work? We do have bread to eat and we can bring food for you, too, if you'd like. That doesn't cost a great deal. A good drink, on the other hand, is hard to come by. If you want to pay us, that's fine. If not, that's fine, too."

We were moved by their words. If the men were not sincere, what stopped them from taking everything from us? Without further deliberation, we handed them three hundred zlotys and some of our possessions. They thanked us profusely. One man stayed to comfort us. The other two left.

Before long, they return with bread, boiled eggs, and a pot of buttermilk.

"Eat, you poor folks. Don't be afraid. If you want to come with us, we'll find you a good hideout for as long as you need. Here in the forest it is not safe."

We are about to accept their offer, but Shmuel Yossel motions to us in the negative. "We'll stay here a bit longer and think it over," we tell them, excusing ourselves.

They do not insist. "By all means! But understand that we don't have much time left."

With a friendly goodbye, they take leave of us, and we remain alone.

Afterwards, Shmuel Yossel explains what a great miracle we just experienced. "You have no idea who those people were! Known murderers with the blood of many on their conscience! I'm afraid to stay here. We are not done with these fellows yet. They may change their mind. Let's leave this place immediately."

We move on, taking shelter in a gully covered with underbrush. As we lie in wait for a signal from Ludwik, we hear gunshots reverberating distinctly in the distance. Hour after hour, the day wears on. It is already dark, but there is no sign of Ludwik. Shmuel Yossel decides to go to Ludwik's house.

He finds out that Ludwik had been looking for us during the day at the spot where he had left us. "How should I know you had to leave your place in the forest?" Ludwik complained. Having heard that the Germans would be returning tonight to search again, he was reluctant to let us back into his house for the night. But when Shmuel Yossel negotiated with him and slipped him a fifty-zloty note, he stopped grumbling.

Soaked from the evening dew, we all return to Ludwik's house. He prepares straw for bedding but does not offer us food this time. As we lie on the straw, we again consider the great miracle we have experienced, and thank Hashem that we suffered only fear.

Ludwik points out that my good suit will arouse suspicion. "People can tell that you are rich Jews," he says. "Here. Put this on." He offers me his old, threadbare winter jacket along with a pair of pants that is so tattered, nearly half a leg is missing. "Incidentally, it'll keep you warm, as the nights are starting to get cold. Hang your suit in my closet — no one will take it." With no choice but to oblige, I don my new uniform, transforming myself into a Purim masquerader.

Soon we hear a noise coming from the barn. The dog barks furiously. Quickly, we put out the candle. Peeking through a crevice, Shmuel Yossel makes out the three bandits. Apparently, they had spied on us and had come to accomplish what they could not do in the daylight. It seems Ludwik noticed them as well. Wielding a hatchet, he is already outside in his pajama pants.

"Get out of here, you thieves! Whom do you want to rob? Me — Ludwik? I'll make mincemeat out of you!"

Caught off guard by this reception, the men retreated.

We realized that staying here, with the bandits keeping an eye on us, was precarious. Although they did not succeed today, how could we be sure they would not try again? We also could not fully trust that Ludwik wouldn't team up with them. Or he might demand more money for our protection than we could pay.

We decided that Shmuel Yossel would go into Szyszczyce in the morning, G-d willing. Perhaps things had quieted down in the village and he could find someone there who would take us in. We would also send a messenger to Dzialoszyce to assess the situation there.

We did not go to sleep that night. Ludwik stood guard. In the morning [Friday, September 4], we asked him to go into Dzialoszyce. He readily agreed but warned, "If I'm not home, who will protect you if the bandits return? All of you had better go to the hilly

terrain at the edge of Szyszczyce. I will bring you bread and milk, and from there I'll go to Dzialoszyce."

With Shmuel Yossel leading us, we leave Ludwik's house. It is not far and he knows his way around. We can see the whole village. It is quiet; there is no sound of gunfire.

Everything Ludwik told us had indeed taken place. Since many Jews were seen fleeing in the direction of Szyszczyce, where the villagers were known across the region as upright Poles, a catastrophe resulted in which more than forty Jews were murdered. But now the search was over.

Ludwik soon arrives, carrying a big bucket with just enough milk to cover the bottom. He hands it to us along with a slab of bread. For his forthcoming trip to Dzialoszyce, he charges us 100 zlotys. "The bread and milk are separate," he explains. "That's on my wife's account." What could we do? We hand him another fifty zlotys, and he is on his way.

Several of Shmuel Yossel's acquaintances in the village come by and share their accounts. They are truly noble people. Some even have tears in their eyes. One, a robust young farmer, stands there wordlessly, dabbing his face so no one will notice he is crying. Shmuel Yossel whispers something in his ear, to which the man nods affirmatively.

"That fellow was Staszek Tetele, a very good-hearted person," Shmuel Yossel tells us afterwards. "He has agreed to let us stay with him tonight. Let's hope this day passes uneventfully."

Later on in the day, we see Ludwik in the distance, staggering towards us in a drunken stupor. Feigning tears, he cries, "Oh, what I have seen! Dzialoszyce is in ruins! Where are my dear *Zyd'kes*? There is not a soul anywhere!"

We learn that Dzialoszyce is still under siege; no one is allowed entry. When Ludwik told the officials that he was there to deliver goods, they reluctantly consented and let him into town. Any Jews

found in the region were assembled at the town hall. There will be another transport, and further searches will be conducted in the surrounding villages.

I do not know whether to believe Ludwik or not. Regardless, I am terribly frightened. We wait impatiently for nightfall. As soon as it turns dark, we slink into the village one by one and take shelter in Staszek Tetele's barn, where his mother awaits us with bread and milk.

Other farmers soon arrive. The village mayor appears and invites all of us without exception, a group of twenty-two people, to his barn. He helps us carry our bundles.

Friday night finds us lodged in the barn of the kind mayor of Szyszczyce, the humanitarian Piotr Juszcyk.

CHAPTER 10

The Kindhearted Mayor

THE NIGHT PASSED QUIETLY. Early Shabbos morning [23 Elul/ September 5], the mayor entered the barn accompanied by his wife, who was carrying our breakfast: boiled potatoes and hot milk.

We had never before eaten food that was cooked by a non-Jew, and to make matters worse, this food was cooked on Shabbos. For a moment, we hesitated. But our cheerful host, noticing our predicament, pointed out the circumstances we were in.

"You'll be able to resume your pious way of life once you're back home. I myself respect and value religious people, no matter their religion. Every person should follow the faith in which he was born and raised. But there are times when you have no choice. You cannot survive without eating and drinking."

We ate the nourishing food, warmth spreading through us.

"You must have been cold sleeping here in the barn," the mayor continued. "We will figure out what to do about that tonight. I have woolen blankets and an old fur that you can use. Let's just see this day through.

"I'll be in Dzialoszyce today. Here in Szyszczyce there is nothing to fear, except for the landowner's despicable German commissar, who shows up regularly once a month and spends the day bustling about, looking for cows or pigs that were not vaccinated. For him, you have to watch out. But we know when he is coming. One person passes the word to the next. That is the degree of solidarity we have in this village. No one will inform on you, even though you are Jews.

"Take a look at how all the villagers are mourning the tragedy that took place on Thursday with Abrams' wife and two daughters. That this should happen in our village and through our fellow Poles no less! One of the girls had just been leaving my farm carrying a pitcher of milk for some Jews hiding in the hilly terrain outside the village. The *Junacy* caught her right here in my yard. When I heard her cries, I raced outside and witnessed the violent struggle. The other daughter was already lying there with her head split open. I ran over and grabbed a *Junak*. 'What are you doing?' I yelled. Thoroughly drunk, he whacked me on the hand with his spade, uttered an obscenity and threatened to take me along to the Germans. I even recognized one of them and marked his name down. There will come a day of retribution. It is not far off.

"See, take a look at this." He offers me some underground newspapers.

I am taken aback. "Underground newspapers?! Aren't you afraid?"

"No," he answers. "From whom shall I be afraid? G-d is the only one you have to fear. We do not have to be on guard here. The Germans are gone and the locals would not betray one of their own. Not one *Junak* originates from this village!"

After telling his wife to take good care of us, the mayor prepares to leave to Dzialoszyce. I ask him to find out detailed news, and give him some addresses where he might learn the fate of my family members. "Very well," he says. "You can rely on me."

We *daven* without *talleisim*. We had not even thought to take a siddur along, and it is the Shabbos preceding *Selichos*!

I am very restless, since I do not know what is happening in Kazimierz either. Had there been an *Aussiedlung* there, too? Where are my parents, brothers, and sister? I am completely cut off from the world. So close, barely seven kilometers from Dzialoszyce, yet it might as well be on the other side of the ocean.

Shmuel Yossel calms me. "We can depend on the mayor for information. Have *bitachon!*" Dear Shmuel Yossel is truly our guardian.

Several hours later, the mayor returns, his usually smiling face looking grim. He tells us that Dzialoszyce is still in a state of unrest. The town is like a fortress — you can neither enter nor leave. As a mayor on official business, he was allowed in. Assembled in the courtyard of the town hall was a new group of several hundred Jews who are to be transported to Wolbrom this evening to join the deportation leaving from there. SS Angels of Destruction were circling around, casting fear upon everyone. They shot a crippled man, a member of the Chaba family that owned a restaurant in the market square.

He did not meet anyone he knew and therefore could not find out anything about my family. He stopped at the addresses I had provided, but they were boarded up. All the stores were closed. He had no definite information about Kazimierza Wielka either. Some said there had been a deportation in Kazimierz; others said not.

We continue to grope in the dark. I cannot allow myself to believe that nothing happened in Kazimierz. For what reason? Isn't it in the same district as Skalbmierz?

Shmuel Yossel brings some plums into the barn and tries to distract us with conversation. "We will not accomplish anything by worrying," he says. "Tomorrow is the Sunday holiday. *Im yirtzeh*

Hashem, on Monday the mayor will go into Dzialoszyce again and we'll know more."

Immersed in thought, each person sits in his own corner. My sister-in-law Tzinne'le is thinking about her two daughters, Chayele and Esther'l. The good-hearted Engineer Szeliga of Nieszkow had promised to send them to a prominent friend of his in Warsaw, where they would live as non-Jews. Granted, the engineer, manager of the sewage construction project in Nieszkow where two hundred Jews worked daily, had previously done us many favors, enabling our family to avoid forced labor. But such a risky undertaking? Sending away two young girls to live as non-Jews! If, Heaven forbid, someone recognized them, would their host still be willing to shelter them? There is no guarantee of anything today. Wouldn't they have been better off wandering together with us and sharing a common fate?

"Just imagine!" Tzinne'le wonders aloud. "Chayele and Esther'l even wanted to take Gittele with them. How would I survive here without my beloved little daughter, who is such a source of comfort to me?"

Meanwhile, our group continues to grow. Whenever the benevolent mayor notices a stray Jew, he welcomes him in and gives him food without asking for any compensation.

It is Monday at last. Good old Ludwik shows up. "Why did you leave me?" he demands.

He tells us frightening news. He heard from his brother who lives in the village that a large search raid will take place here soon. "How can I abandon you in such a time of danger? Since I rescued you in the beginning, I want to help you to the end."

Ludwik warns the mayor not to go into Dzialoszyce. In his superstitious mind, he is convinced that a trip into town is life-threatening. He claims that any person entering Dzialoszyce will be arrested. Hair-raising fantasies! As soon as I press a few zlotys into

his hand, he changes his mind. "If you want to go," he tells the mayor, "I might as well go along with you. Let's find out once and for all what is happening there."

I send along two letters, addressed to Polish friends of mine. Again, we wait impatiently for answers.

Late that evening, the mayor returns. He has specific information this time. A transport of several hundred people had indeed left for Wolbrom on Shabbos. Afterwards, other Jews came out of hiding, thinking the danger had passed. Once again, the new group of Jews was assembled in the town hall. What will happen to them nobody knows. No orders have been given as of yet.

Regarding Kazimierz, the mayor did not have any definite news. He had concerned himself only with Dzialoszyce.

As for my letters — he had brought replies. Two sealed envelopes. He had not read them. With trembling hands, I rip one open. The letter writer informed me that Reizele and little Alte'le had been seen in the market square among the rows of Jews in the first transport. He did not know anything about the rest of my family. According to the second letter, my entire family — all of them without exception — had gone with the transport.

Cold sweat pours over me. My head spins, rainbow-colored dots blurring my vision as the barn whirls around me like a circle of dancers.

What happened afterwards, I do not know.

When I came to, there was a wet cloth on my forehead.

The heartless killers of our people
Tore my heart to pieces, slashed my soul,
When they snatched my cherished daughter in the dawn of her
  youth.
My world turned dark, my soul refuses to be consoled.

The sun of my fortune that set before its time,
My hoped-for firstborn child — where are you?
Are you still among the living???

My heart is searching in the east; my spirit roaming the world.
Alte'le, my beloved daughter, I sought you but could not find you.
O, how I yearn for you — will I merit seeing you again?

In memory of my three-year-old
daughter Alte'le who was taken on a transport on
Thursday, 21 Elul 5702

Chaim Yitzchok Wolgelernter
Tishrei 5703

אזכור לך, דודתי לעשות זמון

יש לעזרים קריא, נשמה שמא

דאן יתן את חמדתי, ישמר נלחמת

וזו תשא לארו ואנא בנויא ונסיי''

יש נשמת שלא ראותא שמא

ראות את ותקמו איזא ?

הכן יחיים זה ??

יש באמת ורוני ססוא רסלא עלוא ...

יולד שאמר שם שליא גל ולאות ...

וזו ןא - ואסא זרות שרקי את ?

לעזה את הבר ... שם שם-שין שלומים ... ... זיף ל ... וזי שלי

ואנא שין ...

CHAPTER 11

Reunited with My Child

I FEEL COMPLETELY WORTHLESS. For what purpose shall I carry on? What can I look forward to after the war, if I survive? Such a difficult battle to wage and what will victory achieve?

Our group here in the barn grows ever larger. On Tuesday morning [September 8], Shmuel Yossel's younger brother Mordechai shows up unexpectedly, a strapping young man with a gentle soul. On the day of the Dzialoszyce expulsion he was in Nieszkow, working at the sewage construction site. When he heard what was taking place in Dzialoszyce, he took shelter with Polish acquaintances in a nearby village. By this time, his mother and Shmuel Yossel had already assumed that he was taken with the transport. The joy at his arrival is great.

"Don't you see?" Shmuel Yossel consoles me. "We, too, thought that Mordechai was gone. Do not believe what people wrote to you. How could they know what happened in that pandemonium?"

A spark of hope began to flicker in my heart. Could it be possible? *Lieber Bashefer, if I ever earned a zechus, may it stand me in good stead now!*

In the afternoon, Shmuel Yossel comes running breathlessly into the barn. "I have good news! I know for certain that your wife, your mother-in-law, and your little son Feivele are here in this area! I have no details yet..."

Half an hour later, the kind mayor returns from Kazimierza Wielka. I had asked him this morning if he could go to my parents' town to find out what was happening there. He hands me a long, detailed letter from my sister Yitta.

She wrote that Kazimierz and Koszyce were quiet. They had feared the worst, but it did not come to pass. Dovid'l and Meir'l went to the Kostrze labor camp, traveling in the car that was heading to Dzialoszyce to pick up Itche Mayer Shochet on that Wednesday. I was supposed to have joined them, but the car was delayed, and by the time it arrived, Dzialoszyce was under siege. Afraid that Kazimierz would meet the same fate as Dzialoszyce, my brothers, along with a few others, continued on to Kostrze. Father went to Wislica (*Veislitz*). Yitta and Mother went into hiding in Kazimierz. But in the end there was no *Aussiedlung*, and none appeared imminent. Father came back from Wislica where he had met my brother-in-law Yisroel Platkiewicz, who was staying there with his wife and two children, his mother-in-law, sister-in-law, and brother-in-law Yoav and family.

Yitta enclosed a letter she had received from Chayele. *I am in Sypow together with my mother and Feivele,* wrote Chayele. *We were robbed. The bandits took all our possessions. I do not know where Chaim'l is, or where Reizele and Alte'le are. Nor do I know if you are still in Kazimierz or whether there was a deportation there, too. I am sending a messenger in the hope that if any of you are still there, you can send us some clothes and let us know the whereabouts of the rest of the family.*

Yitta concluded her letter, noting that she had sent Chayele a few things for little Feivele and asking that we make arrangements to come to Kazimierz.

"Your parents begged me to bring you to Kazimierz," the mayor interjects. "Even though the trip is risky, I promised them I would take you if you want to go."

My joy is not complete, as the report that Reizele and my beloved daughter had gone with the transport is, unfortunately, true.

I immediately dispatch a messenger to Sypow, just two kilometers from Szyszczyce, to bring Chayele here.

Chayele arrives. She is not the same person. Broken, eyes swollen from crying, gentle Chayele had suffered more than the rest of us. With difficulty, she relates the harrowing events she experienced.

"Carrying Feivele in one hand and my rucksack in the other, I left Dzialoszyce together with my frail mother. Not knowing where to turn, we wandered around for a while until we found our way to Latosz in Kwaszyn, who had promised he would take us in if the need arose. He did receive us very graciously, but just when we thought we were safe, he said, 'There is no way you can stay here. The mayor of Kwaszyn has announced publicly that harboring Jews is prohibited. I'm afraid to keep you. However, I have a plan. I will take you to my brother. He will accompany you to his brother-in-law in Dzieraznia who is willing to shelter you.'

"And so Latosz took us to his brother. He, too, was quite friendly. He even insisted on carrying Feivele. On our way to Dzieraznia, we saw two ruffians in the distance coming towards us, carrying heavy sticks. Realizing they were bandits, Latosz's brother ran into the forest with Feivele. The bandits approached Mother and me, and without saying a word, struck Mother's hand with their sticks. 'What do you want?' she sobbed. They kept hitting her until they broke her hand and the pouch she was carrying fell to the ground. They took it and ran off.

"We were on our own. Mother's hand swelled up and turned colors. *Ach*, it was just awful! Soon, Latosz's brother returned, alone,

without Feivele. 'Where is my little boy?' I screamed. 'I put him down on the forest floor,' he answered.

"'Abandoning a child in the forest at night?! Are you out of your mind?' We cried and pleaded with him until he agreed to go and bring Feivele back. After a short span of time that seemed like years, he returned with the child. As for the beautiful winter blanket in which Feivele had been wrapped — that he did not bring back to us. Happy to have the child, we did not say a word.

"In the middle of the night, we arrived at the brother-in-law's house and paid him the full amount he demanded for keeping us until the storm blew over. But first thing in the morning — we had barely slept — he drove us out. Why should he continue to give us shelter? After all, we had already paid him.

"Wandering aimlessly, we did not know where to turn next. We lay down under a big tree in the middle of a field and stayed there for the next two days. Suffering excruciating pain from her broken hand, Mother fainted. I did not even have cold water with which to revive her. Finally, we set out to search for someone who would have mercy on us. With great difficulty, we managed to drag ourselves to Sypow where we found a poor family who let us into their hut.

"Don't ask questions. I have no strength to speak. You ask why I look like this? If I am still alive, I must be made of steel. You surely heard about Reizele and Alte'le... I see you are crying... If you want to survive, you must stop. It is a bitter *gzar din*, a Heavenly decree, and we are no exception. Hashem granted us Alte'le as a gift and He took her back. We must strengthen ourselves."

I contemplate my wife. It is over six years that I have been married to her. Before my eyes, she had now grown to a height of spiritual nobility that I was not able to attain. A woman of delicate disposition, she had acquired an iron strength of character, the soul of Beruriah, the Tanna Rabbi Meir's wife, who waited until Shabbos ended to

show her husband the corpses of their children. And when he began to grieve, she comforted him with these same words: "*Hashem nassan v'Hashem lakach* — G-d gave, and G-d has taken." Chayele had consoled and fortified me.

"Let us thank and praise Hashem that we are here," she continued. "Mother is still laid up in Sypow with her broken hand. Despite everything we endured, we experienced many miracles. The fact that we did not stay in Kwaszyn or Dzieraznia was a miracle, too. The very morning after we left, German raids were conducted, with trained dogs searching for hidden Jews. They found a number of Jews — there were many victims."

"Shall we go to Kazimierz?" I ask Chayele.

"I think that we should wait," she replies. "They say it will be possible to return to Dzialoszyce soon. Let's send a messenger there to find out."

Chayele goes back to her mother in Sypow. I write a letter and ask the mayor to take it to Dzialoszyce and hand it to any Jew he encounters there.

The mayor returns with a reply from my good friend Yakov Nifker.

After the recent, second transport, which departed on Shabbos, wrote Nifker, *people say there will be no further deportations. All the remaining Jews are gathered in the courtyard of the town hall. They are allowed to go out and buy food. Bialabrode is in charge. I have become the interpreter at the town hall. You should stay where you are until I write again and let you know how things are developing. Bialabrode says the Judenrat and the Ordnungsdienst will return from the work camps any day now. Perhaps the community will reestablish itself.*

I ask the mayor to go to Sypow at night to bring back Chayele, my mother-in-law, and Feivele.

Within a short time, my aristocratic, pious mother-in-law had withered. Seeing her with a drooping, broken hand made a very

painful impression on me. This virtuous woman accepted her suffering without complaint. "Let it be like this," she said, "instead of something bad happening, Heaven forbid, to my children."

My precious Feivele, wearing the clothing Yitta had sent him, reached out to me in the dark of night with his little hands — "*Tatteshe!*"

My new-found child recognized me...

Painful emotions and anguished memories stir within me,

As I remember that bitter day — 21 Elul 5702 — when the oppressor burst in.

The stars were darkened; we hoped for a ray of light, but there was none.

Cursed sinners, murderers of the heart of our nation,

Where, O where, did you carry off the pure souls of our brothers and sisters?

Reizele — you blossomed like a rose in the garden of our beautiful family;

You were destined for greatness, with your extraordinary talents and your bright mind,

Your noble spirit, refined soul, and penetrating perception,

Pure heart, charm, piety and devotion.

You aspired, hoped, and fought for life,

Utilized your days productively, benefiting and protecting others

Until your last moment — but you were unable to save your own life.

How can we find consolation? your friends and relatives ask.

And I myself, what answer can I give them?

Reizele, you were plucked together with my beloved daughter,

And so my pain is twice as great. Why should I be bereaved of both of you?

In memory of my young sister-in-law Reizel Platkiewicz,
who was taken away on a transport on
Thursday, 21 Elul 5702

Chaim Yitzchok Wolgelernter
Shevat 5703

ר' עשות ברכים וברכות וברכים כקרתי ואנד

ו' ים ובר - כא עלל תפו - זת שכ הבורד

ז' הטזן בודי נטן יקן נאוו ואזן

ח' בים אנותם בולת ובם אזין

ל' קן לאן? הורשווו ישות הבורות בל אחנן ואחולון —

פ' רחת - רשילש - כוטוש ראן שב חטון הענדרים.

צ' אולות ולבת- יקשוטול וקוקוים ורעון הבשוים

א' בת רח, לפ אזוב, ומדו הכרב

ט' בורת לי, ישת חן, ירצה ומרבב

ק' לית שבש, ורוד בהיש לתת

ר' נ חת בשוים לבוש ולגן ולולש חבש

ש' ב ושבץ האתהן - ובוב את בפ את לא הבבת

ת' ראב לבתים ? יוע אחתונ ברגן וקוקורון

ר' איון לאות, בב ואאש להויבו?

ח' הח אן - רשילש - פן לקלש כ אן ועת

צ' הד שוב אלא פ - פים וה באת שולא שבל ???

שלנ יבר תל רווי האפ ...

Alte'le

You were the first seed in the soil of my happiness,
The blooming flower in the family garden I had just begun to plant.
Your "Tattenyu," trilled in a high-pitched birdsong,
Played on the strings of my heart,
The Song of songs of my life's burgeoning springtime.

With your lively bouncing and fluttering,
You turned the pages of the most beautiful chapter of my life;
The bright, warm rays of your soul,
Reflected in your intelligent, flashing little eyes,
Illuminated the depths of my most latent feelings,
Warming me and filling my spirit with joy.

If the ladder of happiness has a peak,
I reached the highest rung,
For G-d granted me a gift,
You, my precious daughter, Alte Sarah Leah.

The bloody tempest on the Jewish horizon
Ripped the budding rose out of my garden;
The dreadful specter of the tragic transport
Darkened my awakening spring.
My musical strings became stained
With the blood flowing from my wounded heart;
My garden of happiness was flooded
With a deluge of scalding tears.

This *kinah* for Alte'le was written in Yiddish and the original is no longer extant

CHAPTER 12

Yom Kippur 5703 in Kazimierz

WE SPENT ROSH HASHANAH 5703 [September 12-13, 1942] in the mayor's barn. Although we were more than a *minyan* of men, we had neither a *tallis* nor even a siddur, and, needless to say, no shofar. Each person pieced together the holy words of the *tefillos* from memory as best as he could.

No one had any individual, personal pleas. Just one collective request from the Master of the Universe that the new year should bring relief and an end to the plague, at least for the few remaining *Yidden*.

After Rosh Hashanah, I receive a letter from my parents, asking me to come to Kazimierz and assuring me that the situation is stable. All those from Kazimierz who had left to Kostrze, including my two brothers, had already returned home.

Just then the *poritz's* cruel German commissar arrived in Szyszczyce. All of us had to leave the mayor's place and hide in the ditches near the forest. The gusty winds of autumn had already

Tefillos of Rosh Hashanah handwritten by author; *U'nesaneh Tokef* and *L'Kel Orech Din*

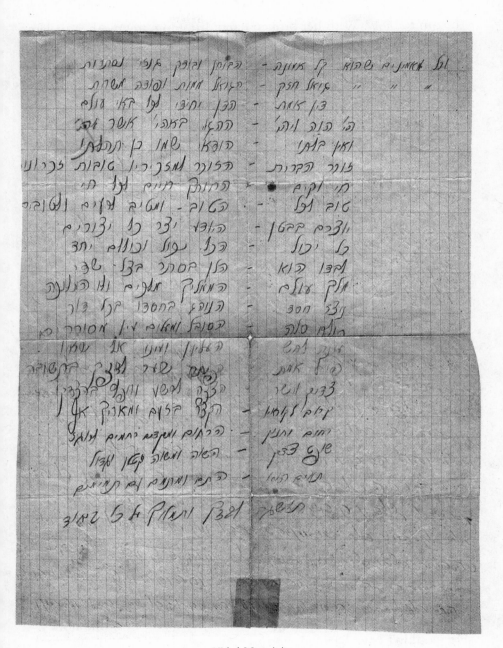

V'chol Maaminim

begun to blow. With her broken hand drooping, my mother-in-law was in terrible agony. My little Feivele, unable to wait for someone to feed him, busied himself with the pacifier in his mouth, took his little pillow, put it under his head and fell asleep. For over six hours he did not have a bite to eat, yet he did not cry; apparently, this child of twenty months grasped the situation. Lying on the wet grass, his face nearly turned blue from cold. We decided not to wait any longer. We would travel to Kazimierz.

At night, we return to the mayor's barn. The wicked German is no longer in the village. On his way out of Szyszczyce, he ran into Rafalowicz, a refugee from Lodz, a quiet, respectable young man who had done business in this area. Without further ado, the German shot him dead.

I tell the mayor of my plan to travel to Kazimierz. He agrees immediately and offers to take us at 1:00 a.m. that night. My brother-in-law Hershel and his family were going to stay until it was safe to go back to Dzialoszyce.

In the middle of the night, Chayele and I, my mother-in-law, and little Feivele set out on the risky journey. We are frightened, but the kind mayor bolsters us.

After traveling some distance, a Polish police officer carrying a rifle blocks our path. Unruffled, the mayor tells him the truth. "These are Dzialoszyce Jews. They want to save themselves. You obviously know what happened there. So what do you want? They are no murderers; they never hurt anyone. Get it?"

"Yes, yes, I understand..." the policeman stammers, "but... but..."

I press a fifty-zloty note into his hand.

"Move along," he says. "Have no fear. You won't run into anyone else. *Do widzenia*! Goodbye!"

The mayor is offended. "You didn't have to give him the money. He wouldn't have harmed you."

We arrive safely at my parents' home. Here in the close-knit circle of my loved ones, my wounds, which had barely begun to heal, opened up again. It was only a few weeks ago that Chayele and I had been here with both of our children; we traveled home a week before the disaster. The joy that Father and Mother derived from my daughter Alte'le is indescribable. She had consumed so much of my parents' energy and worries when she lay deathly ill in the hospital in Krakow. Surely it was Father's prayers that brought about her recovery. At last, they had merited to have her as their guest in good health. A beautiful, bright child, she was the center of attention of the whole town. People could not stop marveling at her intelligent responses...

And Reizele, my soft-spoken, good-hearted sister-in-law, whom my parents considered a member of their own family... How could this have happened?

Hanging prominently on the wall is an enlarged photo of Chayele and me with sweet little Alte'le, vibrant and animated, as if she were alive.

Father is inconsolable. He cries into his tear-soaked Tehillim.

I observe everything around me. Life goes on here. *Yidden* walk in the streets, talking to each other. You can even see them smiling. How can this be? May Hashem help that these people continue to be spared.

At Shlomo Wisnicki's house, they are preparing meals for dozens of refugees from Dzialoszyce. People give *tzedakah* unstintingly.

The next morning, Erev Yom Kippur, Mother wakes me at dawn. "You used to get up early to *shlag kapparos*. Here, I prepared a white rooster for you. Take along little Feivele."

I arise and take my precious child. "This rooster will be our *kapparah*, redeeming us of our sins, my dear child. And may you, little one, our great source of solace, remain ours and not be torn away from your father and mother."

The *shechting* of the chickens and the hurried atmosphere of a traditional Erev Yom Kippur routine took place as every year. But the usual awe for the upcoming Day of Judgment assumed a different aura this year: everyone, even the non-observant Jews, felt a sense of fear and trepidation.

We did not ready ourselves as we did in the past, when each individual would contemplate his own private bundle of troubles and prepare to pour out his heavy heart and beseech the *Ribono shel Olam* for a good year, livelihood, and children. This year we felt a collective responsibility, a sense of accountability for the whole nation. Every person had already experienced in the flesh the impending danger facing us all — the demise of all Jews without exception. Our nation had gone through many difficult times and held on through fire and water. But now, the greater part had already perished, innocent children torn from their mothers' bosoms and buried alive.

Yes, we were getting ready. We would pierce the Heavens, pry open the gates. Miracles must happen. After all, the generation in Egypt did not have more merits than us. We had indeed sinned, but we have undertaken to improve.

The Yom Hadin approaches. We go to Shlomo Wisnicki's house to *daven*. Most of the *mispallelim* are Dzialoszyce *Yidden*, lone individuals who managed to escape. All are brokenhearted, having lost different family members.

Father recites *Kol Nidrei*. As the soul-stirring Skarbover melody surges forth, an intense longing gnaws at our hearts. *Where are all our loved ones...?*

We join in with all our might, like drowning men in a stormy sea clinging to a plank of a sinking ship: "*Vayomer Hashem salachti k'dvarecha...!*"

In the morning, Father asks me to lead the congregation for Shacharis. "You know the pain of the people, so you are suited to be their emissary," he says.

I had never before been the *shliach tzibbur* on Yom Kippur. I *daven*, I chant the *piyutim*; the words emerge as if on their own. "*L'Bochein levavos b'Yom Din* — To the One Who examines hearts." The grief and pain of all the broken hearts gathered here. On this Yom Hadin, we, the remnant of our nation, were all being judged.

Father led *Mussaf*. For the first time, I really understood the meaning of the words, "*Mi bacherev* — who by the sword; *mi baraav* — who by famine; *mi batzama* — who by thirst…" And when we intoned *Eileh Ezkerah*, it was as if the *Asarah Harugei Malchus* were standing before my eyes. This Yom Kippur, I felt neither tired nor hungry. It was an easy fast; may it always be like that.

Father led *Ne'ilah*, too, as if he wanted to achieve it all on this Yom Kippur. For who knew what would be in a year from now?

Ne'ilah: the closing of the gates, the last word of the accused before the verdict is pronounced. We invoke the Thirteen Attributes of Mercy and the merit of Avraham our forefather who offered his only son on the altar of the *Akeidah*. We ask for a pardon and resolve to be upright and pious. Then, the final cry: "*Hashem Hu HaElokim!*"

At night, Father is still in his *tallis* and *kittel*. Like the *kohen gadol* in his white garments after the *Avodah*, he has not finished yet. He is waiting for the moon to appear so he can recite *Kiddush Levanah*. He cannot remember ever having missed it on Motza'ei Yom Kippur.

Outside, the sky is covered with ragged clouds, like blood-smeared pieces of cotton wool taken off a fresh wound. A light autumn rain begins to drip, pressing heavily on our spirits.

The moon did not appear that night.

CHAPTER 13

Return to Dzialoszyce

THE DAY AFTER YOM KIPPUR, Hershel and Tzinne'le's daughter Esther'l came from Dzialoszyce. On the Wednesday evening of the expulsion, at the height of the danger, she and her older sister Chayele had fled to Engineer Szeliga, manager of the work camp in Nieszkow, who had promised to arrange shelter for them with his friend in Warsaw where they would live as gentiles.

She has a long story to tell.

"Yes, there still are decent people in this world," says Esther'l. "Not everyone is possessed by this mad hatred. What Engineer Szeliga did on our behalf deserves to be recorded in the annals of our family.

"When Chayele and I arrived in Nieszkow, the engineer welcomed us like a father. After hiding us at the estate of an acquaintance in a nearby village, he composed a letter to his friend in Warsaw, introducing us as two cousins of his in need of lodging. He then sent for his work foreman, handed him the letter, and instructed him to escort us the entire way until we reached our destination.

"The foreman started out with us, but as we ascended the express train in Miechow for the next leg of our journey to Warsaw, we realized he was gone. Wondering what could have happened to him, we figured he had decided that taking us until Miechow was sufficient! After all, he had already collected payment from us in advance of the trip, so why should he put himself at risk?

"We were on our own. The foreman had the letter with him, and so we did not have the Warsaw address of our hosts. We did remember the name of the people and a house number, but not the name of the street. Since Chayele had been in Warsaw several times in the past, she decided that we should travel on. With a vague recollection of the name of the neighborhood, we arrived and started looking for house number 17 in that area. We found it quite easily.

"The aristocratic, upper-class people who opened the door treated us with suspicion at first. After all, we did not even have a letter to identify us. Once we gave them satisfactory proof, however, they allowed us to come in and gave us an elegant, private room. And that is where we have been all this time.

"But how could we live peacefully in Warsaw when a bloodbath had taken place in Dzialoszyce? I decided to travel back. First I came here to Kazimierz, but no one had word yet of your whereabouts. I then traveled over to Uncle Yisroel in Wislica, where I found out everything...about Auntie Reizele and little Alte'le, such pure *korbanos*... From there I went on to Dzialoszyce, staying with the Nifker family for Yom Kippur.

"More and more *Yidden* continue to arrive in Dzialoszyce. Here, Uncle, I have a detailed letter for you from the Nifkers."

I read the letter. It is from Chaim'l Pomeranz, describing in detail the current situation in Dzialoszyce, the return of the *Judenrat*, and Bialabrode's project of emptying the Jewish houses. He assured me

that if we returned to Dzialoszyce, our house would be opened for us.

Chayele and I decide to travel to Dzialoszyce that night. My mother-in-law, Esther'l, and Feivele would stay in Kazimierz for the time being, until we arranged for our apartment to be opened.

At 3:00 a.m., I set out with Chayele, bidding farewell to my parents' home for the last time.

It is still dark when we arrive in Dzialoszyce. Fire engines and ambulances guard the ransacked city. We go straight to the home of the Nifker family, one of the largest, most distinguished families in town.

Alas, what happened here? Of the eighteen members of the family, only a third had survived. With tears in their eyes, Chaim'l and his sister Lola, the children of our dear friend Yisroel Pomeranz, Moshe Nifker's son-in-law, tell us their story.

"We, the young ones, decided to set out into the world, despite the fact that we had no Polish acquaintances in the area who would take us in. After building a concealed room right here in the house for our father, grandmother, and uncles, we left, with the understanding that they would go into hiding. Apparently, when the time came, they were afraid to carry out the plan, and they all reported to the market square. Had we known this, we would not have stepped foot out of our house. How can we go on living without our dear father? We are orphaned twice over! As for our grandfather in Eretz Yisrael — how can he help us?"

Yes, here in Dzialoszyce, face to face, the communal tragedy begins to unfold in its full magnitude. The suffering of the group makes you forget your own individual suffering.

I go out into the streets. Jews no longer walk through the market square. The Poles look upon every Jew as if he were a murderer, a scoundrel just released from prison. Jews walk only through the side streets and alleyways. The houses are boarded up, sealed with

white paper, deathly silent. In several houses, the beds and floors are stained with congealed blood from the elderly victims who were murdered at home.

Encountering a familiar face, there is such a feeling of kinship that people kiss and embrace one another. Every person has a whole pack of miracles to give over, stories of how he survived. My head is bursting. I cannot bear listening.

I meet my good friend Meir Szulimowicz. He had aged twenty years, this man who had always been full of life. I barely recognize him.

"We did not try to escape," he tells me. "Our entire household stayed in town. We constructed a hideout in the attic for over twenty people. My older son Yossel, employed as the secretary of the public kitchen, had received a stamp from Beyerlein exempting him from deportation. The rest of us entered the hideout, and Yossel walled off the entrance from the outside. We had prepared enough food for two days, certain that in a day or two he would come back to let us out. A few days passed and no one came. Who could have known that Yossel would be taken on the transport, along with the entire *Judenrat*?

"Looking through the tiles on the roof, we could see everything. Don't remind me... The glowing-hot tiles caused torrid heat in the attic. The air was so stifling we felt we would pass out. Our throats burned, but we had no water left; even drinking our own urine could not alleviate our raging thirst. The temperature continued to rise. Some of us already lay unconscious. It was impossible to wait any longer. Better to die from a bullet than this slow death.

"With our last ounce of strength, we called through the roof for help. The firemen came, chopped down the walled-up entrance to the attic, carried out the unconscious, and took us all to the

courtyard of the town hall. Little by little, we came to. Is it any wonder that you do not recognize me?"

He broke down crying. "It's my own fault! I could have been together with my two children in Eretz Yisrael. When my daughter was here a year before the start of the war, she begged me to go back with her. Yes, we are all to blame. Even at that late stage, we could have left Poland, but we did not believe… And even once the refugee situation in Zbaszyn began,[1] it was still possible to escape. Now it is too late — we missed the opportunity."

Our apartment is opened for us. It is just as we had left it. Reizele's things and my Alte'le's little dresses lie around, bereft.

Hershel and his family soon arrive from Szyszczyce. Later that day, Yisroel, too, arrives with his family from Wislica.

"I collapsed several times while escaping Dzialoszyce," Yisroel tells us. "I lost all hope of making it, and begged my family to leave me and at least save their own lives. If they perished along with me, would they be helping me? Suddenly, as if he fell from the sky, a Jewish wagon driver pulled up in a horse-drawn cart. Where he came from was beyond comprehension, at such a time when Jews were prohibited from traveling or even leaving town. Without hesitating, he took all of us in his wagon to Wislica.

"On the way, we encountered a uniformed German officer holding an electric lantern who pointed out the way. 'You must be running from the Dzialoszyce hell,' he said sympathetically. 'Save your lives. Don't be afraid!' We could not understand what was happening.

---

1. Towards the end of October 1938, the German government expelled all Polish Jews living in Germany and deported them back to their native Poland. These Jewish refugees, numbering in the thousands, were held in the town of Zbaszyn (German: *Bentschen*) on the Polish–German border for many months. (Frustrated at his family's ordeals in Zbaszyn, Herschel Grynszpan shot a German diplomat, which became the pretext for the *Kristallnacht* pogrom.)

"That was no ordinary wagon driver," Yisroel and his family state with conviction, "and that officer was definitely no German! They had to have been angels in disguise."

CHAPTER 14

Bialabrode the "*Macher*"

A RED, PUFFED-UP FACE, a pair of beady eyes, and a raspy voice speaking the crude jargon of a Vilna fishmonger — that is the physiognomy of David Bialabrode.

Son of the powerful chairman of the Slomniki *Judenrat*, Bialabrode obtained the post of commander of its Jewish police. His colorful, adventuristic past enabled him to expand his activities far beyond the boundaries of his official position. He established connections with the German authorities, and in the wake of the partial *Aussiedlung* that took place in Slomniki after Pesach, he won the liking of Beyerlein, the newly appointed chief of the Miechow SD. From that point on, Bialabrode could always be found in Beyerlein's company.

His power became ever greater. An automobile was even put at his disposal. There were those who benefited from him and others who were brought to ruin; his name was on everyone's lips. To some Jews he became a legendary figure.

What services he provided for the Germans, nobody knew. Suffice it to say that as soon as Bialabrode arrived in any town with

his automobile, just the sight of his small green cap with the feather on top aroused terror. It meant something new was happening. He carried a leather whip with him all the time and struck innocent Jews no differently than a Gestapo agent. There was speculation that he was even collaborating with the Gestapo, but no one was able to ascertain what his duties were.

During the deportations in the Miechow district, Bialabrode was granted an extraordinary level of authority by Beyerlein, and through his influence, all *Judenrat, Ordnungsdienst* and other Kehillah officials in the entire Miechow region were allowed to stay on during the first round of deportations. Their task was to empty every Jewish home of its contents and sort the possessions into designated storerooms, to be sent to the German *Reich.*

The same was supposed to have happened in Dzialoszyce. Beyerlein had already stamped the identity cards of the Kehillah people, allowing them to stay in town along with their wives and children. However, for unknown reasons, Kunde, chief of the Krakow Gestapo, arrived at the last minute and put them all on the transport. Beyerlein and Bialabrode — or "Dawid" as the Germans called him — came up with a plan. They phoned Müller, the director of the Krakow *Arbeitsamt,* and asked him to separate the young men from the rest of the transport, on the pretense of needing workers for the Krakow-area labor camps. They hoped to find a way to bring the *Judenrat, Ordnungsdienst,* and as many others as possible back to Dzialoszyce to form the same type of liquidation committee.

Their objective was well thought out. In other towns, as soon as an *Aussiedlung* took place, a public auction would be held, wherein masses of peasants would buy the contents of Jewish homes for a few paltry groschen and the German authorities got nothing out of it. With this plan, much would be accomplished, as all Jewish possessions would be gathered in special storage depots. These Jews

would also come in very handy, Bialabrode pointed out to Beyerlein, since they would know where to search and would be able to find items that had been hidden away.

Their strategy succeeded. Müller selected most of the young men on the Miechow transport. They were taken to the Prokocim labor camp near Krakow where all their belongings were confiscated, and three days before Yom Kippur, after working there for two weeks, some fifty former *Judenrat* and *Ordnungsdienst* members were picked up by a special truck and brought back to Dzialoszyce. Bialabrode was waiting to give them instructions regarding the liquidation committee they were to form. Their sealed homes were opened.

The Jews who were assembled in the courtyard of the town hall were given shelter in the large *beis medrash*. The *Ordnungsdienst* men stood guard, making sure no one escaped. The public kitchen was reopened. Little by little, Jews from the labor camps, as well as Jews who had fled to the countryside or to other towns, returned to Dzialoszyce. Those who had large sums to pay off the *Judenrat* were able to get their homes opened. Yossel Richter became the chairman of the *Judenrat*; Kruk, the former chairman, had been deported.

But the *Judenrat* had lost its power. Everything was in Bialabrode's hands. He assigned his own people to supervise the smooth operation of the liquidation process. A committee was formed with a number of groups, each group consisting of one *Judenrat* member, two *Ordnungsdienst* men, and several workers. They opened the sealed homes and carried out the contents, all the while searching for any hidden valuables. The entire booty was then taken to the shul where the items were sorted and sent to designated storerooms. There were many such storerooms: textiles, leather goods, shoes, haberdashery, imported foodstuffs, even old clothes. Every time Bialabrode or Beyerlein came to town, they helped themselves to some items and left.

Beyerlein was delighted with the operation. "You have done a masterful job for the great *Deutsche Reich*!" he exclaimed. "I guarantee that you will be able to stay here as long as you wish. You are a useful bunch of Jews! You're the kind of people we need!"

It was heartbreaking enough to witness hard-earned Jewish possessions and generations-old furniture being carted off by fellow Jews. But even more so was the way it was done — with trademark German precision — and for whom — for the killers of our fathers and mothers!

The members of the *Judenrat* and *Ordnungsdienst*, whose wives and children had been deported just over two weeks ago, were bereft. Some lost their minds entirely, going day by day like automatons to their hated work.

They did it mechanically; it no longer had an effect on them. They took the Jewish possessions out of each home, carefully, so that everything would arrive intact at its proper place, not realizing that when they completed their assignment, maybe even sooner, they would be deported once again. The wicked Germans accomplished this with a particular kind of sadism: having Jews liquidate themselves.

Yes, it reminds me of the *Aggadah* in which Rabbi Akiva asked someone, "What is your sentence in the Next World?" Replied the man: "My Gehinnom is to go into the forest every day with an ax, chop wood, build a fire, throw myself into the fire and get burned. The next morning I arise and repeat the process all over again."

Unfortunately, we are seeing the same Gehinnom unfold here on this world. Large sums of money were given to the selfsame Beyerlein before the *Aussiedlung* in return for a promise that the *Judenrat* officials would be exempt from deportation. Yet they were deported anyway. Why are his guarantees of today any better? Are they not building their own fire, to be burned in it once again?

Nevertheless, people have hope. They still believe that they will be spared.

Life in Dzialoszyce begins to take on an air of normalcy. Jews arrive from other towns in danger, thinking they will be safe here since our town already underwent an expulsion raid. Most of them are not native Dzialoszycers. But the main thing is, there are *Yidden* here again.

The spark of hope ignites: *Netzach Yisrael lo yeshaker.*[1]

---

1. *The eternity of Israel will not be deceived.* This verse [see commentaries on *Shmuel I* 15:29] is often cited to denote the eternal and indestructible nature of Israel, guaranteed by Divine promise.

CHAPTER 15

Appalling News

IN DZIALOSZYCE THIS SUKKOS [September 26, 1942], you could not tell it was Yom Tov. No one put up a sukkah. These days every person's house was a sukkah, a "*diras arai*," a temporary dwelling. Life itself was temporary. Although people were streaming into town from all sides and things had taken on a semblance of normalcy, we did not feel a sense of security.

Appalling news came in from all over. Deportations were beginning throughout the district of Radom. Several partial deportations had already taken place in the city of Radom itself, and shortly before Rosh Hashanah the city was completely *Judenrein*. The expulsions followed a sequence — first the larger cities, then the smaller towns.

As the onslaught neared the town of Zawichost, my sister Matil wrote to us several times, desperately calling out for help. She asked that I provide her with the address of our brother Avramele in Canada. The younger of her two sons, seven-year-old Yechiel Issamar, declared that he would not go on the transport but would

set out into the world. If he managed to save himself, he would need an address to turn to.[1]

Ostrovtze was no more. My saintly rebbe, wearing his *kittel* and wrapped in his *tallis*, was murdered along with his two sons while learning the subject of *kiddush Hashem*.[2]

People arrive in Dzialoszyce from as far away as Opatow (*Apt*) and Staszow. Hearing that an *Aussiedlung* had already taken place here and that Jews were allowed to come back, they took it as an indication that we will be able to stay in Dzialoszyce from now on.

People from Wislica and Pinczow, towns where we ourselves had sought refuge just three weeks ago, come to us now, since these towns are in the Radom district.

And so we run, back and forth. And in Dzialoszyce itself, the ground is burning under our feet.

There is no longer a *shochet* in town. I put my certification in *shechitah* to good use, free of charge. Perhaps in the merit of enabling *Yidden* to eat kosher, Hashem will help. We must try everything.

At the *Judenrat* office, they say in Bialabrode's name that all those who are engaged in emptying the Jewish homes can rest assured that as long as the liquidation process lasts they will be allowed to stay in town and it is even possible that there will be no further deportations in Dzialoszyce. Supposedly, two towns in the Krakow district will be designated as *Judenstädte* where Jews will be allowed to live and Dzialoszyce will be one of them. Similar baseless rumors circulate throughout town, as people try to pacify themselves.

Is it merely coincidence that only Kazimierz and Koszyce remained untouched when every other town in the entire Miechow district was made Judenrein? I wonder. Could it be that the German murderers intentionally

---

1. Ed. Note: Matil and her husband Chaim Yosef Mandel and their children Meir Avigdor and Yechiel Issamar were never heard from again.

2. See footnote in Appendix C for an actual account of what occurred.

left these two towns intact, in order to round up all the new arrivals in the region along with the Jews of these towns?

Beyerlein soothed Bialabrode, pointing out that the newcomers to Dzialoszyce had been put to work in the labor camps of Raclawice and Rosiejow nearby. Raclawice has already been sealed. Barracks were put up where the laborers slept and ate, and just as in Prokocim and other labor camps, the inmates were not allowed to leave. The laborers in Rosiejow, on the other hand, went from Dzialoszyce every morning and returned home at night.

Once again, Jews had to clean the market square. The town hall announced that all Jews residing in Dzialoszyce must have their identity cards stamped every month by the magistrate, just like before the *Aussiedlung*.

The local Poles resumed their feigned cordiality towards the Jews, evidently thinking we were here to stay. And the regional land commissar, though he no longer had any control of the Jews since Beyerlein took over, accepted bribes once again. Naturally, he reassured everyone that there would be no more deportations.

Jews kept coming without stop. One by one, all the Dzialoszycers who were taken off the transport by Müller and sent to Prokocim sneaked out of the camp and returned to town illegally. They were risking their lives, and a number of them, all good friends of ours, were indeed caught and killed. It was heartbreaking to see formerly wealthy Jews, who had lacked for nothing even once the war began, transformed into living corpses, powerless, the light in their eyes extinguished. They stood in line at the *Judenrat* office to get their apartments opened so they could take some possessions before their homes were liquidated.

The Pinchever Rebbe, Reb Pinye'le, who was originally from Sosnowiec but had been living in Dzialoszyce since the war began three years ago, returned from Wodzislaw (*Voidislov*) where he had fled on the day of the Dzialoszyce expulsion. Although Wodzislaw

had undergone an *Aussiedlung* two weeks before us, there was a feeling of unrest there again.

Our home was open to the public. We invited everyone — friends who could not get back into their homes as well as those who had no one left to cook a hot meal for them.

On Chol Hamoed, two sons of Rav Eliezer Epstein, Chaim Meir and Hershel (the youngest), returned from the labor camps. The two of them and two older brothers, Kalmish and Eizik, who could not get out of the camps, were the only survivors of their entire family. The rebbe's apartment and the *beis medrash* were opened right away. We *davened* there and recited Kaddish. An entire town of orphans.

On Shemini Atzeres, we *davened* and conducted *hakafos* in the *beis medrash*. Some *hakafos* they were! It looked more like a procession escorting a deceased tzaddik to his final resting place.

Taking stock of the situation, I wondered, *Was this not also our own funeral procession? Had the sadistic Germans deliberately let us come home to recover and forget our misfortune, only to reopen our wounds and repeat the process?*

On Simchas Torah after *davening*, we received another piece of news: The day before, an *Aussiedlung* had taken place in Wislica. Early in the morning, the town was surrounded by Germans, Polish gendarmes, and *Junacy*. No one was murdered, but in the span of half an hour the Jews were herded into the market square and loaded onto wagons. Three Polish gendarmes from Neustadt, who were well acquainted with *Judenrat* chairman Flaum, allowed him to escape. A man of rare integrity, Flaum declined the favor and stayed with his unfortunate brethren. The transport was taken by wagon to Pinczow and deported along with the Jews there. Within an hour, Wislica was *Judenrein*.

The *Junacy* then went into the Jewish homes, finished off the delicacies prepared for the Yom Tov meal, and looted the possessions.

By the next morning, whatever remained was auctioned off, the apartments were promptly rented out, and the *Aktion* was over.

Gloom and melancholy descend upon us in Dzialoszyce. It seems the expulsion procedure is changing. Things are taking a different turn. No longer are Jews left behind to empty the contents of the homes. There is an auction and it's all over. Apparently, the rumor is true that by New Year's of 1943 no Jew shall be found in the entire *Generalgouvernement*.[3] Why will we Dzialoszycers be an exception? But what can we do...? Perhaps Dzialoszyce will be last and we will be able to remain until New Year's Day? That would give us a few more weeks.

With my previous experience in the textile business, I obtain a position in the textile-liquidation warehouse. My brother-in-law Yisroel joins the group in the food warehouse. We are occupied with work all day. New batches of hard-earned Jewish possessions are brought in daily on wagons loaded to the breaking point with merchandise. Twice a week, Beyerlein or other officials from Krakow arrive by truck to pick up the goods. By the following day, the warehouses are full again.

I cannot sit idle. There is no time to lose — we must make plans for the future. The last minute may be too late.

My mother-in-law, my niece Esther'l, and my little Feivele had come in from Kazimierz. We consult with Esther'l. Maybe we could find a place in Warsaw, where she and her sister were living as gentiles, for my mother-in-law, Tzinne'le, my Chayele and Feivele.

I address a letter to my niece Chayele in Warsaw. We await a response.

---

3. German term for the area of Poland occupied by Nazi Germany

Kinah for Rav Eliezer Halevi Epstein, rebbe of Dzialoszyce

Teardrops flow from my eyes over the loss of a faithful mentor;
With trembling hands, I record these lines as a memorial.
May this be a sign of my esteem, and a final act of kindness.

A man of flawless character, of exalted qualities,
Goodhearted and humble, engrossed in the service of G-d,
Modest and unassuming, he dwelt in the tent of Torah,
A branch of a holy family tree of chassidic rebbes.
This is the true portrait of the tzaddik Rabbi Eliezer Halevi,
Descendant of the Maor Vashemesh.

Torah, avodah and tzedakah converged in his home;
A congenial atmosphere prevailed there
Among a chaburah of like-minded followers.
The brokenhearted and distraught turned there in their hour of distress,
Finding comfort for their anguished souls.

Gradually, his life grew into a spiritual flame,
Glowing like a shining star.
His saintly lineage of chassidic giants
Culminated in his personality
And in the purity of his beautiful progeny.
His friends and admirers bow their heads, and remember with sorrow,
That bitter day — 22 Elul — when calamity struck Dzialoszyce,
Breaking the holy chain and disbanding the group.

סיסי באות נלילית דעין לו אלוא ונין
היבית מודעות ארטלם מדרום אלא עברון
ובא אין וגו באת קמות בוקרום זסא אחרון,

אישות תעימה, קדמת זצות תפוגות
לה אים ונגו, בעולות טסם יטוא
ולסם אומרים, סל הקל, וחמצוע צרת
סלו מא אמות קסמום, וצטו אאמורות
מלא בחורן פלאיות סל התביין
רחי אליערר פלוי ונכו סו וא, צלוד וטסא,

בתרדבת בחיון - קות ווד תורה צעודה ומקא
לתבוית היותה האאוטיברבת סל המחורת התקוניה
ומוב כל קטת דות ווד לוך, קות בורה וטוקה
סוד פלם ואבא נותם לטסו ואאיורה,

עין ווייוניו החוית כה לטלהבת לתנית הבי-חתה
קטב גי ככונה וגאבוד הסרגיעם
טלוות הקאטסא האאוורות בזוגותא קו.בוניות וטלוה
אהדת הצגר סל וטיחקט העצרודה -
ולם הגד - כג אלול - סטו בווטה רטוומסליק הצרוה
וביאגו ואוצוטו - וכבול סאטם- ובכון קטוקא
וטסום צטלות הקאטסא - ונוצוטסא ההחור,

CHAPTER 16

Jewish Slave Labor Camps

IN THE BEGINNING, when the German government established slave labor camps such as Prokocim, Stalowa Wola, and Debica (*Dembitz*) for the Jewish populace, the stated intention was that every Jew would be required to do a two-year stint at forced labor. However, conditions in these camps were such that within a short time even the strongest person perished, or, at best, became crippled for life.

As long as Jewish communities still existed, they would send aid to the laborers in the nearby camps. Our town formed a special committee whose task was to see to the needs of several hundred young Dzialoszyce men who were working in the various camps around Krakow. Before the *Aussiedlung*, we sent a car every week to deliver bread, clean clothing and other necessities. Two men of the *Ordnungsdienst* would go along to deliver the items and hand out letters to the inmates. Sometimes, laborers were even allowed to go home on furlough.

There were also labor camps that were not under government supervision. For instance, Kostrze, where nearly all the Dzialoszycers worked at first, was a labor camp operated by a private German

firm. The director, Kurat, was an entrepeneur who could be bribed, and the overseer, Stieglitz, was a German Jew. Obviously, the conditions there were much better, especially in the beginning when it was summertime and warm enough to sleep in the dilapidated barracks without undue suffering. The laborers were able to survive on the rations they received, 200 grams of bread a day and a small amount of potatoes for the midday meal, since their families in Dzialoszyce were sending food packages. And those whose parents were too poor to send anything received care packages from the committee.

In Kostrze, for a few zlotys you could get out of work altogether. The owner of the camp treated the whole venture as a moneymaking enterprise. The Jewish workers cost him nothing, aside from their starvation-rations, which he compensated for by sending the workers to Krakow to clean the streets and do other similar jobs, earning him a hefty fee from the local authorities. The labor camp was particularly worthwhile; it saved the owner, directors, and all the employees from having to report to the Russian front. As a result, in comparison to other labor camps, Kostrze was considered a Garden of Eden.

Things were very different in the aforementioned camps, which were directly supervised by the Gestapo and the *Sicherheitsdienst*. Ultimately, their true objective was to annihilate the Jewish laborers.

In the beginning of the war, when the agenda against Polish Jewry had not yet taken such a radical course and there was still a slow, systematic process of partial expulsions in the big cities with the small towns remaining unaffected, the labor camps, too, were less brutal. The work was grueling — twelve hours every day including Sunday; the food rations a meager 200 grams of bread in the morning and boiled potatoes at noon; sleeping quarters in makeshift barracks; and discipline, military-style. Still, the inmates were taken to the ghetto to bathe once a week, they received

medical care in the event of illness, and we were able to send them packages.

Later on, however, when the extermination campaign was officially adopted and special SS execution squads began to drive around cities and towns rounding up Jews to be shot and deporting the remainder, the situation in the slave labor camps changed as well. These camps simply turned into a mass grave for their Jewish inmates. Supervision was assigned to Ukrainian guards, who were expressly trained in the art of murdering Jews. Upon arrival, every transport of prisoners was lined up in columns. Two men were selected from each column of twenty and shot on the spot. This was followed by an announcement: "The same will happen to anyone found carrying valuables or more than fifty zlotys of currency!" They were then searched. Naturally, they did not wait but handed everything over immediately. Huge amounts of money and valuables were collected.

Bread was no longer provided; only a small bowl of watery, putrid, maggot-infested cabbage soup. Every day there was a victim; the guards made sure of it by fabricating some crime. All items of clothing, even undergarments, were confiscated. Instead, every inmate was given a paper-thin jacket and pants, which he wore all the time — when these became torn, it was just too bad. Every laborer was assigned a number and was no longer identified by name. Communicating by post or receiving packages was out of the question.

The slightest infraction was punished with a bullet. After a hot day's hard work, if an inmate went past the barbed wire to the filthy water hole to quench his burning thirst, his friends were forced to hang him, and his body would be left dangling for three days. Whenever there was an *Aussiedlung* in the area, a number of men were selected from each labor camp and sent along with the transport.

Under such circumstances, there was nothing to lose. Everyone looked for an opportunity to free himself from this gehinnom. But if a laborer managed to elude the heavy guard, the next morning ten men were hung and the camp was placed under stricter surveillance. The inmates' jackets were marked with an indelible yellow stripe, so that if one did succeed in escaping, he would be easily identified.

Could anyone possibly work under such barbaric conditions? The most robust, able-bodied young men broke down and turned into walking skeletons, unkempt with long, unshorn hair; bellies protruding; dull eyes filled with despair. They no longer reacted to anything done to them.

Every day, dozens of these shadows were missing. Where they were taken, nobody knew. Polish farmers living nearby reported seeing daily transports of prisoners driven into a special barrack standing in the distance. Minutes later the wagons would emerge bearing corpses. Apparently, they are being electrocuted or gassed, said the Poles, since we do not hear any gunshots.

In this manner, one labor camp after another was liquidated.

CHAPTER 17

Moshke

AMONG ALL THE WHEELER-DEALERS who sprang up during the war like mushrooms after a rain, without a doubt first place was taken by Moshke Jakubowicz, known to everyone simply as Moshke.

Hailing from the town of Miechow, where his father worked as a wagon driver, Moshke occupied himself with theft from his earliest youth. He began on a small scale, advancing to become a pickpocket and eventually a safecracker. After working in the field long enough, he wound up in jail.

Sitting in prison for a couple of years shrank his appetite for crime. Subsequently, he settled down and married the daughter of Avraham Frydrych Melker, the poor coal carrier of Dzialoszyce. However, the talent of Moshke's youth often flared up in him, and he conducted a variety of shady deals. When his outraged victims came complaining to his innocent wife, she decided to banish him from the house.

Roaming footloose, Moshke operated a large-scale racket together with other local underworld characters. He continually shocked the town with some new scandal that at times even involved murder.

Though the police realized who had a hand in it, they lacked evidence since the victims were not willing to come forward and testify, knowing their lives would be hanging by a thread.

Moshke cast fear upon the town. When the townspeople saw him in the street, they moved aside, afraid of his gaze. Mothers used his name to threaten their disobedient children.

Some time before the beginning of the war, Moshke disappeared from Dzialoszyce; no one knew his whereabouts. Figuring he must have been imprisoned again, or was perhaps operating somewhere else, the town breathed a sigh of relief.

But with the start of the war, Moshke was back. Rumor had it that he had gained influence with the gendarmerie. Consequently, shopkeepers would turn to Moshke for help whenever the local police conducted a raid and confiscated merchandise. He received everyone most graciously and promised to intervene in exchange for a payoff, which he took in advance. Ultimately, the case would drag on without resolution until the merchant gave up.

One fine day, Moshke was seen — without a Jewish armband — walking in the company of Kowalski, the Polish chief of the Miechow secret police. It was said that Kowalski himself was a former convict and had attained his position specifically because of his expertise in the field of crime. Throughout Moshke's criminal career, he had often crossed paths with Kowalski. Now, in this wartime world of chaos, the two of them decided to use their old acquaintanceship to their mutual advantage.

Moshke was the expert. He was familiar with every nook and cranny in Dzialoszyce and knew where people had stashed away their valuables. He relayed this information to Kowalski, who would then order an official search, even tearing down walls until the fortune a Jew had acquired with years of sweat and toil was found and seized. On top of that, the Jew faced severe penalties for concealing valuables.

Moshke then became the middleman, taking a large sum of money from the unfortunate fellow in return for having Kowalski waive the penalty. On top of that, he proceeded to purchase the confiscated merchandise from Kowalski for a fraction of its value.

These search raids took place daily. Moshke's business was booming. He grew increasingly famous, giving *tzedakah* generously and taking a prominent place in Jewish society.

Moshke gained renown in German circles, too, after Kowalski introduced him to Gestapo chief Rittinger. Moshke promised Rittinger he would reap the benefits. And so, when the formerly well-to-do Meir Owsiany cheated his tenant, the leather dealer Trachtenberg, out of a thousand dollars and they could not reach a settlement, Moshke became the mediator. He took the disputed sum and handed the money to Rittinger, after taking a cut for himself. Trachtenberg and Owsiany were left to deal with the criminal court process.

Moshke's star rose to its peak. He organized his former partners-in-crime into a company of spies, whose job it was to investigate where people had hidden their valuables. As his advisor, Moshke chose Shlomek Leszman, the former owner of several houses of ill repute in Brazil, who had fled that country due to his various misdeeds. Leszman's business intuition would serve him well in this new occupation.

The Jews of Dzialoszyce realized the severity of the situation. Not a day went by without a victim. The nights were not safe either, for Moshke had not abandoned his old profession. If he knew of a hidden treasure that he could appropriate on his own without Kowalski's help, he didn't hesitate to deceive Kowalski as well.

The community turned to Alter Spokojny, a textile dealer who was a former business partner of Shlomek Leszman. He would serve as an intermediary to find out if anything could be done to get Moshke to leave the town alone.

Shlomek used his influence with Moshke to arrange a deal: Moshke would take a monthly fee from all the merchants in return for stopping the raids. A list was drawn up and every shopkeeper contributed a share of the payoff. For a time, things were quiet and the townspeople were satisfied with this arrangement. When Moshke made a *bris*, everyone, including the elderly *rav*, attended. Moshke had become the guardian of the town.

It wasn't long before unrest returned. This time it was even worse. Apparently, Moshke took the opportunity to note the names of those who paid the monthly fee. In this manner, he determined which people still had items of value in their possession. He left it to his spies to unearth these valuables from the most concealed places.

The harsh German decrees raining down upon the Jews were forgotten. There was but one danger: Moshke. Every merchant was at risk of losing the shirt off his back, because in the event Moshke's men did not succeed in finding any merchandise, they took everything a man owned.

Nobody knew how it came to be, but one fine Shabbos afternoon, the Kazimierz gendarmes unexpectedly showed up in Dzialoszyce. They broke into the underworld headquarters where Moshke and his group of some twenty men were playing cards, and arrested all of them, allegedly for gambling. In the morning, everyone was released — except for Moshke Jakubowicz, Shlomek Leszman, and Alter Spokojny.

A Krakow investigator arrived in Dzialoszyce and summoned the prominent Jewish residents to a hearing.

"Why do you pay Moshke a monthly subsidy?" he questioned. The shopkeepers were afraid, and they attempted to deny it. Heavy pressure was applied.

The Pinchever Rebbe was called to the witness stand.

"Tell the court how Moshke broke into the attic of your house at midnight."

The townspeople were forced to admit what was going on.

Moshke became aware of the danger he was in. He contacted his younger brother, one of his loyal collaborators, and asked him to phone Kowalski and Rittinger to come to his rescue, else he would inform on them.

"Tell him not to worry," was Kowalski's reply. "I will come tonight. Have transportation ready near the jailhouse."

Moshke's horse-drawn carriage was prepared. At the specified time, Kowalski arrived, along with some of his agents. He informed the Krakow investigator's team that they could leave. "This case is under Miechow jurisdiction!" Kowalski declared. Apparently, Kowalski did not wish to wait until they learned Moshke's secrets.

The investigator and his group left.

At midnight, Kowalski took Moshke, Shlomek, and Alter out of the jailhouse. "We're escaping," he told them.

No sooner did the carriage leave town limits than Kowalski pulled out his gun.

Bang!

Bang!

Bang!

Moshke Jakubowicz, Shlomek Leszman, and Alter Spokojny, Kowalski's loyal collaborators, were rendered harmless.

"If I didn't do you in, you'd do me in..." he mumbled.

CHAPTER 18

Into *Galus* for the Second Time

POLISH ACQUAINTANCES FROM the surrounding villages begin coming into Dzialoszyce again. They inquire whether all of us are back. Expressing sympathy for the loss of Reizele and Alte'le, they exclaim, "Who didn't know Reizele! Why didn't she come to me? I would have taken her in with open arms. She didn't even look Jewish!"

This time the peasants come en masse; they already know that we will not be staying here much longer. "We have your benefit in mind," they explain. "If you sell us your possessions, at least you'll have some money out of it. With public auctions taking place all over, what do the Jews gain by leaving their things behind?"

Without saying a word, we sell them whatever they want: bedding, clothing, even the clock off the wall, accepting any amount they are willing to pay. We ask only that the buyer at least remember this and take us in should we come in search of refuge. They all give us their word.

Off to the side stands one farmer, not bold enough to make an offer. "I'm a poor man," he says, "and I have no money to buy anything. But if you give me your overcoat, I will light a candle in your memory every year on the anniversary of the *Aussiedlung*. I won't forget the date; I'll mark it down for myself. After all, *Panie*, who will remember you? This way your soul will be purified."

Others promise that if we give them everything we own, they will hide us for the duration of the war. We make deals with various acquaintances to give us shelter when needed. One farmer, a decent fellow by the name of Karol Szita, who lives in a remote area near a forest, guarantees he will keep us for as long as we wish.

We decide that the women will leave to Szita's place while things are still quiet. This would give them time to determine whether they could stay there, now that the weather was turning cold.

They return after a week. Apparently, someone informed on them. The police came, and they escaped just in time.

Our friend Latosz from Kwaszyn had told me about a friend of his, Pietrowski, a poor but trustworthy farmer who lives on the outskirts of their village. Latosz vouched for his honesty. Pietrowski had room for several people, he would provide food, and he had a hideaway that was impossible to find. We could send our belongings to him ahead of time, enabling us to leave Dzialoszyce at the last minute.

We agree to this plan.

In the meantime, a reply letter from my niece Chayele arrived from Warsaw: If we could procure proper identity papers for the women and for Feivele, Mrs. Aubrien, an acquaintance of hers, was willing to bring them to Warsaw and rent an apartment for them where they could live as gentiles.

It is a risky proposition. Even if we could obtain forged papers for the women, they would be in danger of being recognized on the train, and again when they registered in Warsaw. Besides, the way Latosz depicted this new refuge, it seemed redundant to discuss Chayele's letter.

We decide that the women will go to Pietrowski and the men will go along with Shmuel Yossel, who has even agreed to take Yisroel and his family, too. Or perhaps we would be able to stay with the women at Pietrowski's place.

Still, I did not dismiss my niece Chayele's plan. I remembered all too well the few days that my wife and child spent with me in the mayor's barn in Szyszczyce. When the *poritz's* German commissar came to the village and we had to flee together with little Feivele, it was very unpleasant, despite the relatively mild weather. Now, winter was approaching. A grown man could run, if need be, but for a woman and child it would be very difficult. And we could not trust the Poles, even the best of them.

Yes, my niece Chayele's plan is a risky proposition, but with Hashem's help if the journey goes smoothly, they will be safe from then on. In a big city, not everything is scrutinized. It is apparently so, since Chayele has already been there for several weeks and there is no mention in her letter of any problem.

Meanwhile, my wife discussed another plan with a Polish acquaintance of hers in Dzialoszyce. The woman suggested that her widowed mother, who lived alone in a small village near Radom, might be willing to shelter Chayele and Feivele. She would be risking little as long as her boarders possessed the necessary identity papers, for even if they were discovered she could maintain that she knew nothing. Though she was demanding an exorbitant sum, she might settle for less.

The only thing that remained to be seen is whether it would be possible to obtain Aryan papers, as all identity documents must have a photograph and be certified by the county clerk.

My friend Yisroel Alter Nifker tells me he also needs papers for his wife and child. He is considering sending them to his wife's parents in Modrzejow. "Forged identity cards are being produced that are hard to distinguish from authentic ones," he says. "If you'd like, we can arrange it together."

I promptly agree, and we proceed to order the papers.

Time passes, but there is no word on the identity cards. The tension in Dzialoszyce increases. The men who returned from the labor camps now travel back. They would rather work with superhuman strength and live there under terrible conditions than be deported. The people who came from other towns leave as well. Where they will go they do not know themselves, but here it is too dangerous.

The work of liquidating Jewish homes continues. Bialabrode keeps making promises and tells us not to worry at all. "The fact that people are leaving is of benefit to us. The fewer people there are, the better," he explains.

The liquidation of Jewish homes in nearby Skalbmierz has been completed. Accompanied by Bialabrode and two others, Beyerlein drove to Skalbmierz and ordered that its collection of Jewish possessions be sent to Dzialoszyce. Damaged furniture and unmovable items were auctioned off on the spot. The *Judenrat* and *Ordnungsdienst* men were transferred to our town.

On Thursday evening, we learn that the town of Skalbmierz is completely *Judenrein*. Beyerlein himself shot Mrs. Strausburg, a young Jewish woman, for no reason at all, and he beat up the

members of the Skalbmierz *Judenrat* who used to be his best friends. He has shown his true colors.

There is no more time to deliberate. I go at once to Nifker to find out about the papers.

"I don't know what to tell you," he answers me. "I was counting on it. What shall we do now? I heard from reliable sources that things don't look good!"

We send for Pietrowski. He comes from Kwaszyn, picks up our bedding and other essentials, and takes my mother-in-law, Tzinne'le, her daughter Gittele, Chayele and little Feivele back with him to Kwaszyn. The rest of us will stay here yet. I prepare farmer clothes for myself and we wait.

On Shabbos [27 Cheshvan/November 7], there is great unrest. German trucks arrive to pick up the Jewish merchandise from the warehouses.

On Motza'ei Shabbos, a perspiring Nifker comes running in. "The I.D. card is ready but your wife must sign it!"

I send for Chayele. She comes to Dzialoszyce on Sunday morning, signs the papers, and returns to Kwaszyn.

At two o'clock on Sunday afternoon, Mrs. Aubrien arrives at my house. My niece Chayele had sent her from Warsaw. "I was already in the area on Friday, but my friend in a nearby village kept me up," Mrs. Aubrien tells me. "However, I remembered my assignment well. I heard some rumors in the village today. Have I come too late?"

We agree that Mrs. Aubrien will take some of Esther'l's things and return to her friend's house to wait for Chayele, Feivele and Esther'l who will leave Kwaszyn by horse-drawn cart tonight and meet her there. From there they will travel further.

In the meantime, Yisroel, his wife and children, his mother-in-law, sister-in-law, brother-in-law Yoav and his wife and children — ten people altogether — led by Shmuel Yossel and his family, leave Dzialoszyce to a prearranged place in a nearby village. At five o'clock in the evening [November 8, 1942], I leave my house, along with my brother-in-law Hershel, his sons Feivel and Reuven and his daughter Esther'l.

We go into *galus* for the second time.

CHAPTER 19

Out into the World
in Disguise

Sitting in the hut of Pietrowski, our new host in the village of Kwaszyn, we contemplate our current situation. I explain to Chayele that she, Esther'l, and little Feivele must leave now to the village where Mrs. Aubrien is waiting, so that they can travel on to Warsaw.

Chayele has little desire to undertake such a dangerous journey. She is not ready for the new role she will have to play. "What if someone recognizes me?" she cries. "I do not want to part from you again. I wish to share a common fate with all of you, whatever that may be."

I do not relent. "You have to think this through logically and unemotionally. We have a long, cold winter ahead of us and we can not be sure we won't be on the run. Under these circumstances, we'll be unable to help one another. Since you managed to obtain identity papers at the last minute, your primary concern should be to save yourself and our child, as well as Esther'l. With Hashem's help, the trip will pass uneventfully and you will settle down there.

You must be courageous and unafraid. You will be in a position to help us, too, because you'll be free to move around. We do not know how things will turn out here. If the men have no choice but to go to the labor camps, who will send us bread?

"It is a time when every person must decide his destiny alone. One imprudent step may result in very serious consequences. It is not every day that such a good opportunity arises. Mrs. Aubrien is here now, specifically for this purpose. The situation could intensify to the point where she won't be able to come a second time. What's more, especially now while the liquidation process is still going on, Jews will not be so closely monitored. Later, they might pursue every last Jew."

Chayele is dejected, grappling with an inner conflict: *Shall I leave all my dear ones here and part from them once again in order to save myself? What of the risky journey, and even once I arrive in Warsaw — staying there with a little child, a boy at that? But what alternative is there? Not to go? What if I must leave tomorrow when Mrs. Aubrien is not here anymore? Traveling alone is certainly not a possibility!*

Pietrowski sits by the table taciturnly, muttering something from time to time. His silence makes me uneasy.

I approach him. "What's on your mind, *Panie?*"

"I meant maybe two, three people," he replies, disgruntled. "There's a full house here and a crying child to boot!"

He has no patience for this. He is afraid. His son is wanted for labor in Germany, and the Germans could show up without warning.

"If you knew this, why didn't you say so earlier?" I ask.

Chayele overhears Pietrowski's words.

"What do you say now?" I ask her. "It is only the first day. What will we do if he decides tomorrow that he is unwilling to keep Feivele here? Where would we go? For the time being, I have no other place."

With a heavy heart, Chayele agrees to travel to Warsaw. Once again she packs her belongings and bundles up our dear child; the nights are already wintry cold. It is with much emotion that Chayele takes leave of her mother and everybody. Who knows if we will ever see each other again…?

I kiss and embrace my child for a long time. He is my only remaining consolation, upon whom I have placed great hopes. I had already made up my mind that if we survive the war, we shall leave for Eretz Yisrael and raise our child there as a proud Jew that he may yet avenge the Jewish blood that has been spilled.

Now I must again part from my dearest ones and remain alone. And they will have to live as non-Jews in Warsaw. Who knows how long this will last? My child, who is not even aware yet that he is a Jew, will be raised in a non-Jewish atmosphere. At least when his intellect develops, he will know that he has a Jewish father — if his father will still be alive — hidden somewhere. I turn cold and a shiver goes through my bones.

But we may not dwell on it. There is a fire, and we must rescue everything possible. Even if one does not know for sure whether there isn't a fire in the next place, one must first escape certain danger.

Her throat choked with tears, Chayele is unable to speak.

"Hold strong and steadfast," I tell her. "Hashem will help."

With our child Feivele in her arms, Chayele left together with Esther'l to our friend Latosz, who would take them to the village where Mrs. Aubrien was waiting.

"Are you happy now?" I ask Pietrowski.

He shrugs his shoulders and says nothing.

A little while later, he strikes up a conversation with me. "I heard that tomorrow they will begin auctioning off the Jewish homes in Dzialoszyce. I would like to buy one of the apartments, so I need you to give me money."

"Alright," I say. But he continues on to demand a fantastic sum of money, claiming he would take less if our group wasn't so large. I never would have imagined that a quiet, primitive peasant could have such notions. It dawns on me that our stay here will not be smooth and that some of us will have to leave.

He is not done yet.

"There must be a hidden compartment in your house where you stashed your valuables. If someone else buys your apartment and moves in, what will you gain? Tell me where it is and I will buy it and take the valuables."

At my unequivocal declaration that I have no hiding place in my house — I even list the exact contents of our dwelling and tell him he could buy it; it makes no difference to me — he is bitterly disappointed. This quiet man, who presented himself as an honest and straightforward person, was not innocent at all. He had underlying motives from the beginning.

First thing in the morning, Pietrowski took the money and left to Dzialoszyce. He returned at night in a foul mood. He had been unable to get hold of a decent apartment, as the Poles in Dzialoszyce did not allow the peasants from the villages to buy homes that were likely to contain anything of value.

"Woe is me!" Pietrowski cried. "When I finally managed to buy an apartment together with my brother-in-law, there was nothing in it but two broken iron bed frames topped by torn sacks of straw bedding, and a cracked mirror on the wall. Upon seeing this miserable hovel, I ran to recoup my few zlotys. The blow I received on the head from a rubber truncheon made me see stars. I couldn't even bear to bring the beds and straw back with me. Who knows what kind of old, beggarly Jew lived there! Why didn't you tell me?"

Was I supposed to know what he would buy?

"I can't keep such a large group..." he started all over again.

"It's already dark now," I tell him, "but tomorrow some of us will leave."

On Tuesday morning [November 10], Hershel's son Feivel, Mechel Kamelgard, a very fine young man who used to work for our firm, and I leave in search of Yisroel and his family. Perhaps we would be able to stay with them. My mother-in-law remained at Pietrowski's house with Hershel, Tzinne'le, Reuven and Gittele.

We had never before been on these pathways. Trudging through fields up to our knees in snow, we lose our bearings and wander around aimlessly. Wearing my farmer's jacket, overalls and fur hat, I think I am safe; nobody will recognize me. But from all sides, I hear calls of "*Zyd...! Zyd...!*" Afraid to turn around, we run, the wind whipping our faces, our feet soaked from the watery snow.

Just imagine running like this, not knowing where you are going, with a child in your arms, I think to myself. Since Chayele had adamantly wanted us to stay together, she would have been running along with us, too.

Around twelve o'clock noon, on the road to Dziewieczyce, I hear my name being called from the direction of a barn off to the side. There in the cold barn we find Yisroel and his family. His two children, Feivele and Mordche'le, are stamping their frozen little feet up and down. We can hear the muffled coughing of Yisroel's wife, who has taken ill. Shmuel Yossel stands guard outside. Word has it that the police are on the lookout for Jews in the area.

Farmer Franek Baber's barn is my brother-in-law Yisroel's new home.

CHAPTER 20

Final Destruction
of the Remnant

LATE SUNDAY NIGHT, 28 Cheshvan/November 8 [1942], several taxis of SD agents, led by Beyerlein, arrived in Dzialoszyce from Miechow. A number of Polish secret police officers and *Junacy* arrived earlier to join in the final liquidation of the Jews of Dzialoszyce.

The *Judenrat* and Jewish police received an order to round up all the Jews and bring them to the market square immediately. This time around, there wasn't much work to do, as the only Jews remaining in town were the Kehillah officials themselves and a few individuals who were unable to escape or had despaired of life. The others had fled every which way.

Some Jews went into hiding in their homes again, thinking that the *Judenrat* and *Ordnungsdienst* would continue to remain in town. They prepared much larger stockpiles of food in their hideouts, in case this *Aussiedlung* lasted longer than the first.

This time it was Beyerlein himself who very politely informed the *Judenrat* and Jewish police that they, too, must report to the

---

market square. No one would remain in town — the liquidation of Jewish property would continue without Jews. Speechless, they left Beyerlein's office, filled with despair.

The Polish police commander, who had profited in no small measure from the *Judenrat* during the liquidation process, told the Kehillah officials that he could allow them to escape the blockaded town if they wished. A number of them, including Chairman Richter, took advantage of this privilege and fled to Wodzislaw. The rest joined the transport.

An all-night vigil ensued. It wasn't just the few unfortunate Jews on the verge of death who did not sleep that night. Neither did their Polish neighbors and the peasants from the surrounding countryside, who had already begun the inheritance process! They were afraid that the public auction of the contents of Jewish homes that had not yet been liquidated would take place first thing in the morning. Hence, they must not miss out on this last opportunity.

And so, the commotion on this end-of-month, dark, moonless night was as great as on a market day. White sheets, in which a variety of household goods were wrapped, shimmered from afar. Pots and glassware tinkled. The police did not interfere at all; they were busy guarding the Jews.

At dawn, the small cluster of Jews in the market square was marched to the *kolejka*. Among them were *Judenrat* officials and Jewish policemen, led by their commander Hampel. There was no longer need for a special train. A couple of open wagons were enough. This time no crying was heard. The Jews had already learned how to conduct themselves respectably. It was a quiet funeral, without any eulogies or weeping.

Bialabrode accompanied the train to Miechow, where he added the few remaining Jews of Miechow to the transport. He left several *Ordnungsdienst* men there to guard any Jews who might turn up later.

The public auction did indeed begin in Dzialoszyce on Monday. The peasants came from the villages by the thousands. The local police and residents bought the better homes for a few groschen. Volumes of *Shas*, Tanach and other *sefarim*, which the liquidation committee had stored in the women's section of the shul, were sold by the kilo to be used as packing material in shops. The Poles did not know what to do with the Torah scrolls and *megillos*. Why, for half a zloty you could buy a *Sefer Torah*! As a floor covering, it was worth the money.

Dudek the drunkard, the town's outhouse cleaner, who had grown up among Jews, knew their customs, and spoke Yiddish better than Polish, bought a *Sefer Torah* and proceeded to conduct *hakafos* in the middle of the market square. He put on a pair of *tefillin*, wrapped himself in a *tallis* and sang "*Ozer dalim hoshiah na...*" The Poles around him rolled with laughter. Other townspeople who had worked in Jewish homes held up *shofaros* and blew loud *tekios*.

Talleisim, with the *tzitzis* strings removed, were used to make women's garments. Zawartke, the wagon driver for Goldkorn's seltzer factory, covered his mean, one-eyed chestnut horse with the shul's gold-embroidered, bordeaux velvet *paroches* that was reserved for use on Pesach. And instead of the thin ropes that had served him as reins until today, he now had genuine leather reins made from wide *retzuos* that must have belonged to the *tefillin* of the *rav*. Business was in full swing!

On Monday evening the Germans left Dzialoszyce. The Polish secret agents and local police would supervise the remainder of the auction.

Now the serious looting began. First, the police went into the Jewish homes and took the better things for themselves; whatever was left would be auctioned off to the peasants. Next they conducted

searches, chopping up ceilings, floors, ovens, walls, wherever there was a possibility that a Jew might have concealed valuables.

During these searches, they also found live people — Jews hiding in their homes. No longer were such Jews brought to the town hall as in the first *Aussiedlung*. They were now taken directly to the cemetery to be gunned down. Spades stood ready, with which they were forced to dig their own graves. Their fellow Poles did their duties, covering the graves by throwing some earth over the dead bodies.

On Tuesday, the police broke into the hidden room in Meir Szulimowicz's house, which had remained undiscovered the first time. Madejski, the former Dzialoszyce police officer who had become a Miechow secret agent, was the one who found it. There were over twenty people inside.

"Let me live! What will you gain by killing me?" cried Szulimowicz.

Though Madejski had exploited his old friend Szulimowicz many a time in the past, he turned a deaf ear to his plea. "I have no association with Jews!" he snarled.

The group of over twenty Jews was led to the cemetery. Standing before the mass grave, Meir Szulimowicz's last words rang out: "My children in Eretz Yisrael will yet avenge my blood...!" A revolver shot, accompanied by drunken laughter, silenced him forever.

In a house near the Nidzica River, the Polish police came across a set of one-year-old twins who had been left behind by their parents and were barely clinging to life. "Let them learn to swim..." they said, tossing them into the water.

Wagons loaded with all sorts of valuable possessions travel in all directions. They are actually Angels of Death for the small remnant of Jews who are now wandering around seeking refuge in the villages. Yes, the wise and perceptive nation turned out to be terribly foolish in this hour of distress.

We had already learned during the first *Aussiedlung* that safekeeping our belongings with our "good" Christian neighbors only added to our misfortune. Their goal is to inherit our possessions. Thus, they will search us out in order to get rid of us. We should have burned all of our belongings, along with our homes. A town almost exclusively of Jewish houses — and to whom have we bequeathed it? Death is truly bitter, but falling together with the enemy is sweet. *"Tamos nafshi im Plishtim* — Let me die together with the Philistines," declared Shimshon. We Jews knew this thousands of years ago. And here we went so passively. Even the one thing that could have been done — for every person to destroy the contents of his home — we did not do.

In the attic of Yehuda Piekarz, the local police found his son-in-law, Rothblum of Lodz, who had come back to Dzialoszyce from the labor camps. His wife and two daughters had already gone with the first transport.

Rothblum was acquainted with the policemen, as they had been former tenants in the house. "Please let me go!" he pleaded with them.

"Where will you go?" they answered him. "The bullet will find you along the way anyhow. You're better off being buried here in the Jewish cemetery, together with your father-in-law and your friends. You Jews have played out your role here in Europe — you are no longer needed!"

There was no way out. Rothblum was led to the cemetery. He knew where he was going. And why? Because, being a Jew, he was expendable. At least he would be buried among friends. He would feel at home.

Though he was a secular Jew who had long ago broken with Jewish tradition, he requested a *tallis*. This much they did for him.

A "Shema Yisrael!"...and, once more, the space of a useless entity was cleared.

CHAPTER 21

My Sister Yitta — First Victim in Kazimierz

ON SHABBOS [27 CHESHVAN/NOVEMBER 7], my parents' home in Kazimierz was in a state of turmoil, with feverish preparations taking place.

His *bitachon* unwavering, Father paces slowly back and forth, a Tehillim in his hand. It is already two o'clock in the afternoon, and he has not yet finished preparing his customary *shiur*.

"Children, we may not be despondent on Shabbos," he declares. "The merit of our holy ancestors will stand by us. We have a *guter Basheter* — He has helped us in many a predicament. This is a great *nisayon*. Let us strengthen ourselves."

Leaning against her bed, from which the linen had already been removed, Mother, frail and ailing, wrings her hands. Though she has taken each of the prescription medications that are always at her bedside, she cannot calm down. She looks on with a curious detachment at the diligent Yitta, who is quickly packing everything, down to the Pesach cups and decanters, to be hidden. If they survived, it would all be needed.

With a particular earnestness, Yitta wraps up her trousseau, which lay ready since the beginning of the war. This she would entrust to Judge Jan Kotkowski, our family's closest Polish friend, for safekeeping. He had reserved a separate closet for her valuables, even giving her a key to his judicial office, should she need a place to hide in a moment of danger.

Earlier in the day, Yitta had picked up her gentile identity card, complete with photograph and fingerprint, from the magistrate's clerk. She had it all figured out. The entire plan was in place, with precautions taken for every eventuality. Father and Mother would leave late that night with Dovid'l and Meir'l to the village of Jakuszowice — Judge Kotkowski had arranged shelter for them at the court clerk's house. Only Yitta would remain at home. If the situation worsened, she would leave to the judge's office. The key lay in her pocket. Should it become impossible for her to get there — not to worry — she had fashioned an alternate hideout at home, a secret compartment behind one of the walls. Every aspect was strategically calculated.

Later, once she could move around freely with her Aryan papers, she would come up with a plan for our parents. She had sewn into her clothing enough currency to suffice for a while. Anyway, how much longer could the war last?

Neighbors and friends drop by. Noticing the flushed Yitta busy at work, they look on enviously. *She is lucky*, they think. *Nothing will happen to her, chalilah. Leave it to Yitta'le to figure it all out...*

And yet, for all her self-assurance, Yitta feels a sense of insecurity, an inner premonition that gives her no rest.

"Dovid'l," she says to her brother, "somehow I'm afraid. I was too confident... I hope I will not end up like Reizele. I don't know what's the matter with me — I keep dropping things."

Yitta contemplates her packed-up trousseau, each item evoking its own nostalgia. Her mind wanders to Mottel, her prospective

chassan. What more did I need? He expressed clearly and openly that he had never considered otherwise, just that we should wait until things calmed down somewhat... These thoughts cheer her up a bit.

She soon grows despondent again. The work, however, cannot be interrupted, and everything proceeds according to the designated plan. Meir'l carries the most valuable possessions to Judge Kotkowski, who graciously accepts the two large parcels along with the gifts Yitta sent him. "Remind your sister," he says, "that if the situation becomes critical, she need not come to me but should go directly to the judicial office."

At night Father recited Havdalah with the mournful intonation of *Eichah*. Seeing his children's despair, his courage faltered, and the farewell ceremony for Yitta took place in an unending stream of bitter tears.

"May we live to see each other again...!" cried Yitta. "*Daven* that Hashem should watch over me here..." Eyes swollen with tears, they could not look one another in the face. It was like taking leave of a deceased at the cemetery.

Amidst the hurry, Yitta pressed the most recent photo of herself, posing for her Aryan identity papers, into Dovid'l's hand. "Here, hide it on you and keep me in mind. You know how much I loved you all, and you in particular."

The court clerk arrived to help them carry their belongings. To be sure, there was much to carry; Yitta had not forgotten the slightest thing that could possibly come to use.

She escorted her parents and brothers out of the house. *Baruch Hashem they are taken care of*, thought Yitta, sighing from all her hard work. *As for me, if chalilah something bad is destined to happen, at least there will be someone to remember me.*

The night passed with terrifying dreams.

On Sunday morning, although the air was thick with an explosive charge, Yitta wrote a reassuring letter to Father and Mother.

By nightfall, the wings of the Angel of Death could be heard flapping through the air.

Yitta sits all alone at home. As if in spite, the carbide lamp refuses to ignite. Flickering weakly, it casts an eerie shadow on the wall. A gusty wind raps on the closed shutters, as if it has come to deliver dreaded news.

Yitta takes stock of her entire life. Not a blissful moment had she experienced. In our parents' home, because of the ongoing discord with the communal leaders who tormented Father, there wasn't a groschen. Every trifle was attained with great hardship. Her contemporaries, and even younger girls, were already married and running their own homes and looked askance at her ambitions to marry a *talmid chacham*, albeit they did not possess any of her qualities. Yitta's depth and dignified bearing far surpassed the narrow, small-town mentality of the Kazimierz girls. She found her only worldly pleasure and intellectual stimulation in visiting her brother and sister-in-law and Reizele in Dzialoszyce.

Yes, my brother... What didn't he do for me always? Where is he hiding, along with his wife and their one surviving child? How I wish they could have been here now together with our parents! Had they come here during the first Aussiedlung, surely their dear Alte'le would still be among the living. Could anyone have known? Who knows anything nowadays! Just let me make it through the coming day, and I will think of a way...

The thought of tomorrow sends a tremor through her heart, the likes of which she had never in her life experienced.

Suddenly... *Sh! What was that?*

Faint footsteps...getting bolder by the minute.

Oh, someone is knocking on the kitchen door.

"Who is it?"

"*Aufmachen*! Open up!"

In the blink of an eye, the door is thrust open, and the savage faces of two Gestapo men appear.

"Where is the *shochet*?" they shout.

Without waiting for a response, they lead Yitta away. Her heart pounds; her mind works feverishly. *I must save myself! But how…?*

It is a pitch-dark night. Encountering another Gestapo officer, the men greet each other and chat quietly. Taking advantage of the situation, the quick-witted Yitta vanishes into the labyrinth of crowded huts.

After searching to no avail, the officers throw up their hands in resignation, ashamed of themselves. The Jew-girl had defeated the mighty Germans!

My first trial is over, but what shall I do next?

She waits until daybreak. *Going back home doesn't make sense. I have the judge's office key on me. I must go there already. I can't wait any longer.*

Unnoticed, Yitta approaches the large courthouse building. *I made it…*

"*Halt*!" she hears from behind, making her blood run cold.

"Who goes there? Pole or *Jude*?"

"*Jude*," a passing Polish acquaintance confirms.

A blast of a revolver, an inhuman, convulsive scream…and there on the ground lies the lovely, blooming spring flower, wilted, amidst the fallen autumn leaves.

For a time after, there remained a mark, a bloody stain upon the white snow. Polish passersby would stop for a while, and with heads bowed, they would make a sign of the cross and sway sadly, "*Ach*, Irena…"

The vivacious Yitta, the crown of our family, is no more. Already, she belongs to the legendary chain of the *kedoshim* of the past. Standing guard until the last minute in order to save our frail

parents, our unforgettable sister Yitta fell — the first Kazimierz sacrifice on the altar of the new European order.

CHAPTER 22

Living in the Dilapidated *Mikveh* Building

ON MONDAY MORNING [November 9] in the court clerk's dark, foul-smelling pigsty in Jakuszowice, my parents can hardly sit still. Filled with dread, they wait anxiously for midday to hear their first report on the situation in Kazimierz. The hours stretch as long as years.

At last, the clerk returns. His face is grim. In a trembling voice, he relates the morning's events.

"At dawn, Kazimierz was sealed off. The farmers were not allowed in to the market fair. Then, the already familiar procedure followed. The small number of Jews were assembled in one spot and taken to the twelve o'clock train."

"Were there any victims...and do you have information about Yitta?" my parents ask.

He shrugs his shoulders.

"They say..." he stammers, "I don't know...she must have escaped from the transport."

Like a thunderclap on a clear day, his words echoed through the cramped pigsty. Father stooped over like a tree being chopped down and shed his first tear. Wringing their hands, Dovid'l and Meir'l managed to muster up but one word: "*Farloiren!* Lost!"

Having just dozed off, Mother awoke with a start, took one look at Father sitting in the corner, and no longer had to ask. She lay on the straw, her eyes staring blankly ahead, shedding streams of tears.

The court clerk slipped out unnoticed, leaving the unfortunates alone with their misery, each immersed in his own thoughts.

The painful situation now came into sharp focus: their wings had been abruptly clipped. *What shall we do now? Is it possible to manage without Yitta? Is life even worthwhile without her?*

Father already had his approach in place. "We must brace ourselves with superhuman strength," he declared. "Whatever the will of the Creator may be, we must accept it with love. Meanwhile, at least we have a place to stay."

With renewed energy, he began his holy *avodah*, beseeching Hashem with bitter tears. He stood in one place all day like a statue, even abstaining from the bit of bread and water of which he customarily partook at three o'clock every afternoon. He spoke no more. In this short time, he was transformed into an otherworldly being.

Dovid'l and Meir'l decided to put an end to their suffering. But the vision of their father, who had become even more precious and holy in their eyes in these moments, did not allow them to entertain the thought. How could they abandon their parents?

In this manner, the day passed.

Again they impatiently await their host's return. It is quite possible he will have more accurate information. Perhaps he was mistaken. After all, he said he did not know for certain.

The clerk is back. He has no further news except that the *Judenrat* remained in town. "And you must all leave my place," he adds.

"What are you saying? Where do we go? Maybe you want more money?"

No. He is afraid. He will not keep them for any price.

A dark abyss opened suddenly before their eyes. "Have pity on us in this time of danger. Give us one more day!" they pleaded.

With much effort, tears, and money, they prevailed upon their host to let them stay until the following night.

"By tomorrow night, *Hashem Yisbarach* can yet help us," said Father.

A thousand thoughts cross their minds. *Who knows if this isn't the work of Judge Kotkowski? After hearing of Yitta's misfortune, he must have incited the clerk to evict us, so that our possessions will remain his. Perhaps he is even the guilty one in Yitta's death?* Their feverish imaginations conjure up all sorts of ideas. *What are we to do from here on?*

Even in a moment such as this, Father does not lose himself. "The clerk might still reconsider," he reasons. "And if not, we will go to our landlord Gurak, where we lived for close to twenty years. He is the best friend we have. He will give us a place. We have no other alternative."

The next day brought nothing new.

"You must go!" the court clerk stated unequivocally that night.

Having no choice, they pack their bags. Mother, weak and helpless, can barely stand on her feet. Father, Dovid'l, and Meir'l lift the bundles onto their shoulders. They set out, the clerk accompanying and helping them.

As they tread through the meadows, fallen twigs cracking under their feet, every rustle makes their hearts stand still. Refusing to go any further, the court clerk abandons them in the middle of the open fields. Overcome with fright, they envy Yitta's good fortune in having been freed of such dreadful suffering.

With great difficulty, they manage at last to drag themselves into the courtyard of the house they had lived in for so many years.

Their apartment appeared unchanged, except for two white paper strips, like shrouds, sealing the entrance. The entire house, which had once been inhabited by Jewish families, now looked like a tomb in a cemetery.

Father alone goes up to his good old friend the landlord, with complete faith that he will be granted a corner of the barn. But the door is bolted shut. After a while, the malicious landlady opens it and emits a shrill shriek, as if the *Malach Hamaves* himself has appeared before her eyes. The door closes in Father's face.

He stands there begging and calling out to her husband. The door opens again, and the woman throws a piece of old bread to Father, along with a warning: "If you do not leave, I will report you to the Germans!"

More broken than ever, Father shuffled down the stairs.

There is no compassion! From here on, I must devote myself entirely to the service of the Creator. The physical world has no place for me anymore. Perhaps I no longer have the right to live at all? For man was put on this world only to improve it, and to raise worthy generations. When its mission is done, the soul must return to its Source; the number of years is immaterial.

What complaints can I have to the Ribono shel Olam? My daughter and son-in-law and their two children in Zawichost were good Yidden. Their parnassah did not come easily, but that's not important. I, too, was never well off, and when I did have some money I did not use it for luxuries but to support the children in yeshivah, saving every last zloty to send to them so they would remain ehrliche Yidden. Geloibt Hashem Yisbarach, Avramele is a frum Yid in Canada in the free world, doing his holy work. And of Chaim'l I surely had nothing to be ashamed...!

As for the great misfortune that happened with Yitta — can we resist His holy will? Hatzur tamim paalo — the deeds of the Rock are perfect. Who knows His ways?

I have nothing more to do in this world...

Is it so?

After all, my two youngest sons, Dovid'l and Meir'l, are still in my care. For their sake, I must live. I must take care of them. But what am I to do?

Suddenly, it occurred to him. *Past the field is the deteriorating mikveh building, in fact the very mikveh into which I invested so much energy, effort, and money throughout my life. Many times, during the freezing winter temperatures, when there were no funds to pay a caretaker, I was not ashamed to stoke the fire and see to it that taharas Yisrael was guarded. Yes, this zechus will now protect us and it is there that we will be rescued.*

Without further deliberation, the boys stealthily carried several bundles of straw out of Gurak's barn, and they were soon quartered in their new residence.

Every night, Father or the boys slipped out to buy food from their Polish acquaintances. Many did not let them in, bolting their doors as if against some frightening specter. Others sold them food once, charging a hundred times its value and warning them not to come again. When Father went to Judge Kotkowski, who had Yitta's possessions, to ask him for a favor, the judge regarded Father with astonishment and sent him away with some lame excuses. On top of that, he cast fear upon Father, telling him: "They'll search you out. You'd better escape from Kazimierz!"

Father looked up other acquaintances, managing to bring back a stale piece of bread every night. Lying on the straw, Mother suffered without letup. She would gratefully accept the dry bread, sometimes dipping it into *mikveh* water or a bit of vinegar that a Pole had given them. Her weak heart beat ever slower. About her beloved Yitta she never mentioned a word.

One day, she looked out through a crack and noticed her neighbor, Tzirel Miller, who happened to be passing by at that moment. Her fate was the same as countless other Jews who had given their possessions in exchange for refuge with Polish friends, who took it

all and threw them out a few days later like squeezed-out lemons. These Jews were now assembled in the public school building.

Mother learned that Shlomo and Feigele Wisnicki and their children were among those held in this detention center of the living dead, awaiting the implementation of the awful sentence that would release them of their torment.

"What shall I wait for?" asked Mother. "If there exists a way out that can alleviate this worse-than-death suffering, why should I be an exception? Of my beloved Chaim'l, there is no news. If he were alive, he would have moved heaven and earth to find us so we could all be together. I wish to join him..."

She beseeched her husband and sons to have pity and allow her to turn herself in. "I am nothing but a stumbling block to you!" she cried. "Without me, you will be able to save yourselves much more easily. You are not doing me any favors. I cannot take this agony anymore."

"It won't last too much longer," they consoled her. "Soon, soon..."

To this, she shook her head sadly.

CHAPTER 23

Wandering in the Countryside

YISROEL'S HOST WAS A FARMER by the name of Franek Baber, who lived on the Swierczyna road near the forest on the outskirts of Sancygniow. Next to his cottage stood another one, which belonged to his brother-in-law Kantkiewicz. Both men were fine, upstanding Poles, who, despite their poverty, took in anyone who came to them. Soon there were over forty Jews sheltered within the two small dwellings.

However, since Baber and Kantkiewicz were the fearful sort, at the slightest rustle everyone had to run to the shared dilapidated barn, which was the only place to hide. Carrying children and bundles, a group of this size could not remain a secret.

What's more, in order to feed so many people, our hosts had to go into the neighboring villages every day to buy whatever was available. In no time, it became known in the entire countryside that here on the Swierczyna a *shtetl* had formed, which had become the new Dzialoszyce.

The consequences were not long in coming. On Wednesday evening [November 11], Yisroel's third day there, two local Polish policemen showed up. One of them was Stefaniak, a former resident of Dzialoszyce. Having come of their own accord, they led the Jews of one house to the nearby forest and searched them, robbing them of their last groschen and all their bundles. The Jews danced with joy that their lives were spared. The rest of us, who miraculously remained at the second brother-in-law's house, could no longer stay there — the same thing could happen to us the following night.

Shmuel Yossel gathered his family members, Yisroel and his family, and the three of us who had joined them — Feivel Erlich, Mechel Kamelgard and myself. Bundles on our shoulders, our group was wandering once again in search of a place to hide.

Having done business with the peasants in this area for many years, Shmuel Yossel's brother Mordechai had become acquainted with all of them. He could mimic their lifestyle and do farm work as if he were born into it.

"If you are willing to work as a farmhand and adopt the Polish way of life, I'll take you along with me and find a job for you and a place to stay," he offers me. "The farmer clothing you brought along will come to good use. I'll introduce you as my brother-in-law. Peasants take pity on the poor. Just make sure not to slip up and tell them who you really are."

I agree to do whatever he says. Mordechai prepares for himself a similar outfit and hat, and we set out.

The first night, we approach a rich farmer. He gives us food and sleeping accommodations in the drafty barn. It is so cold we do not sleep a wink the entire night. At dawn, after we finally doze off, our host wakes us and sends us on our way.

We continue on to a small hamlet. There we meet Mordechai's old school friend, a quiet young farmer. His wife, a young peasant woman, appears to be a very decent, compassionate person.

Mordechai tells him the purpose of our coming — we are looking for work on his farm.

The farmer consents. "But only as long as things remain quiet."

Our hosts promptly offer us boiled potatoes and hot milk. Since we have not changed our clothes in the last few days and are frozen through and through, we now begin to feel the aftereffects.

We soon go out to the field to do the threshing. I pick up the skill the first time around. I also learn to harness the horses. The farmer is extremely pleased. We eat the midday meal and rest up a bit. Later, we shovel the manure out of the stable. After all, we must prepare a place in the stable to sleep; we no longer entertain greater expectations.

In the evening, the farmer and his wife again give us potatoes and milk. Such large bowlfuls — I had never eaten this much in all my life! I cannot get down to the bottom of the bowl, but Mordechai tells me that a peasant must not leave anything over.

After the meal a surprise awaits us.

"Go into the second room to sleep," says the farmer's wife. "Yesterday we bought a Jewish apartment in Dzialoszyce, so we now have empty beds which are not being used." We do not wait to be asked again.

I immediately recognize Bunim Brener's furniture, his *tallis*, his silk frock, his *tish chalat*. Even his *sefarim* are lying around the room. A picture of the Gerrer Rebbe had already been hung on the wall, among our host's holy pictures.

"Why did you put up this picture?" I ask the farmer. "It is a Jewish rabbi!"

"It is not!" he declares. "It is Pope Benedict. He had a beard, too."

I had no desire to prove him wrong. Let it be Pope Benedict!

The good peasant woman asks me what she can use the matzah bag for.

"Fill it up with hay or feathers — it'll make a good pillow!" I tell her.

She shows me a white *kittel* which she has already washed and pressed. "I'll give it as a gift to the priest. He wears this type of wide vestment."

Lying on the floor are two *mezuzos*, and even a piece of *afikoman* matzah. I pick up the *mezuzos*.

"What are those?" they ask.

"These are sacred Jewish objects that are not allowed to lie around this way," I explain.

Taking the *mezuzos*, they ask me to point out any other items that are holy. "We will pack them in a box and store it in the attic. If there will ever be a Jewish community again, we will donate the contents to the synagogue."

Such devout peasants! They packed up everything: *Chumashim*, *sefarim* on halachah, volumes of *Sfas Emes*, and took it all up to the attic.

Then the woman brings me something else. "I found another sacred object," she declares.

I look. It is a *sheitel*.

So be it. "Pack that up, too," I say.

That night, I took off my farm clothing and covered myself with Bunim Brener's fur-lined Shabbos coat. It was my first good night's sleep in a long time.

In the morning, we found warm water and soap prepared for us. We washed up. You call this *galus*! I could not believe it was all real. Next, the farmer and his wife offered us fresh rolls straight out of the oven. After we ate, we started another day's work — cutting hay, grazing the horses, and drawing water from the well. I already knew how to do it all.

We had a few days of calm. Our hosts became friendlier with us by the day; we were already like family. However, I could not sit

still. In this place, we were cut off from the entire world. I wanted to send a messenger to Kazimierz to find out how my parents were faring, but our host would not allow it. "If you want to stay here, you must cut ties with everyone," he said.

I could not bear staying here any longer — I had to know what was happening. Granted, a few days ago I had met poor Henoch Cudzynowicer, who gave me a report on Kazimierz. He had been there on Shabbos and had eaten by my parents. He told me they were packing up in a hurry and left that night.

But where to...?

In addition, as my Chayele and I had agreed upon, I should have heard from her through our Polish friend Wrubel in Dzialoszyce. I had to send a messenger to Dzialoszyce. But from here it was not possible.

Consequently, on Monday [November 16], a week after the expulsion raid, Mordechai and I decided to leave.

We find Yisroel and Shmuel Yossel in the stable of Wojtek Amerikaner in Szyszczyce. I immediately send messengers to Dzialoszyce and to Kazimierz.

From Chayele there is no news yet. And the reports from Kazimierz are vague. Something about my sister Yitta'le escaping from the transport...

What is that supposed to mean? Where is everyone? And why is there no word from Chayele? I see that I will not accomplish anything with messengers. I must go myself to Dzialoszyce and to Kazimierz.

Everyone looks at me as if I am out of my mind. "He wants to go to Dzialoszyce, where discovered Jews are rounded up every day, where there hasn't been a day since the *Aussiedlung* that doesn't yield dozens of victims!

"And to Kazimierz of all places...!"

Yisroel refuses to let me go under any circumstances. "You will not be helping your parents at all," he says. "Surely they have fled to Krakow by now, and your brothers must be in the Kostrze labor camp, where they stayed once before."

I try sending another messenger, this time with a letter to my friends in Kostrze. But they are no longer there.

I must go to Kazimierz myself to find out everything. I will not let anyone talk me out of it.

"The man is committing suicide..." everyone around me whispered.

CHAPTER 24

My Home in the Slonowice Forest among the *Kedoshim* of Kazimierz

MECHEL KAMELGARD IS THE ONLY ONE who is prepared to join me in this perilous endeavor of slipping into the town of Dzialoszyce.

We set out by foot on Tuesday night [November 24]. Our fear is intense; we imagine that every passerby is looking at us and can hear the loud pounding of our hearts. Yet we encourage each other and continue on.

Finally, the town comes into view. As we walk through the fields near the Catholic cemetery, Mechel changes his mind. He will not go into Dzialoszyce — he wants to turn back. I barely prevail upon him to at least wait for me while I continue into town myself.

I enter through the Chmielow road. Everything is as it always was. People are strolling along; you can't even tell the Jews are missing. The streets are lit by battery-operated lamps. I pull my cap all the way down over my ears and lift up the collar of my jacket.

Who will recognize me like this? Soon I am standing at the door of our friends, the Wrubels.

I knock.

"Come in."

Mrs. Wrubel does not recognize me at first.

"Oh! You did that so well!"

She invites me into the restaurant, locking it from all sides.

"Yes, I have a telegram from your wife," she says, handing it to me.

"Why didn't you give it to the messenger I sent yesterday?" I ask her.

"I was afraid to trust a peasant asking about Jews! How should I know he was genuine?"

I head back, finding Mechel on the outskirts of Dzialoszyce at a Polish acquaintance; he had eaten there. We return safely to Szyszczyce.

My first step has proven successful, and everyone rejoices. I thank Hashem that Chayele arrived safely at her destination.

I immediately begin to make plans for my excursion to Kazimierz tomorrow. Mechel no longer wants to come along, and once again, everyone tries to dissuade me from going. "Be happy that you have news of Chayele and Feivele. What can you possibly do for your parents, that is, if you even find them there?"

The next evening, without telling anyone a word, I set out alone.

With a raging snowstorm swirling around me, I walk to the *kolejka* station on the outskirts of Dzialoszyce. The 6:00 p.m. train is already standing there, ready to leave.

I linger for a moment, deliberating:

If I continue from here to Kazimierz by foot,[1] when will I get there...? I do believe I will have a place to sleep — my parents' landlord Gurak will

---

1. Approximately fifteen kilometers (nine miles)

surely let me in for one night. On the other hand, you can't predict anything
nowadays, and if I am forced to return straightaway, it would be terrible. I
don't think I could endure walking back and forth in one night, let alone on
such a dark, miserable one in the middle of a blizzard, with heavy snow on
the roads.

I hear a call, then a signal from the conductor, and I find myself
inside the railcar — without a ticket. The train is packed with
people. What have I done? Too late. Whatever will be, will be! I
whistle nonchalantly, trying to calm myself. When the conductor
comes along, I slip him a two-zloty note, and he moves on.

I arrive in Kazimierza Wielka. At the station there is no one but
a police officer and several rail workers. If anything has happened,
there is no sign of it here.

I head into the Jewish area of town. It is ghostly quiet. From the
outside, my parents' apartment appears untouched; however, all the
contents have been emptied out. I knock on the closed gate that
leads to the landlord Gurak's apartment. His son Bolek comes out.

"Oh!" he cries. "You are not afraid to come here?"

He is trembling. Not even allowing me into the apartment, he
stands on the steps and tells me everything.

"Yes, they killed your sister Irena. It is true."

I cannot ask him for details, as he is in a hurry.

"Your parents and brothers are here somewhere. I do not know
where they are, but they were not among the 250 Jews assembled in
the school building."

In response to my question as to who those Jews were and what
happened to them, he looks at me with astonishment.

"Haven't you heard anything? The most important people in
town were assembled there — Jews like Yossel Miller and his entire
family, the Wisnickis, the Rozeneks, the Dula family... They had
all hidden in their homes or taken refuge with Polish friends. On
Monday, immediately after the transport left, the land commissar

himself, along with several policemen, approached every Pole, warning each one individually that whoever gave shelter or even a piece of bread to a Jew would have his entire family killed and his possessions burned.

"As a result, all the Jews who had hidden in Polish homes were evicted. These Jews were assembled in the school building. Since there were over two hundred people, the Gendarmerie (military police) inquired of Miechow headquarters: 'What shall we do with them? Will there be another transport?' Came the reply: 'Is there a shortage of earth in Kazimierz?' And so, yesterday they led all the Jews to the Slonowice forest. It took only six men to execute them all.

"*Ach, Panie!* I can't begin to describe to you what was going on in town. Such young, healthy men were among them, and they just let themselves be taken. What a shame! They could have put up a fight. What did they stand to lose?

"Your parents were not there. Your younger brother Marek comes to us often, asking if we have received word from you yet. I warned him not to hang around here anymore, as you can well understand."

He is in a hurry. He claims he is cold.

I tell him where I have come from. "How can I walk back such a great distance now? Let me stay overnight, if only in the barn."

"What are you saying? Do you want to kill us all? *Dobranoc!* Good night!" With that, he left me standing there alone.

I head back. It occurs to me that I might still be able to catch the 8:00 p.m. *kolejka* leaving for Dzialoszyce.

I run, I fly, the 250 *Yidden* hovering before my eyes — nearly the entire *kehillah* of Kazimierz.

Shlomo Wisnicki — such a smart, sensible man, a unique sort of person who went about his way, never raising his voice at anyone. When business was quiet, he could be found occupied with a sefer or a book. A living

encyclopedia, there was nothing he didn't know. His wife Feigele...what a gentle, good heart. How much tzedakah they gave! And the children...

Yossel Miller's family, our neighbors for twenty years. Simple, hardworking people, devout and scrupulous.

Shmuel Rozenek...

Yudel Dula...

Mendel Salzman — even though he was a simple man, he always aimed higher, a real Yid in the full sense of the word.

Couldn't any of them have saved themselves? They had dealt with their Polish neighbors for decades. Wasn't there even one Pole who was willing to hide anyone?

I am already past the town on the path leading to Slonowice. The wind whistles eerily in such a sorrowful, plaintive tune, it seems to me that the 250 *kedoshim*, my friends, are calling to me from the Slonowice forest, asking for something, pleading... My face breaks into a cold sweat.

When I arrive at the station, the train is still standing there. It is delayed; a squealing contingent of pigs is waiting to be loaded. I see nothing. I do not even hear the grunting of the pigs. All I hear are the cries of the 250 people in the Slonowice forest. My chest is so tight I feel no fear, even when two gendarmes, holding a drunk woman between them, stroll by.

I feel as one with those *Yidden*. I knew them from my childhood. Their children were my students...they would do anything for me. And where are my parents and my brothers? Are they not also among them? Did Bolek fool me? Most likely not, for then why would he have told me the truth about Yitta?

When the train spit me out at the Dzialoszyce station, I felt as if I had been violently torn from my home, now situated in the Slonowice forest.

At that very moment, my parents and brothers were sitting in the dilapidated *mikveh* building, ten meters from Gurak's house,

worrying about the fate of their son, who had not made contact with them.

CHAPTER 25

Jewish Dwellings in the Villages

THE VILLAGE OF SZYSZCZYCE became a miniature *shtetl* once again. This time, over sixty Jews found refuge here. Avraham Dula and his family were living at the mayor's house. Yankel Mandelbaum, Alter Kalimacher, Shlomo Kazmierski and Itche Mayer Waga were with Franek Leszczynski. All those of means were at the homes of various other local Poles.

A rumor circulated in the area that until the first of January [1943] there was still time to report to the special cities that had been established for Jews: Krakow for the entire Krakow district, Sandomierz for the Lublin district, and Nowo-Radomsko for the Radom district. Thereafter, if the Germans found a Jew hiding at the home of a farmer, they would burn down the entire village.

Even the quiet, fine farmers of Szyszczyce began to tremble. Although they genuinely wanted to help the Jews — they wouldn't pay a groschen for anything at the Dzialoszyce auction — they were now in an uncomfortable position.

The Jews themselves could not figure out what to do. Avraham Dula sent a messenger to Krakow to his good friend Bialabrode, who had given him a position in the *Judenrat* before the recent *Aussiedlung*, asking him to write back with advice. *Should I come to Krakow?* wrote Dula. *Is it true that the Krakow ghetto will be expanded to accommodate the newcomers? And isn't the journey a great risk?*

He received an immediate reply from Bialabrode: *You should come to Krakow. I guarantee that the Jews will be able to stay here. The trip is not dangerous, as an edict has been issued allowing Jews to travel with assurance until the first of January.*

Without further deliberation, Dula hired a wagon, Waga and Kazmierski a second one, and Zusman Zylber, the recent vice-chairman of the *Judenrat*, a third.

They try to talk us into traveling with them. Yisroel is ready to consent, but his wife is not willing to go. "Why would the Jews of Krakow be privileged characters?" she reasons. "I will not hear of it under any circumstances! You cannot trust the Germans. I refuse to be under their domain."

Shmuel Yossel and Mordechai advise me likewise. "As soon as some Jews leave, the farmers won't be so afraid to keep us. There are too many of us here. All over, everyone knows about Szyszczyce."

Yisroel stays.

The next morning, the wagons returned. The trip itself had gone smoothly; they did not encounter anyone on the way. However, Avraham Dula and his wife and youngest son were searched at the Krakow ghetto gate and arrested by the Jewish police. Rumor had it that foreign currency was found on them.

A few days later we heard that they were killed. Dula's daughter, who tried to intervene, was never seen again. We also learned that a carload of Jews traveling to Krakow from Wodzislaw was detained in Slomniki. All its occupants were shot, including the Pinchever Rebbe, Reb Pinye'le, and his only son Alter'l.

It was becoming clear that releasing false rumors was another German ploy to get Jews to assemble: some would be caught on the way, and the rest would be together in Krakow, eliminating the need for search raids.

We are glad we did not go.

However, here in Szyszczyce, a difficult period begins. With each day that draws nearer to the first of January, the farmers become increasingly uneasy. Every time they go into Dzialoszyce, they return with all sorts of rumors. They begin to hint politely that we should find somewhere to hide before the new year begins. "If we see that things calm down, we will let you come back," they offer.

Shmuel Yossel and his Polish friends, robust villagers, had dug a wide cave in the hilly terrain at the edge of the village. Over thirty people had gone into hiding there, most of them children, whom the farmers were reluctant to shelter from the outset.

Mordechai suggests that he and I and a few other men should dig a second cave. Our biggest concern is Yisroel. Both of his boys, as well as his brother-in-law Yoav's two children, have come down with the measles and are running a high fever. Anyone might agree to keep Yisroel, his wife and their two children. Even Staszek Tetele would not be afraid to take them in, for the children are older and easy to hide. But Yoav's little one is still a young child without the necessary intellect. Besides, a group of ten people is a big undertaking.

I explain to Yisroel that if they split up, it will be much easier to find a place for them all. But he does not wish to do so. "How will they move around without me?" he says. "I am known in the area. The farmers will only take them in because of me. And should Yoav abandon his child? Indeed, in this merit, Hashem will help me."

I do not know what to answer. I wonder whether one may rely on miracles in such a time of danger. Covered with red measle spots, the children lie there motionless. A little warm water is their

only sustenance. Yisroel says Tehillim all day in the foul-smelling stable.

"You'll see," he tells me. "Hashem will send help when we least expect it. I have complete faith that the *yeshuah* can come at any moment."

I seek out Mordechai and Shmuel Yossel to discuss the cave we are to begin working on today. I find them in the old cave, dug by the villagers two weeks ago.

A narrow entryway leads into a wide limestone bunker, the ceiling so low you cannot stand up straight. A metal pail of unpeeled potatoes boils on a small iron stove, producing a thick smoke in the cramped, airless shelter. It is so dark you can hardly see who is there.

By the light of a small kerosene lamp that is missing its glass chimney and smoking badly stands a young, disheveled woman, warming a bottle for her baby. A second child's desperate screams make me shudder. The child's whole face is covered with scabies; only his eyes are visible. He scratches the lesions with his dirty, bloodied nails.

By a second, similar lamp sits Dovid Koppel, picking the disagreeable six-legged creatures that have spread in his clothes like locusts. By the time he finishes one garment, the previously deloused one is full again.

Just today, Shmuel Yossel's child came down with diarrhea. The odor is the last thing that is needed here.

Old Mrs. Koppel carries her grandchild on her shoulders all day, as he is suffering from a severe rash. The child is eating a cold potato. Several washed shirts hang on the stovepipe, but it is impossible to make out whether they were ever white. Kalmen, Shmuel Yossel's brother-in-law, is peeling a carrot. His hands are bandaged; the abscesses he has developed between his fingers torment him terribly.

I cannot bear standing here any longer. My nostrils feel like worms are crawling in them. My eyes tear from the intense smoke. I grab Mordechai and we leave. Only when I get out into the fresh air does it dawn on me where I have just been.

"Is *that* what you would like to fashion for us?!" I ask Mordechai.

"For the time being, we do not need it," he replies. "The farmers will still allow people like us to sleep in a barn. However, after the first of January, if the situation worsens, we will have to hide in such a bunker. But I'll construct a better one.

"Let's go to Tetele. His stable is warm. We'll sleep there tonight. To be in a labor camp in Krakow is surely not better."

That night, the three of us — Shmuel Yossel, Mordechai, and I — slept at Tetele's. It was warm indeed, for me more so than the others, for in the middle of the night, I suddenly felt a stream of hot liquid pouring down on me. Startled, I woke up.

Mordechai struck a match... Tetele's young stallion had selected my face upon which to relieve himself.

CHAPTER 26

A *Chad Gadya* Reenactment

CHANUKAH, THE CELEBRATION of Jewish victory over our Greek enemies, brought a spell of weepy weather. The constant dripping through the barn roof matched the bleakness in our hearts.

If at first the farmers had gently advised us to leave the village for a while, the tone of their voices now increased a notch. In addition, a new crisis presented itself: Polish youths from the villages were being rounded up for labor in Germany. A squad of German cars would arrive unexpectedly, surround a village, seize anyone they found and take them away. These *Aktions*, or *lapankas* as the peasants called them, had already taken place in several villages in the Szyszczyce region. Many an unsuspecting Jew was discovered, too, in which case the host farmer was beaten to a pulp. After that, he would never again harbor a Jew for any price, and neither would his neighbors. Hence, it was to our own advantage to leave Szyszczyce for a while, for if a *lapanka* were to occur here, some of us could fall into German hands and the rest would be evicted.

Once again the question arises: Where should we go?

Mordechai and I had already discussed a cave. Tetele had given us permission to dig in his hillside field on the outskirts of the village. Tomorrow, *im yirtzeh Hashem*, we will begin to implement this plan.

Yisroel's children and his brother-in-law Yoav's children are still sick with the measles. For the time being they have not been evicted yet, but their host Wojtek Amerikaner had already made it clear that the moment things took a turn for the worse, they would have to leave.

The Jews who traveled to Krakow send bad news. There is serious talk there that the entire ghetto will soon be liquidated; women, children and the elderly are due to be deported. Only the slave laborers under *Sicherheitsdienst* jurisdiction will remain. The labor camps run by private firms have already been partly closed down, and the Kostrze camp, where many Dzialoszycers worked, will be closing any day now.

But the labor and conditions under German domain are such that even the healthiest, strongest young men cannot possibly survive. At the 6:00 a.m. wakeup they are given 180 grams of bread along with a bit of warm water for the entire day. Under strict watch, they march to work some two miles from the barracks. Work starts at 8:00 a.m. and continues until 8:00 p.m. The inmates carry heavy boulders and rails for tens of meters. If one is too tired to go on or complains that he is unwell, he is taken with the next transport. The only medicine administered to a truly ill person is a bullet in the head. Half-dead after a two-mile trek back to their barracks, they receive a meager amount of putrid cabbage-and-water and lie down to sleep on hard planks. The camps are under tight security to prevent escape. Should anyone manage to disappear, three of the strongest inmates are selected and the others are forced to hang them on a specially constructed gallows, where they are left to dangle for several days. And where could one escape to anyway?

This week the *Ordnungsdienst* men who remained in Miechow after the last *Aussiedlung* were executed. Along with a number of Jews whose hideouts were discovered, they were assembled and lined up in front of the shul, then taken to a field where they were gunned down one by one, like targets in revolver training exercises.

There was a brawny young man from Slomniki whose wife and only child were next to be shot. As the child was separated from his mother and deputy-*Landrat* Schmidt was getting ready to practice his sharpshooting skills, the Maccabean blood of our Chashmonaic heroes of yesteryear flared up in the young Jew. He ran up to the brazen Schmidt and plunged a sharp knife into his neck. An ambulance took Schmidt to Krakow, but he bled to death on the way. The few remaining Jews in the region reacted to this valiant deed with inner satisfaction, but at the same time they trembled from the possible repercussions.

In the evening, a rumor spreads in Szyszczyce that there will be a *lapanka* later tonight.

I hurry to Yisroel. He stands ready to flee with his sick, measled children in his arms.

The weather is terrible. How can we leave now? But go we must! The Polish boys and girls are also escaping the village. We hope they will not rob us on the way.

The roads are slippery as glass on this pitch-dark night. We hold on tightly to one another. The children are crying. Yoav's wife Elke'le is suffering from pneumonia, which was greatly aggravated the last time the group was on the run. Her every cough echoes through the night like an explosion. Little Moshe Fishele will not leave go of her hand. He desperately wants some bread; because of his illness, he hasn't eaten anything for several days. Yoav trips over a hole in the ground and develops a nosebleed that will not stop.

Yisroel carries Feivele in one hand, and with the other, he supports his wife. With a burst blister from the chilblains affecting

her feet, she can barely walk. I carry little Mordche'le on my shoulders. He hugs me so endearingly.

"Will the war last much longer?" the bright child asks.

Finally, we arrive in Wymyslow, the nearest village. We stop at a farmhouse. Seeing us, the farmer's wife is taken aback. Making the sign of the cross, she lets out a scream. "Holy Mother! Get out of here at once!"

We continue on and meet an old peasant woman, who agrees to take us in. She leads us past a pile of manure into a decrepit, exposed barn. "You can stay here for tonight if you give me a nice woolen dress," she says.

And that is where we sat out the night.

At dawn, I return to Szyszczyce.

There had been no raid after all. Still, Yisroel's host is no longer willing to take the group back in. I beg him to have mercy. "He won't stay with you for long. He must get his sick children under a roof, and then he can look for another place."

Grudgingly, he agrees to allow Yisroel's group back into his barn.

In Szyszczyce, I meet my friend Yisroel Alter Nifker. He tells me that his wife and child arrived safely in Sosnowiec and that conditions there are very good. He and his brother Yakov are staying in a village not far from here. Yakov's wife Nadzia and [his niece] Lola [Pomeranz] are in Krakow with Aryan papers. Chaim'l [Pomeranz] is in a labor camp. Officially there is not one Jew left here in these villages, he informs me.

Then he relates the following news: "Yesterday Bialabrode was killed in Miechow by none other than Beyerlein himself! A vast sum of money and a foreign passport with an alias were found in his apartment; he had planned to flee the country but was caught at the last minute. With this it became clear that Bialabrode's activities had never been clean to begin with. He was the one who had caused Avraham Dula's death, and there were many other victims

on his conscience as well. As soon as he heard about a Jew who still had some money, he would confiscate it through various illegal means. In this way, he lived it up together with the German murderers."

Two days later, Beyerlein was taking a stroll through the Miechow town square, accompanied by two high-ranking Krakow SD agents. Without warning, when they reached the end of the park, Beyerlein received a bullet in the head from one of his escorts. He died instantly.

Apparently, someone had informed the Germans of Beyerlein's participation in Bialabrode's shady deals. Unbeknownst to Beyerlein, a search was conducted in his house, which yielded surprising results: cellars full of gold and diamonds. He paid for it with his head.

It was a true *Chad Gadya*[1] reenactment!

---

1. Haggadah song in which each successive perpetrator becomes the next victim

CHAPTER 27

My Parents' Tragic Demise

FOR THE FIRST FEW DAYS of their stay in the *mikveh* building, my
parents and brothers were able to observe all the proceedings in
Kazimierz. A public auction of the contents of Jewish homes took
place under the supervision of the land commissar and other
important German officials. The better items were taken to the
Rakowski-Banach house, which had served as the *Judenrat*
headquarters. Rakowski, the most influential member of the
Judenrat, had disappeared along with his brother-in-law Yossel
Banach. They were later caught in the nearby village of Topola and
were taken away. Before they left their luxuriously appointed home,
the only one of its kind in Kazimierz, they chopped up the furniture,
broke the glassware, slashed or burned the clothing, and demolished
their entire residence.

Zelig Fischler, another member of the *Judenrat*, fled to Krakow at
the last minute. He had dealt in foreign currency with *Wirtschaft*[1]
chief Zettmeier, who was now afraid that his covert activities would

---

1. *SS-Wirtschafts-Verwaltungshauptamt*-WVHA (Economic-Administration Office of the SS)

---

be exposed. Zettmeier set out to search for Fischler, intending to kill him personally.

A third *Judenrat* member, Mechel Spokojny, a wealthy man who did business with the Polish nobility, arranged to go into hiding with one of his Polish friends. But in the end, he was the only *Judenrat* official who was given permission to remain in town. After two days, he assumed he would be staying on permanently along with two *Ordnungsdienst* men. But as soon as the three of them fulfilled their duties, they were shot.

The local slaughterhouse shared a wall with the *mikveh*, and by listening in on the butchers who gathered there, my parents and brothers were able to find out what was going on. In addition, Father, who went out every night to obtain food, always had the latest news.

When giving or selling food to Father, all his good friends made clear to him that he should not come anymore. They were afraid.

A stranger had arrived in Kazimierz in the wake of the war, a chimney sweep who spoke some German. Rumor had it that he was a German spy. Father had become acquainted with him and now approached him for help. He gave Father a hearty welcome, proceeded to buy whatever he needed without making a profit, and even cooked a meal for him. "Come back any time. Just tell me the night before what you would like, and I'll have it ready for the next night so you won't have to wait," he offered.

For the first time during their whole ordeal, they had warm meals. This infused new life into Mother, who lay on the straw day and night and could no longer even bring herself to swallow the dry bread they had eaten until then. For a few days they began to think their problems were solved, and they decided they would find a way to reinforce the broken window to keep out the winds. The bit of warm food that Father brought lent renewed energy and cheer to all of them.

Unfortunately, on one of his visits to the chimney sweep, Father forgot to lock the door behind him. The landlord's daughter walked in unexpectedly and saw Father. "You had better not do this anymore," she warned her tenant. "They will burn our house down!"

With tears in his eyes, the kind chimney sweep had to obey. No longer was Father able to benefit from his help.

Tough times resumed. Once again, Father had to go out looking for new contacts. The family was overcome with anxiety until his safe return. If not for Mother's weak condition, which necessitated some warm food, they would have abandoned the nightly outings altogether and would have sufficed with one trip to obtain bread for the whole week. Every day they heard of new victims who were caught wandering around at night looking for food. Some were turned in by the Poles; others were spotted by the police.

Father was afraid to return to Judge Kotkowski, who, on his previous visit, had practically told him outright not to come again, since people were aware he was hiding in Kazimierz and visiting the judge.

When my brothers tried to help by setting out on their own to obtain food, they returned empty-handed. Apparently, the Poles took pity only on Father himself.

Next, Father looked up a farmer in Jakuszowice by the name of Wrubel. Before the war, Father would go there to *shecht* animals, and when a cow was found to be *treif*, he would give Wrubel the intestines, as well as the spleen and brains of every calf, free of charge. Remembering Father's kindness, Wrubel offered to cook food every night and bake challah from wheat flour, without asking for any compensation. "If I had a barn, I would certainly shelter your family," he declared. You could barely move in the one-room hut he lived in with a brood of children, one younger than the next. It was a very good solution, all the more so because Father

could reach Wrubel by walking across the fields, without having to pass through Kazimierz.

With food taken care of, things went smoothly for a few days. But now a problem arose. The butchers who worked in the slaughterhouse next door had become aware that Jews were hiding in the *mikveh*. They did not report this to the authorities, but they did repeat it to others, until even the young children were talking about it. One day the village veterinarian approached the *mikveh* window and told Father, "People know about this place. It may become dangerous for you here. For your own good, I advise you to leave."

What were they to do now?

Father recalled that our neighbor, Moshe Federman the butcher, had mentioned that he had prepared a hideout in Gurak's barn loft. "Let's go take a look," Father said. Indeed, Moshe was there with his four children and one other person.

And so, on Thursday night [November 26], after more than two weeks of living in the *mikveh* building, my parents and brothers moved into their landlord's barn. Living conditions were better here and things were much easier. Father no longer had to go out, since Moshe and his children brought food every night.

Father fasted and *davened* all day. His whispered prayers could often be heard: "*Please let me survive to see the yeshuah, but if not, let me at least merit to die among Jews and to be buried with taharah in a Jewish cemetery.*" Father had always been scrupulous with ritual purity, immersing himself even in the winter in freezing water. His devotion to this aspect reached the most exalted levels.

Three days later, on Sunday night, Moshe went out as always to buy food. Seized by an impulse, he slipped into a Polish neighbor's storage room for some flour, without telling anyone where he was going and what he was doing. The Pole saw Moshe, followed him to his hideout, and informed the Polish police.

It is one o'clock in the morning. Everyone is sleeping. The bales of hay are pushed aside and light fills the hideout, followed by the harsh voices of the Polish police. The situation is hopeless.

Dovid'l and Meir'l, panic-stricken, could not bear witnessing this catastrophe. An inner force took hold of them. Barely dressed, they jumped off the roof and disappeared into the dark of night. Several gunshots accompanied them but failed to find their mark.

Father and Mother were searched, and everything was taken from them. Together with Moshe, who was wounded by a bullet, they were led to the school building.

Several hours later, the two brothers instinctively found each other in the dark *mikveh* building. Wordlessly, they clung to one another — a shadow remaining of the Wolgelernter family.

The following evening, Monday, 22 Kislev/November 30 [1942], as night fell upon the Slonowice forest, the second chapter of the tragic demise of my parents' home came to an end. The light which had illuminated our life's path for so many years was extinguished.

"*Caw*...! *Caw*...!" Flocks of black crows flying overhead eulogized our saintly parents, who had just been buried — not among Jews, and without *taharah*.

CHAPTER 28

My Brothers Resolve to Save Themselves

IT IS THE THIRD DAY since the devastating calamity that befell my brothers. An early winter snowstorm blows in through the crevices of the dilapidated *mikveh* building, the wind howling an eerie tune befitting the mood. Twilight envelops the dark ruin. Visible from a distance through the broken windowpanes, the world is blanketed in snow-white shrouds. It seems as if all of nature commiserates with these two fading souls.

Barely dressed, and frozen through and through, they conduct an ongoing discussion as to whether it is still worth living after suffering such irreparable wounds.

"Does this world offer anything that promises to lighten our great tragedy in some way?" ponders the elder one. "Am I not better off putting an end to my misery by swallowing the powder I carry with me, and joining our exalted parents and sister?

"Even if we were to set out into the world as we are, without clothing, to fulfill our one remaining desire to search for our

brother and share with him the tragic fate of our unforgettable family members, can we be certain that we will find him? With death lurking at every turn, it is quite likely that we will perish somewhere along the way. Wouldn't it be more sensible if it happened here, so our young blood will flow together with the blood of our loved ones?"

It is the final reckoning of two lost, grappling souls. The decision must be reached today. Weakened from three days without food and the frigid cold that penetrates their every limb, staying here any longer is impossible.

"I have made my decision," the elder one says, renewing the conversation. "My life no longer has worth or substance. On the third of September, in the Dzialoszyce market square, my fantasy was crushed, my hope extinguished, leaving behind a rip in my heart that has filled with blood and tears. Why go on living and cause misery to another with the shadow of sadness that will accompany my life's path forever? If I did not carry out this desperate step until now, it was only because I wanted to survive to see our beloved sister happy.

"Later, our dear father held me back. On Sunday night, when we stood face to face with the frightful Angels of Death who came to take us under their wing, I could not bear the sorrow of witnessing the tragic epilogue of our dear parents. I wished to put an end to my young life. But Father, his countenance reflecting his unflinching *bitachon*, told me: 'You may not do so, child. Save yourself now!'"

A choked sob interrupts his words. "Brother!" cries the younger one. "Your heart is not entirely broken. A spark of hope still flickers. Out in the world, beyond the barricades, past barriers we have not yet crossed, someone is waiting for you who will bring you great happiness. Your wandering soul will yet find a *tikkun*. Do you have the right to tamper with your destiny?"

The mystical silence of *Ne'ilah* reigns, the rhythmic beating of two broken hearts the only audible sound as exhaustion overtakes their limbs. Involuntarily, their eyes droop shut.

A light slumber enveloped them, carrying them high up into the worlds of the Heavenly empire, through the tree-lined boulevards of the *Asarah Harugei Malchus* and other *kiddush Hashem* sacrifices.

So many familiar faces. So much splendor and glory...a labyrinth of palaces and gardens...a pure Gan Eden atmosphere. What is this?

Oh! Our saintly Father is also here. Perhaps we are imagining? No, it is surely so. Indeed, Father is seated in one of the splendid halls, wearing his bordeaux velvet tish chalat, his shtreimel crowning his head. Immersed in a Midrash open before him, his face radiates a saintly light.

"My children," he called out in wonderment. *"What are you doing here? How did you get here?"*

"Dear beloved Father! We have nothing to live for. We want to be here with you. Do not make us leave!"

"No, my dear children!" Father replied. *"One may not do so. Go back and Hashem Yisbarach will be with you. Somewhere in the world, your brother wanders, anxiously hoping to hear from you.*

"Kinderlech, go to your brother. Stay together. It won't be long before you will be saved. Forge new links in the chain of our exalted lineage. Remain devout, proud, good Yidden. This will be a tikkun for our neshamos so our bodies will rest in peace. Along with your mother and sister, I will intercede for you. Together with our holy ancestors, we will implore before the Kisei Hakavod that you be protected from all hardship. For until the destination, the path is yet strewn with thorns. Have bitachon...!"

Awakening with a start, the brothers broke into a cold sweat. Their decision was finalized: They would set out and save themselves.

CHAPTER 29

The Kaziel Family

ON THE OUTSKIRTS OF SKALBMIERZ, not far from the bridge, there stands a small, nondescript house, much like all the surrounding houses. In two small tidy rooms lives the family of Stefan Kaziel.

A middle-aged man of about fifty, Stefan, a former railway machinist, had lost his job in the wake of the war. A deep, perceptive sort with an open-minded, big-city *Weltanschauung*, he could not adapt to the narrow mindset of the simple peasants.

Stefan sits isolated in his home, a loner, brooding over his past achievements and fantasizing about the glorious future that awaits him, a qualified craftsman.

As soon as justice triumphs over the world, my material career will be assured! Besides, I am not that hungry for money. Just let redemption come for mankind, liberation from the dark barbarism that has suddenly poisoned all of Europe. Yes, it is shameful to admit, but it is a sad fact — we are spitting in our own faces. Loyal Poles, yesterday's avowed Democrats, have abruptly cast off their convictions and made common cause with the murderous Germans.

Stefan's robust physique had deteriorated. The constant reports of atrocities had sapped his energy and spirits and affected his heart. Just today, they had arrested several Jews, whose only crime was that they were born Jews. They were executed like the most loathsome criminals. And it was his fellow Poles who had turned them in.

He could still visualize Brener, his hardworking Jewish neighbor, being led away, his innocent eyes pleading from afar: "Save me!"

Ach, it was awful! And what offense did my former tenant Lewkowicz commit? What a gentleman he was, a decent, upright person. Did he rob anyone?

They say that Jews took control of all commerce. Did anyone stop the Poles from doing business, too? There is a need for every type of profession. It so happens that the Jews were experts in this field. Are we better off now that they are not here anymore? On the contrary, everything is in short supply and the prices for any available products have risen drastically. Besides, were the Jews allowed entry into any other occupations? Why, a Jew could not even get a job as a janitor!

And to think that our own townspeople would assist our mortal enemy, who stabbed our independent republic in the back! Can we be sure the Germans won't extend their treatment of Jews to include ethnic Poles? Haven't they already done so by expelling our Polish brethren from the areas of Posen and Silesia?

You blinded, misguided people! I believe that in the big cities this would not happen. Not only would an intelligent man of conscience refuse to help the German murderers, but he would surely help the oppressed. Here, people are afraid. If I didn't have such corrupt neighbors all around me, I would rescue these persecuted Jews...

Such are the thoughts of Stefan Kaziel, as he smokes one cigarette after another.

His wife, a charming blonde woman with a good-natured smile that conveyed her energy and initiative, was forced to become the

provider of the family ever since her husband lost his position. She was not accustomed to this, having had at her disposal his substantial monthly salary that had sustained a comfortable lifestyle. Exhausted from a full day of work, she sits down to eat her lukewarm dinner with scant appetite.

Their two pretty, blonde daughters are finishing their homework and getting ready for bed.

Unexpectedly, the door opens. Two young men quietly slink in like thieves. They are frozen through and through. Dressed only in thin pants and summer sandals, they had wrapped themselves in a tablecloth that Judge Kotkowski of Kazimierz consented to give them from all the possessions their murdered sister had left with him.

They had wandered through the countryside, where death lurked at every turn, searching for their lost brother. On the way, it occurred to them that Yitta had told them about a close friend, Magda Kaziel, living in Skalbmierz. They decided to stop at her house, hoping she would allow them to spend the night and recover from three days without food and sleep.

"We are brothers of your friend Irena," they explain. "Would it be possible for you to let us stay overnight? A stable is good enough. Have pity on us. We are exhausted, brokenhearted and bereft."

Two tears, like round pearls, welled up in the woman's kindly eyes. The young men reminded her of her good friend, who had tragically perished.

"Sit down, you poor souls," she said. Not letting them say anything more, she promptly placed her unfinished food before them. "Relax... I'll have something hot ready shortly."

Paying no heed to their objections, she went right into the storage room and brought in some wood. Soon, there was hot coffee.

It was beyond comprehension. *Is this all a dream? To be sitting in a house with non-Jews serving us food and preparing coffee for us?! These people must be malachim!*

The woman would not let them talk. "Eat first and regain your strength," she said, sitting opposite them with a motherly smile. Lost in wonder, they realized that there were still good people in this world, people with compassionate hearts.

How fortunate we would be if they gave us shelter here, they thought. *In this warm, idyllic nest, we would surely be out of harm's way. O Hashem, show us miracles! But we nurture vain illusions. They do not appear to be living in comfort, and even if that were the case, could we expect them to sustain us? After all, the people with whom we left our possessions drove us away and refused to give us anything, and they were high-ranking people in society. If a judge, who administers justice and defends morality, could act that way, what can we expect from ordinary citizens? We should be grateful that they welcomed us with such hospitality even though we could not offer any money. But to think that they will take us in when we don't have a groschen to our name is a futile fantasy. Let's just hope they give us a place for tonight.*

Apparently, the wise, sensitive woman noticed their worried expressions. "You can sleep here," she consoled them. "Don't even mention it. I know everything you've been through. We heard about it. Your sister's death shook me up completely. It took me a long time to recover.

"You are bereft, and I realize that finding your brother is your sole remaining purpose. But it's late and you are tired. I'll fix a bed for you so you can rest up."

Without further ado, she carried in the leather-upholstered chairs from the other room. Pushing them together, she fashioned a bed. "Have a good night. Do not thank me... I don't want to hear. You don't owe me anything. Sleep well."

Though the brothers had not slept for three nights, they could not fall asleep. They were astounded by the few moments spent among these people. *In the middle of a cruel, stormy sea, did there still exist such a tranquil island? Could fiery compassion blaze within the hearts of such simple, commonplace Poles? And towards whom? Towards Jews, who have a price on their heads!*

They have taken us in with open arms and given us food and a place to sleep. Even the stable would be a luxury for us, but seeing our condition they made us a bed in their home, without asking for any compensation. And why all this? Simply because the woman is a friend of Yitta's! Perhaps our saintly sister is indeed interceding on our behalf. O, Ribono shel Olam, help us in our time of need... They continued to *daven* all night.

Neither did Magda and her husband sleep that night. The gentle woman, overcome by the tragedy of these two young people, had so strongly restrained herself from showing emotion in their presence that she broke down crying in her room.

The measured, cool-headed Stefan calmed his wife. "Now is not the time for sentiment. It won't do them any good. We ought to rescue these people, but first we must think logically whether it is feasible from a practical standpoint."

"We will rescue them!" replied Magda.

"*Mamusia*, let's hide them!" begged their two little daughters, who were lying in their beds. "Such quiet, fine young men... Why shouldn't they live?"

"But I see that they don't even have any clothes," remarked Stefan.

"That's not a problem. You have more than enough clothing from our good times."

"What about food?"

"We have a cellar full of potatoes. It should last for the duration of the war. And in the meantime, we will search for their brother.

You know me, Stefan. When I make up my mind, no hardship exists that can stop me from carrying out my goal."

Stefan agreed. He knew his Magda all too well.

With these thoughts, the woman drifted into a troubled sleep that gave rise to a jumble of dreams. Hovering before her was the image of Yitta, her vivacious, murdered friend, eyes filled with tears, arms outstretched, pleading: *Dear Magda, save my orphaned brothers who have just arrived at your home. Remember how you told me before the calamity that if things got bad I should come to you for shelter? So I'm asking you now to rescue my brothers. I perished due to the betrayal of a Catholic Pole. Now you, with your noble Christian soul, should demonstrate that not all Poles are poisoned with this blind hatred. Whom did I harm? Take my wandering brothers into your care, so that I can rest in peace."*

"Be assured, my friend, that I will do everything I can," replied Magda. *"I will not send your brothers away, and I will help them find their missing brother. It is our holy purpose, Irena."*

Shaken by her dream, Magda arose with a start. She woke up her husband Stefan. "We will save these young men!" she declared.

In the little house of the Kaziel family, a provisional verdict was issued, reinstating life to two of those condemned to death by the twentieth-century German Inquisition.

CHAPTER 30

People with a Conscience

ON THE NARROW-GAUGE RAILWAY that ran between Kocmyrzow
and Charsznica, there was always a great deal of activity and a crush
of people on the Kazimierz-Dzialoszyce route.

Before the war, the town of Dzialoszyce was the center of
commerce for the entire region. Every day the Jewish merchants in
the surrounding villages would come into town by *kolejka* to shop
for merchandise; the fare was only a few groschen.

With the onset of the war, despite Jews being prohibited from
traveling by rail, the *kolejka* became more crowded than before.
Polish dealers and black marketeers took the place of the Jews.
Looking for instant riches, they traveled back and forth every day,
smuggling whatever commodities they could obtain. With each
person boasting of his business acumen to the next one, the noise
and chatter was deafening. New horizons had opened for these
low-class Poles who had suddenly become prosperous achievers.

The Jews were the main topic of conversation.

"So there!" exclaimed one passenger. "We thought we wouldn't
be able to manage without them, that we would be unable to exist.
Our governments constantly discussed how to wrest commerce

from Jewish hands, but their brilliant minds were never able to come up with any solutions. It's a new world now. Did it hurt us if they had to shoot a couple of Jews? True, murder wasn't necessary. They could've deported all the Jews and resettled them in the *Kresy*[1] to work in the labor camps.

"If any of them do come back after the war, they can forget about returning to business. We have already learned the field quite well. Besides, they won't have capital to invest, as any money they took with them was certainly confiscated, and here in the walls of their houses they will not find their valuables anymore."

A middle-aged man with a handlebar moustache and a venomous smile could not forgive the speaker for his sympathetic declaration that murdering the Jews was unnecessary. "What?!" he cried out. "They should have killed all of them, even the little ones, down to the youngest children! For when they grow up, we'll have the same situation again. They are our enemies. The German *Fuehrer* is an expert on the Jews. As for the German occupation of our Polish homeland, I'd sooner have it this way than have Poland dominated by an alien people."

"In actuality, the Jews did not rule us," his seatmate countered. "Even if you are correct that the Jews usurped it all — commerce, the press, crafts — we still had the option of forcing them out. After all, the government was under our control. But no one could figure out how to lead the country. Had our *Endecja*[2] leaders won power, they would have resolved the problem in a humanitarian manner without running afoul of the rest of the world. Now, with that dictator, we no longer have any say. He tells the world that our

---

1. Polish term for the territory comprised of the eastern borderlands of Poland, incorporated into Soviet Russia in September 1939

2. *Narodowa Demokracja* (National-Democratic) party, known as *Endecja* for its acronym ND, the main nationalist political movement; the party placed anti-Semitism at the center of its platform and aimed to exclude Jews from Polish social and economic life.

people, the *Junacy*, are the ones committing atrocities against the Jews. He even arranges for photos to be taken of Poles beating Jews. What do we gain from this? When peace is reached, the Jews abroad and the Jews who return from the transports will take revenge on us. What did we need all this for?

"Yes, I agree that there were too many Jews here. But the issue could have been handled in a much better way."

The moustached man would not submit to his neighbor's viewpoint. "You are an agent of the Jews!" he retorted. "Would the *Endecjas* have solved the Jewish Question? I was also a party member before the war, but I saw that it was all worthless. And the *Ozon*[3] party people, too, were only concerned with their own pockets. The *Judenfrage* was merely a propaganda tool. This had to happen. A pity they didn't shoot all of them! As for the deported Jews, I do not believe they will return. If you say it is so, then we are indeed in trouble. I am less afraid of the Jews abroad than of these Jews. It would be awful if they came back..."

The discussion flared up.

Traveling among the dealers was a young blonde woman, Magda Kaziel of Skalbmierz, who could not restrain herself.

"No!" she declared. "An honorable Pole with a Christian soul may not condone such shameful violence, the likes of which history has never before seen. I, who had to take up trading because of the war, have no claims whatsoever against the Jews. Would they have stopped me from doing so before the war? Did they seize anything that was rightfully mine? How can one justify the murder of an entire people, moreover the murder of little children, solely because of their sin of having been born Jews? How can a man with a

---

3. *Obóz Zjednoczenia Narodowego* (Camp of National Unity), known as *Ozon* for its acronym OZN, a pro-military party formed in 1937, which portrayed Jews as unassimilable and demanded their mass emigration.

conscience, who has children himself, say a good word about such horror?

"Yes, only someone who appropriated a Jew's possessions could talk like that! Before their catastrophe, the Jews trustingly left everything with Poles who were ostensibly their good friends. It would be a shame for these Poles if they had to give it all back. As long as the valuables remain with them, they are agreeable to having the Jews killed. Such people couldn't care less about Poland's autonomy!

"You, sir," she said, pointing to the man with the moustache, "there is no doubt that you have Jewish property, lots of it, or a man of your years wouldn't speak this way. That is why you are so scared at the mere mention of the deported Jews returning. For who knows if the very Jews who left their possessions with you will not indeed return one day?"

All eyes turned in the man's direction. He tried to respond but could only stammer incoherently.

Aha! The woman had hit the mark, as if she were witness to it all!

"As for me," she continued, "three weeks before the Dzialoszyce *Aussiedlung*, I bought a cloak from my good friends at the Platkiewicz firm and put part of the bill on credit. If I knew where they were now, I would go there by foot to settle my debt, even though my finances are bad. Who knows if they even have bread to eat? Such respectable people! They can't even get around. Since I am free to move about, I hope G-d helps me find them so I can pay up. That's what an honest Christian should do."

All the passengers are stunned by her words.

Seated off to the side is a dapper young man with eyeglasses, nervously smoking a cigarette. Despite being engrossed in a book and appearing to have little interest in the whole discussion around him, he cannot sit still. He rises from his seat, elbows his way

through the throng and unobtrusively taps Magda on the foot. Then he moves on and returns to his place. The quick-witted woman immediately realizes that this fellow has something important to tell her.

She waits for him at the station.

"You can get specific information about the Platkiewicz family from a man living near the Szyszczyce forest," he states tersely.

"Do you know for a fact? Are you sure you're not making a mistake?" she asks. "Do you mean the Platkiewicz family that has a son-in-law from Kazimierza Wielka?"

"There is no mistake," he confirms.

At that, Magda decides she will not travel further on business but will return home first to the two bereft brothers and gladden their bitter hearts with the news she has learned.

She presses on. "Was anybody from the family killed or deported?"

An unequivocal "no."

At her request for his name, she receives an answer: "It's not important. What's more, if you are interested in their welfare and you are in a position to help them, you should do so, and you, too, should not disclose your name or any details. The most important and greatest key to success is secrecy."

With that, the young man said a friendly goodbye and was gone.

The man was Engineer Szeliga.

CHAPTER 31

Finding My Brothers

AT DAYBREAK ON ROSH CHODESH TEVES [December 9], Mordechai, his cousin Itzik (Yehoshua Lipavker's son) and I began digging a cave in the hillside behind Staszek Tetele's field. It was a snowy, wintry day. The work proceeded at a brisk pace, and by midday we had dug a hollow large enough to accommodate several people. With a few finishing touches and a supply of straw, the dwelling would be complete.

At three o'clock, we returned to finish the job. Mordechai was the first to enter the cave. As he stepped inside, a chunk of earth tore loose above him, and before he could manage to escape, the entire dugout collapsed on top of him.

Itzik immediately began removing the fallen earth. However, it soon became clear that the work was not progressing quickly enough, and in the interim, Mordechai was in danger of suffocating.

I ran into the village for help. Tetele and two other robust peasants immediately came with me, bringing along their spades. Within minutes, they pulled out the unconscious Mordechai. The earth in

that location was too soft to suit our purposes. All the villagers came running, gaping at the wondrous scene.

Shmuel Yossel was there, too, speaking to a young Polish woman whom he had met on the way. Noting his Jewish appearance, she had asked him if he knew anything about the Platkiewicz family. He pointed at me.

The woman, wearing a fur jacket and carrying a walking stick, makes a pleasant impression. She calls me over to the side, takes out a long letter and wordlessly hands it to me, waiting a few paces away for me to read it. I instantly recognize the handwriting of my youngest brother Meir'l.

We have been dealt a tragic blow. We are twice orphaned. Father and Mother are no longer with us. Yitta was killed, too. She was the first victim in Kazimierz. Barely dressed, we miraculously managed to escape under gunfire. The woman bearing this letter is our guardian angel. She rescued us. We have no possessions. If you are able to send us some clothes and a few groschen, you can trust the woman...

The letter continued on — it was more than eight pages long. But I could not read any more. The words would not stand still, dancing on the paper, which was spinning like a carousel along with everything else around me.

I could not come to terms with what had happened. *How long was it since I had been in Kazimierz? According to Meir'l's letter, exactly two weeks ago they were still alive. That meant that they were in the mikveh in Kazimierz while I was talking to Gurak's son Bolek. And he had no idea where they were.*

If only I had known... It would have been so easy to bring them here, and we would all be together now.

I had already found out earlier about Yitta's death and had acclimated myself to the tragedy. But to hear that Father and Mother had perished, too! How could it be? Couldn't Father have escaped together with Dovid'l and Meir'l...?

First page of Meir's letter to Chaim Yitzchok

The woman approaches me.

"Excuse me, if I may," she says. "I am waiting for you to write a reply to your brothers, and I want to return home before it gets dark. I won't be able to find my way at night."

"I'm coming with you," I tell her. "No, I'm not afraid at all," I add. "I want to be together with my unfortunate, orphaned brothers. Their last remaining purpose was to find me. Now that they have achieved their goal, I, too, have the same wish. But first I would like to go to Dzialoszyce to my friend Wrubel with whom I stored my belongings, and pick up some clothing for my brothers. As for you, *Pani*, if you want to wait for me, fine. If you cannot wait, I will write a few words to my brothers, and I'll find my way to your house later."

"I'll wait," she replies. I find a place for her to stay.

I head to Dzialoszyce myself, for the second time. But this time I am no longer afraid; my mind is occupied with other matters. My feet carry me along as if I am flying, and before I know it I am there.

It is late at night when I return to Szyszczyce, bringing with me some clothes for my brothers. The woman is too tired to travel. On her way here, she did not have exact directions and she had gotten lost. We decide to leave at dawn.

Unable to absorb the great tragedy, I could not sleep that night.

Can it really be true? How will I bear hearing the sad reality from my brothers?

My saintly father... His countenance alone was enough to infuse me with strength and bitachon whenever I went home to my parents' house in Kazimierz! After a visit with Father, I was so uplifted that my whole life took on a new perspective. How proud I was of my dear father.

And Mother, ailing, melancholy from her constant suffering... Still, whenever I came home, there was an air of celebration in the house, and her somber eyes would light up with joy. Perhaps that was her only pleasure in

life. Nothing was more precious than the motherly emotion she displayed towards me.

In one fell swoop, it has all disappeared. Kazimierz no longer exists for me. I no longer have parents. I have been orphaned of both at the same time. I was not there at the moment of their departure from this world; did not ask forgiveness; did not say Kaddish; did not sit shivah. I do not even know where they are buried, so I can pour out my bitter heart at their kever. I am an orphan — orphaned of a saintly, beloved father who was murdered. A father who could have lived, who should have lived, who wanted to live...

The bit of straw under my head was wet with my tears.

Shortly after 6:00 a.m., I wake the woman and we set out. With the Polish woman confidently accompanying me, it wouldn't occur to anybody that I am a Jew.

On the way, she met a friend of hers.

"Aha, Magda, you found yourself a companion!"

"Yes, indeed I did. If you look, you find," she replied with a laugh.

"I have good luck," she said, turning to me. "If your brothers stay with me, they'll be safe. You can see for yourself that everything is turning out well. If you wish, *Panie,* you are welcome to stay together with them."

I do not yet know what to answer. I just want to be there already.

We arrive safely at her house. She tells me to go into the next room; she will stay in the kitchen, so as not to intrude.

All the wellsprings opened up. The world ceased to exist. Three individuals with one torn, blood-soaked soul reunited in that small room.

"We escaped in our undergarments," my brothers tell me tearfully. "We did not even have a chance to take along a picture of our saintly parents. We did not intend to rescue ourselves. In fact, we planned to commit suicide, but Father stopped us, telling us it is

forbidden. 'Save yourselves!' he cried out to us. That was his last wish.

"The way things turned out, we can clearly see that our survival was unnatural. As we were fleeing, the police shot after us but missed. Then, without clothes or money, we found our way here. These are not ordinary people but angels. Formerly of Kazimierz, the woman is Yitta's friend. Indeed, Yitta had told us that her Polish friend in Skalbmierz offered to hide her, but we only thought of it when we were desperate.

"Yes, our dear sister was always devoted to us. She wanted to save Father and Mother, too, but she did not succeed. Now we are all alone."

"Look, this is the only thing remaining of her," Dovid'l says. "In the last minute before we parted from one another, she gave me this as a keepsake. I carried it on my heart, the place from which she was torn...such a lovely, blooming flower."

He hands me the picture of Yitta.

May G-d bind the soul of my father
To the lofty realm of the holy and pure ones
Who gave their lives and publicly sanctified G-d's Name.
All his life he did G-d's work with faith and sincerity,
Engrossing himself in Torah study and prayer with fasting and asceticism.
A branch from a tree of righteous, rabbinical ancestors,
He was cut down during the harvest of blood.

Alone in the loft of a cowshed I sit,
Enveloped in my double mourning;
Concealed in this hideaway, my soul cries out
And accepts G-d's awesome judgment,
Yisgadal v'yiskadash Shemei rabba — May His great Name be exalted.

Father, you always humbled yourself,
Before the individual and the congregation.
In your final days, you prayed persistently for a Jewish burial.
Father, Father! Crown of my life! Is this the reward for Torah?
Why did this happen to you?
Why did you not merit to be laid to rest in purity...?

Dear brothers!
That a holy spark was ignited in your hearts,
That the fear of G-d and religious zeal were rooted in your soul,
Inspired by the tzaddikim whom you frequently visited;
All the Torah that you acquired,
Spending the prime of your lives learning in yeshivah —
Who made it all possible? Who cleared the path for you?
It was our sainted father, who dedicated his life,
To raise you in the tradition of your holy forefathers.

Who did not hear of our father's achievements and noble character?
His good heart, his tender soul, commiserating with every person's pain,
His acts of kindness, the way he exerted himself to benefit others,
His home open to every heartsick and dejected person,
How he spent the better part of his day in intense prayer,
Weeping, fasting, abstaining from earthly pleasures.
Humility, submissiveness, compassion, and respect for rabbinic leaders
Were the treasured qualities imprinted in him by his mentor,
The saintly Ostrovtzer Rebbe.
And many years earlier, when he was yet a young man,
The saintly Rebbe of Chentshin, too,
Recognized Father's qualities and treated him with love and esteem.

I appeal to you, our ancestors,
The Chozeh of Lublin, the Zichron Shmuel, and Rav Issamar of
  Konskowola,
Exalted tzaddikim who devoted their lives to publicizing G-d's Name:
Clear the way for your saintly descendant and disciple,
A link in this great chain of holy men.
Elevate him, lift him into your Heavenly sphere,
Into the palace of the holy and the pure.

In memory of my father, my mentor and teacher, Yeshayah ben
Yechiel Issamar Wolgelernter zt"l, who was killed al kiddush
Hashem, Hy"d, on Tuesday, 22 Kislev 5703 in his hometown of
Kazimierza Wielka

By his son, Chaim Yitzchok Wolgelernter
Teves 5703

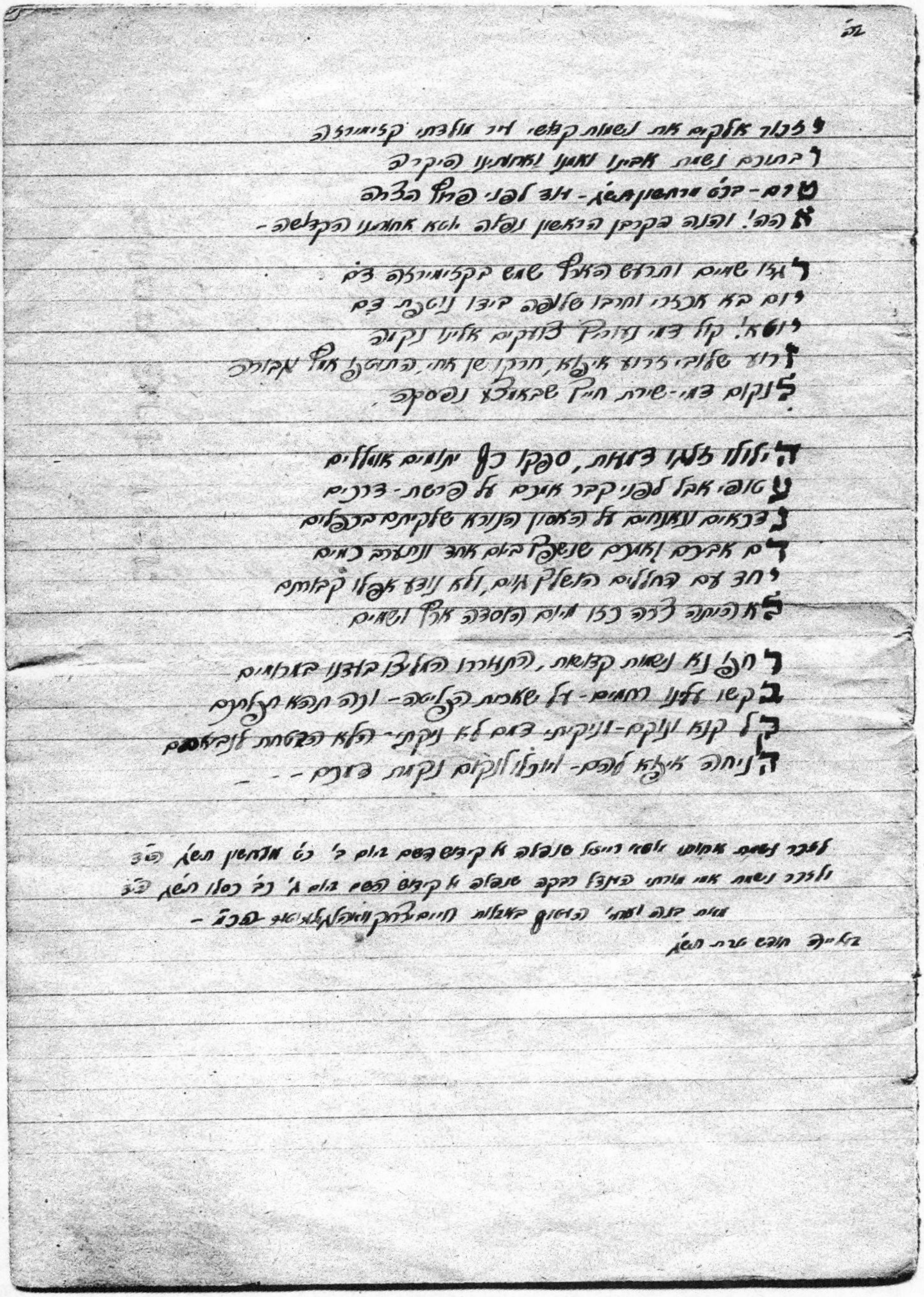

May G-d remember the souls of the kedoshim of my birthplace
    Kazimierz,
Among whom are the souls of our father, our mother, and our dear
    sister.
On 29 Mar Cheshvan 5703, even before calamity struck the town,
Alas, the first to fall victim was our saintly sister Yitta.

The heavens trembled, the earth quaked,
The sun stood still in Kazimierz,
On the day the killers came, their blood-soaked swords drawn.
Yitta! Your young blood cries out to us for revenge!
Arm in arm, we brothers shall grit our teeth,
Gird ourselves with valor and might,
To avenge the song of your life that was so cruelly cut short.

Bereaved orphans, wail, let your tears flow,
Clap your hands in sorrow,
Enshrouded in mourning,
Before your mother's grave at the crossroads,
Bemoaning the double tragedy that has befallen you —
The blood of your father and mother, spilled on the same day,
Flowing together like water,
Their corpses flung into an unknown grave, along with the other slain.
A calamity like this has not happened since heaven and earth were
    created.

Rouse yourselves, O holy souls, awaken and plead for us on high,
Beseech G-d to have mercy on us, the surviving remnant,
And thus should be your prayer —

"O vengeful G-d! Keep the promise You made to their prophets:
'I will not forgive the blood that was spilled.'"
Ease the plight of the remnant,
So that they may avenge your blood.

In memory of my sister Yitta Reizel who perished al kiddush Hashem
on Monday, 29 Mar Cheshvan 5703, Hy"d
And in memory of my mother Hendel Rivkah who perished
al kiddush Hashem on Tuesday, 22 Kislev 5703, Hy"d

By their grieving son and brother,
Chaim Yitzchok Wolgelernter
In the loft, Teves 5703

CHAPTER 32

At Yisroel's Refuge

A SOFT KNOCK ON THE DOOR interrupted us. The kind woman entered.

"I did not want to disturb you until now," she says. "It's enough. It won't help anyone if you get sick."

She serves us a meal on a clean, properly set table, as if we are guests.

"Like in a Jewish home," my brothers comment. "You can't imagine how decent these people are. They sincerely and wholeheartedly want to rescue us. If you wish, you can stay here with us. But if you prefer to go back to your family members in Szyszczyce, we would like to join you there even though the conditions here are much better.

"If we do decide to stay here, Magda has already devised a plan. Her mother lives in the adjoining apartment, which also consists of two small rooms. Since she lives alone, she does not need both. Magda would break through the common wall and put up a door, annexing the extra room for our use. Once the door is concealed with a curtain, no one will suspect that there are people living

behind it. In the meantime, until the work is completed, she would put us in the loft above the stable."

For now, I am unable to give a definitive answer.

"I must go back to everyone in Szyszczyce," I tell my brothers. "In the meantime, you stay here, and I will come from time to time to look in on you. Traveling is dangerous but not too bad at night. Later, we'll have to make a decision whether to stay here or there."

This place appeals to me. I lie down to sleep on the elegant, wide couch. It is a dream for a Jew to sleep in a house in these times!

At night, I returned to Szyszczyce.

I found Yisroel in a new place. He was staying with Jozef Juszcyk, known as *Bogac*, "the rich man." The wealthiest person in the village, the only thing he lacked was a bit of decency. Wishing to gain a reputation as an upright fellow, Jozef had taken in Yisroel's group of ten so the villagers would say that he was bighearted and a man of compassion.

In the process, he also had "compassion" on their clothing and other belongings. "Should all this fall into the hands of the Germans? What for! It is only right that you give it to me rather than to them."

For that reason, he did not demand money for sheltering Yisroel. "Poor soul, you need the money to live," he said. "Clothing and other valuable items will do." And he was an expert, too, when it came to choosing fine things!

His wife, a broad peasant woman, worked up an equally broad appetite — for at least half a dozen dresses and a couple of woolen coats. After all, she had snagged the wealthy Platkiewicz clan! As soon as there was the slightest commotion in the village, she was the first to relay the news, her watery eyes blinking as rapidly as her words.

Yisroel's family did enjoy some comforts. I must have found favor in Mrs. Juszcyk's eyes for she showed me the horse stable, which

was partitioned with wooden boards into two sections, one for horses and one for pigs. "I took all the pigs out of the stable so Yisroel's family could have the entire pigsty to themselves," she said proudly.

Straw, on the other hand, was something she could not offer. After all, on her eighteen acres of pastureland, where could she find straw? Especially since there had been a poor crop this year!

"Anyway, they won't be cold," she insisted. "The stable never gets cold. Our farmhand has been sleeping there all his life and he never once got sick."

Yisroel is content to have roomy quarters, even though there is no straw and the ground on his side of the stable is perpetually wet, being that Juszcyk's big plow horse does nothing all day but eat, drink, and relieve itself. Needless to say, the stench in the stable is so thick it is almost tangible. Yisroel makes light of it all.

"Our exile here and all Jewish suffering in this war is a punishment for our sins and should serve as our atonement," he says. "You saw yourself that a person can endure anything. You know how gravely ill I was the first time I had to flee. Nevertheless, since it was Hashem's will that I be saved, He sent a wagon. Now that I must keep a special diet, I get to eat warm black bread and boiled potatoes. We just have to *daven* that things should not get worse, and have *bitachon* that relief can come at any moment."

Even his two children, Feivele and Mordche'le, already know this. Having just recovered from the measles, their faces are pale and sickly. They can barely eat the watery potato stew. Hoping I have perhaps brought a pat of butter or a few cubes of sugar, they run up to me, their skinny, frozen fingers groping in my pockets.

"Finish up, Feivele, and say some Tehillim," Yisroel says to his son. "Hashem helped and you recovered. You should continue to *daven* that the *yeshuah* should come already. You have no sins, so Hashem will listen to your *tefillos*."

"If little children have no sins, then why does Hashem punish them?" the intelligent child asks.

Hmm...

Is there any way to answer this question...?

Yoav is busy with his little son Moshe Fishele. Since the child could not be washed during his bout with the measles, his scalp had become infected by scabies, which spread so quickly it nearly covered his entire head. His curly locks of hair protrude like tall reeds in a marsh. Yoav continually smears oil on the inflammation, a tried-and-true peasant remedy. His wife Elke'le is asleep; she stays up nights watching over the child to make sure he doesn't scratch his scabs.

Yisroel's wife Feigele stands near the small window, washing the only shirt that was left after all the laundry was stolen from their new quarters.

Yisroel's mother-in-law Malka'le, practical as ever, had procured a pair of big boots. Even after wrapping her feet in thick woolen rags, she had plenty of space left for storage. Ha, ha! No one was going to steal her possessions so easily! She keeps them near her at all times. Ever since Yisroel's laundry was stolen, she sits on her bundles all day. If she leaves for a short while, she puts her daughter Sur'cik in charge. Although the girl does not take after her mother — she is not nearly as sharp — she is smart enough to sit on the bundles.

Malka'le had even come up with a solution for all the possessions she left in Yisroel's house in Dzialoszyce. Before leaving, she had carefully packed all her things and placed them in a cabinet, locking it and taking the key with her. "Look, here it is!" she tells me, showing me the key.

A meticulous woman with a keen memory, she still remembers, over thirty-five years after her wedding, what she cooked on the first day she began to keep house. The quilt covers and pillowcases

of her trousseau are still as good as new, the monograms, embroidered with Russian letters, still bright. She is wearing a thick woolen dress that her mother had inherited from her own mother-in-law! It has finally fulfilled its destiny.

Because of her temperament, she has very little tolerance for the children and criticizes whatever they do; nothing is good enough. During the frequent quarrels that ensue, the raised voices in the stable are loud enough to be heard from a distance. At such times, Yisroel is beside himself and declares that he will not stay together with them, as he cannot endure the fighting.

But as soon as I point out to Yisroel that this arrangement is not a solution and they must split up since it is impossible for so many people to live together, he immediately calms down.

"In this *zechus*, Hashem will help..." he says.

CHAPTER 33

Gittele — A Young Victim

ONE DAY [at the end of Kislev/beginning of December 1942], Pietrowski declared in no uncertain terms that he could not continue to shelter my mother-in-law, Hershel, Tzinne'le, and their children, Reuven and Gittele, who had remained in Kwaszyn after the rest of our group left. They begged and pleaded with him, to no avail.

In the middle of the night, he ushered them out of his house, accompanied them for a short distance, and left them under the open sky. All night long they wandered through snow-covered fields. At daybreak they found their way to Franek Szczubial in the hamlet of Debowiec.

Franek took the group to his neighbor Stak Winiarski, an absentminded young peasant who had managed to make a small fortune through illegal means. His wife was a typical, crude peasant woman with a low character. Now that she had come into money, she desperately tried to play the role of an educated, upper-class woman. She wore elegant clothing on an ordinary day and styled her hair in the latest fashion, though much to her distress her flaxen,

stick-straight hair refused to curl. When talking to people, she would keep her calloused hands out of view lest they betray her lowly origins. Mrs. Winiarski was the authority in the house.

Standing before her now were five frightened Jews who had walked all night with their bundles on their frail shoulders and were shivering from cold. The youngest was trembling violently; she had taken ill from the exertion of carrying her rucksack in the frigid weather. They anxiously awaited a favorable response — to be allowed in, if only in the stable together with the cows and pigs.

Her heart softening at the sight, Mrs. Winiarski consented. She demanded a hefty sum but promised to include food and any other necessary items. "I'm not doing this for the money," she explained. "I'm taking you in only because I feel sorry for you." Apparently, her delicate, noble sensitivities could not bear to see people wandering about with nowhere to go.

What's more, she realized that she knew these Jews. "For the Platkiewicz family to be in such a state is just awful!" she cried. "I will bring you something warm to eat right away and a thermometer to take the child's temperature."

Life in the foul-smelling pigsty turned out to be very difficult. In Pietrowski's place, they had stayed in a room and always had hot meals. When they needed something, he would go into town to get it for them. Here the conditions were unbearable. Mrs. Winiarski barely showed her face in the stable and gave the group strict orders never to come into the house. "We always have people coming by," she warned.

If there was no bread left in Szczubial's shop by the time they got there at night, they would not have any bread to eat the following day, since they dared not venture out during the daytime. The lukewarm black brew called "coffee" often came as late as eleven in the morning, and the midday meal, which they paid for separately, consisted of nothing more than boiled potatoes and water, which

was brought to the barn whenever Mrs. Winiarski remembered to send it. And although she owned two cows, she refused to provide a drop of milk, even if they paid for it.

When they needed warm water for Gittele, the despicable maid was unwilling to ask her mistress. And if they ever took some fresh straw to sleep on, she made a huge fuss. "There'll be no straw left to bed down the pigs!" she would shriek.

Little Gittele was truly not well. They tried every home remedy and medicine, one pill after another, to bring down her temperature, with no results. Always a healthy, strong child, she lay there, her body weakened, her once bright-red lips pale and parched. Something had to be done.

In the evening, Mrs. Winiarski arrived to milk the cows. Tzinne'le approached her, crying bitterly. "She remained my only consolation, this exceptionally intelligent child of mine! I did not want to send her along to Warsaw with my older daughters Chayele and Esther'l, afraid of what would happen to her. And how would I have lasted all this time without her? Now she is burning with fever. I don't know what's wrong with her. Poor girl, she doesn't complain, but her every groan tears my heart to pieces. Who knows what she has come down with? Please have mercy, *Pani*. We'll pay you good money. Take her to a doctor. No one has to know who she is. I'll cover her with a blanket so she won't be recognized."

Although Mrs. Winiarski was afraid at first, her stony heart was stirred. The next morning, she harnessed her wagon and took Gittele to Dr. Kozak, who diagnosed the child with pneumonia. This was somewhat of a relief, since pneumonia was not life-threatening in a child this age. In fact, the doctor did not even prescribe any medication.

For the next few days, her condition remained stable. Suddenly, one night, the door of the barn was yanked open. Three bandits barged in and ordered everyone outside without delay. Terrified

and disoriented, the sick Gittele ran out into the snow, barefoot, dressed only in a nightgown. The bandits grabbed some money and vanished.

Immediately, the child's temperature shot up. Nothing could be done to strengthen her weak body. Her once sparkling eyes took on a glassy look. When she heard the others whispering about her critical condition, Gittele cried out, "Why aren't you doing anything to save me?"

They decided to appeal to Mrs. Winiarski again and ask her if she could take Gittele to Dzialoszyce to see Dr. Grebowski. Though she was not willing to go alone, she agreed to go together with Mrs. Szczubial. With the child well wrapped in a blanket, the two women rode into town.

Dr. Grebowski determined that Gittele had typhus fever; she would have to be admitted to the hospital. But how? In the Dzialoszyce hospital, they would recognize her right away, the little criminal.

To make things worse, Mrs. Winiarski told them that the Dzialoszyce police had heard about the break-in and would surely come to Debowiec to conduct an investigation. "You must leave, the sooner the better," she declared.

They hired a horse-drawn wagon and traveled to Szyszczyce with the sick child. Here they moved in with an impoverished peasant living in a tiny, one-room hovel. The ill-tempered peasant woman stood there glaring at them resentfully.

Gittele's weak legs can hardly hold her up, but there is no room to sit anywhere, let alone to lie down. They are forced to stay in a barn again, where the cold wind blows in from all sides. Two dark rings encircling her eyes, her gaunt face contorted with pain, the child pleads for something to eat.

O Merciful Creator! What sin is this innocent child guilty of? I think to myself. *She endured everything just like the adults, running along with*

them and carrying her heavy backpack. She was saved from the murderous hands of the Germans only to be lying here critically ill, while in Dzialoszyce there is a large hospital that was built with Jewish money. Shall this precious child perish?

Gittele grows weaker by the minute, her forehead intermittently breaking into a cold sweat. Hershel continues to whisper tear-filled *tefillos*. Tzinne'le's wellsprings have already dried up. Her heart contracts with pity as she watches her beloved child desperately fighting for life.

Her body racked with pain, the child cannot lie on the hard barn floor any longer. Goodhearted Mordechai, Shmuel Yossel's brother, holds her in his arms.

"I was hoping that Hashem would help me..." With these words, the flickering light of Gittele's soul was extinguished.

The prematurely severed, youngest branch of the Erlich family was laid to rest in the shade of the old willow tree on the outskirts of Szyszczyce [on 13 Teves 5703/December 21, 1942].

With the participation of a *minyan* of *Yidden*, I, too, said Kaddish before the fresh *kever* of my dear niece Gittele, one single Kaddish for the souls of my saintly father and mother.

The tender and delicate Gittele, crowning glory of the family,
Escaped the roundup along with us,
Surviving as a source of solace to her parents.
Her intelligent mind and enchanting looks
Pointed to a promising future for this young girl.

A brutal fate abruptly slashed the thread of her life;
In a stable in the village, on 13 Teves 5703,
Before her eleventh birthday,
Her gentle heart was shattered,
The light of her soul extinguished.

A barren tree on her grave in the valley of Szyszczyce
Calls out in wonderment upon this age-old, obscure enigma:
"Why did this happen? What sin did this young girl commit?"
The tree's branches groan as it wails a sad lament,
For the crown of the family,
The severed bough buried underneath.

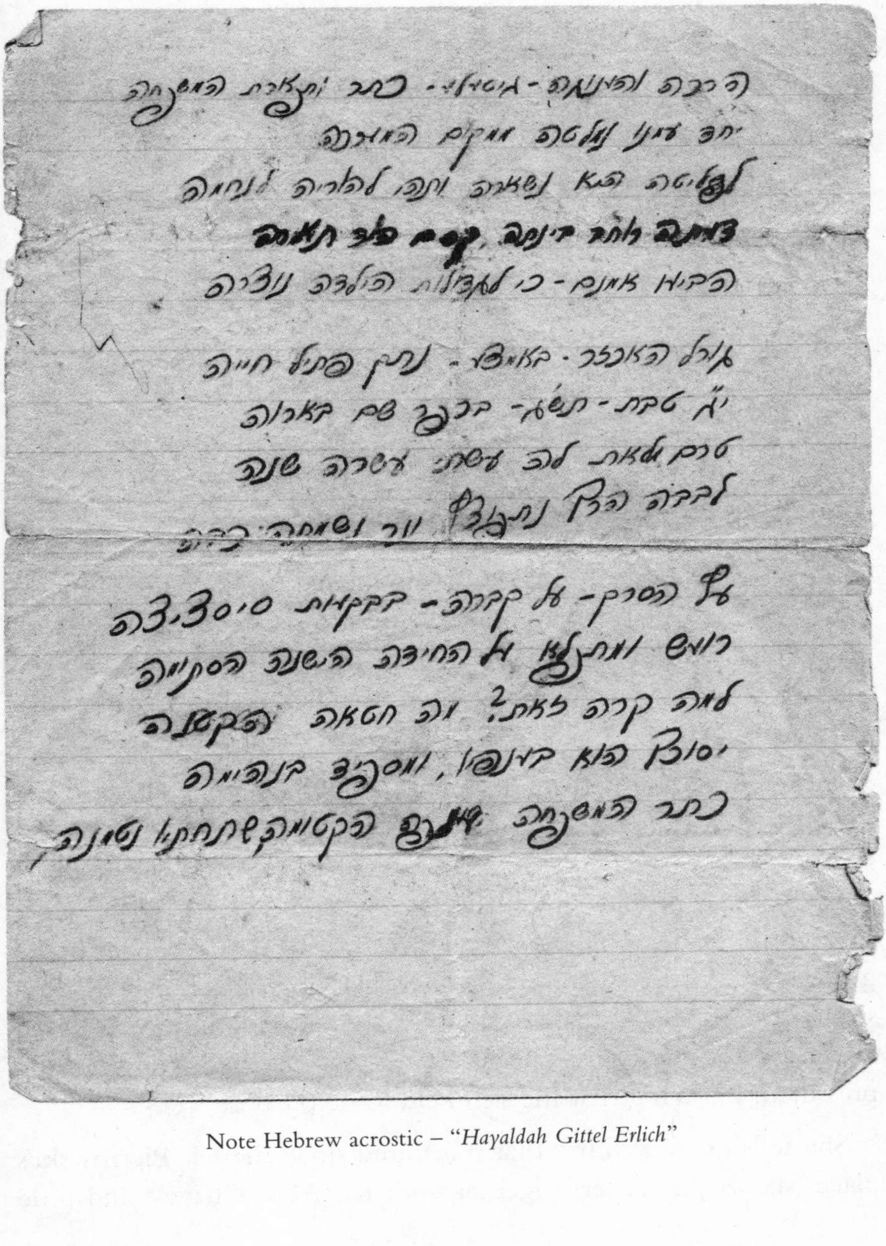
הרבה [illegible] - [illegible] - כתב ותעודת המשפחה
יחד עמן נלקחה ממקום [illegible]
לגליציה היא נשארה ותקוה להוריה לנחמה
[illegible] [illegible] [illegible] [illegible] [illegible]
הבינו אמנם - כי לגדולות הילדה נועדה

גורל האכזר - [illegible] - נתק פתיל חייה
י"ג טבת - תש"ג - [illegible] שם באדמה
טרם מלאות לה עשתי עשרה שנה
לבדה [illegible] [illegible] [illegible] [illegible]

על הסרק - על קברה - [illegible] [illegible]
[illegible] ומתנצל על החידה [illegible] [illegible]
למה קרה זאת? זה חטאה הקטנה
[illegible] הוא [illegible], [illegible] [illegible]
כתב המשפחה [illegible] [illegible] שתחתיו נטמנה

Note Hebrew acrostic – "*Hayaldah Gittel Erlich*"

CHAPTER 34

You Are a Jew

THE DAY AFTER THEIR GREAT TRAGEDY, my brother-in-law Hershel and his family and my mother-in-law moved to the home of Jedrze Kula. Though Kula was an anti-Semitic peasant, his poverty and greed for Jewish money outweighed his hatred of Jews. He allowed the two women to sleep in the house; the men had to stay in a barn once again.

Meanwhile, Hershel and Tzinne'le's two daughters, Chayele and Esther'l in Warsaw, were anxious to know how their family was faring. And so, Esther'l took the risk of traveling to Szyszczyce. This fifteen-year-old child had already endured so much. How many times had her life hung by a thread as she defied danger in the guise of a gentile, all the while strengthening herself and holding steadfast in the belief that at least her parents and family were living safely in the peaceful village of Kwaszyn. She struggled and prevailed, knowing that life still held some purpose.

She tells us everything that transpired since she left Pietrowski's place [six weeks earlier] together with her Aunt Chayele and little

Feivele, accompanied by the kind Mrs. Aubrien who had come especially from Warsaw for them.

"All day that Monday we stayed with the estate owner's wife in a village near Slaboszow. She was afraid to keep us any longer, so we hired a wagon at night to take us to Miechow where we would catch the train to Warsaw.

"True, we had forged papers, but what of it! The slightest blunder on our part could have betrayed us. What's more, it turned out that we were traveling during the most dangerous time possible! That very night, all remaining Jews in the Miechow region were in the midst of being rounded up and deported. Hundreds of wagons filled with men, women and children were heading to the train station. Their cries and wails broke the stillness of the night.

"Mrs. Aubrien, Aunt Chayele, carrying little Feivele, and I made our way between the wagons towards the platform. The various Gestapo members, secret agents and Polish policemen accompanying the Jews illuminated the area with searchlights that pierced through us like spears, so afraid were we of being discovered. Mrs. Aubrien nearly went out of her mind from terror. When Feivele began to cry, Aunt Chayele stuffed a handkerchief into his mouth so as not to attract the German murderers' attention in our direction. She had wrapped a black shawl around her face so no one would recognize her.

"We could hardly get onto the crowded platform, where the scenes unfolding before us were so shocking they made our hair stand on end. Little children — live children! — were stuffed into paper sacks, which were tied and tossed into the boxcars.

"At last we managed to board our train, and after a harrowing trip we arrived in Warsaw. As we were descending from the railcar, a secret agent detained us. He released Mrs. Aubrien and me but led Aunt Chayele and Feivele away. Apparently, he suspected they were Jews.

"At the Gestapo headquarters, Aunt Chayele begged for mercy. 'I want to live yet!' she cried. 'You must have a child — certainly you have a mother. How can you kill me?' The agent took pity on her, accepted a bribe and let her go. How long it seemed until we finally saw them return.

"We took a horse-drawn cab to the lodgings that Mrs. Aubrien had arranged for us. But the carriage driver realized we were Jews and he, too, had to be paid off.

"At last we arrived at our destination. But on the long trip, Feivele had caught a cold that soon developed into pneumonia. He needed to be admitted to the hospital. We were very anxious, as they would easily discover that the boy was Jewish. Aunt Chayele decided to confide in the intelligent young doctor. 'Nothing will happen to you here in my office,' he reassured her, 'but you must be very careful in Warsaw. It is becoming increasingly dangerous for Jews in this city.'

"Aunt Chayele was especially afraid to remain in Warsaw, since the secret agent had recorded her name. She recalled a conversation with a Mrs. Pawlowski back in Dzialoszyce. The woman had told her that her mother-in-law might be willing to rent out a room in her cottage in Jedlnia, a village near Radom. I set out with Mrs. Aubrien to look into it. With no address and without even knowing the old woman's name, we approached the Catholic priest, who directed us to the right place. The woman, however, had no idea what we were talking about; her daughter-in-law had never mentioned anything to her. After we made a phone call, her grandson arrived from Dzialoszyce and the matter was straightened out. I traveled back to Warsaw, picked up Aunt Chayele and Feivele, and we settled down in Jedlnia.

"But I could not sit still," continued Esther'l. "At all costs, I had to come and see how you were doing. And now, to hear this tragedy with Gittele... Couldn't she have stayed with me in Jedlnia or with

Chayele in Warsaw? With her fluency in Polish and her cleverness, who would have discovered she was Jewish? I cannot believe that Gittele is no longer alive. And that she died a natural death? She was such a healthy, vibrant girl..."

Esther'l contemplates her mother. She is not the way she used to be. And her father, ever cheerful and full of *bitachon*... What has happened to him?

"It is a Heavenly decree," Hershel consoles his daughter. "We do not know what our own fate will be. Do you think we are secure here? We have to *daven* fervently. My child, you and Chayele are living in Warsaw as non-Jews. You should know that you are playing the role of our ancestors, the Spanish Marranos. Hashem will help you. As for us, we couldn't have led such a life, and so we pray that Hashem will protect us here.

"Come what may, the two of you should always remember that you are Jews! *Yidden!* Gittele, our innocent child, died as a Jew. As much as you can, refrain from doing things that are forbidden — because you are a Jew!"

She would remember her father's words well.

On the train ride back, there was a crush of people. A fat Polish smuggler-woman jostled her way through the railcar, shouting, "We are as crowded as the Jews on the trains!"

Esther'l felt as though she had been stabbed by a needle.

A young rogue with whiskers sidled over to her. Gesticulating with the glove in his hand, he announced, "In my town, the police caught a *Zyd*, dressed in one of those long black coats. Guess what they did with him?"

"They finished him off for sure!" everyone answered.

"*Ach*, never! Our people have noble hearts. They did not kill him, Heaven forbid! They made him perform in the town square so the townspeople could watch the sight. The Jew stuck the hem

of his coat into his belt and began to dance. Ah, what a wonderful show it was!"

The passengers burst into uproarious laughter.

"Too bad you weren't there to see it!" he said, casting his eyes upon Esther'l to see how his story had impressed her.

Esther'l nodded and gave a forced smile. But inside, her emotions churned. She had to turn away so people would not notice her cheeks flaming with agitation. *Who knows who that poor Yid was!* She wanted to tear off her mask and spit in the face of that ugly, despicable creature. But she had to control herself. She must live yet, if not for her own sake, then for her dear parents in Szyszczyce. *They could never have endured such a thing!* she thought to herself.

And when another passenger began to tell about a Jewish girl who was caught with forged papers, Esther'l could hardly contain herself; she felt she would explode.

Her father's last words rang in her ears. It seemed as if everything — the wagon wheels, the locomotive, and all the people on the train — all of it was screaming out to her:

"You are a Jew...!"

CHAPTER 35

Dangerous Journeys

ON THURSDAY NIGHT [December 24], when I went back to Skalbmierz after two weeks to visit my brothers, they were no longer in Magda's house. Magda had already exchanged houses with her mother and moved next door, and the wall separating their apartments had been broken through. In the meantime, she had put Dovid'l and Meir'l in the barn loft above the pigsty.

When I came up there, besides for the two of them I found three other occupants: Mrs. Esther'ke Zylberminc of Pinczow and her two children.

At the beginning of the war, when Pinczow was burned down by the Germans, Esther returned to live with her parents in Skalbmierz. Her father, Yankel Lewkowicz, had been a tenant of Magda's parents for over thirty years, so that Esther and Magda were born and raised in the same house and grew up like sisters.

Before the first expulsion raid in Skalbmierz, Esther asked Magda to take her in. At that time, the situation in town was critical and no one knew what to expect, so Magda advised Esther to hide in a nearby hamlet for a few days until things settled down. Esther

followed Magda's advice and went into hiding together with her unmarried brothers Yerachmiel and Ezriel; her husband did not want to live on the run and decided to join the transport together with Esther's father and sister. After the *Aussiedlung* ended, she came out of hiding along with other local Jews and returned to live in Skalbmierz.

During the second expulsion raid, Esther wandered from place to place in search of refuge. Now that Magda was sheltering my two brothers, she agreed to take in Esther and her two children, ages eight and five. Her two brothers were hiding elsewhere in town.

At night Esther would often go around town, collecting debts from local farmers with whom her family had conducted business in the past. She felt she needed the money to survive.

Stefan and Magda advised her not to jeopardize her life doing that. "Everyone in town knows you and someone might betray you, especially since you are collecting money. If a debtor is loath to pay you, he may follow you to determine your whereabouts and all of us will be caught."

Indeed, the water carrier had already reported to Magda that people were whispering that Esther'ke was hiding in town — and where else if not with her good old friends?

Nevertheless, Esther could not be swayed. "I must go. I need the money," she said. "No one will betray me."

A few days passed. For me, who was used to moving around, life here was very uncomfortable. All day we had to lie under the bedcovers that Magda had given us, as it was unbearably cold in the exposed loft. I was extremely restless and bored stiff throughout the long days and even longer nights. My back began to ache from lying in one place.

After these few days here, I wanted to go back to Szyszczyce. Yisroel and his family were at Jozef Bogac. My mother-in-law was with Hershel and Tzinne'le and their son Feivel at Jedrze Kula.

Their son Reuven was with Franek Szczubial in Debowiec. A refined young shopkeeper, who could be clever when the need arose, Franek had constructed a hideaway in his stable where he sheltered Yonah Friedman from Dzialoszyce. He was therefore willing to take in Reuven as well.

I lay in bed thinking: *In Szyszczyce, various situations arise, and my relatives there cannot move about. I'll go back to Szyszczyce. On the way, I'll stop in Dzialoszyce at the Wrubels where we stored our merchandise. Whatever they give me will be useful, since the peasants prefer textiles over currency. Besides, my brothers need money to pay Magda. So I must go...*

It is a clear, frosty evening. I set out in the snow, the cold stinging my feet. I had walked these roads countless times. I am no longer afraid, albeit Jews discovered in the Dzialoszyce region are regularly shot. There is a crippled *Volksdeutsche*,[1] a lone SS stand-in, stationed in the provisions warehouse. Before the first *Aussiedlung*, he asked my brother-in-law Yisroel to give him a dress for his wife. Now he is in charge of the executions. Neither do the Blue Police stand around with their hands folded. But all this does not scare me.

With my fur hat pulled down over my ears and a leather-belted heavy jacket over riding breeches with black stripes down the sides, I look like a forest watchman. When I add in some whistling and the casual discharge of a couple of Polish vulgarities, I believe I can pass for a racially pure Aryan.

I walk through the town of Dzialoszyce. Although it is still early, only 7:00 a.m., it is already broad daylight, yet there is not a person in sight.

I observe the town. *What has become of it? What happened to its homey atmosphere, the hubbub of people strolling in the market square, the ringing laughter of red-cheeked children sledding down from the top of the hill behind the church, across the full length of the market square?*

---

1. Term for ethnic Germans living outside the *Reich*

Did we perhaps overstep our boundaries? When one is a stranger, one behaves accordingly. Maybe we were not permitted to laugh so exuberantly in galus? Today, we in Szyszczyce and the Yidden in other villages are not laughing anymore, surely not strolling. We were in galus all along, not in our own homeland.

Yet many of our people thought they had it all figured out. If a fifteen-year-old boy took out his first book from the public library, he already considered himself an intellectual. He would engage in political discussions, develop grand ambitions, and involve himself in party debates for days on end. And if he went once to empty a Keren Kayemet[2] tzedakah box, he considered himself an idealist, an activist for the Zionist cause.

But this castles-in-the-air wisdom was of no use to any of us, especially at the end, when we plainly saw the storm winds blowing from the German west. What is left of all this? A dark void. A deserted market square where you can do whatever you want; nobody is going to stop you.

The Poles have not yet fully occupied the large houses around the market square. On the ground floors, most of the windows are dark, like sightless eyes. I am more afraid of walking in the alleyways than of the Germans themselves. Houses with knocked-out windowpanes gape at me like skeletons risen from the grave, with sockets in place of eyes; doors torn down, floors ripped out. The tannery area looks like it has been through a bombing raid. All the empty structures were demolished for firewood by the local population.

I arrive at the Wrubels. When I had called on Mrs. Wrubel a few weeks ago, she had received me graciously. Today she is decidedly cooler. "How is it that you are not afraid to come here so often?" she wonders aloud. "Just this morning the Gestapo came to Dzialoszyce and rounded up several Jews. They no longer have to search for them. When the Jews realize it is too difficult to remain

---

2. Jewish National Fund, established in 1901 at the Zionist Congress in Basel

in hiding, they give themselves up. Indeed, Yossel Cudzynowski, the cattle dealer, turned himself in today together with his two grandchildren. And Bunim Brener's wife went to the Polish police, handed them whatever money she still had, and asked them to shoot her so she could be buried next to her husband. Naturally, they promptly fulfilled her wish."

Mrs. Wrubel tells me other, similar stories. Apparently, she is not eager to part with more of my merchandise, so she tries to tempt me to give myself up, since, as she puts it, "it will be impossible to survive in the villages."

I wonder whether she truly knows of some impending danger hanging over our heads. Be that as it may, one thing is certain: She will not live to see me turn myself in! Would she betray me herself? That much she wouldn't do at this point.

Mrs. Wrubel gives me some of our textiles. I light a cigarette and move on.

On my way home, I had a minor incident in the village of Labedz. It was past nine o'clock at night and the watchman stopped me. I did not wait to hear what he wanted but quickened my stride instead. He followed me for a while but could not catch up with me.

It was after ten when I arrived in Szyszczyce. I had already stayed with Hershel at Kula's place last time, so now I went to Yisroel.

In his residence in Jozef Bogac's stable, the day is just beginning. Since it gets dark at 3:00 p.m., everyone goes to sleep and awakens, refreshed, at 10:00 p.m. Afterwards, they hold discussions until morning dawns. Yisroel's mother-in-law reminisces about things that happened decades ago, they argue a little, and make plans for after the war. Their hands keep busy, too, scratching the lice that plagues their bodies.

They are delighted to see me and envy my boldness. But I collapse onto the damp, moldy floor, thoroughly exhausted; I have no

energy left to answer all their questions. Hunger gnaws at my innards. All they have to offer me is a piece of half-baked black bread, the center as sticky as a *fluden* cake, some bitter-tasting potatoes, and icy water. I do not even wait for my clothes to dry. The damp bread, the cold water — everything tastes fine to me.

When I fell asleep under a trough in a corner of the stable, I was oblivious to the world around me and the long *galus* night disappeared.

CHAPTER 36

A Chain of Tragedies

AS ALL THE RUMORS of impending raids died down, life in Szyszczyce stabilized and the remaining Jews in the village settled into a routine.

Yisroel and his family stayed with Bogac; my mother-in-law and Hershel and his family stayed with Kula. There were a number of other families as well: Yankel Mandelbaum, his wife, and their sixteen-year-old son Hershel at Franek Leszczynski; Alter Kalimacher, Mrs. Grynfeld and her fifteen-year-old daughter at Magalski; Shlomo "Shpitz" Goldkorn, the photographer, and his son at Zacharjasz; Mendel Dula's wife, his two sons and a son-in-law at Woznicki. The wealthy Abish Granetman, for whom a few zlotys now had to be collected every week, was also here in the village, wandering from place to place. Askiel, a youth with a handlebar moustache that made him look like a born peasant — you could not tell he was Jewish — was dubbed "the Jewish mayor" by the villagers. He was here along with his brother Landek, a similar type, and their parents and sisters.

In addition, the cave in the hillside behind Tetele's field was home to over thirty people. The Poles called it the "Jewish ghetto" and

considered it a religious duty to help the occupants by bringing them food and other necessities.

The people of Szyszczyce became accustomed to living with the group of Jews in their midst. For their Christmas dinner, they asked the Jewish women to prepare some traditional Jewish delicacies. The Jews felt obligated to taste all the various foods and participate in the religious ceremonies being observed that night. Aside from this occasion, though, they generally felt comfortable among the villagers and would join the nightly gatherings at the mayor's house along with the village elders for a few drinks and a friendly chat.

During the time I was in Szyszczyce, I no longer slept in Yisroel's stable. Yankel Mandelbaum's host Franek Leszczynski invited me to stay in his place free of charge, so I stayed there together with his other tenants. Yankel and his wife conducted themselves as if they were at home. Every week I *shechted* a goose for them and joined them at their meals. There was nothing more to do but *daven* that things not get worse before redemption arrived.

On the night of New Year's Eve [Thursday, December 31, 1942], I returned to Skalbmierz to visit my brothers. I found them still living in the loft; they had no desire at all to move back into the house. Though life in the uninsulated loft was difficult, with freezing winter winds and snow blowing in through the cracks, they had acclimated themselves to it. By now, they had already arranged for everything. Having found Gemaras, *Chumashim*, and other *sefarim* left behind by former tenants, they were able to learn. They even blocked off one corner of the loft with bales of hay, where they placed two buckets, so they would not have to venture to the outhouse.

Their food, which consisted of coarse black bread and black coffee for breakfast, boiled potatoes at noon, and a repeat of breakfast for the evening meal, was brought to them by their host Stefan, Magda's husband, every day at the exact same time to the minute.

He did this with utmost secrecy and caution, so that no one would notice, because his mother-in-law, Magda's mother, in contrast to her daughter, was a most unpleasant woman of whom my brothers were very wary. She kept her cow in the stable directly underneath the loft; hence, they had to stay on guard constantly. As soon as they heard her coming into the stable, they did not dare move until she left.

In the shared courtyard lived a tenant, a young fellow who used to be a coachman. He conducted his current business dealings only at night when everyone was sleeping. Since Stefan had to pass the man's window in order to get to my brothers, he carried their meals in the same buckets he used to feed his two pigs. As soon as he got into the stable and saw that no one was there, he would deftly take out the food, go into the storage room and climb up to the loft. At night, either Stefan or Magda carried away the two waste buckets to be emptied. They would not let my brothers attend to it, for fear that someone would notice.

That's how cautious and secretive Stefan and Magda were. Yes, Magda kept the advice Engineer Szeliga had given her on the train — secrecy — to the fullest meaning of the word! For this reason, my brothers preferred to remain in the loft rather than in the house, where it would be impossible to be as careful. If someone were to show up at the house, it would get too complicated for Stefan and Magda. After all, they were only human.

That evening, when I came into Magda's house, she said to me, "Just this very minute, Esther'ke went into town, as always. All our attempts to dissuade her have been unsuccessful. We are very afraid something might happen to her. Maybe you can prevail upon her to stop going. After all, it is in your own best interest, because if Heaven forbid something happened to her, you could all be caught, too. Her older brother Yerachmiel is here now. He came to look

after the children while she is away. Talk to him. Explain to him the gravity of the situation."

Naturally, I promised to take care of the matter.

I discuss it with Yerachmiel. He agrees. He tells me he has spoken to his sister about this on more than one occasion.

Exhausted from my trip, I soon fell fast asleep, unaware whether Esther returned to the loft that night.

It is already broad daylight when I awaken to the sound of Magda's trembling voice speaking to Yerachmiel. I approach them. Magda is unrecognizable, tearing her hair out, her face flaming. She cannot stop crying, though she makes an effort to talk as quietly as possible so the children should not hear.

"What happened?!" I ask.

"Awful, the worst… Esther'ke is not alive anymore! When she went last night to collect money from one of her debtors, the woman, an underworld character, refused to pay up. Apparently, she followed Esther, and while Esther was at the next debtor's house, a Polish policeman arrested her and put her into jail. He then called in a loathsome *Volksdeutsche* from the Kazimierz gendarmerie who regularly comes visiting his girlfriend in Skalbmierz. Minutes later, Esther'ke lay dead in the jailhouse courtyard. In fact, she is still lying there unburied. The whole town came running to see; after all, everyone knew her. And the word is out that she was hiding by Magda Kaziel and that her two children are still here.

"What do we do now? The police might come here any minute and search the house, especially since people say that Esther conducted all her affairs from here. My childhood friend…such a young woman! I cannot bear it. I can't go out into the street. The distress on my face will be the confirmation everyone is looking for."

It is a terrible predicament. Yerachmiel is in a state of shock. I cannot discuss anything with him.

Realizing that something is amiss, the children's ears perk up. "Where is our *Mamusia*?" they ask.

"She went to Krakow, precious children," Magda answers them.

They do not say anything more.

Magda calms down somewhat, and Yerachmiel, too, collects himself.

"There is no time to spare," I say. "First, the children must leave. We adults will stand ready in case we hear the police arriving. Even once they are in Magda's house, we will still have time to jump down into the field through the small door in the loft. It is surely not the best idea to escape in broad daylight, but we may have no choice."

Yerachmiel comes up with a plan. He will arrange for a Polish woman who ferries Jews to safety to bring the children to his uncle in the Krakow ghetto tonight. Later, he will travel there himself to take care of them. Even though he still has a safe hideout in Skalbmierz, he feels he cannot leave the two bereft orphans alone in Krakow with his uncle.

All day, Magda watched the two children. The day passed without incident. At night, Yerachmiel bundled them up — Magda wanted to keep one child, but they did not want to part from one another — and brought them to the Polish woman. They arrived safely in Krakow.

A few days later, Yerachmiel, too, went to Krakow. We received a letter from him asking us to send him bread since he was working in a labor camp with very meager rations. He wrote that his uncle and the two children were taken on the very next transport that left Krakow.

Since the children were gone, Yerachmiel decided to return to Skalbmierz. He did not succeed. He was caught trying to escape from the labor camp, and his fellow Jewish inmates were forced to hang him.

With this, another link was added to the long chain of tragedies.

At this point, I could not leave from here so easily. I had to wait and see if my brothers would need to leave Magda's place entirely, in light of the recent events.

We began to consider the idea of having my brothers join the rest of my family in Szyszczyce. Aside from the fact that people in town were talking about Magda harboring Jews, which made staying at her house dangerous, we also saw clearly the consequences of a Jew being out on the streets. And here I was going back and forth regularly.

I was sure I could succeed in finding a refuge in Szyszczyce for my brothers without too much trouble. We agreed that as soon as I went back to Szyszczyce and found a suitable place, I would send a Polish acquaintance to escort them so I would not have to make the hazardous trip again. They would be ready at a moment's notice.

In the meantime, although the days passed uneventfully, lying flat on my back day and night was not pleasant. It was worse than prison. Solitary confinement makes life very dreary. It could either turn you into a full-fledged madman or, on occasion, into a fine philosopher. The former is more easily come by.

I decided to take preventive measures.

CHAPTER 37

Harrowing Experiences

AFTER TWO WEEKS IN MAGDA'S STABLE, I trekked back to Szyszczyce. It was a dark, moonless night and snowing heavily. On top of that, I was weighed down by some of Dovid and Meir's possessions that I had taken with me to lighten their load in case they would need to leave suddenly.

This time I did not take the Dzialoszyce route. Because of the heavy snowfall, I went by way of Kwaszyn, walking on the main road where the snow accumulation was not as great. I intended to spend the night there.

I arrive at my friend Latosz's house. As always, he gives me a friendly reception and we converse easily.

"What's new in the neighborhood?" I ask.

Immediately grasping the intent of my question, he answers, "Unfortunately, there is tragic news. This week they rounded up ten Jewish people in Szyszczyce and took them away."

With every fiber of my being, I control myself from displaying my inner turmoil. *Ten people...Ribono shel Olam! Who else if not Yisroel's group is exactly ten?* I quickly change the subject, sit for a few

more minutes chatting, then take my leave, abandoning the idea of spending the night there. I must find out what is going on in Szyszczyce, though walking through the rough terrain will not be easy, especially now that everything is covered in snow. But what could I do... I must go.

I begin trudging through the fields in knee-deep snow, resting every few steps. I cannot see my usual familiar route; all the narrow pathways are covered over. I follow my intuition alone.

Soon I feel feverish and parched. In the distance, I see the light of a house. Mustering up all my energy, I reach the little farmhouse.

"Please let me come in," I plead.

"I don't conduct dealings with people at night," a man answers me through the door.

"Just give me some water!"

"I don't have any," is his response.

I could not go on. My strength was exhausted, my thirst raging.

"Just a drop of water!" I beseech him.

"If you don't leave of your own accord, I'll turn the dog on you!" he threatens.

What shall I do? Perhaps I should go back to Kwaszyn to Latosz? No point in that — I might be halfway to Szyszczyce by now.

I linger for a few more minutes and continue on my way.

I had noticed footprints in the snow that seemed to lead somewhere. I follow the tracks, and, after several meters, I come upon a well of water in a pit. It is not too deep. I take a slipper out of my rucksack, bend down and scoop up water, again and again. I can hardly drink enough to quench my thirst.

I do not see any more footprints. They came to an end at the well. I continue on aimlessly. I feel so feverish, I'm sure if I were to take my temperature now the thermometer would burst. Even after throwing off my heavy jacket, followed by my sweater, I still feel hot.

Judging by the trees I can see up ahead, it appears that I am near the rugged area bordering the village of Szyszczyce. I sit down for a bit, then go further, the drifts getting deeper and deeper until the snow reaches my neck. Now I am in serious trouble. I dare not take another step or I may fall in and be unable to get out. I try to backtrack, which means starting all over again, blindly. Who knows if I will yet reach civilization tonight?

I get down on all fours. I believe I see a light...yes, a window! I move towards it. It is the village of Wymyslow! Just another short stretch and I will reach my goal.

The moment I collapsed breathlessly into Yisroel's place and saw them all there, I forgot the entire ordeal.

"What time is it?" I ask.

"Just past nine thirty."

It had taken me over three hours to walk from Kwaszyn to Szyszczyce instead of the usual twenty minutes.

At last, I find out what happened. Two Polish policemen from the village of Gory had arrived in Szyszczyce. They rounded up a group of Jews — not Yisroel's group — and demanded a sum of money, which they gladly handed over. Half an hour later, the Jews were released.

Yisroel actually sees the whole incident in a positive light. "This shows that we don't have to be afraid of the Polish police," he says. "As for the Germans, they surely won't come here. They have more important assignments than driving around the hamlets searching for a few Jews."

Filled with *bitachon*, Yisroel agrees to have my brothers come here. "These trips back and forth to your brothers are no laughing matter!" he declares. He hands me a thermometer, but I no longer need it. My fever is down — I feel much better.

I could not sleep that night from the excitement and joy of finding all of them safe. *I could squeeze one of my brothers into the stable here,*

but it would be better to find a place where the two of them could stay together. Surely, that shouldn't be too difficult to achieve...

In the morning, I met up with Shmuel Yossel and told him the situation with my brothers.

"By all means!" he said. "Not to worry. We'll be able to find a place."

Since there was no immediate urgency to bring my brothers here, I stayed in Szyszczyce at Franek Leszczynski, Yankel Mandelbaum's host, for the next two weeks.

Suddenly, alarming news began to circulate through the village: In Marianow a farmer was shot to death for sheltering Jews... Another farmer had his place burned down... The rumors began to pelt us like hail.

Yisroel's landlord Bogac dug a pit under the stable floor where Yisroel and his family could hide in case of a search. The fearful Kula, who was sheltering my mother-in-law and Hershel and his family, refused to do the same for any price. "I've had enough," he said. "It's time for you to leave."

But where to? For the time being, it was still quiet in Szyszczyce. On the other hand, we could not wait until the last minute, especially with two frail women — my elderly mother-in-law and Tzinne'le — who might not be able to make a quick escape.

Since Kula was not bold enough to tell them outright to leave, he kept bringing fresh news: this one was hung, that one was shot... This had such a bad effect on the women's already frayed nerves that their health began to decline. They could not even eat anymore.

An idea occurred to me: How about bringing my mother-in-law and Tzinne'le to my brothers' place?

When I proposed this to them, I also made them aware of the difficult conditions in the loft. "You will need strict discipline — you cannot utter a single loud word. The greatest hardship of all is the cold. The food is very meager. Milk and butter can only be

obtained once a week on market day, and you cannot ask for anything better or burden Magda and her husband with buying this and that, as it is imprudent for them to be seen going back and forth too often. On top of all this, you would have to pay in currency, not like here in the village where you can pay for everything in textiles."

Sure enough, their initial reaction was not favorable. After all, here at Kula they were in a warm house and had all the milk and butter they desired. On the other hand, none of it was worth the terror they were experiencing.

And so, this past Friday [January 29, 1943], when Kula came back drunk from Dzieraznia and reported that things were heating up in Szyszczyce, they were ready to agree to anything as long as they could live in peace.

I hired a messenger to take a letter to my brothers, letting them know that we were considering joining them in Skalbmierz in light of the recent developments in Szyszczyce. *Please ask Magda what her terms would be if we all came to the loft*, I wrote. *The main thing we ask of her is to dig a pit under the stable floor for us to use in the event of a search. Please send a reply back immediately with the messenger.*

On Motza'ei Shabbos, when my brothers were told that a messenger was waiting for them, they were sure he had come to take them to Szyszczyce. They packed all their belongings and went down to Magda's house. They were in for quite a surprise.

After a long conference with her husband, Magda agreed to take in only my mother-in-law, Tzinne'le, and Hershel, and to make the necessary preparations we had requested of her.

Upon receiving the reply, Tzinne'le did not want to wait another minute. She was prepared to go with me by foot on Sunday night. Hershel would arrange for Feivel to join Reuven at Szczubial's place in Debowiec and would then travel to Skalbmierz by wagon with our mother-in-law. The plan was alright with me.

Sunday [January 31] turned out to be a nice day with light frost on the ground but no snow. We would be able to go.

At two o'clock in the afternoon I am at Yisroel's place apprising him of Tzinne'le's decision, when his landlord Bogac comes charging in. "Quick! Into the *skrytka*! The Germans are here in the village! They are already searching Wojtek Amerikaner's place!"

Immediately, I run over to Kula's house to tell everyone. But just as I pass Tetele's house, Shmuel Yossel's sister comes out of the barn, screaming, "Run for your life! They're already at the next courtyard!"

The two of us dash up the hill towards the forest. Behind me, I hear a shout: "*Jude, komm her!*"

I turn around. Standing about ten meters below me is a German in civilian clothes. I run like mad. A revolver shot rings out behind me. I do not look back now but continue running up the hill with all my might.

Only after I covered a considerable distance without hearing anything did I turn around again. From afar, I saw the German arresting Yankel Mandelbaum and his wife and son. I could not linger on to see what would happen. I did not continue running but proceeded at a steady pace, looking back every so often.

Not even ten minutes later, I saw a German in the distance riding a horse in my direction. There was no time to waste. I took off my heavy jacket and ran full speed into the forest. When it became very dark, I finally paused to look around and get my bearings — I was on the far side of Dzieraznia.

I had never been in this area before. Without asking anyone for directions, I walked until I managed to find my way to Kwaszyn. From there I continued on to Skalbmierz to my brothers.

I could not go back to Szyszczyce now, though I was deeply worried about the fate of my family there. The German who had shot at me had been standing just past Kula's vegetable patch...

And what happened to Yankel and his family after they were taken away? What miracles I had experienced! First the bullet missed me. And if the German had not caught Yankel, he would surely have caught me, or at least taken aim at me again.

I told all this to Magda and asked her to go to Szyszczyce first thing in the morning to bring everyone here. But she did not think it advisable for her to show up there so soon after a German raid.

That day was one of the worst days of my life.

CHAPTER 38

Rescued from Danger

On Tuesday [February 2, 1943], Magda traveled to Szyszczyce. That one short day seemed like years as my brothers and I waited anxiously, hoping she would return with good news.

At eight o'clock in the evening, a horse-drawn sleigh pulled up in front of the house. They had arrived. Quietly, one at a time, Magda led my mother-in-law and Tzinne'le into the house.

"Where is Hershel?" I ask.

"He went to Debowiec to make arrangements for Feivel to stay with Szczubial. *Baruch Hashem* everyone is alive!"

They proceed to tell us the events of the last two days:

"We were inside Kula's house while the German stood just past the garden, shooting in your direction. You could imagine our emotional state. Kula's wife and children almost went out of their minds. What were we to do? We were doomed. Kula himself, though, did not lose his composure. At this most dangerous time, he led us into the barn. After burrowing a hole deep into the haystack, he pushed us in, blocked the opening with sacks of grain,

and left. Kula's family remained in the house, kneeling before the pictures of their holy saints and praying on our behalf.

"The German spotted Yankel Mandelbaum and his family running away. Since he was closer to them than to you, he gave up pursuing you and turned in their direction. We had no doubt they would be killed on the spot. However, the kind mayor of Szyszczyce, bold and unafraid in the face of danger, appeared on the scene. Hearing that the German knew some Polish, the mayor reasoned with him: 'What will you gain by shooting them? They will perish regardless. Just take their couple of zlotys. It's a sin to waste a bullet on a Jew!'

"The mayor's suggestion met with the German's approval. He took a hefty sum of money, a watch, and a few other items, gave Yankel and his family a murderous beating and let them go. He then demanded a horse from the neighboring farmer Wlodarski to go chasing after you. Hearing the German's intentions, Wlodarski gave him an old one that was unfit for riding. The German soon returned, roaring, 'This horse is worthless!' He grabbed another horse and set out again.

"Riding along, he noticed footprints leading to the cave in the hillside, but by the time he got there, everyone was gone. The villagers had warned the inhabitants, and they all escaped, except for one member of the Abrams family who was still there. The German took aim with his revolver, shooting him in the arm. Figuring he had finished him off, he left to continue his search for you, but when it grew dark he returned to the village.

"Meanwhile, two other Germans were conducting house searches. After failing to find any Jews, they warned the villagers they would be back later in the week. Early that evening, they left in their taxi.

"We figured you had gone to Skalbmierz and would send a messenger the next day to bring us over to your place. Since we

were afraid the Germans would return, we sat in the haystack all day, nearly suffocating. Monday passed without incident.

"This morning the Germans came back and threatened to burn down the village. A great uproar ensued. Before leaving, they arrested the mayor and took him along in their taxi, announcing that they were going to shoot him. The villagers were wailing.

"Kula kept running into the barn. 'What do you want from me?' he cried. 'Please leave!'

"We pleaded with him. 'Where should we go? You're sending us out into mortal danger!'

"He wouldn't hear of anything. We gave him all sorts of valuables to keep us another hour, even half an hour, since we were still hoping a messenger was on the way. When he came to tell us that a woman was asking about us, we immediately understood who she was and went into the house. The young woman introduced herself as Magda and stated that she had come from Warsaw bearing a letter from the children. She handed us your letter, then turned to Kula and explained: 'I am a smuggler and I will be escorting them to Krakow. All I need is that you arrange transportation so I can take them to the *kolejka* station.' She told us she would gladly take us immediately but it was too risky during the daytime. We were to be ready as soon as it turned dark.

"Meanwhile, the mayor came back. They had driven him until the village of Wolica and threatened him with the worst if he would not reveal where Jews were hiding. The mayor remained steadfast and did not let a word slip. 'I did not become a mayor in order to search for Jews,' he told them. 'That is not my job. If you kill me, so be it. I'm not afraid of death.' The Germans were so taken aback by the mayor's courage that they released him with a brotherly slap on the back.

"Even so, the villagers were no longer willing to harbor the Jews, for fear the Germans would come again. Since they had already

shown up twice, it seemed certain that someone had informed on the village. Yankel Mandelbaum left Franek Leszczynski's place and went to a fellow by the name of Wozniak in Debowiec, who offered refuge for a day or two to those who had nowhere else to turn. Although Bogac had already dug a *skrytka* under the stable, he was no longer willing to shelter Yisroel's group. However, as long as we were at Kula's place, he was quiet and let Yisroel stay. At night, when the horse-drawn sleigh was already standing in front of Kula's door, Yisroel came over. 'Bogac ordered me to go!' he cried. 'Since he heard that you are leaving, he is not willing to keep me any longer.'

"What were we to do? Should we not leave Kula...? We decided on a plan. Hershel and Yisroel would take some of the remaining textiles that were stored with Bogac and distribute it among their Polish acquaintances for safekeeping. They would then leave to Debowiec, where Yisroel and his family would have to find a place to stay until things quieted down in Szyszczyce. After arranging for Feivel to stay with Szczubial, Hershel would wait in Debowiec until you could bring him here.

"Our trip to Skalbmierz was fine and we thank Hashem that we made it. If only Hershel, too, would be here already!"

In the morning, although they were not used to drinking black coffee, my mother-in-law and Tzinne'le ate their meager breakfast heartily. After two such harrowing days, all they wanted was peace and quiet. It was cold in the loft, but they had both brought along feather quilts for this purpose. They were happy to be here; everything was fine.

Magda had not sat idle. In order to dig a bunker for us as I had requested, she had exchanged her stall with her mother's, which was bigger and situated exactly beneath the loft. She made a hole in the floor of the attic, so that in an emergency we could slip out of the loft and climb down the ladder into the pit under the stable

floor below. Another advantage was that she could hand us food through the opening without having to go into the storeroom. She kept her two pigs in the stable under us, so it would appear that she was bringing food for the pigs.

Magda's tenant began digging the pit. In order not to arouse his suspicion, she told him that she needed it as a hiding place for her two young daughters, because of an impending *lapanka*.

By the time I left on Thursday [February 4] to pick up Hershel, the makeshift bunker was ready.

I arrive in Debowiec. Yisroel and his family are with Stak Winiarski, Hershel's former host. As bad as it was when Hershel had stayed there, now it is many times worse. They are practically fasting. They have not received a morsel of warm food, despite paying endless sums of money. The boorish Mrs. Winiarski comes in regularly, demanding that they leave immediately. In this way, she extorts as much money from them as she can. If not for the bread Yisroel occasionally obtained from Szczubial's shop at night — they did not dare venture out during the day — his family would have starved to death.

When I came in, the children fell upon me, looking to see if I had any food for them. I had a few roasted potatoes and a slice of bread and butter. They grabbed it. What joy! It was the greatest treat. The somber stable came alive with the children jumping up and down with excitement. Dear little Mordche'le kept on kissing my hand, grasping it with his cold, skinny fingers. "It's so good when Uncle Chaim'l comes! Don't go away!"

I promise the children I will come again and bring many good things.

In spite of it all, Yisroel's spirits had not fallen. "What's in the newspaper?" he asks me. "Staying with Winiarski is our worst suffering yet. I have *bitachon* that we will surely be redeemed from

here. And if G-d forbid not, I will go back to Bogac. He assured me that if I returned to him in a few days, he would take me back."

I meet up with Hershel at Szczubial's place. Franek had agreed to have Feivel join Reuven and Yonah Friedman.

I stayed with Yisroel all day on Friday [February 5], since the *poritz* in Szyszczyce had told me to come to him on Shabbos to collect the money he still owed my family.

On Shabbos morning, Hershel and I walked to Szyszczyce, but when we called on the *poritz* he told me he was short of funds. "Come back next week Friday or Saturday," he said. I had no choice.

We waited until it got dark before setting out to Skalbmierz. The conditions were not good for walking — the roads were wet and muddy. We got a bit lost but finally arrived safely at Magda's house, bringing with us some sugar and butter from Szyszczyce.

It wasn't long before the new occupants adjusted to the difficult life in the loft, keeping military discipline and talking in whispers.

By this time, after so much wandering, I was eager to rest up a bit. But I had to go again, just once more. The *poritz* had told me to come to him at the end of the week.

And so, on Wednesday night [February 10], I set out to Szyszczyce for the umpteenth time.

CHAPTER 39

The Situation in Szyszczyce Becomes Critical

COLD, WET WEATHER, the kind that penetrates your bones, enveloped me on this trip to Szyszczyce. As soon as I took my first few steps, an ominous feeling gripped me; my instincts foretold trouble. I considered turning around. Something was holding me back from going. But I knew that if I did not go, there was no one else who could collect the debt from the *poritz*, and we needed the money to pay Magda. Maybe later we could arrange for Chayele and Esther'l, Hershel's daughters in Warsaw, to send us currency so I would not have to go on such dangerous expeditions all the time.

I proceed on the Drozejowice road. Even though it is the main thoroughfare, nobody drives it at night. I plan to sleep in Kwaszyn and continue on to Szyszczyce before dawn.

I arrive at Latosz's house. He responds coldly. Gone are his friendly receptions. I cannot understand what has prompted this sudden change.

"The villagers say I have dealings with Jews," he explains. "What do I need that for?" He is extremely displeased that I visit him so often.

He hems and haws when I ask if I could spend the night. "I'm afraid to let you stay in the house, but you can sleep in the barn," he finally says.

It seems we have already lost this refuge, too. I will no longer be able to come here. Everything is slipping out from under our feet. It is a miracle we still have Magda's place.

At daybreak, I arrive in Szyszczyce. Here, too, all our good friends had undergone a transformation. A storm was brewing in the atmosphere.

"It would be most appreciated if you did not show your face in the village for a while," they all tell me plainly. "Granted, last time we came through unharmed, but who knows what could happen next time? Any day now we are expecting a *lapanka*. That much we know for sure."

I stop by Bogac to see if Yisroel had returned there. "I have no intention of taking them back in," he declares. Yisroel and Yoav had left nearly all their possessions with him, so he had nothing more to gain by sheltering them.

His stout wife comes out of the house. "They really put me to shame," she complains in her shrill voice. "After seven weeks of staying here, they did not trust us with their belongings but took everything away to my brother-in-law Tetele. I don't ever want to set eyes on them again!"

Poor woman! Such heartache and humiliation! It bothered her that Yisroel had distributed some of his merchandise and did not leave every last thing with her.

Seeing that I could not stay there, I went directly to the *poritz*.

"Come back Saturday first thing in the morning when I'm still home," he tells me. "By then, I'll surely have the money for you."

I buy some provisions — butter, eggs, bread, and milk — to bring to Yisroel, place everything into the farmer's basket I have with me and start on my way to Debowiec.

As I approach the hamlet, I notice a civilian on horseback, armed with a rifle, riding through the fields opposite me. By his green cap with a feather on top, I can tell right away that it is the *poritz's* despicable German commissar. Running away is out of the question. I gather my courage and walk with my head held high, looking straight at him and whistling. He rides right past without even giving me a glance. Feeling reborn, I wipe the cold sweat from my forehead and continue on my way.

At Yisroel's place, I come upon pale, frightened faces. "We saw that accursed German through our window and thought he would come in to search our place!" they explain. "What's more, Mrs. Winiarski plans to send us away tonight. Szczubial told her that German secret agents are definitely coming."

My visit calms them somewhat, as they hope I might have a solution.

"I would like to go back to Szyszczyce," Yisroel suggests. "Bogac promised to take me back in."

"I was there already," I tell him, "and he has no intention of taking you and your family back in."

They are speechless.

Still, Yisroel does not lose hope. "I'll go there myself," he says. "Maybe I'll prevail upon him."

Yisroel asks me to go with him. But the many kilometers I already traversed today and the fright I just underwent have so drained me that I am about to collapse. "Let me get some rest and then we'll go," I reply.

Yisroel understands. "I would have gone with Yoav," he excuses himself, "but he has been gravely ill all week. His temperature is

almost 40 degrees (104°F) and we don't even have warm water for him to drink."

I shudder when I see Yoav lying motionless with a wet rag on his forehead, a corpselike grimace on his ashen face.

Grimy and unkempt, the children stand around the basket of food I have brought for them, fidgeting uncomfortably in clothes that haven't been laundered or changed in several weeks. They drink up the raw eggs — there are no cooking facilities here — and eat the slices of bread and butter. Their wan faces shine.

No sooner do I sit down than Mrs. Winiarski enters the stable with a final ultimatum: "You've got to leave tonight!"

"The situation is not all that bad," I reason with her. "You have a good cellar. In the worst case, they could go down there to hide. Besides, I am going with Yisroel to Szyszczyce to find a different shelter."

At dusk, Yisroel and I set out to Bogac.

We discuss, we plead, we promise the world, but he will not hear of it. His wife would not even talk to us.

We return to Debowiec and beg Mrs. Winiarski to have mercy. After we give her two new dresses and a sizeable sum of money to let us stay at least over Shabbos, she finally relents.

"What will you do after Shabbos?" I ask Yisroel. "Now you see that you cannot go on like this. Nobody will keep a group of ten people. Even Bogac told you clearly that at most he would take back five people. If you want to survive, you must split into two groups."

Yisroel does not respond to this. "In the meantime, why worry?" he says. "By the time Shabbos is over, Hashem will help us!"

What more could I do?

On Friday [February 12], I return to Szyszczyce, planning to wait there until I could see the *poritz* on Shabbos. There isn't a single Jew

left in the village. I stay with Franek Leszczynski, Yankel Mandelbaum's former host, who is none too pleased that I am there.

"I will leave tomorrow and will not show my face here again any time soon," I assure him. "But I must stay here tonight."

He is afraid. "We are expecting the Germans to come," he says.

"I'll stay awake all night," I offer, "and if I hear anything suspicious, I'll leave immediately."

The good peasant consents. "Actually, I think tonight is my turn to be the village watchman," he says, "so it works out well. If I hear anything, I'll come to alert you."

At night, when it is already very dark, Yankel Mandelbaum and his wife and son appear.

"What happened?" I ask.

"The villagers in Debowiec know for certain that secret agents will be arriving in the morning to search for Jews," Yankel explains, "so I had to leave. And where else should I go?"

Before I can manage to ask any further questions, Yisroel shows up, too. He tells me the same. "Mrs. Winiarski came into the stable screaming that if we did not leave on our own accord she would call the agents herself. Of course, the money and the gifts I gave her were all for naught. We had to leave Debowiec. After arriving in Szyszczyce, we went to Bogac, but he refused to let us in. Seeing that he could not shake us off, he arranged for a young ruffian to yell, 'The Germans are here!' Thinking it was true, we turned back. Our whole group is now sitting in the wet snow on the footpath leading to Debowiec."

Yisroel alone had come here to speak to me. "Save us...!" he pleaded, sobbing like a child.

I was seething with indignation. "I told you it would be impossible for all of you to stay together! Who will let you in at such a dangerous time? Why don't you want to split up? How can you help everyone else if you yourself are in a helpless position? Don't

you have pity on your own children? What can be done now and how can I help you at a time like this?"

I speak to Franek.

"Absolutely not!" he declares. "How can I possibly take them in?"

I follow Yisroel, wading through huge mud puddles as rain comes down in buckets. After several detours, we finally reach the group.

Yoav is lying there. It's hard to believe that this is a live human being. Elke'le's coughs and Feivele's sobs echo like cannon shots through the quiet night. Sitting on the bundles in the watery snow, everyone is soaked through and through.

We gather the children and the bundles and head back into Szyszczyce. To whom we do not know. We just go. Feivele stumbles and falls. He cannot get up. Apparently, he has broken or sprained his leg. He grits his teeth in pain but does not cry. I lift him onto my shoulders.

We come back to Bogac's place. The doors are bolted. We knock. There is no answer; apparently he is pretending to be asleep. The barn and the stable, which were always open, are now locked. We try a second house, a third… No one is willing to let us in, certainly not a group of this size. To our good fortune, I notice that the small stable belonging to Bogac's mother is open. We go in and put the children to sleep.

Yisroel is content already. "I'll talk to the old lady tomorrow and offer her a few zlotys. I'm sure she'll agree to let us stay," he says, thanking me for saving him.

I return to Franek. Yankel Mandelbaum is reading a letter from his two sons, who are in a labor camp. They write that the situation there has improved.

Cold and wet, with my boots full of water, I cannot regain my bearings. But no sooner do I stretch myself out on the straw than Franek appears, trembling so violently he can barely speak. "They're here! Several wagons loaded with Germans are at Wojtek

Amerikaner's farm. I heard loud screams coming from there. Who knows if they haven't caught some Jews! Escape as fast as you can!"

I am outside in a flash, Yankel shouting after me to wait. I can hear the wailing and crying carrying across from the other end of the village. Searchlights cast their beams upon the muddy fields. In the pitch dark, feeling the terrain with my hands to see if there are any pits, I run wherever my instincts lead me.

Before long, I reach the forest. I am soaking wet. Although I see that no one is chasing me, I cannot continue standing there.

I make my way down the hillside towards Ludwik Juszcyk's house. As it is very slippery, I lie down and roll to the bottom of the hill, thanking Hashem that I haven't injured myself.

Ludwik promptly opens the door. "Ah! Why haven't you come here all this time?" The shrewd peasant offers to let me sleep in his bed. "Your friend Abish Granetman is here, too," he adds.

I tell Ludwik what is going on in Szyszczyce.

"I will not sleep tonight," Ludwik says. "I must stand guard in case the Germans make their way here."

I feel hot and cold all over and a fit of shivers comes over me when I think of Yisroel. What will be with him and his family? Where could they run? His unfounded optimism would be his own undoing. The thought of his two precious children makes my stomach sink. And what of Feivele's injured foot? In spite of his great pain, the intelligent child did not even cry, for fear that someone would hear.

Oy, Ribono shel Olam! You created so many forms of affliction and torment in the world. Must only the small Jewish nation suffer? And for how much longer...?

CHAPTER 40

My Miraculous Escape

AT DAWN ON SHABBOS MORNING [8 Adar I/February 13, 1943], I ask Ludwik to go into Szyszczyce to find out what happened last night. He refuses to go for any price. "I'm a tough fellow," he says, "but not when it comes to the Germans. And they may still be in the village."

I step outside with Abish Granetman. We stand on the path, waiting. Perhaps one of our friends or acquaintances will come by. Before long, we see Shmuel Yossel and Mordechai walking towards us. They had heard about the raid but do not know any details.

We decide to go to the cave on the outskirts of the village, hoping to find someone who can tell us what happened. Indeed, we find quite a crowd. Yankel Mandelbaum and his family are there. Yisroel and his entire group are there, too, but they are barely recognizable.

Two puffy red eyes staring out at me from a mass of mud — that is Yisroel. Feivele lies on the floor, blue from the cold. His knee had swelled up, but no one knows what to do about it. Mordche'le is thoroughly frostbitten and cannot even move his fingers. Feigele and her mother are disheveled, sitting helplessly with their hands on

their faces. Elke'le is at her deathly ill husband's side, wringing her hands in despair. The children pull at her dress, begging for food. It is a dreadful scene.

Tears streaming endlessly from his swollen eyes, Yisroel is unable to utter a single word. At last, he begins to tell us what transpired in Szyszczyce.

"We were in Bogač's mother's stable, sleeping so soundly that we were completely unaware of the commotion at Wojtek Amerikaner's place. A few German soldiers even came to Bogac's house and knocked on his door. When he opened it, they roughed him up and left without bothering to peek into the tiny, dark stable. Despite all this, we did not hear a thing.

"At dawn, however, when the old woman came in and discovered us, she ran to her son and raised a hue and cry. Bogac came running over, warning us, 'If you do not leave immediately, you'll be in serious trouble!' Having no other alternative, we took shelter here in the cave. But what shall we do now?

"The Germans who raided Wojtek Amerikaner's farm last night did not come to Szyszczyce with the intent of searching for Jews," Yisroel continues. "There had been a robbery at the local mill, and suspicion fell on Wojtek. Two wagons brought a company of eighteen German soldiers from Dzialoszyce. They gave Wojtek a thrashing, confiscated all his possessions, handcuffed him and took him to town.

"The Germans took the opportunity to stop at several houses in the village, beating people indiscriminately. When they stopped at the mayor's house in the middle of the night, his two strapping sons, afraid they would be seized for labor in Germany, jumped out of bed and fled. Upon entering, the soldiers noticed the empty beds with mussed-up, still-warm covers and asked the mayor who had been sleeping in them. He could not tell the truth, for fear they would demand that he turn over his sons. By his lack of a ready

response, the Germans came to the conclusion that Jews had slept there. They whipped the mayor until he lay unconscious in a pool of blood.

"Initially they had wanted the mayor to direct them to the cave, the so-called Jewish ghetto, that night. But seeing his current condition, they said they will come back tomorrow, that is, Shabbos, so he could tell them where the Jews are hiding.

"Franek, who was on watch duty, also got a beating. It has reached a point where the villagers have declared, 'If a Jew shows up in Szyszczyce, we will personally tear him to pieces!'"

I ponder the situation. *How can I go into the village under these circumstances? On the other hand, I must get the money from the poritz. What's more, how can I abandon Yisroel and his family? Time is running out. They must be rescued immediately, or some of them will perish, whether or not the Germans return today. Yoav, Feivele, and Mordche'le will not survive the frigid cold in the cave.*

I made my final offer to Yisroel. "You see now that the situation is critical. Your clothes have already caught fire. You cannot wait any longer. This is my plan: I will risk my life to take you, your wife, and your two children along with me to Skalbmierz in a hired wagon tonight. I'll find a place in the area for us to stay until nightfall. I do not even know if Magda will allow us in, but I believe that if we beg and implore her to let you stay for a short while, she will not turn us away."

At this point, Yisroel is ready to agree to anything, but when he repeats my offer to Feigele, she does not respond. Her mother, who has been sitting frozen in her place, seemingly oblivious to her surroundings, suddenly awakens from her stupor. She whispers something into her daughter's ear, whereupon Feigele announces that she does not want to go along.

"How about if I take Yisroel and the two children?" I ask.

"Definitely not!"

I thought I would lose my mind. "Do something!" I appeal to Mordechai and Shmuel Yossel. "You see what's going on!"

After talking it over, Mordechai says that he knows of a farmer in a hamlet a few kilometers away, who might take them in. But they would have to wait until dark to go there.

Yisroel embraces this plan. "Now that we are settled, you can go off to see the *poritz*," he tells me.

Though I do not favor the idea of having them stay in the cave all day, there is nothing more I can do. As I take my leave, Yisroel's children grab onto me, wanting me to stay. Everyone speaks out against my going into Szyszczyce. "The villagers will stone you!" they warn.

But I must go.

"Come back here again if you can…!" I hear Yisroel calling after me.

Once in the village, I steal over to Franek's house. Sitting like a mourner, with head bowed and eyes downcast, he recounts the events of the previous night.

"The Germans will surely be back today," he concludes. "As a close friend of yours, I am telling you: Run wherever your feet will carry you. Do not stay in Szyszczyce another minute! And tell the people in the cave that they should leave immediately."

I hurry across the fields to the *poritz*. With a minimum of conversation between us, he hands me the money he owes, in a hurry to get me out of his house.

By sunrise, I am on my way. At this time of day, it is not safe for me to walk on the roads. Since I have no place to stay, I sit for several hours in the hilly terrain on the outskirts of Szyszczyce.

At midday I continue on. In order to avoid the main road where wagons travel, I walk through the village of Drozejowice. I am almost at the far end of the village when I hear a vehicle approaching at high speed. Turning around, I see two German army wagons.

They must be the same ones that were in Szyszczyce last night, heading back from Dzialoszyce for a second round.

In a flash, I am in the fields looking for a place to hide. But no more than twenty meters behind me, one of the soldiers chases me on foot.

"*Halt!*" he shouts.

When I do not stop, a shot rings out.

As I continue running, I notice a peasant woman coming out of a little farmhouse with a burnt roof, closing the door behind her and bolting it with a chain — a sure sign that no one remained at home.

Without a moment to lose, I race over to the house, silently remove the chain and enter the front room. Seeing a ladder standing there, I climb up, ducking down to make sure no one can spot me from the outside through the exposed roof.

There is a thick layer of straw in the attic, protecting the house from rain. I stretch out flat on the floor, quickly cover myself with the straw and lie there holding my breath, fearing the worst. Barely do I finish throwing the last piece of straw on myself when the door of the house is thrown open.

The German soldier enters, looks around for a few minutes, then leaves. A moment later, he comes back in and starts climbing up the ladder. *This is it... I am doomed.* He stands in the attic for a short while, scanning it carefully, then goes back down.

I hear many loud voices outside. It seems all the soldiers are looking for me. Straining my senses, I peek out from beneath the straw and see the peasant woman being led by the arm.

"Where is the fellow who escaped from us?" they interrogate her. "Where is he hiding?"

She has no idea what they are talking about.

"*Kreuz-Donnerwetter!*" they shout, slapping her. "If you don't tell us, we'll burn down your house!"

I am in grave danger. *O Merciful G-d!* I pray. *It is not yet three months since I was orphaned of my parents. Shall my two-year-old son, my one remaining child, now become orphaned, too, of a father whom he hardly knows? If I perish here in the fields of Drozejowice, there will be no witness to my death, and my dear Chayele will remain a tormented agunah for the rest of her life. Tomorrow night is our seventh anniversary. Shall our happy married life come to such a tragic end?*

Today, the eighth of Adar, is the yahrzeit of my grandfather Rav Yechiel Issamar. Zeide! For whom have I undertaken this dangerous trip if not for my brothers, the children of our exalted father, your son Yeshayah! Shall your yahrzeit, a day when the soul rises to a loftier realm, be stained by the blood of your murdered son's child?

After all, I am only living for my wife Chayele, for our one and only innocent little child, and for my rescued brothers who have not yet experienced happiness. Shall the hands of the murderers succeed in destroying all these lives at once? I want to live to avenge the blood of my parents and sister...!

At that moment, I made a decision: *I would not fall into their hands alive!* Taking out the razor blade I carried on me, I held it close to my throat and observed the ensuing events.

The peasant woman crossed herself and swore by all her saints that she knew nothing. I saw one soldier hold her to make sure she did not escape, while the others tossed straw and grain out of the adjacent barn. "He's got to be hiding right around here!" I heard one German shout.

I am still in great danger...they may decide to come up here again.

I watch as several soldiers move on to search the neighboring houses. A few continue to stand outside, holding onto the woman. I feel like my eyes are popping out of their sockets. How long the search lasts, I cannot determine.

The soldiers return, unsuccessful.

"It can't be!" I hear one of them insist. "He must be here somewhere!"

Again, they begin to flog the peasant woman, threatening to demolish her house. By now, not only do I see death before me but I already feel it; every one of my limbs has gone numb.

Suddenly, it grows quiet: one minute, two, three…

I peek out again from under the straw. I do not see a soul. My heart slowly resumes beating. I wait a bit more…I do not hear a thing. I wait for what I estimate to be half an hour…still quiet. Then, I hear the crack of a whip. The wagons must be leaving. With Hashem's help, the danger has passed.

I lie motionless in the attic until it becomes pitch dark; I cannot be sure they haven't left one of their men behind. Then I climb down the ladder, approach the woman and ask her what happened.

With tears in her eyes, she tells me the whole story.

"Are you sure they are gone?" I ask her.

"They did not leave anyone behind," she assures me.

"I am the one they were looking for," I inform her, offering her some money. After all, it was because of me that she received a beating.

She declines. "Thank the good Lord, I am glad that I truly did not know you were up there!" she says. "This way a person was saved through me. I do not want a reward for that." She would not even tell me her name.

The next morning, back in the loft in Skalbmierz, Magda relayed the conclusion of the previous day's events, which she had heard from a Drozejowice villager.

The Germans barged into a house where some young peasant boys were playing cards. Identifying one of the boys as the supposed escapee they were searching for, they beat him savagely, forcing him to confess why he had run away.

The fellow remained unconscious for four straight weeks.

CHAPTER 41

A Great *Baal Bitachon*

FOR DAYS AFTERWARDS, I was in a state of melancholy, unable to find my bearings. Life no longer held any meaning for me. I could not sleep at night; terrifying dreams tormented me, and I often woke up screaming. Under normal circumstances, I would have required medical treatment to restore my shattered nerves, but that was obviously out of the question now. I wanted to cure myself by repressing the recent events, but they seemed to thrust themselves into my consciousness of their own accord.

Whenever thoughts of Yisroel and his children crossed my mind, my uneasiness intensified. *Who knows what is happening there? Why haven't we heard from him?* Right before I left, Yisroel and I had agreed that he would write to us as soon as he was settled in the new refuge in Waridlow where Mordechai was planning to take them that night. By this time, a few days had gone by with no word from him.

I just hope he got there safely. A letter sometimes gets lost, I consoled myself. *Besides, Yisroel couldn't have gone to the mailbox himself. Perhaps*

he gave it to someone and the person forgot to mail it, or lost it... Anyway, what good is worrying?

A few more days passed, and still there was no word from Yisroel. But when a letter arrived from my wife Chayele, I began to feel better.

Everything is in order here at Mrs. Stepanowa's place in Jedlnia, she wrote. *Our Feivele is busy playing and is doing well. Let's remain strong... it will be good.*

The letter strengthened and encouraged me. I realized that I have to stay alive, if only for the sake of my beloved little son. Chayele wrote that when she spanks him he says, "I will go to *Tatteshe!*" So he has to have a *Tatteshe*, my sweet child.

Yet I so wished to hear good news from Yisroel. Upon my return to Skalbmierz, I had asked Magda if she would have taken in my brother-in-law and his family. "It would have been difficult," she answered, "but had you brought them, I wouldn't have turned them away." Knowing this pains me all the more.

A few days later, we receive a letter from Debowiec from Hershel's sons, Feivel and Reuven. *We are no longer at Szczubial's place,* they wrote. *Although our rent was paid up until the first of March, we had to leave long before that. Secret agents showed up to conduct a search. Apparently, someone had reported to the Germans that Szczubial was harboring Russian spies. We had to flee to another farmer, where we stayed in a pit under the stable all day. At times, we even had to run and hide in the fields. We lived through terrible days and wonder if we could join you. If so, perhaps you can come and pick us up.*

There was not a word about Yisroel.

How could I possibly go to Debowiec? We ask Magda to travel there and assess the situation. As to whether she would take in my nephews, she says, "I have no choice. I must. We'll have to enlarge the *skrytka*."

She leaves, taking along our letter to Feivel and Reuven, in which we asked them to send us a detailed reply in the event they could not return with Magda at this time. And above all — to let us know Yisroel's whereabouts and how he is faring.

Magda returns alone.

"I could not bring them today," she explains, "but it is quiet in Debowiec now and it should be safe for them to stay there another few days. In the meantime, I'd like to make sure the *skrytka* is ready before I go back to pick them up next week."

She did have a long letter for us, in which Feivel elaborated on the turbulent events of the past two weeks.

Every few days there were house-to-house searches in the area, forcing us to spend entire nights lying in snow-covered fields. We experienced so many miracles it is impossible to put everything in writing.

Then there were a few words written in Hebrew, apparently so my mother-in-law and Tzinne'le should not understand:

Uncle Yisroel and his entire group were killed two weeks ago on Tuesday, 11 Adar I.

Hershel, who was holding the letter, nearly dropped it. I pretended to wipe perspiration off my face with a handkerchief, so my mother-in-law should not notice the tears flowing from my eyes. I could not hear or read any further. I lay down under the bedcovers and pulled the blanket over my head.

I tried to gain control of my emotions. I had not imagined, even before the letter arrived, that Yisroel was doing well. I had prepared myself for such news, braced myself so it would not have such a strong effect on me. After all, I had experienced my own life hanging in the balance and I knew that every person was accountable for his own fate.

Nevertheless, those few Hebrew words had such a devastating impact on me that as I lay under the bedcovers, a fresh wellspring

of tears opened. My temples pounded like a drum. I held both hands to my throbbing head to keep it from exploding.

I perused the letter again. There were no further details.

Tzinne'le read it next.

"What do these Hebrew words signify?" she asked.

"Uh…nothing. Just regards from Yisroel."

"So why didn't he write in Yiddish?"

"Do I know? Feivel probably wanted to demonstrate his aptitude in written Hebrew," was all I could reply.

On Wednesday the following week, Magda traveled to Debowiec to pick up Feivel and Reuven. But on Thursday morning, she returned alone again.

"What happened?" we asked.

"I got lost and wandered about all night," Magda explained. "By the time I made it back to Skalbmierz with the boys, it was daylight already. I did not want to bring them into the house in plain view, so I found shelter for them underneath the bridge by the river. It's a good hiding place; nobody ever goes there. As soon as it gets dark, I'll bring them here. I had no choice."

Feivel and Reuven arrived at night. We assailed them with questions, my mother-in-law most of all. "Where is Yisroel?" she demanded.

Feivel answered the way I had prompted him in my letter — that Yisroel had gone to Waridlow together with Shmuel Yossel and Mordechai.

Upon hearing that, my mother-in-law calmed down somewhat. "I just hope and pray to Hashem that this bitter war will not last too much longer and that we will survive to see each other again," she said. "If only I could be together with my devoted son already!"

Once my mother-in-law and Tzinne'le were asleep, Feivel told us the whole story, beginning with the fateful Shabbos morning when I left Szyszczyce.

"A squad of German secret agents arrived in Debowiec on that Shabbos morning [8 Adar I/February 13]. All the Jews escaped. Hidden in Szczubial's stable, we were the only ones who remained in the hamlet. The Germans searched the place thoroughly but did not find our hideaway. After that, Szczubial refused to keep us any longer. He took us to Muszial, an impoverished farmer. We hid in a pit under his stable. A few times, we had to run into the field and take cover in a ditch that he had dug for us. It was only through miracles that we survived.

"Later that Shabbos, at three o'clock in the afternoon, a unit of Polish policemen from the village of Gory arrived in Szyszczyce. Accompanied by the German commissar and a number of Polish peasants in several wagons, they went straight to the cave and surrounded the whole area. Uncle Yisroel and his group, Yankel Mandelbaum with his wife and son, Abish Granetman, Shmuel Yossel, and a few others — eighteen people in all — were inside.

"As soon as Shmuel Yossel realized what was happening, he fled. They did not succeed in catching him. But when Yisroel tried to do the same, one of the peasants seized him. He begged and pleaded for mercy. Upon hearing the name Platkiewicz, the Pole released Yisroel, advising him to run away as fast as he could. When Abish Granetman attempted to escape as well, he was gunned down on the spot.

"When Yisroel saw his family being loaded onto the wagons, he came back and gave himself up. Since the Polish police were in charge, he thought he would be able to pay them off, just as a few weeks earlier when ten Jews in Szyszczyce were arrested by the Gory police and subsequently released for a few zlotys. After all, Yisroel was an expert in business negotiations.

"The occupants of the cave were rounded up and taken to Gory, where they were stripped of their possessions and thrown into jail. The local mayor was ordered to provide them with food. They

remained there until Tuesday when a special German unit arrived from Busko. Since the Polish police and the German commissar were not willing to shoot the prisoners, the German agents entered the jailhouse.

"The villagers who told us the story could hardly bear to describe the scene that followed. Little Mordche'le, lying ill with fever and too sick to get up, was shot to death in his cell. Seeing this, his mother Feigele fainted. Before she regained consciousness, they put a bullet through her, too. The peasant women did not even wait until Feigele was dead before ripping off her clothes and carrying her body into the forest.

"The rest of the group was led away, Yisroel carrying Feivele because of his injured knee. When they reached the forest, they were lined up and murdered one by one with revolver bullets. After pulling off the clothes from the corpses, the peasants buried them all in a mass grave, except for Yankel Mandelbaum's strapping, sixteen-year-old son Hershel, who struggled in the throes of death while the curious Poles looked on, wondering how long he would last. When he finally succumbed after eight hours, the peasants threw him into a separate grave."

This was the final chapter in the life of the great *baal bitachon*, Yisroel Platkiewicz, the surrogate father of our family.

What didn't he do for us all? Upon his father's passing, the burden of taking care of his widowed mother and his young orphaned siblings fell upon the shoulders of fifteen-year-old Yisroel. With honest, conscientious, superhuman toil, combined with his brilliance and aptitude, he achieved his noble goal of supporting the family in a respectable manner. He accorded his mother the greatest respect; she was his role model, embodying the ideal of saintliness.

Frugal and content with little, he himself did not indulge in the family's material comforts. He was careful not to wrong anyone,

striving to live his life by the laws and ethics of the Torah and to raise the children in that spirit.

In the most difficult moments of our lives, Yisroel's unshakeable faith and words of consolation pointed us in the right direction, like a flash of lightning on a dark night.

Not only did he extend himself for his own mother and siblings, but for his wife's family as well. He would not abandon his mother-in-law and brother-in-law; he knew they would be defenseless and vulnerable without him. Unfortunately, calamity befell them nonetheless, and it did not spare this great *baal bitachon*. While trying to rescue helpless victims drowning in a stormy sea, he himself was swept away.

This righteous person, who believed firmly that Hashem could send salvation in the blink of an eye, had no place amidst the anarchy and pagan ideology preached by Hitlerism. And so, this pure, unblemished sacrifice was offered along with millions of others on the altar of the great *Akeidah* of European Jewry.

Could there exist a human heart that does not skip a beat while carrying out the execution of such precious children? Cursed be the mothers who gave birth to such creatures! Let a public zoo be established, in which an iron cage will display the German beast who stretched out his hand to murder little Mordche'le.

We cannot ask questions. If the fervent Tehillim recited in the corner of Bogac's stable by the pure, innocent ten-year-old Feivele did not reach the Gates of Mercy, then surely a steel barrier has been erected to prevent such holy prayers from penetrating.

May the cup of anguish be full already. And may redemption come for the few survivors of this bloodbath, who hope for a better world where they will see revenge against those who attempted to mercilessly tear out the Jewish people by the roots.

Racheim Hashem al she'eiris Yisrael — O Hashem, have mercy on the remnant of Israel!

My elderly mother-in-law sits hunched over her book of *techinos*, crying hot tears that she merit to see her son Yisroel in this world. But at that very moment, his *neshamah* already hovers in the Heavenly spheres in the Next World, in the embrace of his father who was also taken in the prime of his life.

11 Adar I. This day will serve our family as a symbol of idealistic devotion. And Yisroel's memory will take its rightful place in our broken hearts, alongside my martyred parents and sister.

O "Tzvi Yisroel" — Glory of Israel!
Upon the heights lie the slain,
How have you fallen among the mighty![1]

My wounded soul is bathed in the blood of my martyred relatives,
My heart torn to pieces by the dreadful events,
Bowed in somber mourning, tears flowing from my eyelids.
Before my tears could dry and my cuts could heal,
Along came your fresh grave,
And the bitter weeping resumes anew.

All your life, my dear brother-in-law,
You were a father to us, seeking only our benefit.
Since your youth, you set this as your purpose.
Woe is to us!
For in the awesome bloodbath and destruction of our nation,
You, too, fell among the heroes, together with your wife and your two
    precious sons.

My whole being yearns for you, my dear brother-in-law
And I voice my grief with a lament.
I am pained over you, my brother,
For you did not leave behind
A remnant within our nation.

In memory of my brother-in-law Yisroel Tzvi Platkiewicz who perished al
kiddush Hashem with his wife Feige and their two sons, Shraga Feivel and
Mordechai, Hy"d, on Tuesday, 11 Adar I 5703, in the village of Gory in
the district of Pinczow

Chaim Yitzchok Wolgelernter, Nissan 5703

---

1. **Hatzvi Yisroel** al bamosecha chalal eich naflu giborim (Shmuel II 1:19). The author uses this verse as a play on the full name of his brother-in-law — Yisroel Tzvi.

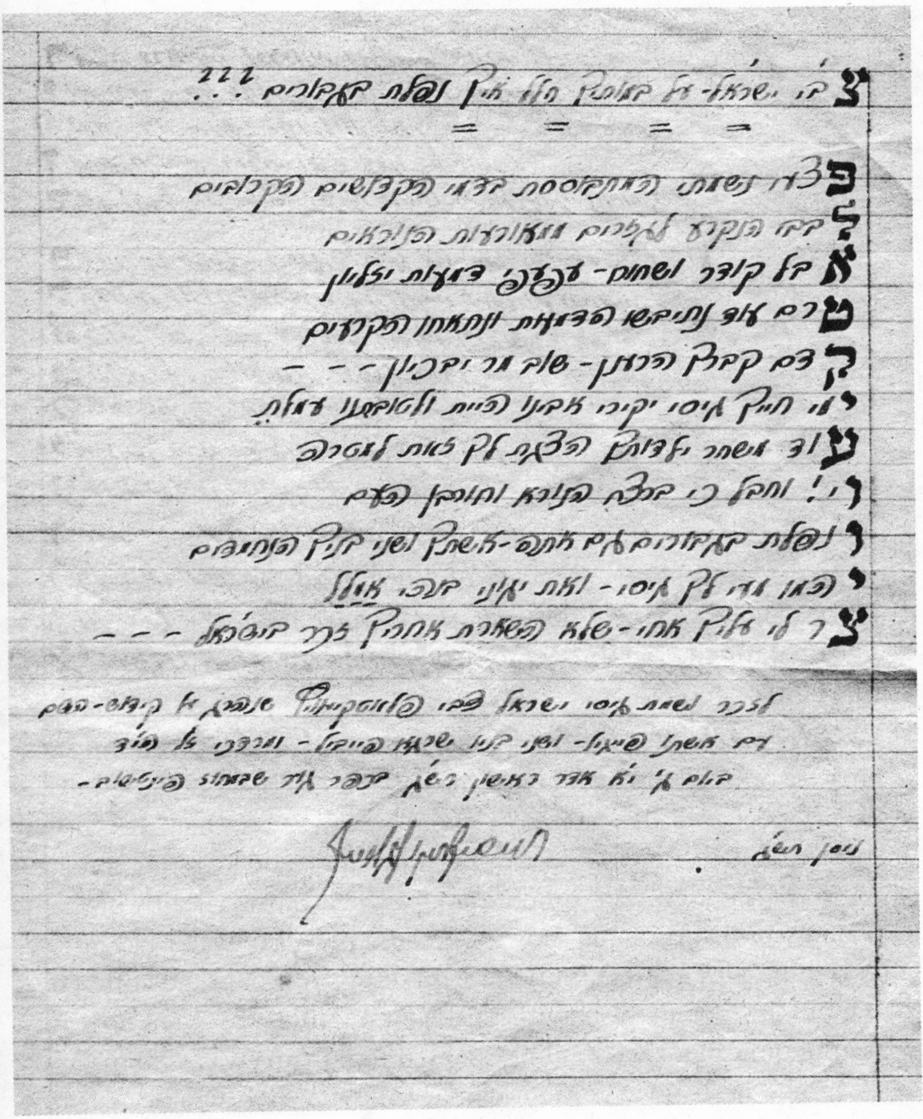

CHAPTER 42

The Conscience
of the World

INEVITABLY, OUR LIVES GOT BACK on track. Time slowly healed our fresh wounds. We dared not mention a word about the tragedy if we wanted my mother-in-law to survive. The conditions in the loft were difficult enough.

We became accustomed to the daily menu of coarse black bread with a bit of black coffee and a scant portion of boiled potatoes. To us, the food tasted like the most luscious delicacy. When the salty potatoes made us thirsty and we had no water to quench our thirst, we found a solution. We simply removed one of the tiles from the roof and scooped up some snow. We could not store water because, after standing for a few minutes, it would turn to ice. Magda offered to fatten the potato dish with lard, but we did not want to eat anything unkosher that was not essential to our survival. Obtaining butter was a luxury we could no longer allow ourselves, since I had given up on my trips to Szyszczyce. But we were happy that at least we could stay together.

Whenever there was any unrest in Skalbmierz, Magda would promptly alert us. We would quickly climb down the ladder to the stable and lower ourselves into the pit underneath. Magda would then close the trapdoor and spread manure over it. On several occasions, we had to hide there for a full twenty-four hours. The dreadful heat and stuffiness in the cramped, dark pit made it difficult to breathe. If that wasn't enough, the bodily fluids of the pigs standing in the stall just above our heads dripped down on us. Yet we accepted all of this with equanimity, glad that at least we were not forced to run. As soon as Magda gave us the signal that the German murderers had left, we would go back up to the loft. After such an ordeal, it took us a while to recover.

Our one concern was what would happen if we ran out of funds to pay Magda. Our survival was now a question of money. Since I had not wanted to keep too large a sum with me, my wife Chayele had most of our gold coins. We had to find a way to exchange them for zlotys and have the currency brought here.

We wrote a letter to Hershel's daughters, Chayele and Esther'l, turning to them for help since they were living as gentiles in Warsaw and were able to move about freely. Everything now depended on their response.

Before long, Esther'l arrives in Skalbmierz, accompanied by a Polish woman, an acquaintance of Chayele's from Warsaw. Just a sixteen-year-old child, Esther'l had become a mature adult. She grasps our situation immediately.

I ask her if she could go to my wife in Jedlnia from time to time to pick up some gold coins, exchange them for zlotys in Warsaw and bring us the money. She says she will think it over.

She tells us of the various difficulties her elder sister had to contend with. At one point Chayele's identity was nearly discovered, but now she has a good position as a bookkeeper in the office of a

German firm that works for the army. She receives a respectable salary and mingles in high society.

Esther'l had visited the Warsaw ghetto several times. She describes the fierce battles taking place there now in the streets. "The Jews erected barricades. Standing on the rooftops, they opened fire and threw hand grenades at the disoriented Gestapo units that had come to liquidate the last remnants of the ghetto. The Jews refuse to be victims any longer! Every day scores of German soldiers are killed. Their commanders do not know how to deal with this situation. Every house is a fortress. The Germans have already sent in planes to bomb the ghetto houses from the air, but the Jews are holding out heroically!"

At last, the time had come to wash away our stain of disgrace: that we allowed ourselves to be led like sheep to the slaughter. To a certain extent, Warsaw has restored our honor. Had the revolt taken place earlier when there were still over half a million Jews in the city, things might have turned out differently. Couldn't the Jews of the smaller towns have managed to obtain weapons, too, and done the same?

Then again, Jews were not thinking in terms of resistance. They were expecting to buy their survival by paying a fortune in goods and money. And they relied on Roosevelt coming to their aid. *America and England will surely help us*, they believed. *Mankind will never swallow such barbarity against defenseless people. The conscience of the world will cry out in protest! The Pope, spiritual head of Christianity, will surely issue a strong condemnation.*

That was the level of trust the Jews had in the conscience of mankind.

But who is mankind — and what is mankind? Man has an inborn tyrannical instinct to dominate his kind. And it is a world where the end justifies the means. If the end can be achieved through the respectable mantle of democracy or other grandiose slogans, all the

better. If not, the bloodshed that is used to reach the goal reveals the true character of mankind.

America and England, the two wealthy powers who control most of the world, could easily afford to uphold their charming ideals and show a modicum of tolerance for the most vulnerable creature in the world, the Jew. But let the Jews obstruct just one tiny cog in the great master engine and these countries, in total disregard for their own principles of democracy, will allow the Jew to be disposed of with the selfsame totalitarian means — bloodshed.

It hasn't been all that long, just over three years, since ships packed with homeless Jewish refugees sailing for Palestine were left stranded on the seas, only to be attacked from the air by British planes, while small roving bands of Arab terrorists, unchecked by the British, were killing Jews daily in Palestine. Even today, after nearly four years of war, England is still powerful enough to rule colonies and territories all over the world. Can't they control the Arabs in Eretz Yisrael?

The real truth is that the British intentionally refrained from controlling the Arabs, appeasing them at the expense of the Jewish victims. Now, too, the western powers try to win the sympathies of the occupied, oppressed nations of the world by broadcasting all sorts of cliches promoting justice and human rights. But are they helping the Jews?

We experienced the same in Egypt of old, a country that worshipped the sheep, the most gentle of animals. Yet this did not stop the Egyptians from brutally trampling an entire nation — enslaving six hundred thousand men, forcing them to do backbreaking labor, and murdering their babies.

After their defeat in the First World War, the Germans found themselves without territories and colonies to dominate. So they formed the National Socialist (Nazi) party, with the first paragraph of the party platform beginning with *"Juden."* Why? Because

dominion over the Jews is, after all, the easiest! Initially, the Germans did not employ such drastic methods; evidently, they were afraid of world opinion. Later, they realized they could openly adopt the most radical and despotic means of oppression without anyone stopping them.

And still, the Jews relied on the world!

England must be pleased with the current developments. For them, the Jewish problem is solved. No more bother, no one to hassle them for immigration certificates to Palestine, nobody to remind them of the "national home for the Jewish people" which Minister Balfour had promised the Jews quite a number of years ago. No longer will they need to debate the connotations and implications of the term "national home."

As far as they are concerned, the war could last indefinitely. The phlegmatic Englishmen have all the time in the world. And the most important factor in waging war is money, of which they have more than enough. Open a second front, a third front... They know exactly what to do, without anyone instructing them.

By the time the terms of a peace treaty will be dictated, the British will have landed on the European continent, and the German fortifications and submarines will be nonexistent. In the interim if an entire people — the people that gave the Bible to the world — goes under, so be it. No doubt, the Archbishop of Canterbury will compose a special prayer memorializing the Jewish nation, to be recited in all the churches of England.

In a similar vein, upon Roosevelt's initiative a committee was created that will attend to the needs of the suffering Jewish survivors, provided there will be any survivors. A number of times, Roosevelt even went on radio to publicly express his sympathy for the Jewish people. What more could he do? After all, with his paralyzed legs, he can't be expected to come here.

Even so, he does not sit idle, what with the ongoing conferences taking place. Just recently, a conference was called for the start of the new year, which was to determine the location for the next conference, which in turn would establish the agenda for the conferences to follow.

And this is the world the Jews relied on.

CHAPTER 43

Yizkor

SINCE THIS YEAR [5703] was an *iber yahr*, the Yom Tov of Pesach fell well into spring.

Fragrant air wafted in through the cracks in the roof of the loft. The earth shed its wintry white garments and donned its verdant spring cloak. The sun, too, awakened from a long winter slumber, wiped the raindrops off the earth's weepy eyes, and stood ready to serve the world with its loving rays.

Double windows, insulated all winter with cotton batting to keep out the bitter cold, were now thrown wide open. Children played outside in front of their houses. All of nature had come back to life.

But our death sentence is still in full force. It is only two days to Pesach, the season of our freedom, which we had fervently hoped would usher in our redemption. Unfortunately, all we have is hope.

We had already explained to Magda that we are not permitted to eat bread on Pesach and asked her to cook potatoes and borscht for us, or beans if necessary. And so we prepare for the Yom Tov, my brother-in-law taking the lead. The devout Hershel, who always

scrupulously observed every *minhag*, conducts the search for *chametz*. And on Erev Pesach in the morning [April 19, 1943], he vigilantly ensures that we do not eat bread after the prescribed time.

On the first night of Pesach, after the *Shemoneh Esrei*, Hershel recites Hallel with great fervor. Yes, a song of praise! I am reminded of the Gemara that says: At the Splitting of the Red Sea, when the Egyptians were drowning, the angels wished to sing a song of praise. However, Hashem exclaimed: *"My handiwork is drowning in the sea and you recite a song of praise?"*

Ribono shel Olam, Your handiwork, the Chosen People, the children of Avraham, Yitzchak and Yaakov, the descendants of the people You redeemed from Mitzrayim, are drowning in a sea of blood. How can we sing a song of praise?

When the angels came before the Throne of Glory carrying the babies that had been entombed alive by the Egyptians, they said, "Look what happened to Your children!" You immediately gave the order to Moshe: "Go and redeem the nation!"

Ribono shel Olam! How many innocent Jewish children have perished already! When will You send our redemption?

We have a guest. Hershel's daughter Chayele has come from Warsaw. We are overjoyed, as eight months have gone by since we last saw her. She has brought us money. The plan we had discussed with Esther'l had worked out well.

Chayele can barely speak Yiddish anymore. Is it any wonder? She lives under the guise of a gentile with an assumed Polish name and must guard against the slightest slip that might betray her identity.

What an ironic twist of fate! The Jews merited to be redeemed from Egypt because they did not change their names and language, and now Jews attempt to save their lives by adopting a foreign language and changing their names!

"It won't be too much longer," Chayele consoles us. "Momentous events are taking place that will soon decide the course of the war.

The defeat of the Germans in Stalingrad is unique in the history of warfare."

My mother-in-law listens attentively to all this. The difficult conditions in the loft no longer bother her. She takes everything in stride — the coarse bread, the black-colored liquid that serves as coffee without a bit of saccharine to sweeten it; sometimes a day can go by when we don't even get that much. Emaciated to half her weight, my mother-in-law spends her days crying into the tattered *Shevet Mussar*[1] she found here. All she wants to know now is whether we will be able to leave the loft before the last day of Pesach.

"Why specifically the last day, *Babbeshe*?" asks Chayele.

"My darling child! On the last day of Pesach, we must go and say Yizkor in memory of all the innocent martyrs who are surely in the Heavenly spheres by now, and we will ask them to intercede for us on high."

We all bow our heads in grief. Which one of us did not have family members who were already in the Next World, pieces of ourselves torn away, leaving rips so large they could never be repaired, people who were once living personalities and were now mere names on a long list, to be remembered in the all-encompassing word: *Yizkor*.

Yizkor...

Remember, G-d, the soul of my sainted father Yeshayah ben Yechiel Issamar who was murdered al kiddush Hashem, and shelter him under Your wings in the lofty realm of the holy and the pure.

Remember my sainted father who occupied himself with Torah and mitzvos all his life. For forty years he covered the blood of the fowl he shechted. But his own blood was shed without being covered.

---

1. Early eighteenth-century work of ethics by Rabbi Eliyahu Hakohen of Izmir, Constantinople, translated into Yiddish and Hebrew

In the most frigid winter weather, he walked miles to find a kosher mikveh, encouraging others, too, to be scrupulous about ritual purity. But he himself was buried without a taharah.

All his life he gave tzedakah and did acts of kindness. Did he not merit having the ultimate gemilus chessed performed for him...?

Yizkor...

Remember, G-d, the soul of my mother, Hendel Rivkah bas Meir, who was murdered al kiddush Hashem.

Although she was frail and sickly all her life, she was staunch and stalwart in spiritual matters, keeping our family from being swept up in the current of modernity. With her weak constitution but strong character, she stood guard like a steel barrier, not allowing the winds of change to cross the threshold of her home. May her soul, too, reside in the Heavenly sanctuary of the kedoshim.

Yizkor...

Remember, G-d, my sister Yitta Reizel who was murdered al kiddush Hashem.

It is difficult to fathom that the vivacious, dynamic Yitta lies motionless in a dark grave in a Christian cemetery, that a life that held so much promise has turned into a legendary heroine of the past.

She wished to save our parents, to fulfill the fifth commandment — Honor your father and your mother. Was the reward of longevity to be granted her only in the Next World...?

May her pure young soul rest in the Heavenly realms.

Yizkor...

O Father, Mother, and Sister — Remember my dear little daughter Alte'le, your own flesh and blood, who was torn away from us and disappeared without a trace. Where is she...? Which world does she inhabit, together with her dear aunt Reizele?

Dear Father and Mother, remember your three sons, condemned to death but fighting for their lives like drowning men in a stormy sea holding onto a

plank of their shipwrecked boat. May the blood that our family has shed until now be enough.

Remember my wife Chayele and my only son Feivele. May he live to see his father in person, the father he knows only through what his mother tells him. May I merit raising my child to be a proud, good Jew, which is what you strove for in this world.

And we will remember...

We will remember you, our sainted parents who were murdered along with hundreds of thousands of other Jews as sacrifices on the altar of *kiddush Hashem* in this painful era of *chevlei Mashiach*... We will remember the seeds you sowed in our childhood years. May they yield the results you endeavored to produce.

We will remember the holy sparks of our illustrious ancestors. May they ignite into blazing rays of light that will illuminate your dark graves, conveying to you the consolation and pride of having left behind a righteous generation.

We will remember you, dear sister Yitta... If there existed a scale by which loyalty and devotion could be measured, surely your heroism would have reached the peak. We will remember your selfless acts, which you paid for with your young life. Your deeds will endure for eternity and your memory will forever remain in the innermost recesses of our hearts. If any member of our family survives, let him take pride in the crown jewel of our family, who bore the name Yitta!

[After the war, Dovid Wolgelernter related: "When my brother Chaim Yitzchok read the Yizkor chapter aloud in the loft, his eyes were swollen with hot tears. We all wept along, sensing that the Yizkor also alluded to us, though our souls were still clinging to our gaunt, emaciated bodies."]

CHAPTER 44

The Tide Begins to Turn

MONDAY [JULY 26, 1943], one of the last hot summer days at the end of Tammuz, dawns fair and bright. The sun strides easily across the cloudless blue sky, generously casting its rays upon the world. From afar, through the attic cracks, a lovely panorama of ripe grain is visible in the fields. All of creation is alive, inhaling summer in its full blossom and splendor.

An opposite phenomenon exists in the loft. Our hearts are cheerless and heavy. We spend our nights fighting the tiny brown creatures that have launched an all-out offensive against us, even as their larger brown-shirted comrades are in the midst of being stamped out on the Russian front by the Red Plague.[1] The lice attack us mainly at night, and we are vastly outnumbered — that is, unless we should manage to procure a few extra pairs of hands! After several sleepless nights that seem more like years, we are utterly spent. We see no way out.

---

1. Epithet referring to Communism

Granted, the Germans are being pounded into a bloody pulp on the battlefield. On the western front, the Allies have already taken the little Mediterranean island called Lampedusa and are poised to vault into Sicily. They are beginning to carve up the occupied territories. But what will come of it?

Just recently, the *Duce*[2] delivered a speech, publicly declaring that he and his colleagues are confident of victory and will yet return to take North Africa. Apparently, the imminent British defeat of Italy is no cause for concern. Who are we to think otherwise? If Mussolini says so, he must know better!

Then there was the summit between the *Fuehrer* and the *Duce*, which was no simple matter. The Krakow gutter tabloid *Ganiec* reported a news item all the way from Tokyo, stating that Japan is keeping a close eye on this meeting that is sure to have significant and surprising political repercussions.

Things are heating up. The world is at a crossroads, while we lie in a loft for nearly nine months, waiting anxiously for an Allied victory. It is most unpleasant.

Immersed in thought, I do not notice our hostess entering, a smile lighting up her face. She has brought our breakfast consisting of warm water. In order to give it some color, she adds a substance which she calls "coffee," though it has absolutely nothing in common with the latter.

I had learned from experience that if Magda was smiling, she must have some good news to report, albeit not always did it prove to be true.

"I can tell that you have good news, *Pani*," I say.

"Don't ask! It's over!"

"What happened?"

"It's over! It's over!" she yells.

---

2. Italian for "leader," the title assumed by Benito Mussolini, Fascist dictator of Italy

Realizing that I will not get a straight answer out of her, I ask, "Will we be able to leave any time soon?"

"Not yet. For that you must wait a bit longer. But Italy is surrendering! The Pope was assassinated! A revolution is underway in Germany! The Polish army stationed in Turkey is advancing through Spain towards the Black Sea and our forces will march into Poland through Lithuania, bypassing the Russian army..."

She is not done yet.

"There was heavy bombing in the Turkish capital — what's it called again — Naples! The trains are no longer running."

She got completely carried away, and she still had more to tell. My head began to spin from this hodgepodge of incoherent information that stuck to me like peas on a wall. There was just one thing I did understand: Magda was no expert on geography. To her, Naples was the capital of Turkey and Spain was situated on the Black Sea. But at least I knew from this whole muddled collection of sensational reports that something was in the offing. There was nothing more to do but wait for the next issue of the *Ganiec* newspaper.

In honor of the big news, we received a better dinner today: a two-course, no, a three-course meal — potatoes and water, garnished with parsley greens. It looked appealing and we ate with a much improved appetite, lightening the atmosphere in our prison cell. I just hoped that at least some of the news would turn out to be true.

The tabloid finally arrives. We search for corroboration of Magda's reports, but there is nothing. A black cloud darkens our newly brightened horizon. It was all a bluff, an illusory soap bubble. Apparently, Magda intended nothing more than to pour salt on our open wounds. What a mean woman!

Suddenly a small, innocuous tidbit catches my eye: "Mussolini resigns. Marshal Badoglio forms new government."

What is this? So something *is* happening after all! Had the omnipotent *Duce*, who only recently declared that he would return to capture North Africa, been forced to leave his *Palazzo Venezia* in Rome? He himself — the founder of Blackshirt Fascism, who emulated Hitler's despicable theory of racial supremacy?

After a twenty-year reign, have you, Mussolini, suddenly been ousted like a rabid dog by your own Fascist brethren? You entangled your peace-loving nation in an alliance with Germany, to curry favor with your murderous mentor who promised you the world for supplying him with soldiers. You delivered fiery speeches attacking Roosevelt and Churchill and threatened to return to the North African front. Yet, after one bombardment of your city of Rome by the Allied quad-engined bomber planes, you backed down, disregarding what you said only a day before.

You are not done yet. Not only will history judge you as a wicked dictator, but a verdict awaits you by your own fellow Fascists, your former followers. So in the interim, Comrade *Duce*, you'd better prepare a hiding place for yourself. History repeats itself. You're lucky you came out alive from this ugly state of affairs. As for your friend and mentor — certainly a worse fate awaits him.

Yes, the tide has truly turned!

My frail and emaciated noble mother-in-law, who suffered so much throughout this time and endured our prisoner's existence like the rest of us, noticed our surprised and joyful expressions. "Is it really true?" she asked.

"Yes, it's true! We will soon be liberated!"

At that, a spark of happiness lit up her weary eyes.

"*Oy, Ribono shel Olam,*" she sighed, "may I live to see my children again..."

CHAPTER 45

Not a Trace of Jews

[Ed. Note: The first page of this chapter is not extant; therefore, the events leading to the author's trip to Dzialoszyce are unknown.]

WE ARRIVED IN DZIALOSZYCE at ten o'clock at night. Our friend Jan refused to let us in. We were already thinking of going back, but having survived the hazardous trip, were we to leave empty-handed?

We wait out the night in a storage shed and return to Jan at dawn. He opens the door, greeting us with the old, familiar refrain: "You dared to come at such a time?! Just yesterday, Hershel Grzes and his wife and child were discovered and shot to death. Actually, things like that rarely happen these days, for the simple reason that there are no Jews left here anymore. Over the past year, they got rid of all of them."

Not only had the living Jews been eliminated, but even the Jewish cemetery had been ravaged, along with the surrounding grounds. The better marble monuments were carted away and the simple headstones were chopped up to be used for road pavement. The entire cemetery is plowed over. One cannot tell there was ever anything there.

The big shul will be converted into a public bathhouse. The small homes on the side streets were torn down and sold to the peasants for firewood. There is no vestige of the house of the rebbe, Rav Eliezer Epstein.

The town is unrecognizable. Everything has been erased in such a systematic manner. The final destruction is complete.

Later in the month of Av [August 1943] —

On this upcoming Tishah B'Av, with the desolation of our hometown of Dzialoszyce fresh in our minds, we in the loft will have a keener understanding of the lament of Yirmiyahu Hanavi. The prophet's words have now taken on new meaning.

"*Eichah yashvah badad* — Alas, she sits in solitude! The city that was great with people has become like a widow."

CHAPTER 46

Tishah B'Av

WE FOUND OUR TERRIBLE TRAGEDY mirrored in the words of the *navi*.

During the mad and frenzied rush of our day-to-day lives, had any of us ever paused for a moment to reflect upon the fiery expressions of fury of the prophet Yirmiyahu, upon his foretelling of the *Churban*? Indeed, not only did he predict the destruction of the Beis Hamikdash, but also our present *churban*, the current *"Valley of Slaughter."*[1]

Large and small will die in this land; they will not be buried and no one will eulogize them... No one will break bread for their bereavement to comfort them about the dead...about their father and mother...[2]

Yes, whom was Yirmiyahu referring to in this verse if not to our generation? And what is the *"Valley of Slaughter"* if not the unknown destination to which millions were transported, a *"land of waste and desolation"* where they perished of hunger, where innocent children

---

1. *Yirmiyahu* 7:32
2. Ibid. 16:6–7

along with the elderly were left unburied to become *"prey for the birds of the sky"*?

Did anything like this happen at the destruction of the first or the second Beis Hamikdash — that survivors should be unable to fulfill the traditions of mourning for their parents?

Those who survived the *Churban* did not continue to remain in mortal danger. Clearly, the *navi* meant us, the few individuals in hiding, who cannot even properly mourn our closest family members.

The only solace we find here to dispel the pain are the volumes of Mishnah and Gemara and other *sefarim* in the loft. At least we can learn mishnayos as a merit for the *heilige neshamos*.

And in the endless sea of the Talmud, this petty and insignificant world fades into nothingness...

[The remainder of this diary page is torn off and is not extant.]

CHAPTER 47

Shabbos Nachamu

"*NACHAMU NACHAMU AMI* — Comfort, comfort My people, says your G-d."

Like a healing balm, the prophet Yeshayahu's words always soothed the hearts of a people enveloped in collective mourning for the *Churban*. After the three weeks of *Bein Hametzarim*, during which specific customs and centuries-old traditions weighed heavily upon the soul, the words of comfort in the *haftorah* of Shabbos Nachamu drove away the dark clouds of the past and brought a message of redemption and hope in a bright future. *O herald of Zion...say to the cities of Judah, behold, your G-d!*

With what bitter irony do these selfsame words ring in the ears of the few Jews who are still in hiding, where even their miserable prisoner's existence is not assured. We are engulfed in mourning that is unlike that of generations of Jews who grieved over the destruction of the Beis Hamikdash, the resulting exile from our homeland, and the loss of thousands of Jewish lives. For the events of the *Churban* retained a spark of consolation. In the heart of the misfortune there arose the city of Yavneh and its Sages, under the leadership of the great Rabbi Yochanan ben Zakkai. This infused

the strength and hope necessary to endure the deathblow and to await with eagerness the great salvation predicted in the words *"Nachamu nachamu ami."*

But our grieving seems to have no end. It is almost a year since our loved ones, fathers, mothers, brothers, and sisters were wrenched from our midst, infants torn from their mothers and taken away — but not into exile. Countless places of worship have been destroyed. Millions, not thousands, have been murdered, entire families spanning several generations wiped out without any survivors.

And the process is not yet over. Every day, after almost a year of wandering in this gehinnom, another tormented Jewish soul is pulled out of his hideout, with a bullet from the Polish Blue Police serving as his final atonement. Did not the anguish and travail he suffered all this time suffice to purify his soul? Unfortunately, it is the second clause of Yeshayahu's prophecy that has come true: *For she has received from the hand of Hashem double for all her sins.*

What shall be *our* consolation? How can our great pain be alleviated? What can heal our open, bleeding wounds? Weeks go by without a glimmer of hope. The day of vengeance is still far off, and who knows if it will ever arrive?

Perhaps the Allied bombardment of the city of Rome, mentioned in today's paper, shall be our consolation. For it was the Romans who destroyed the Beis Hamikdash, resulting in this two-thousand-year *galus* that is a direct cause of our current suffering. Jerusalem and Rome are inversely related. *Lo nismala Yerushalayim ela mi'churbanah shel Romi* — Jerusalem will only flourish once Rome is destroyed. Now that the destruction of Rome is materializing, we have reason to anticipate the fulfillment of the other half of the promise — the rebuilding of Yerushalayim. May this be our consolation, our *"Nachamu nachamu ami."*

As for our heroic *kedoshim* in the Next World who are gone without a trace — what will be their consolation?

It is exactly fourteen years since my oldest brother Avramele left Poland for Canada. In my mind's eye, I can still see the tearful scene in my parents' home as vividly as if it happened today.

Mother, wringing her hands, lamenting, "I raised a son for over twenty years, undergoing worry and aggravation, until, with Hashem's help, he grew to be a pious, respectable young man. I had hoped to see nachas from him...and now I am sending him away to a strange country across the ocean. Who knows if I will ever see him again?"

Father, sitting in another corner... Even he, with his strong nature, could not control his emotions at this moment and wiped away tears. "All my life I strove to leave over a frum and devout generation. And now, just like that...to send away a son? What will become of my child there?"

Yes, in my parents' home that year, it was indeed a mournful Tishah B'Av.

It is true, my dear Mother, you did not live to see him again. It was a sorrowful day for you when he left. Dear Father, you hoped for and endeavored to raise a righteous generation. You feared for Avramele, since he was leaving for Canada. But today, Mother, he is the source of your consolation. And you, Father, may rest in peace. Your offspring will survive; your memory will live on — through Avramele.

This train of thought brings me to ponder the significance of my own physical existence. I wage a tough, grueling battle so that I may live to see revenge for the blood that was spilled and to raise a new generation with a bright future. As for me, bruised in body and spirit with irreparable wounds, is my own life still worthwhile? Might it be the will of the Almighty that even the lone Jews who have survived until now shall not evade the harsh Divine decree?

Let my dear, beloved little son, out in the world together with his mother in the guise of Aryans, live to see revenge and salvation.

And that will be *my* consolation, my *"Nachamu nachamu ami..."*

CHAPTER 48

Yahrzeit of a Town

THE YAHRZEIT OF THE *KEDOSHIM* of Dzialoszyce falls on 21 Elul.

A full leap year has passed since the twentieth-century Torquemadas, in the name of their *Fuehrer*-god and his prophets, carried out a bloody auto-da-fé in my hometown of Dzialoszyce against the defenseless Jews, the heretics of the depraved German creed. It is already a year since the swastika-emblazoned *Junker*[1] troop train laid the cornerstone for the new murderous German order in Europe. Three pits, filled with 1500 martyrs, are the foundation of this new civilization, and the sealed cattle cars packed with thousands of Jews are its edifice.

Did these peace-loving human beings disturb anyone's tranquility? In the vast world, did this small band of people take up anyone's space?

---

1. The honorary title *Junker* ("young nobleman") came to refer to members of the landowning nobility of Prussia and eastern Germany. The younger sons, who did not inherit land, often joined the army.

The echo of my child's voice reverberating, "*Tattenyu!*" leaves me no rest. And the thought of Reizele's hand reaching through the tiny lattice opening of the cattle car, beseeching, "Save me...!"

No doubt the sweet, lilting voice of my little Alte'le and the singsong Semitic melody of Uncle Yosef Shaul learning mishnayos did not harmonize with the harsh cacophony of the beer-guzzling Germans' hoarse Nordic voices.

Surely the slender, delicate Reizele must have disrupted the development of the big, heavy Bertha.[2]

Or perhaps the paralyzed ninety-six-year-old Rav Mordechai Staszewski was one of the authors of the *Protocols of the Elders of Zion*?[3]

And why shouldn't the six-month-old baby be trampled to death by a Prussian boot or killed by the iron stake of a Polish hero as due punishment for his subversive, anti-Hitler activities?

No, the modest and pure Jewish family life could not coexist with the *Kraft durch Freude*[4] theory.

Everything was achieved on that black day, Thursday, 21 Elul 5702.

Space was cleared on the European continent for the expansion of the venereal-diseased pure Aryan blood.

The sadistic instincts of the helmeted German beasts were sated with the clotted blood and marrow of the unburied Jewish corpses.

---

2. Apparently a reference to the super-heavy cannon known as "*Dicke Bertha*," developed by the Krupp company before WWI. It is said to have been named for Bertha Krupp, heiress and owner of the huge Krupp industrial empire, which became the chief producer of armaments for Nazi Germany and used tens of thousands of slave laborers during World War II.

3. Published in Russia in 1905 and disseminated internationally in multiple languages, it described a meeting of Jewish leaders, the so-called "Elders of Zion," and their conspiracy for Jewish global domination. Although it was discovered to be an anti-Semitic hoax, it was publicized extensively by Nazi Germany and its myths were exploited by Hitler.

4. "Strength through Joy," abbreviated KdF; large state-operated propaganda organization in Nazi Germany providing organized leisure trips and events for the German work force and later for the Wehrmacht troops.

They marched back from the execution site with the triumph song of Horst Wessel[5] on their lips: "When Jewish blood spurts from the knife, all is well with us..."[6]

Kaddish — a *tikkun* for the *neshamah* on the yahrzeit.

The final deathblow of the bloodthirsty regime will be the *tikkun* for the *kedoshim* and our revenge.

---

5. Nazi party activist and SA (*Sturmabteilung*/Brownshirts) leader who was glorified as a martyr of the Nazi movement following his murder in 1930. Wessel wrote the lyrics for a song, known as the *Horst-Wessel-Lied*, which became Nazi Germany's national anthem.

6. "*Wenn das Judenblut vom Messer spritzt, dann geht's nochmal so gut.*" These lines are part of the *Lied der Sturmsoldaten* (Stormtroopers Song), sung by the SA during street parades, along with the Horst Wessel song.

CHAPTER 49

Breaking the Tablets

AT MIDNIGHT, THE STRIKE of the twelfth hour,
When G-d, cloaked, as it were, in mourner's attire,
Moves from His Throne of Justice to His Throne of Mercy,
He sheds a tear over the destruction of the Temple,
Over the ravaged Altar and the cessation of the offerings.

At that moment, the fledgling Gestapo priests — *pirchei kehunah*,
Garbed in brown vestments and turbans of steel,
With automatic pistols their *klei shareis*,
Offered up Jewish sacrifices on the new altars —
The deep, freshly dug pits.

Little children, newborn babes instead of turtledoves and pigeons,
One-year-old boys in place of one-year-old sheep,
Aged men and women, tzaddikim, unblemished burnt offerings,
Their blood was sprinkled on the base of the altar-pits,
And the fragrance of incense — of disinfectant and congealed marrow,
Rose up to Hashem as a *rei'ach nicho'ach*.

Singing Levite songs of praise — the Horst Wessel hymn:
"When Jewish blood spurts from the knife, all is well with us,"
The newly composed *Hallel Hagadol*;
The libations were fulfilled in the local tavern
With wine, cognac, and alcoholic beverages,
The remainder of the night spent in wanton abandon,
Drunken orgies with brazen harlots.

You, the survivors who witnessed the bloody tragedy,
You, the firebrands saved from the burning altar:
Take the millions of skeletons out of the mass graves,
Erect a tower to reach the seventh heaven,
Step up to the Throne of Glory and ask the Man clothed in linen,[1]
If this is how the Pangs of Redemption are supposed to appear,
About which our great Sages prayed:
"*Yeisei v'lo achminei.*"[2]

If it is so,
Then remove the sticky fatty marrow
From the bullet-pierced skulls,
And grease the wheels of Mashiach's chariot,
Which have become rusty
During the two-thousand-year wait.
Dry up the mud-covered road
With the ashes of the burned Torah scrolls.

---

1. *Levush habadim* — a reference to the angel Gavriel (*Yechezkel* 9:11); see *Sanhedrin* 98a; see also *Eileh Ezkerah*, the Yom Kippur prayer of the Ten Martyrs — Rabbi Yishmael ascends to Heaven and asks the *levush habadim* if the decree has come from G-d.

2. *Let Mashiach come, but let me not behold him* (i.e. suffer the accompanying events) [*Sanhedrin* 98b].

Build an arch from the bodies of the holy tzaddikim,
And let the torn black-and-white *talleisim*,
The symbolic flag of Torah, black fire on white fire,
Fly above, lowered to half-mast,
Let the unborn children of the murdered pregnant women
Parade in front of it.

But if we were not deemed worthy of the *Geulah*
Because of our sins and impurity,
Then, O Mashiach, drive along the new *Autobahn*,
Paved with the tombstones of Jewish cemeteries,
And press forward into the Third Reich to Hitler's tzaddikim.

An honor guard of demons, born in the twilight of Jewish existence,
The bodyguards of the mighty Ashmedai-*Fuehrer*,
Will anoint King Mashiach
On the banks of a great river flowing with Jewish blood,
Whereupon a comprehensive report will be issued
Of the gigantic extermination campaign.
All of the barricades have been removed,
By means of stoning, burning, beheading, and strangling,
The *even negef*[3] of Your revelation.

Master Mashiach, you can saunter,
From east to west, from north to south,
You will not find a trace of Jews.
A swastika-cross in the form of a guillotine was placed
In the Sanctuary of European Jewry;

3. Tripping stone; see *Yeshayahu* 8:14 and *Sanhedrin* 37b/38a

Scrolls of immoral pagan law,
Inside the Ark, in the Holy of Holies,
In place of the Tablets.

Watching from the distance, Satan rubs his hands with glee,
Roaring with laughter at his triumphant victory.
It is truly the ideal of the End of Days,
The unity and peace of the time of the Redemption.
Tumah and *Taharah* have sealed a pact,
Kedushah has surrendered to the *Sitra Achra*.

CHAPTER 50

My Dream[1]

IT IS ONE OF THOSE LONG, bitter cold nights of Kislev [December 1943]. Outside, winter is in full force. As we lie here inside this attic prison, condemned to death by the murderous German civilization, snow blows into the loft through the cracks in the dilapidated roof and walls. The wind howls an eerie, mournful tune befitting our despondent frame of mind. We fortify ourselves against the intense cold by lying curled up under bedcovers that are so grimy you cannot tell they were once white.

The oppressive atmosphere is broken only by the whispered voice of my pious mother-in-law reciting entire *techinos* from memory as she fervently entreats the Almighty to bring an end to our dreadful suffering. At times the sound of a deep sigh of resignation and despair emanates from another corner.

As I lie pressed between my two bereft, orphaned brothers, jumbled thoughts swirl like images in a kaleidoscope through my hazy mind. *Merciful Creator! Will our tormented souls ever find peace? Is*

---

1. Ed. Note: Excerpts of an overlapping, Hebrew-language version of this chapter have been incorporated within the translation.

there still hope for those broken limbs that fell off the great altar upon which myriads of the finest and best of our nation were brought up for slaughter?

Over a year has passed since the bloody storm that uprooted our dearest loved ones, leaving a gaping, festering wound that has not yet begun to heal. And still, the sharp sword of Damocles continues to hang over our heads.

We are already resigned to our prisoner's existence, the meager diet of dry bread and boiled potatoes, unwashed clothing, and the nightly battle with the little brown creatures that have occupied our cell, conducting a nocturnal offensive against our gaunt flesh. Some days we are forced to hide in the airless pit under the stable floor in a crouched position while the waste from the pigs seeps down onto us.

It is already a year of living in a gehinnom of suffering. Our strength is waning, our bodies are emaciated as skeletons, our eyes hollow with apathy. And there is no relief in sight.

Magda's attitude towards us cooled over time. In the beginning, she appeared to be an angel of mercy, spreading her wings over us and emphasizing with heartfelt emotion that she had no intent other than a holy zeal to rescue us from Hitlerite cruelty. Her once fiery idealism has since become tainted with materialistic motives. She even stopped the special meals she used to prepare now and then for my mother-in-law. My entreaties that she take pity on the frail old woman, who is in imminent danger of dying, have no effect on her whatsoever. She no longer has any compassion.

On the other hand, it is not surprising at all. The corrupt propaganda campaign conducted daily by the German murderers in their venom-filled newspapers, the mudslinging against international Jewry that precipitated the present war, enabling Germany to expand its absolute power and to subjugate the Aryan nations, poisons everyone and incites the occupied nations against the Jew: the eternal enemy. All at once, they can justify the terrible massacres

they have committed against European Jewry, their political failure, and their loss at the eastern front. It is all the fault of the Jews.

I remember when we wandered through the countryside immediately after our expulsion from Dzialoszyce. The Polish farmers sympathized with us. There were even some who took Jews into their homes. But now everything has changed. The *Narodowa Demokracja* (ND) party, already known for its hatred of Jews even before the war, experienced a resurgence. Thanks to Hitler, the *Endecjas* found an opportune time to implement their schemes, so that those individuals who managed to escape the Gestapo sword fell into their hands. Today a Pole would not endanger himself and shelter a Jew for any money. The villages are empty of Jews.

Magda knows all too well that we cannot budge from here. She takes advantage of our helpless situation in a mean-spirited way, extorting everything possible from us. She waits for the month to end so she can increase the rent. She allows us to stay only because she senses that we still have a few more zlotys. Without a doubt, once the supply is exhausted, we will be cast out, since she, too, has come to regard us as lowly, worthless creatures meant to be tormented and uprooted. Our money reserves are gradually dwindling, and if the war continues to drag on, we are in danger of finding ourselves in the same predicament as a year ago.

So what was the point of going to all this trouble for the past year? Aren't the heroic kedoshim who died al kiddush Hashem and who now bask in the shade of the Shechinah to be envied?

Similar despairing and pessimistic thoughts gnaw at me day and night. Oblivious to the cold and everything around me, my mind drifts to my days of learning Torah in yeshivah. I search the world of the spiritual. Perhaps there I will find an answer to my muddled doubts.

Soon I sink into a deep sleep. And there before my eyes stands my saintly father. The sight of his sincere, loving image intoxicates me

with indescribable happiness. The sound of his soft and cheerful voice rings in my ears.

"A great question you have asked, my son. You should know that this is a tremendous test. The present period is extremely lofty. Our forefather Yaakov wished to reveal the End of Days, but it was hidden from him. Now, however, the revelation of the End is beginning.

"In the *Likutei Baal HaTanya*, the concept of the End is explained as '*keitz kal basar* — the end of all flesh.' The light of the spiritual *geulah* cannot be revealed before the total obliteration of the corporeal, the negation of the physical flesh. Removal of this screen allows the force of *ruchniyus* to rise and to cleave to the Heavenly, eternal Source. Indeed, the mission of man in this world is towards this goal — to reinforce the spiritual and to elevate the *neshamah*, the G-dly part of man, to its lofty Source.

"The topic of *kofin oso ad sheyomar rotzeh ani* — forcing a person until he says, 'I agree'[2] — is difficult to understand. If in fact one does not want, how is it useful to coerce him? The Rambam explains that the *neshamah* itself desires the good, but being bound in the *guf*, the body, the latter interposes and prevents the person from clinging to the mitzvah. However, coercion, the subduing of the physical matter, brings to the fore the positive will of the *neshamah*. Once the person is aroused to *teshuvah* and abandons his sins, his physical self, too, becomes refined and elevates itself to the spiritual.

"It is for this reason that the world is akin to a *bei hilula*, a wedding hall, for just as a *chassan* on the day of his wedding is forgiven all of his sins and becomes a new being, so is the task of every person in this world to strengthen himself to abandon his sins, thereby elevating his *guf*.

---

2. In certain instances of vows or divorce proceedings, a rabbinical court may force an individual to act. See *Rosh Hashanah* 6a and *Yevamos* 106a, *Mishneh Torah Hilchos Gerushin* 2:20.

"The death of a person also cleanses him of sin. Therefore, the day of the yahrzeit is called a *'hilula,'* a wedding, for every year it evokes the day of his death when his sins were cleansed. Hence, the *neshamah* rises on high to a more exalted level.

"The subject of *Kiddush Hashem* is very lofty; not every mind can grasp it. By giving one's life for the sanctification of the Name of Hashem, the *neshamah* reaches the summit of its elevation, and this is literally *'keitz kal basar.'*

"And although there is none higher than those killed *al kiddush Hashem*, nevertheless the agony of exile and wandering is no simple matter either. These are the birth pangs of Mashiach. Regarding this time, our Sages have said: *'Echoz v'al tachmitzenah* — Hold strong to it and don't fail it.'

"No, my son, you may not despair! Every great achievement is attained with hardship. The birth of a child also involves pain and sacrifice, and today you are experiencing the birth of a *Geulah* and the blossoming of a new and better world. And that is why so much blood is being shed.

"As for the question of why so many tzaddikim have perished — that is in a heavenly realm. But know that by giving one's life *al kiddush Hashem*, the soul offers itself as a *korban* to the Creator of the world.

"My child, your suffering in exile cleanses you so that you will be worthy. Do not question it, but accept it with love, lest you weaken. Strengthen yourselves and do not give up, for redemption is near..."

I awoke awestruck, beads of sweat covering my body, my knees shaking. In this first year following my father's death, it was the first time I saw him in a dream. No longer did I have any doubts. Now I understood the purpose of our suffering.

I resolve to accept it with love. A spark of hope and comfort ignited in me.

That day, 22 Kislev, was the yahrzeit of my saintly, martyred parents.

CHAPTER 51

Refuge in Debowiec

IT IS ONLY A SHORT TIME since we moved to our new quarters, the drafty barn loft of a corrupt farmer in Debowiec by the name of Biskup. Like murderers in search of a City of Refuge, we found a haven in this tiny hamlet. We have not yet acclimated ourselves, not yet recovered from our recent tumultuous experiences.

After more than a year in Magda's loft, we were sure we would stay there until the end of the war. We had long ago resigned ourselves to our difficult, confined existence, not to mention our constant hunger. We waited out the days, hoping there was something to look forward to. Suddenly one day, without warning, Magda discarded us like squeezed-out lemons. We could not believe our ears when she came in and announced that we had to leave.

"*Pani*, what's the matter with you?" we cried. "How can you poke fun at us? We are but shadows of our former selves!"

"No, I do not mean this as a joke," she explained coldly and categorically. "I'm afraid that someone informed on me. The Germans might come and search my house."

We implored her to have mercy on us. "How can we leave in our famished, weakened state, especially on this moonlit night?" Barely clinging to life, my mother-in-law was beside herself.

Magda offered no response. All we could see before us in the dark loft were her two venomous green eyes, unblinking as she pronounced a death sentence upon the eight of us.

As we prepared to leave, she covered her eyes with her hands, feigning tears as if she were sorry for us. She played the act further with mock words of comfort. "As soon as the storm blows over, you can come back to me. In the meantime, you might as well leave your things here. Everything will remain untouched. Why drag those heavy bundles along with you?" Apparently, she was very concerned that we not overexert ourselves carrying our possessions.

Surely, the taste of death could not be more bitter than on that Friday night[1] when we left the cell we had been imprisoned in for over a year. The consequences of our yearlong starvation diet became apparent with our first few steps out of the loft. Dizziness overcame us and our knees gave way. We stumbled and fell.

Magda slammed the door shut behind us as if banishing some nuisance. With a wave of the hand, she was rid of us. She had already bled us dry, extracting a fortune in money, clothing, and textiles. What did she need us for any longer?

We began walking, the moon shining upon us. I led the way, supporting my shrunken, emaciated mother-in-law by the arm, the others following behind. Our caravan of people walked with one aim: to leave the town of Skalbmierz as quickly as possible. But where should we go? This no one knew. We trudged on, at times crawling on all fours across the rugged terrain. We did not see a soul.

---

1. Ed. Note: Based on the author's description of the weather and full moon as well as his letter to his wife (see *Survival and Renewal*), it appears that the group left Magda's loft in Skalbmierz in mid-Shevat/beginning February 1944.

As we neared the village of Kwaszyn, it began to rain heavily. In the distance, I could see the first house, where our old friend Latosz lived. It occurred to me to approach him for help. Perhaps he would shelter our group. Certainly, he would let us spend the night if we left by morning. Why, he already had many of our valuables!

I knocked. When the door opened, we were greeted by a shrill shriek. The old woman berated and cursed her daughter for opening the door. We would have to move on. The young woman was kind enough to give us directions to Pietrowski, where we had stayed for two weeks after the second *Aussiedlung*.

The rain continued to come down in buckets and my mother-in-law had to be carried. We made it to Pietrowski's house with great difficulty. He opened the door and explained that his wife was in labor and he could not possibly let us in.

We continued on our way. I guided my sister-in-law Tzinne'le through the knee-deep mud puddles, stopping to rest after each step. With our last ounce of energy, we all plodded on. The rain stopped and with Hashem's help, after more than seven hours of walking, we arrived in Szyszczyce in the middle of the night.

Stealing into the mayor's open storage shed, we lay down to sleep on the ground. At daybreak, Hershel and I called on the mayor. He received us quite graciously but explained that he was gravely ill and could not shelter us. "What's more," he added, "the murderous *Narodowa* party officials in Wolica are keeping an eye on me and have searched my place several times. They even fired warning shots into my house. Altogether, it is dangerous to stay in the village, since they have spies here as well. Your lives are hanging by a thread!"

With great reluctance, he consented to our plea to let us stay in his barn until nightfall. We prayed fervently, hoping the day would not end, for where would we go then? But in this bitter war, were the entreaties of *Yidden* fulfilled? Surely steel-and-concrete

fortifications were erected before the Gates of Mercy so that our prayers could not penetrate.

When it turned dark, Hershel and Feivel went to their former hosts and offered any price for one night's shelter. They soon returned, their efforts unsuccessful.

The mayor's wife drove us out of the barn. We went back to the exposed shed and sat there in the cold. What were we to do? I was at my wits' end. The raw blisters on my feet were torturous and I was shivering. Soon the mayor gave us an ultimatum. If we did not leave, we would be in trouble. Our situation was hopeless.

Feivel and Reuven suggested that we go to Debowiec where they had stayed last year and sneak into Szczubial's open barn without his knowledge. There was no other alternative, but I did not have the energy to go any further with my sore feet. I believed that one of my acquaintances would allow me, alone, to stay for a day. My two brothers, however, refused to part with me and so the three of us decided to stay in Szyszczyce.

Hershel fell upon me, bidding me the farewell of one who is sentenced to death and feels the noose tightening around his neck. I felt a stream of hot tears on my face, heard his choked voice in my ears. "If you survive," he cried, "I ask you to be a father to my two unfortunate daughters who are out in the world under assumed identities. Remind them that they are Jews, children of their father and mother, who were not spared the tragic fate of millions of other Jews."

I was left speechless and could not formulate a coherent response. I simply did not know how to answer him.

Only after they left did I slowly begin to absorb Hershel's words. He had spoken out of complete resignation and despair, without a shred of hope. Indeed, his request rang like a last will and testament. What did he mean that I should be a father to his children? Was I guaranteed to survive? Even if I did, how would I be capable of

fulfilling such a task? And how could I convey such a message to his two grown daughters? In the current replay of Haman's decree, these girls were playing the part of Queen Esther, sustaining our group all this time. Should they not merit seeing their father Mordechai[2] alive?

My brothers and I wanted to run after Hershel's group and share a common fate, but nobody stood to gain from that. On the contrary, five people were more likely to find shelter than eight. Besides, we would see what tomorrow would bring. We could not deliberate much longer than that.

The mayor's wife returned. I ran into the mayor's house, imploring him to have mercy and allow my brothers and me to stay for just one more day. I showed him my swollen feet. But I no longer recognized the mayor. He was a changed man. "If you don't leave, I'll hand you over to the authorities!" he threatened.

We left. I knocked on doors, Tetele's and others, but no one answered. Next, I tried Bogac. Apparently, he was afraid we had joined the partisans, as he let us in for the day and was very accommodating. He thought we had come to forcibly reclaim the possessions that Yisroel had left with him. Altogether, his whole conduct baffled me — it was too good to be true. I began to fear that he was planning to betray us.

We decided that as soon as it got dark, we would go back to Skalbmierz, for we could not imagine that any peasants in this area would shelter us after the bloodbath that had taken place here a few months ago. Virtually all the Jews had been eliminated, either by the Germans or, even more so, by the *Narodowa* collaborators headquartered in neighboring Wolica. We had no choice. We would cry and plead with Magda to let us in again. After all, she did say that if a few days passed quietly, she would reconsider.

---

2. A reference to Hershel, whose full name was Mordechai Tzvi

In the interim, we lay down in the drafty loft of Bogac's barn. With the wind blowing in from all sides, I could not possibly fall asleep; the narrow mattress and cover that our host had grudgingly given us barely sufficed for one person, let alone to keep the three of us warm. As I lay awake, I heard the dogs barking and thought I heard footsteps as well.

It seemed like a figment of my wild imagination: I received word that *baruch Hashem* the others were alive and had reached Debowiec, where they found a refuge that at first glance seemed quite satisfactory. They had some food to eat and their frozen hands and feet were able to recover from the harrowing ordeal of wandering around during the most frigid winter weather. They said that the three of us, too, could join them in Debowiec.

—

That a Polish peasant was still willing to risk his life these days, and that here in Debowiec, a burial ground of Jewish victims, we encountered six surviving Jews hiding in this very barn[3] — it is like a dream, a Heavenly revelation.

Soon after my arrival, I hear a voice calling up to the loft in Yiddish. There are *Yidden* here! Real living Jews, lone survivors who had experienced indescribable miracles. Their accounts

---

3.   Ed. Note: In a Yiddish-language chapter submitted to the *Sefer Yizkor shel Kehillat Dzialoszyce V'hasevivah* [translated in the *Dzialoszyce Memorial Book*, JewishGen, Inc., 2012], Dovid Wolgelernter expounded upon the events in this last chapter of his brother's diary: In mid-1943, the peasants in the Debowiec region, in fear of their lives, evicted the Jews they were harboring. With nowhere else to go, many of these Jews hid in the wheat fields, where the Nazis soon hunted them down, leaving their bodies lying among the wheat stalks; the corpses remained there until they were buried by Polish farmers during the harvest. Chaim and Roza Smolarczyk; their three children, Genia, Rivka, and Berl; and Roza's brother Zelman Gerszonowicz, who were staying at Franek Szczubial in Debowiec, were among those who were forced to leave. They took refuge in a hillside cave until their hideout was discovered, at which time they miraculously escaped and returned to Debowiec. These six Jews were living in a cramped pit under the floor of Biskup's barn for five months by the time the author and his group arrived in the loft above them.

overwhelm me. I realize that the troubles we endured are only a fraction of what they have gone through. These simple, earnest, good-hearted people are as overjoyed to see us as if we were their blood brothers.

"Are Jews still alive?" is the first thing I want to know. "Does our race still exist?"

"Yes!" is the answer I receive. "Jews still exist. But a different sort. These are not Jews in hiding, but young Jews, so-called partisans, who live openly and freely in the forests. With weapons in hand, they engage in battle with a powerful, brutal enemy that vastly outnumbers them. An enemy that murdered their fathers, mothers, sisters, brothers, and children. This small band of martyrs fearlessly avenges the blood of our people."

I cannot believe that the stories they tell about these Jewish warriors could be true; they sound like the stuff of legend. How can a handful of young Jews be capable of fighting the Germans? And aside from the obvious enemy, even worse are the Polish collaborators from whom it is impossible to protect oneself.

I lie there thinking. As I doze off, I am awakened by the loud barking of the dogs. I am very uneasy… I think I hear footsteps. But it soon grows quiet and I calm down. It must have been my wild imagination.

Just as I fall asleep — it is at least 4:00 a.m. by then — I feel a hand shaking me.

"What's the matter?" I ask, alarmed.

"Chaim'ke, wake up," someone whispers into my ear. "The Jewish partisans, four of them, are here."

Before I can orient myself, I hear the traditional *shalom aleichem* greeting and feel a warm Jewish hand reaching out to greet me in the dark. Approaching me with brotherly friendliness is the leader of the partisans. Although I cannot make out his face, hearing his *mamme lashon* I recognize thirty-year-old Avraham Szajnfeld, a

poultry dealer from Dzialoszyce. Father used to *shecht* chickens for him.

He tells the familiar, tragic refrain: he lost his father, mother, sisters, wife, and — his voice cracks — his only child, a three-year-old boy, a wunderkind. This proud Jewish fighter who feared nothing, this hardened Jewish warrior who had washed his hands in pulsing German blood, broke down at the mere mention of the name of his innocent child Shimmele. He has but one goal in life: to spill as much German blood as possible. *Revenge! Revenge!* With bated breath and intense concentration, I listen to the tales of his valiant battles.

As day dawns, I see the resolute and fearless look on his face, the fire of vengeance flashing from his eyes. This is how our heroes of old, the Chashmonaim, must have looked. I feel insignificant, small and humble in the presence of the great, proud Jewish soul found in the slight build of the young man sitting beside me. Here is a man living with purpose, a man who spills the blood of the murderers with his own hands, avenging the lives of my father and mother, my sister Yitta, and my beloved, unforgettable child. This man takes action so that my loved ones might rest in peace in their dark, unknown graves. If I had not felt embarrassed, I would have kissed him.

Later, the other three members of the group come up to the loft. There is Berel Jakubowiec from Dziewieczyce, an old friend of mine, a bright young man. He lost everything — his five brothers, fellow partisans; his parents; his nephews and nieces. He is completely alone. All he has is his rifle. This gives him the strength to go on. He, too, has a rich, heroic past. He has already avenged the blood of over twenty murdered family members.

The third partisan, Nosson Kielcer, is a wealthy textile dealer from Kozlow, where he owned two houses and was a distinguished member of his community. The sorrow of his tormented heart, the

painful memory of his young murdered wife and two children, is soothed only through his automatic pistol, which he immerses in the blood of the beastly murderers.

The fourth partisan, Avraham "Pelon" Fuhrman,[4] the youngest of the group, has also scored a respectable record of dead Germans.

"You see," they explain, "if our entire unit of twenty Jews would still be alive, the situation would look a lot better. But after a Pole betrayed us, the Germans ambushed our position and killed most of our comrades. In the meantime, we wander around. As soon as the weather warms up, we will regroup and return to the forest, and you will once again hear of our exploits."

I am stunned, completely hypnotized by their tales of vengeance against our bloody enemies. We need Jews like these. More power to you, dear brothers! May your courage continue to be strengthened.

I bow my head with respect and honor before such proud, valiant Jewish heroes. My spirits were uplifted, my soul rejuvenated by these four young men during the few days of their stay here.

[This is the end of the diary of Chaim Yitzchok Wolgelernter Hy"d.]

---

4. In his later years, Avraham Fuhrman recalled the spiritual fortitude Chaim Yitzchok and his family members exhibited. "They ate kosher food only — Biskup's wife brought eggs and potatoes to the loft — and they spent their time *davening* and learning." Furhman also elucidated some of the many moral dilemmas that arose. "Chaim Yitzchok wished to accompany me on my expeditions; he feared for my safety since I was so young. On the other hand, he felt his place was with the group. One day he did decide to come along with me. We partisans had a twofold mission: kill or sabotage Germans, and help Jews survive by any means possible. When Chaim Yitzchok witnessed our methods of extorting provisions from the Poles, he himself was loath to eat the food, but at the same time he said to me in a fatherly way, '*Mein kind, ess gezunterheit* — eat in good health, my child.'"

EPILOGUE

By Dovid Wolgelernter

Excerpted and translated from the
handwritten, Yiddish-language Epilogue
penned in the postwar years

To turn the pages back and recount all the events of one's life would be very difficult, since one does not remember everything and some things prefer not to be remembered. For us war survivors, relating our horrific experiences is to relive misfortunes whose suffering and anguish are unfathomable, reopening wounds which have not healed to this day, and will never, ever heal.

The pen is too weak, paper inadequate, to describe the greatest churban in the existence of the world. Nevertheless, it is worthwhile to convey even a drop in the ocean of our bitter tzaros to those who were not there and cannot imagine it. Only our deep longing for a better tomorrow gave us the strength to endure. At every opportunity, with every slight improvement, we thought, "Soon, soon the yeshuah is coming." But alas, after our group wandered and hid for nearly two years, only two of us remained.

It would be a great injustice on our part if we forgot the kedoshim as if they never existed. It is a holy obligation upon us to preserve their memories. And so the task of writing the epilogue to the Sefer Hadma'os, the unfinished, tragic story written by my brilliant elder brother Chaim Yitzchok Hy"d, has fallen on my shoulders.

Epilogue

IT WAS SIVAN, A WEEK after Shavuos, the beginning of June 1944. Outside, the fields of Debowiec were covered with sprouting greenery. The fragrant scent of spring wafted through the cracks in our barn loft.

We lay on the straw in a state of despair — Meir and I, Chaim Yitzchok, his mother-in-law Yachet Platkiewicz, Tzinne and Hershel and their sons Feivel and Reuven. Two partisans, Avraham Szajnfeld and Berel Jakubowiec, had decided to stay with us.

With no progress on any front, prospects for the war's end were dim. Although we had survived thus far, our refuge was uncertain once again. Our host Biskup was a volatile and corrupt peasant who continually threatened to evict us unless we gave him more money.

When we heard him climbing up the ladder one day, we figured he was coming to harass us as usual. His changed expression, however, told us he had good news.

"The Allies landed in France!" Biskup announced. "They are advancing upon Germany from the west!"

We were sure he had concocted the report in order to extract a reward from us, but he showed us the headlines in the latest newspaper. Concealing our excitement, we promised him money for liquor if he brought us the next day's paper. We could not sleep that night as we anxiously awaited Biskup's arrival with the morning news.

It was true! The Allies were pressing forward on all fronts. The journalists and pundits opined that Roosevelt, seeking another term in office, had stepped up the pace of the war to prove his mettle to the American voters.

We calculated that at this rate the war could be over in less than three months. Filled with euphoria, we began to discuss the future. My thought-out, practical brother Chaim Yitzchok, however, responded coolly to the news and warned us not to forget our precarious position. In fact, it only reinforced his sense that we would be wise to seek a more secluded and reliable hideout. The two partisans suggested a possibility in another hamlet.

Hershel, who was a great *talmid chacham*, agreed, noting that in the *tefillah* of *Hoshanos* we recite: "*Shalosh sha'os, hosha na* — During the three hours, O Hashem, please help us!" He inferred from this verse that even in the last three hours of one's ordeal, when salvation appears imminent, one cannot become complacent.

The rest of us accused the two of them of creating complications with their unwarranted pessimism. "Hashem helped us all this time," we argued. "Surely we will be redeemed soon."

Maintaining that one may not rely on a miracle, Chaim Yitzchok set out the following week with Avraham Szajnfeld and Berel Jakubowiec to search for a new shelter. We waited anxiously for three days until they finally returned, reporting that they had found an isolated farmstead on the outskirts of Berel's hometown of Dziewieczyce. The farmer, comfortable enough to supply us with abundant bread and other food items, needed extra money to cover the expenses of his daughter's forthcoming wedding. He had therefore agreed to take us in as long as our stay there was kept strictly secret, which suited us perfectly.

We all agreed to the idea of moving to the new hideout, and we began to ready ourselves. However, we could not leave until Hershel and Tzinne's daughter Esther'l came from Warsaw with money —

it was four weeks since she had last been here and she was due to visit us again in two weeks.

The next morning, Friday, June 16, we prepared a telegram addressed to Esther'l and asked Biskup to have his wife send it when she went into town. To our great surprise, he informed us that Esther'l had just arrived from Warsaw. We were overjoyed, especially since she confirmed that the war was indeed coming to an end.

That night, Chaim Smolarczyk and his brother-in-law Zelman Gerszonowicz paid us a visit. They were delighted that they had come just in time to see our important guest, who was beloved by all like an only child. We prepared a festive meal with the eggs, butter, and two fresh loaves of bread they had brought. Eating bread to our fill felt like a long-forgotten Yom Tov! We sat around chatting until late into the night, momentarily forgetting our difficult circumstances.

Zelman Gerszonowicz, 1950s

It was only in the morning that they explained the purpose of their visit: they had come to warn us to leave this place, the sooner the better. The day before, they had heard from a trustworthy Polish acquaintance that there was talk in the area that Biskup was harboring Jews. "If people are speaking about you openly, it is no small matter!" Chaim and Zelman cautioned us. "Do not put your lives at risk. The war might drag on. Every day is of the essence."

We decided to move to the new refuge at once. Esther'l would come along with us before returning to Warsaw. This way she would be able to find us on her next trip.

But how could we let our landlord Biskup know that we were leaving? He craved the fat fee we were paying him. On the other hand, if we left without notifying him, he would surely search us out and betray us.

We told him the truth. "We are leaving because there is a rumor circulating in Debowiec that you are harboring Jews."

He vehemently denied it. Clearly, he did not want to lose his profitable enterprise. The rumors did not concern him in the least. He figured the Germans would no longer be raiding the villages. And if the anti-Semitic Polish *Narodowas* found Jews in his barn, they might kill the Jews but would not harm him.

We paid no attention to his assurances and continued with our preparations. Two days before our planned departure date, we reassessed the situation: perhaps it was too risky for eleven people, carrying bundles on their backs, to travel together in one large group. Besides, it would be beneficial if a few of us went ahead and readied the new hideout.

Feivel Erlich and I were chosen to go ahead, escorted by Avraham Szajnfeld. At nightfall, I prepared a revolver — by now we had obtained and learned how to handle firearms — and we filled several rucksacks with most of the possessions in the loft, so that the larger group would be able to travel unencumbered.[1]

We agreed that if the three of us did not return to Debowiec the next night, the others would assume it was safe for them to leave on the following night. Berel Jakubowiec, armed with a rifle, would accompany the second group.

---

1. Ed. Note: In all probability, Dovid Wolgelernter carried his brother's writings with him to the new hideout at this time, saving the diary for posterity.

Mindful of the risk we were undertaking, our farewell was protracted and tearful. "May the *malachim* guard you on your way," eight voices fervently wished us, and we set out.

What are we doing? I reflected as we walked along under the dark, moonless sky. *Could we trust our new host? We do not even know him. Somehow, he seemed too eager to take us in. Are we going straight into the lion's den?*

Feivel interrupted my train of thought. "I think I see two men over there at the edge of the forest!" he whispered apprehensively. I pulled out my handgun, just to be sure. Coming closer we saw that the figures were merely two dead trees.

We continued on, treading lightly, the slightest rustle making our hearts pound so violently we could count each beat. When a faraway house light turned on, illuminating the night, we waited until it was extinguished before proceeding.

Oh, when will our sins be atoned for? I thought. *Do we Yidden deserve to be punished more than any of the nations? Are the rivers of innocent blood not full enough? How much longer will we have to prowl through the night like thieves?*

We soon made out three more figures in the distance. From their movements, we had no doubt this time that these were people. Not taking any chances, we fired at them and watched with relief as one man fell and two fled.

At 2:00 a.m., we finally arrived at our new quarters. Quietly, we squeezed into the barn through a loose board in the wall.

Our host, Julek Sito, entered the barn at daybreak. He seemed like a decent fellow, but we had learned that looks could be deceiving. He began to fashion a hideout out of piles of grain, leaving an opening on the side for an entrance. He then provided us with more bread than we could eat and plenty of potatoes, milk, and eggs. How fortunate that we would all be able to regain our strength before liberation!

Julian [Julek] Sito

We slept well that night.

In the morning, Sito brought us the newspaper. Russian forces had taken Vilna and were advancing on Grodno. In the west, too, the Allies were advancing rapidly. But our thoughts were focused on the members of our group who were scheduled to arrive that night.

After it grew dark, the three of us began peering through the cracks, straining our ears to pick up the sound of approaching footsteps. It was a pitch-dark, rainy night — 1 Tammuz, June 21, 1944. Hour after hour passed. At dawn we began to worry. Once the sun rose, they would no longer be able to travel. I banished the uneasy thoughts that entered my mind. They had probably postponed the trip because of the bad weather.

Exhausted from our all-night vigil, we lay down for a nap. No sooner had we dozed off than our host entered the barn. His expression told us that he had significant news. Probably a report from the front lines.

"Eight rich Jews were discovered and murdered in Debowiec!" he blurted.

His announcement hit us like a thunderbolt. Unaware of our relationship to the victims, Sito continued to relay the details. I could not listen any further. My head spun, my knees buckled. Everything turned black before my eyes. Choked with tears, Feivel and I could not utter a single word.

How had this happened? How could the Angel of Death have struck them down on the very night they were supposed to join us?

Our ominous premonitions had come true. Had the vile Biskup killed them himself? Was he an accomplice in their murder by *Endecja* (ND) party members? My face was aflame, my mind bursting with grief and guilt. What had I done? Why had I so easily parted from my brothers?

Dear beloved brothers of mine, why have you left me behind? I wept. *What am I worth without you? What purpose shall I live for and how will I continue on my own? Would that I had been taken together with you!*

In one fell swoop, twenty-one-year-old Feivel Erlich was bereft of his parents and two siblings. Following in the footsteps of his devout father Hershel, Feivel declared: "'*Hashem nassan v'Hashem lakach* — G-d gave and G-d has taken.' Only after Hashem takes back do we fully appreciate what He had given us."

Indeed, as I lay there in a daze, I visualized the images of the *kedoshim*, each one a priceless treasure.

Chaim Yitzchok, my saintly older brother, a tremendous talmid chacham with a brilliant mind, one of the outstanding talmidim of the Ostrovtzer Rebbe Reb Yechezkele... A shining star on the Torah horizon, he was the pride of our family. We bowed our heads before him with respect for his depth of understanding in all areas as well as his extraordinary personality. Anyone who became acquainted with him was enamored with his warmth and friendliness. He cared for me with his heart and soul, as a father to his child. All my life I looked up to Chaim'l, proud that he was my brother. Now, after twenty months in hiding, his promising future was gone, vanished, and along with it my own prospects, too.

Meir Shmuel Eliyahu, Meir'l, my younger brother, whose soul was bound with mine... When our lives were spared and we found each other in the Kazimierz mikveh, we promised we would never separate from one another. Come what may, we would share the same fate. "I will help accompany the women, who are in a weakened state, on this difficult trip," offered Meir. "We will be together again in a day." But, alas, this bitter tragedy had mercilessly separated us forever, and I was alone... What a tall, distinguished-

looking young man Meir was, wise beyond his years, a gifted scribe with a great future before him. The Angel of Destruction had wiped it all away.

Yachet Platkiewicz, Chaim'l's devout, pure, righteous mother-in-law... She spent her days in the loft davening and saying Tehillim with its Yiddish translation. She refused to compromise on her standards of kashrus. "Babbeshe, how will you have strength to survive?" Feivel and Reuven asked her. To which she replied: "Don't we say every day, 'Hanosein laya'eif koach — G-d is the One Who gives strength to the weary!'" She accepted her suffering with equanimity, living with the hope that she would survive her travails and continue her life of generosity and good deeds. Sadly, it was not to be.

Hershel (Mordechai Tzvi) Erlich, a great talmid chacham and yerei Shamayim... A disciple of the Sochatchover Rebbe and a ben bayis by the Kozhiglover Rav, Rav Aryeh Frommer, Hershel observed the mitzvos scrupulously and carefully guarded his speech. During our time in hiding, his mouth did not cease to utter words of Gemara, mishnayos, or tefillos that he remembered by heart. His concern for all of us in the loft was boundless; I had lost in him a devoted father.

Tzinne Erlich, a soft-spoken, refined, righteous woman, mother of five outstanding children... She accepted the difficult conditions without complaint and endured the tragic loss of her youngest, Gittele, who took ill during their wanderings from one hideout to another. Now, the dragnet of death swallowed her, too, along with her husband Hershel and two more precious children, Reuven and Esther'l.

Fifteen-year-old Avraham Reuven Erlich... What an exceptionally bright boy he was; his father placed great hope in him. They learned together from memory day and night in the hideout. His soul, too, had been plucked by this unnatural death.

Sixteen-year-old Esther Erlich... A lovely rose, a remarkably intelligent girl who risked her life to save her parents, visiting us regularly to bring the money we needed for our survival. Her arrival was always greeted with joy and festivity. With a comforting word for each person, she infused new life

into our group. "Don't worry, Babbeshe," she would tell her grandmother, "it won't be too much longer. For every day of suffering, you will be granted a good year." To her father she would say, "I never forget that we have a G-d Who will take pity on us. Pray that I be safe on my dangerous travels." To us she said, "You have lost your devoted sister Yitta'le. I will be like a sister to you and help you just as I help my own family." Indeed, we saw in her our unforgettable sister and found solace in her presence. Now the light in her eyes had been extinguished in the prime of her life, reopening my wound.

Berel Jakubowiec, a courageous partisan who sacrificed his life to help us... He was to be the leader and protector of the group. Instead, he fell victim along with the others even before setting out on the risky journey. The last survivor of a family of heroic brothers, he had escaped many a danger. Not one German whom he encountered had slipped his grasp. Now he was unable to elude his own murderer.

When I came out of my reverie, I contemplated whether I had anything left to live for. My cherished sister Yitta had been gunned down by a German soldier as she tried to slip into her hideout in the Kazimierz courthouse. My beloved parents were shot dead in the Slonowice forest. This tragedy was my third heavy blow.

Turning to Avraham Szajnfeld, I cried out, "Was our suffering of two years for naught? How long can a person endure such pain? I have decided to take my life."

At that, Avraham jumped up. "You should drive such thoughts from your mind!" he chided me. "How would that benefit the unfortunate victims? Perhaps your life was spared so you could avenge their innocent blood. Perhaps you were saved because you are destined to tell future generations what the Germans did to the Jewish nation. I know how much you have lost, but it is all part of the collective suffering of our people. And our Sages say that just as one blesses G-d when good things happen, one must bless G-d by reciting 'Baruch Dayan ha'emes' when bad things happen.

"Look, dear Dovid," he continued. "From now on I will be your brother. We will stick together. Wherever you go, I will go. Let us continue to have faith that this bitter war will come to an end and the cup of pain and sorrow will be full at last."

Avraham Szajnfeld

The exalted perspective of this noble Jewish partisan lifted my spirits.

I thought of the two remaining orphaned Erlich children — Chayele (Helenka), living in Warsaw with false papers, and Feivel, with me in our new hideout. *May the remnant of their distinguished family live on and avenge the blood of the kedoshim*, I prayed.

I thought, too, of Chaim Yitzchok's unfortunate widow Chayele and their young orphaned son Feivele who barely knew his extraordinary father. Unbeknownst to them, while living with false papers at Mrs. Stepanowa in Jedlnia, their crown had been taken, their sun had gone down, plunging their lives into darkness. Maybe we would be able to help them somehow.

In the weeks that followed, we were consumed with grief and had to use all our energy just to go on living. At the same time, the news from the battlefield became very encouraging. The Germans were suffering one defeat after another and the Russian army was coming closer every day. We could hear the sound of artillery shells exploding in the distance.

One Friday night our host came up to the barn loft. "Several houses in the village are on fire. My farm may be next," he said.

"I'm going into the forest to take shelter until the battle ends. Do you want to come along?"

"No, we'll stay here," we replied, afraid the villagers would discover us.

Later that night, Sito returned from the forest and came running up to the loft. "You are free!" he cried at the top of his voice. "You are free! The Russians are here!"

We were speechless. Should we rejoice? Should we laugh and dance with happiness? Overwhelmed with emotion, we broke into uncontrollable sobbing, spasms of pain and grief mingling with gladness and relief. It was only a few months since our loved ones had perished. Couldn't they, too, have lived to see this moment?

You are free! the farmer had shouted. But what did that mean? Where were our parents, brothers and sisters? Where was our home? Where were we to go? Bewildered, we did not know what to do next. Sito suggested that we stay a while longer until things settled down. His wife came in to share her joy with us, apologizing that the meals

Sito's daughter (c) and her family, with whom Dovid Wolgelernter maintained contact for many years

were not always perfect. "But the main thing is, you are free," she said.

Impatient to see the world, Avraham went to Dzialoszyce. There he met hundreds of Russian soldiers, many of whom were Jews. They had learned of the *churban* of the Jewish people and the torment we had gone through. There were no other Jews in town. We thought we must be the only survivors of the inferno.

Gradually, Jews returned from the camps and from various hideouts: emaciated skeletons, lone survivors of entire families and villages. We grouped together, sharing stories of both loss and survival. One man told me the following incident:

"A few months ago, three of us were on the road one night when we saw three other men in the distance. Suddenly, a revolver bullet almost hit me and I fell from fright while my two friends fled. Can you imagine? I nearly became a victim in the last weeks before liberation!"

When I questioned him, I realized that these were the men Feivel and I had fired at, thinking they were the enemy! Such was the vulnerability of a Jew during those tragic times.

Avraham, Feivel, and I moved into an apartment in Dzialoszyce near my sister-in-law Chayele and her little Feivele, who had returned from Jedlnia. For a long time, I walked around hunched, with my head down; in our attic hideouts we had been unable to stand fully erect. And, like other survivors, every time I stepped outside I looked around furtively to make sure I was safe. Fear was a constant companion.

After a few weeks, Avraham Szajnfeld left for the city of Pinczow, where he had received a prominent position in the police department in recognition of his partisan activities during the war.

As for me, penniless and without decent clothes or shoes, I decided to travel to my family home in Kazimierza Wielka, where

some of our possessions were hidden. Avraham gladly agreed to come from Pinczow to escort me.

~

I walked through the streets of my hometown with a pounding heart. Polish acquaintances recognized me. "Ah, the rabbi's son!" they exclaimed, their smiling faces belying their discomfort at seeing a former Jewish neighbor returning. I could not look at them. By not helping us on that ill-fated expulsion day, every one of them was guilty in my eyes.

The Jewish area that had once pulsated with life was now empty, bleak, and eerily quiet. Arriving at the house where we used to live, I felt dizzy and faint. Willing myself to hurry and take care of what I had come for, I knocked on the door. The lady of the house told me that her husband had died. Assuming a pained expression, she wrung her hands and declared, "When the Jews were deported from Kazimierz, I could not eat all day!"

I asked her about the things we had hidden in the attic.

"I don't know anything about that," she replied. "My husband took care of such matters, but he passed away." Seeing the uniformed Avraham with me, she added, "You are welcome to go up to the attic and look around."

With a trembling hand, I removed the board, revealing the neatly wrapped parcel containing our possessions. Everything was in perfect order. Yet it granted me no pleasure. It only awakened the memory of when we had all stood there. "Let our worldly goods disintegrate," we had prayed, "as long as we live to come back here together." Sadly, neither prayer was fulfilled. Everything was as good as new, but to my great grief and heartache, the rest of my family was not here with me.

First I unpacked my father's new *bekeshe*; the *gartel* and the yarmulke were in the pocket where he had placed them. I could still hear him say, "When the war is over, I will put it on for the

first time and say *Shehecheyanu*." Near it was the beautiful dress my mother wore only on Yom Tov. In its pocket I found the tear-soaked handkerchief she had used on her last Yom Kippur when she *davened* for us to be saved from the impending disaster. Next, I took out Meir's Shabbos suit, which was folded together with mine. My suit had found its owner, but who would wear my brother's suit?

Stored in a separate box were my sister Yitta's clothes and part of her trousseau, set aside for her future marriage. I found the challah cover and the Pesach matzah cover she had skillfully embroidered, but who would use them? Each article stared at me blankly, reminding me of my dear parents and my beloved sister and brothers.

Noticing my tearstained face, Avraham quickly boxed the items and tied up the cartons, and we traveled back to Dzialoszyce. It took me a long time to recuperate.

⚡

I tried to start life anew, but it soon became apparent that living among the anti-Semitic Poles was fraught with danger. Not a day went by without reports of Jews around the country being harassed or attacked, even killed, by Poles who apparently could not accept the fact that Jews had survived and were returning to their hometowns. Since Jews were more vulnerable in the smaller towns, Feivel and I decided to leave Dzialoszyce and relocate to the city of Gleiwitz in western Poland where there was a larger survivor population.

Before leaving the region, we were determined to find out where our murdered family members had been buried. Five of us traveled to Debowiec on that day one year after the tragedy: Chayele, little Feivele, Feivel Erlich and I, escorted by Avraham Fuhrman, fellow partisan and cousin of the murdered Berel Jakubowiec.

Biskup, who had undoubtedly taken part in the massacre, stayed out of sight. We went up to the barn loft. Our hideout was untouched; everything was as it had been a year earlier.

If this place could speak, I thought, *it would tell us of the last minutes of the kedoshim before their souls ascended to Heaven. We would surely hear how they begged for their lives: "Don't kill us! What harm have we done to you? Why would you murder innocent people?" But it was all in vain. Their pleas fell on deaf ears. The Poles callously butchered eight pure souls.*

Why...?! Why...?!

We could not ask questions. It was a *gzar din*, a Heavenly decree. The Gates of Mercy were closed. And we, the survivors, had to go on with our anguished lives.

A neighbor showed us the spot where the bodies had been hastily buried in one grave. The earth was still fresh. As we stood there with bowed heads and aching hearts, I was reminded of the verse, *"Mah nora hamakom hazeh* — How awesome and holy is this place!"

Sobbing bitterly, Chayele threw herself on the *kever*, grieving for her dear mother, eldest sister, and beloved husband Chaim'l, the light of her life.

Avraham Fuhrman

We stayed there for a long time, absorbed in our sorrowful thoughts. It was difficult to tear ourselves away, but at last Avraham told us it was time to leave. I said Kaddish with little Feivele.

"When is Father coming home?" he asked sweetly. His mother had always assured him, "When we come back home to Dzialoszyce, *Tatteshe* will join us and we'll be together again." How he longed to see the father he remembered only through the picture he clutched.

We left, feeling dejected and inconsolable as after a *levayah*. Our only solace was the thought that there remained one glowing ember of the radiance of our glorious family: young Feivele, a bright child, who we trusted

would follow in the footsteps of his great father and forge a new link in the golden chain of tradition of our saintly ancestors.

After pondering the tragic ordeals that we endured, one must conclude that a Divine Hand directs the world. Despite the great catastrophe that befell us, unparalleled in the history of mankind, and despite having lost our greatest tzaddikim, the Jewish nation has risen once again. Netzach Yisrael lo yeshaker. Hashem has not abandoned His people.

For over twenty-six months, I was sealed off from the world. Nature, which was created for every living creature down to the smallest worm, did not exist for us. After liberation, the first time I saw a Yid, I fell upon him and was unable to speak. We did not need to speak. Our eyes told it all. We had been orphaned as one. Thus, for me, every gathering of Jews is a great simchah.

We may not allow the churban to break our spirits and strip us of our emunah and bitachon.

Dovid Wolgelernter, 1996

Because at the same time that we looked death in the eye on more than one occasion, we saw and had opportunity to be convinced of the Hashgachah Pratis, the Heavenly determination of the destiny of every individual Jew who was saved from the hands of the murderers.

It was extremely difficult for the survivors to make a decision to go on with normal life. We were so depressed, so broken physically and mentally, despairing of life and pessimistic about the future. But we came to the realization that we must continue to build and create new generations and that this would be the greatest revenge against our enemies who desired to exterminate the Jewish nation, to uproot the Jewish tree at its roots.

How true are the words of our Sages: "Even if a sharp sword rests on a person's throat, he should not refrain from praying for mercy."

BOOK TWO

Survival and Renewal

PART ONE
By Chayele [Wolgelernter] Finkelstein[1]

I WAS HAPPILY MARRIED and a mother of two young children when the Germans besieged my hometown of Dzialoszyce.

On September 2, 1942, moments before the start of the *Aussiedlung* in which 1500 Jews were murdered and thousands deported, I fled to the countryside along with my mother and nineteen-month-old Feivele. After several harrowing days, we found a peasant who agreed to shelter us until the storm blew over. In the interim, to my great anguish, I learned that my beloved firstborn child Alte'le, who was not yet three years old, was among those rounded up in the market square and deported to an unknown destination,[2] along with my sister Reizele.

---

1. Based on oral testimony provided in taped interviews conducted in 1993 and 1994 by grandson Chaim Yitzchok Wolgelernter; a 1998 letter to the family; and many conversations over the decades. Portions of the narrative synopsize, or elaborate upon, corresponding parts of the diary.

2. Later determined to be the Belzec extermination camp, where over 500,000 Jews were gassed to death upon arrival from March to December 1942. Only a handful managed to escape.

I soon reunited with my husband and other family members who had taken refuge in another village in the area. Shortly before Sukkos 1942, when it seemed the worst was over, we returned to Dzialoszyce.

It wasn't long before we began to hear rumors that a second *Aussiedlung* was imminent. Chaim Yitzchok, who could not pass for a non-Jew, procured forged identity cards for me and for Feivele, and in November 1942, our entire family went into hiding once again.

I desperately wanted all of us to stay together. However, life in hiding, my husband pointed out, meant confinement in decrepit barns, exposure to frigid winter weather, a meager diet, and the possibility of having to flee at a moment's notice — hardly sustainable conditions for a young child.

When Mrs. Aubrien, a Polish officer's wife who had frequented our textile shop, agreed, for a hefty sum, to accompany me and little Feivele to Warsaw, my brother Yisroel warned: "Dear sister, do you realize that each infraction — leaving town limits, traveling by rail, and possessing forged identity papers — is punishable by death?" I knew, too, that even if I did reach Warsaw safely, life in disguise was fraught with danger and required extreme vigilance.

I was despondent and torn.

With Chaim Yitzchok's urging, I made the wrenching decision to go my own way, so that our lone remaining child might survive. I took leave of my husband, my mother, my sister Tzinne'le and her family, and brother Yisroel and his family — never to see them again.

Escorted by Mrs. Aubrien, I set out with Feivele and my niece Esther'l, who was returning to Warsaw to rejoin her older sister Chayele. Unwittingly, we left at a particularly dangerous time: a deportation was in progress at the Miechow rail station. Sheer miracles saw us through the daunting challenges of our journey.

Then, just as we alighted from the train in Warsaw, a Gestapo agent in civilian clothes stopped us. Mrs. Aubrien, who bore impeccable papers, insisted that she had met us on the train. He released her, along with blonde, blue-eyed Esther'l. Feivele and I, and the porter as well, were taken to Gestapo headquarters. May I always have the strength to pray as intensely as I did when I climbed the stairs of the Gestapo building that day!

The agent sat down at his desk in the corner of a large office, studied my identity papers and wrote at length in a notebook. Uniformed officers and civilians alike walked back and forth through the office. No one took any notice of us, nor did anyone ask the agent what he was doing or who we were; apparently, he was a very important personage. I stood there composedly, masking my inner anxiety and fright, while Feivele played with some objects on the desk. Suddenly, the Gestapo agent looked up at me and said, "I suspect that you are Jewish."

"That is not true," I stated emphatically.

He repeated his assertion three times. Each time I denied it. Then he said, "You will have to defend yourself before a higher authority."

I remained silent and did not plead for mercy. He continued writing notes. Suddenly, he directed the porter, who had been standing there listening to our exchange, to leave the office.

Turning to me, the agent asked, "Do you want to live?"

"Do *you*?" I countered. "How much is it worth?" I had a substantial amount of currency with me.

"One thousand zlotys," was his answer.

I handed him the money. He took my hand and said, "May you survive the war and live happily."

Over the years, I often pondered: *No Jew who entered those portals exited a free man. Surely this was no real Gestapo agent but Eliyahu Hanavi in the form of a Nazi officer!*

Chayele Wolgelernter's false identity card

When I left, I was convinced that the agent would have me followed. The elderly porter was afraid to take me to my destination. There I stood outside the Gestapo building in the virtually *Judenrein* city of Warsaw, with my suitcases on the stairs and a heavy child in my arms. Taking pity on me, the porter agreed to carry my baggage down for an additional fee. Esther'l, who had been anxiously waiting nearby, was relieved to find me unharmed.

For three weeks, we were forced to keep moving, as one landlord after another suspected that I was a Jew. Although I had excellent forged papers, I could not register as a legal resident of Warsaw since I bore no documents verifying my place of origin.

Desperate, I recalled an ill-reputed Polish teacher in Dzialoszyce who had mentioned that his mother might sublet a room in her cottage in the village of Jedlnia near Radom. Since it was a journey of some 120 kilometers (seventy-five miles) from Warsaw, Esther'l traveled there with Mrs. Aubrien. The village priest directed them

to the elderly widow, who agreed to take us in for a substantial monthly fee.

It was November 30, 1942 when Helena Palek, twenty-two-month-old Felusz Palek, and fourteen-year-old Marisia Novak arrived in Jedlnia.[3]

Mrs. Marta Stepanowa was a devoutly Catholic, old-school anti-Semitic woman who genuinely believed that Jews use Christian blood for baking Passover matzah. She took us in primarily for monetary reasons. As the widow of an army officer, her government pension was a mere 250 zlotys a month; hence, the tenfold monthly rent she demanded of us made her risk worthwhile, especially since we bore Aryan papers. Only due to Chaim Yitzchok's foresight in acquiring gold coins at the start of the war was I able to pay such a

Mrs. Marta Stepanowa, 1947

Mrs. Stepanowa's daughter Krystyna

3. Esther'l — "Marisia" — alternated between her aunt Chayele in Jedlnia and her sister Chayele — "Helenka" — in Warsaw. In addition, she spent short periods of time with her parents and siblings when delivering funds to the group in hiding.

sum. Nonetheless, she was a decent person who took a liking to me and treated me hospitably.

Ironically, her anti-Semitic views safeguarded our identity. It was a while before anyone suspected that this woman's boarders were Jews. In addition, since she was a well-liked, respected person, I was fairly certain the villagers would not inform on us.

Religious zeal was another motive. Mrs. Stepanowa tried to convince me that the Jewish nation was suffering retribution for spurning Christianity. She encouraged me to come to church with her, in the hope that I would agree to be baptized. This was her opportunity to save three souls! I had no idea how to conduct myself there but was obliged to go along. Little Feivele came, too,

(l-r) Chayele Wolgelernter, Krystyna, daughter of Mrs. Miredski (owner of cottage)

Feivele, mid-1944

dressed for the occasion, and I was fortunate that he had not yet learned to speak Yiddish else he might have betrayed us. One day, I was called upon to sing in the church choir. After that experience, I avoided going again.

From November 1942 to February 1945, although I lived in comparative safety and ease, I faced the challenge of caring for my young child alone while vigilantly guarding our assumed identity. I was also plagued with unrelenting anxiety over the fate of my husband, mother, and siblings. I knew that they were living in various hideouts under dreadful conditions and were at great risk of being discovered.

After the group found refuge in Skalbmierz, and later in Debowiec, Esther'l or Chayele would travel there from time to time to deliver funds. This enabled me to hear news of my family members and to correspond with them.[4]

Letter received by Chayele Wolgelernter from her mother and husband hiding in Magda's loft in Skalbmierz [January 1944][5]

Lieb kind Chayele,

First I must thank you for the treats you sent. We enjoyed them very much.

You write that you feel sorry for me for having only dry bread to eat. Let me tell you, do not have any heartache about it. Praised be G-d that I can eat the slice of dry bread. May Hashem help us not to lack anything, and may we be liberated very soon.

My dear child, I beg of you to see to it not to let your little boy stay in the house by himself, if at all possible. And please buy a pair of shoes for him.

4. Only the letters *received* by Chayele are extant.

5. Ed. Note: The setting of each letter has been determined from its contents.

Imagine how I feel, Chayele, realizing that fourteen months have gone by since I last saw you, and the same goes for Yisroel. At least you keep me informed, but I have not heard from Yisroel in a long while. May G-d help that we should see each other again very soon.

I implore you — don't get upset about anything. Remember, nowadays nobody has it easy. May Hashem help us and save us, amen. I have nothing more to write — my eyes are melting with tears. May G-d help us to be redeemed soon.

Regards to Esther'l and to your dear little son. May we see each other again very soon,

Your mother

P.S. Please do not send us anything as it is too much trouble for you.

My dearest one and only Chayele!

I write to you again in Yiddish, the language of our happiest times, and it is precisely because of those times that I direct these lines to you. You punish our darling child, my only consolation, the innocent little angel who shares our dismal fate? He knows his father only through the stories you tell him. In his imagination he dreams of meeting me. He is happy with every smile you grant him. How can you be cross with him? Let me assure you that this affects me more than him. I endure my present gehinnom only in the hope of seeing both of you again.

Believe me, although I am far away from you and do not experience all the details as you do, I understand the causes of your aggravation just as if I were there with you. But you should understand that the whole situation we are in is unnatural. In today's chaotic, abnormal times we must not allow ourselves to get upset over these things, but should daven to Hashem to bring salvation.

Chayele, why don't you buy a pair of shoes for our child? I am sending you two pieces of leather, and I ask that you have a shoemaker fashion a nice pair of shoes for him. If the leather is not suitable, go ahead and sell it, and let the shoemaker produce a sturdy pair of shoes. I am also sending you my suit. Please have it cleaned and pressed, because I have no space for storing it here. Besides, a

situation may arise in which we will need to sell it — after all, nowadays you never can tell what surprises are in store for us — so it is best that you keep the suit. With Hashem's help, if you will not need to sell it, so much the better.

Our financial situation is as follows: For November and December we paid 8000 zlotys each month — Magda took advantage of us for those two months. However, for the month of January we convinced her to settle for 5000zł. What will be in the coming months I do not know. I want to point out that although we have been staying at her place for more than a year, we cannot figure her out. She is a strange and unpredictable woman. Occasionally, she goes crazy, treating us cruelly and acting as if she might turn us in, and we think that we are finished. Then again, at times she acts kindly and humanely. One thing we know for sure: she has an insatiable craving for money, and that is our salvation. That is why I keep urging you to collect as much as possible of the outstanding debts from our Polish acquaintances, so that we will not have to rely on changing the last of our gold coins. As I mentioned numerous times, we must reserve the gold coins for an emergency when we will need it to save ourselves. One may not rely on a miracle that the war will end shortly. We have heard such reports over and over again. I am not saying that the end isn't near — with Hashem's help anything is possible — but it is wise to have reserves on hand.

We had made several plans for Helenka's current visit. She was to go to Dzialoszyce, spend the night at Mrs. Piestrzeniewicz's house and go around making collections from there. At this time of year, when the daylight hours are short and the nights are long, one can move about with confidence and much could be accomplished. But my plans came to nothing. My old sense of egotism took over. Wouldn't it be easier if I went? However, for the time being, I do not feel that I should be the one to go. Helenka says that she will try to get Mrs. Wisniewski and Esther'l to go. She is afraid, and I cannot prevail upon her. I just know one thing: When times were good and we could travel freely without obstacles, nobody did anything. We must all bear the guilt for neglecting to arrange for debt collections more often during the good times when things were easy. Unfortunately, the past

cannot be retrieved. So now it has to be done this way. I have no solution for the problem. The money will last until it runs out. That is the reason I am sending you my suit to have on hand for an emergency. And perhaps Hashem will indeed help us before then. Do not worry about me. G-d will not abandon us. He has saved me from greater perils. Nothing will happen because of a lack of money. You know how we live here. Baruch Hashem we have dry bread and potatoes to keep us alive. We hope and pray that we should at least have this much until we are rescued.

But I beg of you once more to have mercy on me, on yourself and on our child, and do not cause yourself any aggravation. Our boy should not be deprived of anything, not even a smile. Please write and let me know that you had a pair of nice, sturdy shoes made for him. Let Helenka mail your letter in Warsaw, or perhaps Esther'l will come here and bring it along.

Helenka tells me that Mrs. Stepanowa is sometimes annoyed with you. You chop wood and do other similar things on Sunday. Is it worth it? Just remember that you should thank Hashem every minute of the day that you are in a house with our sweet little child. That is no small thing. We are sitting here for the second winter in a cold, drafty barn loft, and we thank G-d for that, too. It no longer bothers me. I have a whole day to learn a little bit of Torah — it just so happens that I found sefarim here from a previous Jewish tenant. The rest of the day I record everything we have gone through. I am sending you herewith a chapter of my work.

Strengthen yourself, Chayele. With Hashem's help we will be liberated very soon. Regards to Esther'l, and loving kisses to my dear child.

With fervent longing,
Your Chaim

Letter received by Chayele Wolgelernter from her husband
hiding in new quarters in Debowiec [winter 1944]

Dear Chayele,

I send you herewith a poem that I composed especially for you. It is just a fragment of my large collection, the fruit of my literary creativity. Don't scan it casually — contemplate and feel it. For it expresses my heart and soul, tears and blood. Too bad that I cannot send you all my writings on various themes. From time to time I will send you something.

I also devoted a special chapter[6] in my "Book of Tears" to Mrs. Stepanowa, which I will translate into Polish. I am sure she will be pleased. Esther'l will tell you more about it.

In short, if G-d helps us and we survive, I aspire to take a place in the literary world. This is only thanks to the war — I would have gladly given up this career and kept my old one.

Chayele, I hope that by Esther'l joining you, your situation will improve. It will be easier for you when you need to sell something. In general, taking care of everything yourself is not easy, but that is the way it is. Be strong and full of hope.

Our situation here has temporarily worsened. We had to vacate our quarters for a short while, and that's why Esther'l had to go back. But with G-d's help everything will blow over and things will work out. Esther'l will tell you everything. If she can stay with you, so much the better. If not, maybe she can stay with Helenka.

Chayele, I remind you again, whether Esther'l stays with you or not, see to it to go out and buy butter, milk, and some meat. You are allowed to eat non-kosher meat on my responsibility. It is a question of saving your life — you must have strength to survive. And in light of our staggering expenses, spending a few hundred zlotys more each month won't make a difference. I believe you sent someone to collect

6.   See Appendix B: *Righteous Gentiles*

unpaid bills from Mrs. Piusi and Mrs. Wrubel, and I am sure Mrs. Yanowski paid an installment. We won't go bankrupt, chalilah. With G-d's help we might even have a new source of income. Esther'l will explain everything.

I am sending you now the items from Wrubel. You'll see if you can sell them. You should always have some money in reserve as well as valuables to fall back on since one never knows what might happen.

Don't worry about us. True, we had to leave temporarily, but thank G-d we have a place to stay, and maybe it will be even better. So you see, baruch Hashem we are not in distress.

When Esther'l or Helenka come next, please send along a detailed letter and a picture of you and our little Feivele. Let me know if Mrs. Yanowski has a little boy's suit for him. Or maybe you can have a suit made from Esther'l's jacket — she says that she can't wear it anymore. It would make a nice summer suit. Esther'l tells me that he has no undergarments. My poor little boy! For the time being I cannot send any clothing of mine. I gave everything away to people who are more destitute. With Hashem's help, I will find an opportunity to send some fabric.

Please write to me about everything, with all the particulars. But use the mail as little as possible, and certainly do not send a registered letter. In a small village, such letters arouse suspicion.

Again, if you can earn money by selling some of our merchandise, that would be best. Although we still have enough gold coins in reserve with Helenka, we need to save it for an emergency. You never know, in a time like this a situation may come up where extra currency would be very helpful.

I repeat, do not worry about us. We thank and praise Hashem that we left that mean and dishonest Magda. Over here things are better all around. The main thing is, be strong! With G-d's help, this will all pass, and perhaps it is not so far off.

You, Esther'l, and Feivele should eat and drink whatever is available. I give you permission to eat everything. Please send a letter at the earliest opportunity.

Make sure to give me a comprehensive report and include a picture. Let me know if you like my writing — it is my daily occupation in these times. Everything else you will hear from Esther'l.

> My heartfelt wishes to you along with my precious Feivele,
>
> Chaim'l

Now, dear Chayele, besides the fabric I prepared for Esther'l to take, I am also sending you a batch of material cut to size into six sections. A neighbor of ours cut the material but he does not have a shop to do the sewing. If I had ready-made garments, they could easily be sold, but the cut sections are just lying around and not coming to any use. I explained to Esther'l how these sections should be sewn together. Please go to a tailor right away and have him produce the garments. It shouldn't cost a lot. When it is done, send everything back here at the earliest opportunity. If you can sell them there for at least 200 zlotys apiece or better, go ahead and sell them. But you should definitely send two or three garments here. I am also including brown thread to make three small satchels from the material. Please take care of this right away, and send the garments as soon as you have a chance.

Chayele, remember, if anyone goes to the Polish woman, please write a note asking her to let you have the few meters of green cloth lying covered up in her attic. My trousers are worn out and it's a shame to put on my new ones for I may have to sell them. Besides, I need a durable pair. If you can have trousers made of that green material, you can estimate the waist more or less, and the length should be one meter. That should be long enough, for I push the ends into my boots. Otherwise they wear out in no time. And it is a pity to ruin my good suit. Once again I ask you to write to me and to take care of the abovementioned things. Regards from everyone here, and in particular from your dear mother,

> Chaim'l

Ode to Chayele[7]

When you extend your arms embracing our child,
Clasping him close to your motherly heart,
Suddenly, the hermetically sealed gates of sadness
Of my troubled, anguished spirit
Swing wide open,
And a gentle breeze of hope wafts in.
Yes, all is not lost;
My life is still worth living.

For there is Feivele, my ray of consolation,
Lighting up the dark abyss
Of our shared tragedy —
Our never-to-be-forgotten Alte'le,
Torn away from us.

Here in the putrid Debowiec pigsty
I sense the aroma of his youthful, springtime fragrance
Intoxicating me, banishing the murky mist
That oppresses our souls like a turbulent nightmare.

Chayele, tell our darling little son
About the condemned-to-death father he does not know;
Let the innocent, pure little child
Pray to Almighty G-d, the Merciful,
To call an end to our suffering and distress,
That I may merit to live to see you both again.

---

7. These stanzas comprise the second half of an intimate poem in which the author expressed his yearning for his beloved wife and child.

Letter received by Chayele Wolgelernter from her mother, brother-in-law
Hershel Erlich, and husband hiding in Debowiec [March 1944]

Lieb kind Chayele,

I really have no particular reason for writing to you. I pray that Hashem help
us. My dear child, I want to tell you not to be too strict on yourself. Indulge a little.
Have a hearty meal and drink a cup of milk to give you the strength to endure
everything. Dear child, may G-d help us to be set free from this bitter galus. I have
nothing else to report. May Hashem Yisbarach help us soon. I can write no more for
my heart is melting, my eyes brimming with tears. My best wishes to you and your
dear child. May Hashem help that we see each other again,

Your mother Yachet

P.S. As a special request, dear child, I ask you to live in harmony with Esther'l.
You know that peace is the underpinning of the world. True, there is no peace
today, but we hope that G-d will help us. And so I ask you, dear child, to be kind
to Esther'l. After all, she is my grandchild, just like one of my own children. Dear
Chayele, I write from the depths of my heart! Oh, how I long for the moment when
we see each other again, I hope very, very soon.

My dear worthy sister-in-law,

I take this opportunity to write a few lines to you. I know and feel that you
esteem and trust me like a devoted brother. Therefore, allow me to write a few
words of mussar. Esther'l told us that you look emaciated and that you are very
tense. That is hardly surprising, seeing that we are living in a time of unequaled
harshness. That's why we must strengthen ourselves and place our hope in Hashem
Yisbarach. Our very existence is a string of wonders and miracles, and we trust that
Hashem will help us so that we will once more rejoice. But we have to weather the
storm!

My Esther'l does not feel well. She has a cough. I know that you live on a meager
diet. You make do without butter, sugar, and flour. But you are committing a
grave sin. You know that in Heaven every Jewish child is as precious as a diamond.

That's why you must guard your health. I beg of you for your own sake and for my Esther'l's sake, take care of yourself and eat a better dinner. If you have pity on yourself and on my child, Hashem Yisbarach will have pity on all of us, and He will help us and deliver us.

Best regards to you and your dear son. Hoping to be reunited soon,
Your brother-in-law Tzvi

Dear Chayele,

I am very surprised that you did not send me a letter with Esther'l. I found out that you keep up your ascetic diet of dry bread and potatoes without any proteins. You are afraid that you will run out of food. I even thought of not writing to you anymore. Well, if your mind is made up, what can I do? But the situation we are in is too dismal and grave, and you have too much heartache and pain as it is, that I should add to your misery by not writing to you. But I want you to know that the grief your conduct is causing me is greater than the pain you are suffering. I cannot understand why I deserve this.

Let me point out one thing. I personally was forced to live the austere lifestyle you are leading. I know all too well what it means to survive on a mere crust of dry bread. When we left our hideout in the attic of the nasty Magda, we were half-starved. Baruch Hashem, we now have plenty of bread and a few eggs and we eat a satisfying supper. You should be happy and thank G-d that we pulled through after this harrowing existence. May Hashem continue to protect us and may we all be reunited soon.

Why do you fret and worry so much? Granted, money is an important factor, but it is not the main thing. We have seen great fortunes being lost overnight. If G-d protects us, money will not be a problem. Besides, since our expenses run into the thousands every month, the cost of a pound of butter, a few eggs, and a little sugar is of no consequence. Yes, we should try to have Mrs. Wisniewski collect as many unpaid bills as possible. This should not be overlooked. But skimping and being anxious won't do you any good. On the contrary, it will make you sick and sap your strength. And what's the point? Worrying about tomorrow makes no sense. You don't even know what will happen in an hour, or even a minute, from now.

If Hashem Yisbarach grants us life, you have to be strong and in good health. Don't think that after a long period of starvation you can quickly recover your strength. Getting back on your feet takes a long time. Chayele, I implore you to take pity on yourself, on Esther'l, on our child, on your frail dear mother, and on all of us. I want you to buy butter, eggs, and sugar every week without thinking twice.

That way you won't be tense and high-strung. And if you are calm and in good health, our child will behave well and not be jittery and naughty. As for Esther'l, it is your responsibility to see to it that all her needs are met. A child her age requires all the essentials for growth and development. You are taking the place of her parents — you are her guardian. Knowing this gives me the satisfaction and courage to go on living. Don't hesitate, and don't worry about the finances. You won't be short of money.

I am sending you my suit. Please have it cleaned and repaired. It got torn on a nail in Magda's attic. I don't mind if you have to sell it as I have no space for storing it. Meanwhile see to it that Mrs. Wisniewski goes out collecting unpaid bills. Maybe she'll raise some money, and with G-d's help things will work out.

Lately our stay in Magda's attic became intolerable. Esther'l will give you a full report of the circumstances of how we left. At first I was afraid Magda might blackmail us, but she didn't dare because she was afraid of me. When I told her I was going to join the Polish underground in the forest, she gave back all the things she stole from us. If I had a gun, she would have returned all the cash she squeezed out of us and money would be the least of our problems. Esther'l will tell you everything. But the main purpose of my letter is to urge you to eat plenty of nourishing food.

You mentioned to Helenka several times about your earrings. I want you to know that I have them here. I did not sell them. I am sending you a few pieces of soft leather. They are poor quality, but you can have a pair of shoes made out of them for our child. Or if you need a pair of sandals for yourself you can use the leather for that. Make sure to have a pair of shoes made for our child right away. Spring is just around the corner. The child has to be outdoors and he needs new shoes.

Don't worry about us. We thank G-d Who has not abandoned us thus far and we trust that He will continue to help us. No doubt you know that there are other Yidden here with us, and good Jewish partisans often come by, too. Maybe Shmuel

Yossel will pay us a visit one of these days. Just don't worry about us. Let's hope and pray to G-d that the end is near, and we will see each other before Pesach.

Erev Pesach is two weeks from this Friday. I suppose you will not want to eat chametz. Chayele, you should bake matzah, or bake cakes with wheat flour mixed with eggs but without a drop of water, like egg kichlech. Under the circumstances, I permit you to bake such cakes, even on Pesach itself. They are not chametz and are absolutely kosher. Everyone can eat them. That's what you should do. As far as we are concerned, if at all possible we will do the same. Beans, kasha, and millet may be eaten without concern. You should also buy fish. Remember, do not be tight-fisted. Since we don't know exactly when it is, make sure to keep Pesach until after Shabbos, meaning until Sunday.

Neither you nor Helenka should send mail too often. You understand that in a small village a farmer receiving a lot of mail arouses suspicion. Also, please send your letters to Helenka, so that we will receive one letter rather than two. By the same token, don't be concerned if you do not hear from us regularly. It is quite complicated to get someone to go into town to mail a letter.

That's about all for now. Further details you'll hear from Esther'l. Be well, along with our sweet darling son. Everyone over here sends regards. If I have the opportunity, I will send you a kosher chicken. I repeat, please keep sending Mrs. Wisniewski to Dzialoszyce to make collections. Any amount we can raise helps. Esther'l will fill you in on everything else.

Your Chaim

A Bitter Liberation

In June of 1944, Esther'l traveled to Debowiec and never returned. Thereafter, I received sporadic word from my brother-in-law Dovid, but nothing from my husband. For eight long months, I could neither substantiate nor allay my awful suspicions.

At last, in January of 1945, the village of Jedlnia was liberated by the Russian army. It wasn't until a month later, when Russian soldiers were everywhere, that I felt safe enough to leave.

First, I needed to find a doctor for Feivele's eye inflammation. Four years old by then, my little boy walked alongside me on the road towards the city of Radom. I hoped someone would give us a lift for at least part of the sixteen-kilometer (ten-mile) distance.

"I must get to Radom to see a doctor," I called out to an approaching Russian officer with several medals on his chest.

"Unfortunately I cannot take you there, as the war is not over yet and I am still on duty," he replied in Russian. "But keep going. Perhaps someone else will take you."

We walked on. A while later, an army jeep stopped for us. Feivele sat on the driver's lap and played with the levers and buttons on the dashboard. As we traveled, we encountered an unforgettable sight: scores of dead German soldiers lining the ditches alongside the road, and in the distance, horse-drawn carts collecting the corpses.

When we reached Radom, we called upon Mrs. Miredski, the dentist who owned Mrs. Stepanowa's cottage. On her visits to Jedlnia, she had often brought her young granddaughter to play with Feivele. Mrs. Miredski directed us to a doctor.

While in Radom, I learned that a Jewish committee had been formed to help the survivors in the region.

"Where and how did you survive?" the director questioned me.

Upon hearing of my travails, he exclaimed, "One has to bow to you! You must be a righteous woman to have made it through the war with such a small child, in that nest of anti-Semites no less!"

At the committee office, I met a man from Dzialoszyce, an acquaintance of our family.

"Do you know anything of my husband...my mother...my sister?" I asked eagerly.

"No, I do not," he replied, "but your brother-in-law Dovid sent me to Jedlnia to look for you. Mrs. Stepanowa told me you had gone to Radom. I can accompany you back home to Dzialoszyce."

He waited in Radom while I returned to Jedlnia to pack our belongings.

Though Mrs. Stepanowa was losing her source of income, she wished us a kind farewell. I was forever grateful to her, and we corresponded for a number of years.[8]

⚹

Returning to my hometown was no simple matter. There was no public means of transportation in war-torn Poland in February of 1945. I was grateful to have someone to escort me, first to Kielce with an overnight stay there, then to Pinczow, and finally to Dzialoszyce.

It was only when Feivele and I reunited with my brother-in-law Dovid Wolgelernter and my nephew and niece, Feivel and Chayele Erlich, broken remnants of a once large, flourishing family, that my fears were finally confirmed. The stark reality engulfed me: My beloved husband Chaim Yitzchok and our cherished little Alte'le, my dear mother Yachet Platkiewicz, my sister Reizele, my sister

Chayele (Helenka) Erlich, 1947

Feivel Erlich, early 1950s

8. The letters from Mrs. Stepanowa are still extant.

Tzinne'le, her husband Hershel and three of their five children, my brother Yisroel, his wife Feigele and their two young sons, my in-laws Rav Yeshayah and Hendel Rivkah Wolgelernter, their son Meir, daughter Yitta, daughter Matil and her husband Chaim Yosef and their two young sons...

They were gone.

Since my apartment was now occupied by Poles, an empty apartment that had once belonged to another Jewish family was assigned to me and Feivele. My brother-in-law Dovid and my nephew Feivel stayed with us in Dzialoszyce.

Shockingly, though Feivel was a mere twenty-two years old, his hair had turned white. Apparently, this phenomenon resulted from the intense terror he had experienced as German soldiers poked their bayonets into a haystack he was hiding in.

As I met other survivors, I realized that children of my son Feivele's age were a rarity. In fact, even older children who had survived in hiding were undernourished and sickly, their growth stunted. *Baruch Hashem*, Feivele was lively, robust, and healthy since he had eaten well and had even been able to play outdoors while in Jedlnia.

I turned my attention to gathering as many family valuables as I could. Escorted by a Jewish police officer [Ed: presumably Avraham Szajnfeld], I entered my mother's apartment. The kitchen was ransacked, the stove dismantled. But in our apartment, behind a tile in the kitchen wall, I found the box Chaim Yitzchok had hidden. In it lay a substantial amount of promissory notes and American dollars.

I also approached several Polish acquaintances in order to retrieve the clothing and textiles we had given them for safekeeping. My efforts were unsuccessful. Finally, after one Polish couple returned some of the many items we had deposited with them, I was

emboldened to ask them for my sister's fur coat. Although they claimed the Gestapo had confiscated it, along with the remaining contents of our suitcases, I was sure I recognized the coat their daughter was wearing.

To be fair, some kindhearted Polish neighbors were genuinely happy to see us. Walking on the streets of Dzialoszyce one day, I met a Polish doctor. He greeted us joyfully, exclaiming, "Whom do I see!" and proceeded to purchase a length of white cloth for a doctor's overcoat from the meager inventory of textiles I had been able to recoup. Later, Zelman Gerszonowicz told me that this doctor had risked his life by treating hidden Jews in the dark of night. In recompense, Zelman sent him clothing and money for decades.

I also traveled to Sosnowiec with my nephew Feivel, who wanted to reclaim his parents' business. Needless to say, he failed.

Plainly, surviving Jews were not welcome in the liberated country of Poland. We were free, but afraid for our safety, especially in the villages and towns. Dovid and Feivel decided to relocate to the larger city of Gleiwitz in western Poland, where many survivors had been given apartments formerly occupied by Germans.

Before leaving the region, they were determined to find the burial place of our murdered relatives. On 1 Tammuz/June 12, 1945, the day of the yahrzeit, Avraham Fuhrman escorted us to the hamlet of Debowiec.

A villager showed us the spot where one could clearly see a mound of fresh earth. Overcome with emotion, I swore I would not leave Poland without exhuming the remains and taking them with me. Naturally, I was unable to fulfill my vow during those chaotic and dangerous times.

⚓

After Dovid and Feivel left Dzialoszyce, I no longer had any reason to stay in my hometown. That Friday, I returned to the

Polish couple and asked them if they could at least give me one of my empty suitcases. I told them I would soon leave forever.

"Why not stay a few more days!" the woman urged.

I persisted with my plans, hurrying to the kind doctor late at night on Motza'ei Shabbos to collect the money he owed me for the fabric.

On Sunday morning, when the woman saw me heading to the *kolejka* with little Feivele, she again suggested that I stay until Tuesday. Undeterred, I continued on my way.

I later learned that her son-in-law organized a pogrom in Dzialoszyce on that very Sunday evening, June 17, 1945. Five *Yidden* were murdered. Our lives had been spared again, just in time.

Refugees

In Gleiwitz, Dovid, Feivel, and I received an apartment with three rooms and a kitchen. We remained there for approximately one year.

During that time, a Vaad Hatzalah delegation headed by Rav Yitzchak Halevi Herzog, Chief Rabbi of Palestine, was in Europe,

Dovid Wolgelernter (l), Feivel Erlich (r), Chayele Wolgelernter (seated), 1946

(l-r) Chayele Wolgelernter, Dovid Wolgelernter, Feivel Erlich, identity of uniformed officer uncertain, Feivele, 1946

calling on the Vatican to return Jewish orphans hidden in monasteries and churches. Chaim Yitzchok's cousin Rav Sholom Pinchas Wohlgelernter, an American rabbi and officer in the UNRRA (United Nations Relief and Rehabilitation Administration), was a member of the delegation. He tracked us down and helped us begin the lengthy emigration process.

Rav Yitzchak Halevi Herzog in center, Rav Sholom Pinchas Wohlgelernter to his right

Feivel and Dovid wrote to Avraham Szajnfeld that in light of the tense situation in Poland we had decided to leave the country without delay. They advised him to quit his prominent position in the Pinczow police department and come along with us. He replied that he needed more time to settle his affairs and that eventually he would join us.

Sadly, a short time later, we were notified by the Pinczow police department that Avraham had died. We soon learned the facts: Avraham Szajnfeld had been lured into an ambush, forced into a

sack and thrown into the river. This gallant partisan, who had outwitted the German enemy, had fallen at the hands of his Polish colleagues who could not swallow the idea that a Jewish survivor had become a government official. This incident only strengthened our resolve to leave the country at once.

After the Kielce pogrom of July 1946, when Poles brutally murdered more than forty Jews, it became clear that the soil of Poland was burning under our feet. There was no longer any place for a Jew in this country.

Rav Sholom Pinchas immediately obtained space for us on a Mizrachi refugee transport to Diablice, Czechoslovakia leaving Poland the following Shabbos. No documents were required. Since it was a matter of *pikuach nefesh*, he stated that it was permissible to board the train on Shabbos.

We stayed in Diablice, near Prague, for several weeks. Among the refugees was the young Rav Yitzchok Dov Kopelman, later the famed *rosh yeshivah* of the Luzern Yeshivah.

Feivel Erlich left Czechoslovakia for England on a youth transport arranged by Dayan Grossnass. After learning in the Staines Yeshivah for a few years, he married Brenda Neufeld and settled in London. They had five children and numerous grandchildren. His sister Helenka married Jonathan Dresner, one of the prisoners rescued by Oskar Schindler. After Jonathan finished dental school in Germany, the couple immigrated to Israel. They had two daughters and a number of grandchildren.

Along with Dovid, I was transferred to Strasbourg, France as part of a large group of refugees awaiting our turn for *aliyah* to Eretz Yisrael. There we spent the Yamim Tovim of 1946. We lived in a large community building on the Rue Sellenick that served as a home for refugees as well as an orphanage. Here, too, my Feivele was an exception, as most of the children had survived the war in Russia and were quite a bit older.

In Strasbourg, medical treatment was available and various lessons and courses were offered. I completed a nursing course, earning a diploma as a medical assistant.

When all the children were thoroughly examined, tuberculosis was discovered in Feivele's lungs, apparently caused by living in very close quarters with many refugee children. I was completely shattered and felt I would have a nervous breakdown. Feivele was taken to a hospital in Strasbourg, then to the resort area of Schirmeck, where Dovid was working for the refugee administration.[9]

Dovid Wolgelernter with Feivele in Schirmeck, 1947

After a time, Feivele was x-rayed. Since he had not had sufficient bed rest, he had not recovered at all. Before returning to the United States, Rav Sholom Pinchas Wohlgelernter came to visit me again, along with his younger brother Rav Elimelech. When he asked what he could do for me, I replied, "At all costs, I must go to Switzerland in order to save my

---

9. During this time, Avraham, the eldest of the Wolgelernter brothers, who had been living in Canada since the late 1920s, found Dovid's name on a survivor list printed in the newspaper. He corresponded with his only surviving brother and arranged for his immigration to Toronto. There, Dovid married Mindel Zilberstein, a fellow Holocaust survivor. They had two children, Yeshayah Baruch and Chava Hendel (Twersky), and a number of grandchildren. Dovid Wolgelernter lived to learn that his brothers' remains were found and reinterred in Eretz Yisrael. He passed away in 1996.

child." Switzerland was known to have the best facilities to cure this malady.

Dovid Wolgelernter and Feivele surrounded by refugee children in Schirmeck, 1947

Rav Sholom Pinchas Wohlgelernter in Schirmeck, 1947; Chayele Wolgelernter is at far left

It turned out to be quite difficult. Rav Sholom Pinchas exerted great effort, even writing to Federal Counselor Max Petitpierre. Fortunately, his efforts were successful, and we arrived in the Swiss village of Leysin, a famous health resort, in July 1947.

Feivele was admitted to the Rose des Alpes sanatorium, under the care of a world-renowned tuberculosis specialist, Professor Auguste Rollier. The refugee committee arranged living quarters for me for six months in an apartment owned by a Jewish doctor, during which time I was able to visit Feivele every day.

Thereafter, I went to live in the town of Montreux an hour away, which had a small but vibrant Jewish community, where I rented a furnished room from a Jewish family. I managed to visit Feivele at least once a week.

I did not have many gold coins left, but I learned to sew handbags and thus earned my keep. The work kept me occupied and did me good, though I was usually exhausted by the end of the week. The Landau family, wonderful people whom I cannot forget, kindly invited me for Shabbos meals. I also grew close to the Sternbuch, Botchko, and Weingort families.

Feivele stayed in Leysin for over a year until he was fully cured. In 1948, he was transferred to a children's home, administered by Mrs. G. Goldberg, in the country air of Mont Pelerin above Vevey. His stay there was funded in part by the Swiss Jewish Refugee Relief Agency. After Feivele was there for a year, there was an attempt to smuggle him to Israel without my knowledge, but thanks to the intervention of Rabbi Dr. Theodor (Binyomin Zeev) Weisz, the new *rav* of the Orthodox *Israelitische Religionsgesellschaft* (IRG) of Zurich, this plan was foiled.

Chayele Wolgelernter, c.1948

PART TWO
By Feivel Wolgelernter

IN 1950, WHEN I WAS nine years old, my mother married my unforgettable stepfather Yisroel Mordechai (Motel) Finkelstein, joining him in the city of Regensburg in Bavaria, Germany. The *shadchan* was our family friend, Chaim Pomeranz, a native Dzialoszycer who was my stepfather's business partner in the Penna Feathers and Down Company. The company eventually grew into a leading wholesaler of feathers and down, and manufacturer of pillows and comforters.

My stepfather treated me as his own child in every respect. My mother could now afford to send me to the well-known Jewish boarding school, the Institute Ascher in Bex, Switzerland. There my Jewish education began in earnest.

Chaim Pomeranz

In 1951, my brother Yaakov Yechiel was born. Two years later, in 1953, our family immigrated to Toronto, Canada, where we had

several relatives — Uncles Avraham and Dovid Wolgelernter; my father's cousin Rav Yaakov Yitzchok Wohlgelernter, elder brother of Rav Sholom Pinchas; and my stepfather's younger brother, Uncle Moishe Fishel Finkelstein.

Unfortunately, my parents did not succeed in establishing a profitable business in Toronto. After my bar mitzvah in early 1954, they returned to Regensburg, where they lived for the next twenty years, engaging in myriad *tzedakah* and *chessed* activities. Their home became a haven for *rabbanim*, *roshei yeshivah* and *meshulachim* visiting Munich, who did not hesitate to take the long detour to Regensburg. While Papa drove them around to collect funds, my mother washed their clothes, and had a hot meal ready when they returned. My stepfather was the *gabbai* of the city's shul, as well as the *gabbai* of the Rabbi Meir Baal Haness-Polin charity. My mother regularly sent bedding and substantial sums of money to needy brides in Eretz Yisrael.

I stayed on in Toronto for two years, attending the Eitz Chaim Talmud Torah school headed by Rabbi Chaim Nussbaum. I boarded at the home of R' Yisroel Yitzchok Cohen, a Holocaust survivor who later authored the poignant memoir, *Destined to Survive*.

In 1955, after completing the first year of high school, my class broke up and most of the boys transferred to the Telshe Yeshivah in Cleveland. Since I could not adapt to the American mindset and way of life, I went to learn in the Letchworth Yeshivah in England, upon the strong recommendation of my cousin Feivel Erlich. There I became very close to his family.

After a while, I began longing to return to Switzerland. In 1958, I enrolled in the Yeshivah of Luzern under Rav Moshe Solowiejczyk. Thereafter, I boarded at the home of Rav Avraham Kuflik in Zurich for four years while I attended the Institut Minerva for my high-school diploma and subsequently studied for my master's degree in electronic engineering at the ETH Zurich.

At Feivel Wolgelernter's engagement, April 1964; (l-r) Yisroel Mordechai Finkelstein, Feivel Wolgelernter, Rav Mordechai Yaakov Breisch, Rav Moshe Chaim Schmerler

In 1964, while still a student, I married Rachel, the younger daughter of the well-known Leon and Minouche Erlanger-Silbiger of Luzern.

We have two sons, Chaim Yitzchok, married to Sari Brandeis, and Yisroel Naftoli (Nafti), married to Tovi Kolman; and three daughters, Tirza Ruchama, married to Ezra Bloch; Chana Breindel, married to Moishi Bollag; and Rivka Yachet, married to Shloimi Leiner. Our sons and sons-in-law are noted *bnei Torah*, following the example of their ancestors, and have granted us a lovely bunch of grandchildren and several great-grandchildren.

My brother Yaakov Yechiel Finkelstein married Rachel Orzel of Basel, Switzerland and settled in Toronto, where he is known as an outstanding *talmid chacham*. They have five married children; their three sons and two sons-in-law are all upstanding *bnei Torah*.

In 1972, my parents liquidated the Penna Feathers and Down Company and went into retirement, settling in Zurich.

After a protracted illness, Papa passed away in 1989. He is buried on Har Hamenuchos-Tamir. Two of my grandsons are named after him.

Living near us in Zurich until the ripe old age of nearly ninety-four years, Mother was spirited and mentally alert until her final days. The way her face lit up when she spoke about her childhood and the early years of her married life in Dzialoszyce demonstrated how happy she had been then. Occasionally she would also talk at length about her harrowing experiences during the Holocaust. She lived to see some three dozen great-grandchildren.

Yisroel Mordechai Finkelstein

A day after Shavuos of 2006, just two days before the wedding of her eldest great-grandchild, my mother passed away. She was laid to rest alongside my stepfather on Har Hamenuchos. Within the year, Nafti's wife Tovi gave birth to a baby girl, whom they named Chaya Rechel.

Chayele [Wolgelernter] Finkelstein

Through an extraordinary turn of events, my mother lies buried just a few steps away from the *kedoshim*, including her mother; her sister; and her first husband, Chaim Yitzchok Wolgelernter, my father, *Hashem yinkom damo.*

POSTSCRIPT — 1993

Finding the
Family Grave

By Feivel Wolgelernter

"LET US TRAVEL TO POLAND," my mother would tell me from time to time once I became of age. "I would like to see Dzialoszyce again...and maybe we could also find the grave of our dear ones."

When I asked her if she knew where our family members were buried, she would reply evasively, "Let's just go and we'll find it."

In my profession as an engineer, I always required precise data before embarking on any serious endeavor; hence, I did not even contemplate the idea of going to Poland, especially since travel to and within Communist Poland was no simple matter. Moreover, I feared the emotional effects the trip would have on my mother.

Never revealed to me — neither by my mother, nor by my uncle Dovid Wolgelernter during my trips to Toronto or in our frequent correspondence and phone conversations — was the fact that my mother and Uncle Dovid, Feivel Erlich, and I, escorted by Avraham Fuhrman, had visited the burial place of our murdered relatives in

June of 1945. Somewhere in the tiny hamlet of Debowiec, Poland, less than five kilometers (three miles) from Dzialoszyce, there was an unmarked grave in which lay the eight *kedoshim*.

I can only surmise that the trauma must have caused this information to be suppressed.

✦

Years later, in March of 1993, I unexpectedly learned that the location of the grave was indeed known.

Hoping to glean information that would help decipher the diary, my son Nafti, then living in Israel, attended an annual meeting of elderly Dzialoszyce survivors. There he was hailed as the grandson of Chaim Yitzchok Wolgelernter and great-grandson of the famed Yachet'l Platkiewicz.

Subsequently, my cousin Feivel Erlich suggested that Nafti establish contact with another resource: Avraham Fuhrman of Ashkelon, the former partisan who had often visited the group in their Debowiec hideout.

"Did you ever visit the gravesite?" Fuhrman asked Nafti.

"No," was Nafti's reply.

"Why not?"

"Because no one knows where it is."

"I know exactly where your family members are buried!" Fuhrman declared.

Galvanized by his newfound knowledge, Nafti contacted Moshe Spiegel, the administrator of a *chevra kaddisha* in Bnei Brak, who had many years of experience locating graves in Eastern Europe for reinterment in Israel.

"It is quite possible that we can find the grave," Spiegel asserted.

Fuhrman then contacted his cousin Marian (Mayer) Boruchowicz, who, as a young child during the war, had been hidden by Franek and Maria Szczubial of Debowiec. After his adoption by the Szczubials at the age of eleven, Marian stayed in Poland and became

completely assimilated. He confirmed that the location of the gravesite was known in the village, and gladly offered to assist us.

I remained skeptical, but when Nafti persuaded me that this mission was more than just a fantasy, I engaged Spiegel's services. He would be assisted by Baruch Goldberg (Har-Zahav), a veteran member of the *chevra kaddisha* of the Israeli army.

Moshe applied to the Polish government for the necessary permits and took care of all other preliminary arrangements.

Less than a month later, our expedition was underway.

Sunday, 27 Nissan 5753/April 18, 1993[1]

At 10:30 a.m., I board the plane from Switzerland to Poland with my sons Chaim Yitzchok and Nafti.

After landing in Warsaw Airport, we find our prearranged Jewish driver, Yankel Czyc. He takes us to the Hotel Mercure near the former Jewish quarter of Warsaw.

On our visit to the city's huge Jewish cemetery, we encounter hundreds of people, among them many dignitaries who have come to participate in the commemoration of the fiftieth anniversary of the Warsaw Ghetto Uprising.

Most of the cemetery is neglected. The crumbling tombstones and dense trees growing out of the graves create a ghostlike atmosphere. We say Tehillim at a number of *kevarim* of tzaddikim.

After we strike up a conversation with an elderly Jew, Avraham Prajs of Gur, he offers to take us to his hometown. In Gora Kalwaria, we see the once vibrant Gerrer *beis medrash* and the Jewish cemetery and say Tehillim at the *ohel* of the Chiddushei Harim and the Sfas Emes.

---

1. Based on my daily log at the time

On our return to Warsaw, we visit the infamous *Umschlagplatz*[2] and other former Jewish sites. There is absolutely no trace left of the ghetto; everything is new. Only a few street names remind us that hundreds of thousands of Jews once lived here.

Around 9:00 p.m., we meet with Moshe Spiegel and Baruch Goldberg in the Menorah Restaurant for supper and formulate our plans for the next day.

Monday, 28 Nissan 5753/April 19, 1993

At daybreak, we begin our journey south towards Miechow. Moshe and Baruch travel with their driver, Adam Neuschewski, in a grey Ford van provided by the Office of Foreign Graves. It is equipped with digging tools, sheets, and two coffins; a large cross hangs in the rear.

Chaim, Nafti and I follow in a taxi with our driver, Richard Karpfman. We discover that he had a Jewish father who was murdered in Treblinka. To my surprise, my long-forgotten Polish mother tongue slowly comes back to me as we converse.

The sky is overcast, giving way to light rain. Riding along well-paved, straight roads bordered by extensive birch forests, we pass many signs pointing to towns whose names recall the country's rich Jewish past.

Ahead of us, the van exits towards Miechow, where Moshe will pick up the digging permit. Our taxi turns east, past my birthplace of Dzialoszyce and on through the countryside to the tiny, primitive hamlet of Debowiec.

We arrive there at 10:30 a.m. The villagers do not seem surprised to see a group of visiting Jews. Apparently, Moshe Spiegel laid the groundwork for our coming.

---

2. Collection point where Jews were gathered for deportation from the Warsaw ghetto

We meet with fifty-five-year-old Mr. Szczubial and his wife. He is the son of Franek and Maria Szczubial, who provided shelter and aid to a number of Jews, including some of our family members. He gives me a copy of his parents' Yad Vashem certificate. The elder Mr. Szczubial died eight years ago, and his wife five years later, both well into their eighties.

Yad Vashem certificate awarded to Franek and Maria Szczubial

They take us to their niece, thirty-two-year-old Alexandra Kopczynska, whose husband Jan is the village mayor. She speaks some English and is friendly and helpful. "My grandparents loved the Jews," she tells us, "especially your family."

At Alexandra's, we meet sixty-eight-year-old Bronek Gala. With a mysterious smile fixed on his face, he appears a bit senile, but supposedly he knows where our family members are buried.

With the air of one harboring a deep, dark secret, Gala leads us down the beaten path that serves as the main road to the edge of the village. Turning right, we cross a barren field, then a strawberry field, until we reach a U-shaped depression, three meters (ten feet) deep, filled with trees and shrubs. "There they lie!" he proclaims, pointing to a spot along the steep incline. "This is the place where Biskup buried eight people."

He then continues 100 meters to the left, stops, and points again. "Another body was buried down there," he says. We later find out it was Avraham Fuhrman's stepmother.

Noticing our skepticism, Gala insists that his information is accurate.

Just before noon, Moshe and Baruch arrive with the digging permit from the Miechow Ministry of Agriculture. Almost simultaneously, a small blue bus from Katowice pulls up. Four men descend. Marian Boruchowicz has come to assist us, bringing along two robust Polish diggers and Mieczyslaw Leszczynski, a cousin of the Szczubials, who had lived with them in Debowiec.[3]

Not relying on Gala — the spot he indicated on the steep slope seems a most improbable place to bury eight bodies — the men begin to dig a little further down the incline where the ground levels off. They are soon assisted by the strapping Wozniak brothers

---

3. Mieczyslaw Leszczynski helped the Szczubials shelter and aid the Jews in their care, for which he, too, was designated a Righteous Gentile by Yad Vashem.

of Debowiec. The villagers gather to watch the scene. It is the event of the decade for these simple folk.

After much exertion, a couple of trees are felled and a trench 2 meters long by 1½ meters deep (approximately 6½ x 5 feet) is dug.

Nothing is found.

12:00 noon —

During the midday recess, we go back into the village and have a look at Biskup's place. His stepsister, an old crone, is the only person still living in the wooden farmhouse. The ramshackle barn, inhabited by chickens and pigeons, is the place where my father's heartrending chronicle ended. Nothing but a couple of rusty milk containers indicates that a group of people once lived in the hayloft. We note the secret trapdoor above the underground pit and the ladder leading down to it from the loft.

Biskup's barn

At the entrance to the barn; Feivel Wolgelernter second from right,
Marian Boruchowicz third from right

The loft

Ladder leading from the loft to the underground pit

Area of barn floor covering the trapdoor to the underground pit

Standing outside in front of the barn, I wonder, *Is this the very spot where my father was murdered in cold blood on that moonless night, 1 Tammuz 5704, forty-nine years ago?*

According to Marian Boruchowicz, if Biskup did not commit the murder himself, he certainly was an accomplice. Avraham Fuhrman, on the other hand, who as a former Jewish partisan operating in this area did not accompany us for fear of reprisal, had shared with us his conviction that the group was murdered by Polish partisans or bandits.

One thing is certain: Biskup was a wicked, untrustworthy person, who was loath to lose his profitable source of income. Did he exact his revenge upon his Jewish tenants who were preparing to leave in search of a new refuge?

We will never know.

Monday afternoon —

We return to the digging site. Two elderly Polish women stridently assert that Biskup dragged the bodies out of the village after they had become bloated, and buried them in a different spot, some twenty meters (sixty-five feet) further.

Since the women make a far more intelligent impression than Gala and their claim is convincing — the level ground they indicate is a more likely place for a grave — we all move to that part of the U-shaped depression, and work begins anew.

The men dig three more trenches, unearthing the skull of a small animal, the foreleg of a cow, and a small, unidentifiable bone.

I realize that we may have to dig up an area 20x20 meters — approximately 4,000 square feet — to a depth of 1½ meters (five feet). It is an impossible endeavor.

"*Da-da-da-da...*" Jan Wozniak begins to regale the crowd by mimicking a bulldozer. He suggests that we hire a "*mechaniczki*" in Kazimierza Wielka, the nearest industrial town.

Not taking him seriously, Moshe announces a sizeable reward to the person who correctly identifies the gravesite. We give the diggers some vodka, and they intensify their efforts.

Further work yields no results and we become increasingly discouraged. Finally, at 6:00 p.m., Moshe asks the Wozniak brothers to direct us to a bulldozer operator, and work is halted for the day. I reward the diggers for their work and we leave for Kazimierza Wielka.

Monday evening —

I observe the village where my father grew up. Kazimierza Wielka had developed over the years into a large, thriving town. The long-gone Jewish community, led by my grandfather Rav Yeshayah Wolgelernter, had been a tiny fraction of the population; there are no signs of its absence.

After locating the address of the bulldozer operator, we find the factory closed for the day.

We continue south to Krakow. As night falls, a beautiful, medieval city unfolds before us. We view the interior of the Tempel Synagogue. At the Rema shul, we meet the president of an aging two-hundred-member congregation, and recite Tehillim in the adjacent ancient cemetery at the *kevarim* of the Rema, the Bach, and the Megaleh Amukos.

After an exhausting day, we check into the Hotel Forum for the night, fervently hoping that on the following day our efforts will be rewarded.

Tuesday, 29 Nissan 5753/April 20, 1993

The day dawns warm and sunny. Moshe and Baruch travel back to Kazimierza Wielka to arrange for the bulldozer.

In the interim, my sons and I head to the town of my birth. As we near Dzialoszyce, we note the old *kolejka* rails crisscrossing the

countryside, wending their way towards what was once a bustling commercial center.

In contrast to Kazimierza Wielka, Dzialoszyce had declined sharply since its prewar heyday. Half a century later, there still is a visible, gaping void left by the expulsion that drained the town of 80 percent of its population, as well as its economic and cultural vigor.

Memorial for the *kedoshim* of Dzialoszyce

We stop at the police station. The young chief, Adam Porebski, is friendly but treats us with a degree of suspicion, a residual characteristic of the recently ousted Communist regime. He escorts us to the site of the razed Jewish cemetery where a new

Feivel Wolgelernter (c) with his sons Nafti (l) and Chaim Yitzchok (r) at the monument

monument, erected by the Rozenek family, memorializes the 1500
Dzialoszyce *kedoshim* massacred by the Nazis in September 1942.

Porebski arranges for the retired Professor Stanislas Greda, who
speaks a fair French, to act as our guide. With pictures from Chaim
Pomeranz's sister Lola who had visited Dzialoszyce some years
earlier, we find the house where I was born and lived with my
parents and sister Alte'le next to my maternal grandmother and her
famous textile shop.

▲ Walking through the town of
Dzialoszyce

◀ Feivel Wolgelernter (l) and son
Chaim Yitzchok (r) in front of the
Platkiewicz family apartments and
shop, Dzialoszyce, 1993

"Ah, I remember the Platkiewicz family well," an elderly man tells us.

"I lived opposite them," a woman adds, introducing herself as Maria Markewicz, née Praszu.

We visit the ruins of the once magnificent Dzialoszyce shul. The roof, adorned with elaborate frescoes, caved in about fifteen years ago, our guide tells us. The floor is overgrown with wild grass and shrubs. The *beis medrash* building nearby is in slightly better condition, but lies abandoned. Across from it is the former *mikveh*.

We thank the professor, and with a feeling of emptiness, I take leave of my hometown.

Noon —

Chaim, Nafti and I arrive back in Debowiec just before noon. A bulldozer is already at the digging site, excavating strips of earth twenty meters (sixty-five feet) long to a depth of twenty centimeters (eight inches), uprooting trees and dumping heaps of earth. Moshe tells us that it took an hour to convince the bulldozer operator to drive down the steep slope.

Though the soil is light and sandy, and a few minutes yields a day's work of half a dozen men, nothing is found.

When work stops at 12:15 for the midday break, I am nearly ready to concede defeat.

Tuesday afternoon —

Having heard of the reward offer, the elderly Stanislaw Granek, a contemporary of Gala and former resident of Debowiec, arrives from Busko. He points to the exact position on the slope that Gala had indicated. The two peasant women now retract their claim and concur with the men.

At 12:45 p.m., work resumes. We instruct the bulldozer operator to dig directly into the slope. Moshe and Baruch walk alongside,

peering closely at the mouth of the huge shovel as it burrows into the earth.

Mouth of the shovel at the digging site; Baruch Goldberg (Har-Zahav) supervising

At 1:00 p.m., they spot a human bone, then another. There is indeed a grave well into the incline, precisely where Gala had pointed at the beginning!

Its mission accomplished, the bulldozer leaves. Baruch takes over, hollowing out the site mainly by hand. Chaim and Nafti assist.

Grave

Slope

Villagers survey the gravesite area

Chaim Yitzchok looking at the grave

Although it is difficult for me to pull myself away, I go up to the top of the depression, since it is halachically forbidden to look at a parent's remains. My sons continually take pictures and keep me informed.

I take out my Tehillim. As if of its own accord, it opens to Chapter 94: *Keil nekamos Hashem* — "Almighty of vengeance, reveal Yourself..."

How fitting, I reflect.

Moshe and Baruch begin the difficult process of identifying the skulls and bones based on factors we had heard from surviving family members — my grandmother had lost her teeth with age; my father and uncle had both been over 1.8 meters (six feet) tall; my teenaged cousins had been short and slight in build. It appears the victims were shot or clubbed to death.

I tear *kriah*.

All of us are overcome with emotion, particularly Nafti. Having immersed himself in my father's writings for many years, he had become intimately familiar with his grandfather as a living personality. Now, the tragedy penetrates his consciousness in a palpable manner.

Paradoxically, although I am an *avel* until nightfall, I am filled with elation and gratitude to *Hashem Yisbarach* for enabling us to bring our family's remains to *kever Yisrael*. What a remarkable *chessed* my son had performed for me by spearheading and goading me to proceed with this unusual mission. Orphaned at a tender young age, I would now be able to *daven* at my father's *kever*.

It is difficult to separate the remains; apparently the bodies had been carelessly thrown into the earth. The work continues for several hours, as Chaim, Nafti, Moshe and Baruch laboriously and reverently sift the earth for smaller remnants. The bones are sorted to the extent possible within the parameters of *kavod hameis*, and laid on eight sheets.

Nafti and Baruch digging for remains

By late afternoon, 29 Nissan 5753/April 20, 1993, we had found the skeletons of eight people, not more and not less. There was not a shred of doubt: It was my family.

- Yachet Platkiewicz, my grandmother [1879-1944]
- Tzinne Erlich, her oldest daughter, my aunt [1901-1944]

- Mordechai Tzvi (Hershel) Erlich, Tzinne's husband, my uncle [1898-1944]

- Esther Erlich, their daughter, my cousin [1928-1944]

- Avraham Reuven Erlich, their son, my cousin [1929-1944]

- Berel Jakubowiec, Jewish partisan guarding the group [c.1921-1944]

- Meir Shmuel Eliyahu Wolgelernter, my uncle [1920-1944]

- Chaim Yitzchok Wolgelernter, my father [1911-1944]

At 5:30 p.m., the van pulls up to the edge of the grave. The large coffin is brought out and the sheets are tied into bundles and placed inside it.

With his peculiar smile, Gala requests payment for the trampled berry fields. I hand him some bills, as well as the sizeable reward he has earned. As I liberally dispense dollars and expressions of gratitude, I think to myself, *These Poles are marvelous people, entirely different from their predecessors.* I resolve to give a generous gift to the village of Debowiec.

At 6:00 p.m., the coffin is carried into the van and, at our request, Adam discreetly removes the cross. Both vehicles are ready to leave.

My sons and I walk back into the village — Nafti to

(l-r) Baruch Goldberg (Har-Zahav), Feivel Wolgelernter, Moshe Spiegel

Biskup's place to take a few more pictures, Chaim and I to take leave of the Szczubials. The vehicles will pick us up from there.

When they do not arrive, we return to the clearing and are shocked to find that the villagers have blocked the roadway with a tractor and a barricade of trees. A heated argument is in progress, chiefly instigated by the two peasant women, whose shrill voices rise above the ruckus. "They must pay for every uprooted tree!" and "Twenty minutes from here, they used to burn the likes of you!"

I learn firsthand that my mother and other Holocaust survivors were not exaggerating when they maintained that the prevalent, virulent hatred towards Jews was transmitted through the generations in mothers' milk.

We are seven men, but we stand no chance against the brawny peasants. Moshe has already offered a small sum. I double it. As the mood gets uglier, Chaim leaves to fetch the mayor, who suggests we pay restitution and take a receipt. I redouble my offer, and after a short conference, the villagers accept. We get into our vehicles and hurry out of Debowiec, the age-old lesson of anti-Semitism rendering our expenditure worthwhile.

<hr />

On our way back to Warsaw, I called my mother, who was in Canada after spending Pesach in Toronto with my brother and his family. I instructed her to tear *kriah* and sit *shivah* until nightfall. This opportunity to properly mourn her first husband, her mother, and her sister proved to be a cathartic experience for her.

On Wednesday morning, April 21, Chaim, Nafti, and I took a flight back to Zurich. Later that day, Nafti and his wife Tovi flew back to their home in Israel.

Using his connections and a measure of resourcefulness, Moshe Spiegel unexpectedly managed to transport the remains that very evening on his return flight from Warsaw to Israel.

The following day, Thursday, April 22, Moshe informed us that Rav Wosner had ruled that the *levayah* was not to be delayed. It would have to take place before midday on Erev Shabbos! I barely made it onto the plane to Tel Aviv.

In the interim, Nafti had to make immediate arrangements for a burial place. His efforts to purchase a site near the grave of my stepfather in the Perushim section of Har Hamenuchos-Tamir in Jerusalem were initially met with much reluctance. Never before had the *chevra kaddisha* administration encountered such an unusual situation.

As the *kedoshim* had been buried together for forty-nine years in Poland, their remains would now, too, be buried in a *kever achim*, as dictated by Rav Wosner. Three adjacent graves were converted into four, connected to each other below ground; my father and his brother Meir were laid to rest at the far left.

On Erev Shabbos, 2 Iyar 5753/April 23, 1993, a *levayah* was held with some sixty close friends and relatives in attendance. Among them was Avraham Fuhrman. Several Dzialoszycers, including Chaim Pomeranz and Kalmish Epstein,[4] were also present. Nafti eulogized the *kedoshim*. Feivel Erlich and I said Kaddish. There was not a dry eye.

Two months later, on 1 Tammuz 5753 — the forty-ninth yahrzeit — we gathered again to erect a monument above the grave, which would tell the story to generations to come.[5]

"G-d, bare Your arm against the cruel sinners. Earth, cover not their blood."

---

4. Son of Rav Eliezer Epstein *Hy"d* and pupil of my father

5. Many newspapers reported on this story at the time. I wrote an article as well, describing this extraordinary event in the April 30 and May 7, 1993 editions of *Die Jüdische Zeitung* in Zurich and in the June 1993 edition of *The Jewish Observer*.

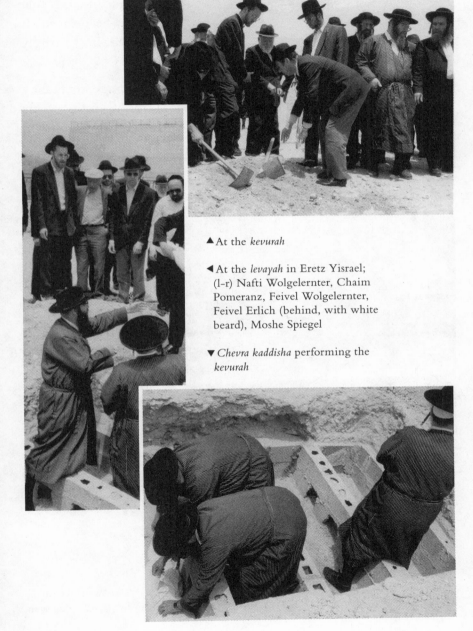

▲ At the *kevurah*

◄ At the *levayah* in Eretz Yisrael; (l-r) Nafti Wolgelernter, Chaim Pomeranz, Feivel Wolgelernter, Feivel Erlich (behind, with white beard), Moshe Spiegel

▼ *Chevra kaddisha* performing the *kevurah*

The monuments on the *kever achim*

Close-up view of inscription for Chaim Yitzchok Wolgelernter *Hy"d*

The Jerusalem Post, International Edition

The Jerusalem Post Magazine

ארבעים ותשע שנים הם חיכו

■ סיפור קטן, רב עוצמה, בשולי החיים ■ ארבעים ותשע שנים המתין ר' פייבל וולגלנטר לרגע הזה. כמעט יובל לאחר שנשרד מאבני, הביא את עצמותיו לקבורה ■ במרומי הר המנוחות נכרה קבר אחים. שמונה בני משפחה שנרצחו והושלכו לקבר אי שם בלב השום מקום, יומן מפורט שכתב בעיצומם של ימי האימה, מתוד כל פרט. פרקי תיעוד, פרקי גבורה, פרקי אמונה ■ רצח בפולין, מצבה בירושלים. הי"ד ■

י. אהרונסון

Yated Ne'eman, Hebrew-language edition

"ספר הדמעות "עולה לירושלים

קיומו של נדר לאחר מ"ט שנים

י. אונגלר

איזהו מקום הקבורה

Hamodia, Hebrew-language edition

They Waited for Forty-Nine Years For Burial

By Y. Aharonson

R' Feivel Wohlgelernter waited forty-nine years for this moment: almost a jubilee after parting with his father, he was able to bring his remains to proper burial * A mass grave was dug on the heights of Har Hamenuchos and eight members of his family who had been murdered and cast to some unknown grave in some unknown place finally found their proper resting place * A detailed diary written in the throes of those fearful times documents every development. * Murder in Poland, a tombstone in Jerusalem, may Hashem avenge their blood!

It happened two months ago on Har Hamenuchos in Jerusalem. After the gravestone was erected, R' Feivel Wohlgelernter finally returned home, his stormy spirit allayed. An odyssey of pain, wandering and travail has finally come to a peaceful end after forty-nine years. His relatives, killed in cold blood under the silent trees of a forest in Poland, have been brought to their final resting place.

This story could have been without an end and the family could have continued to wonder where the ignominious burial place of their loved ones was actually located. It had happened on a notoriously cold Polish night, they knew, in notoriously cold blood. Not even a simple stone marked the spot. Hardly any memories.

After the devastating war, after

An odyssey of pain, wandering and travail has finally come to a peaceful end after forty-nine years.

having lived through the horrors and the bloodshed, R' Feivel was able to rehabilitate himself completely. Yearnings for a childhood home which he never knew, had to be shunted aside, only to surface time and again, like an unwanted, annoying guest, before they could be repressed again, until a wrath which barely receded but was repeatedly tucked away in the chambers of his heart, was finally soothed. He did not let time serve the murderers. His family was finally given a proper Jewish burial, almost fifty years after that terrible moment.

His father, the one he had never had the privilege to know, dogged his footsteps like a shadow. Yet his tender hand seemed at hand to help him along through the difficult times of life. He had been a mere baby when it had happened, but throughout his life, for forty-nine years, he had yearned to see his father given a proper burial. The promissory note was now mature and paid up; his prayers had been answered and the debt cancelled.

Chapters of Faith

This tale has lots of holes and gaps in it; it was not written in one sitting. Even after reading the diary of his father, a most detailed one, which survived in the hands

Nine thousand people had resided here before the war, eight thousand of them Jews. Now, only 1,700 people lived here.

of R' Feivel's uncle, there remain unanswered questions. The terror gelled into words; the pain clothed in print; thoughts, doubts, episodes

of bravery and faith, are all bound up between its pages.

On the day of his wedding, Feivel's uncle, brother of his murdered father, gave him the diary as a memento. The dark clouds that hovered over the skies of European Jewry are fully documented. Dzaloshitz, a typical Polish city, began sipping from the cup of bitter brew. The first transport, it was called in dry terms.

R' Feivel's father had been a man of letters. While still studying under the Rebbe, in yeshiva, he had been the only one allowed to write during shiurim. The Rebbe, so a seat mate of his would relate, would say, "He is the only one whose understanding of the matter was not marred by the act of transcription."

In his diary, with a sensitive pen that seeks to touch the truth, he documented those dreadful times. Day by day, each day with its dole of suffering, were recorded by his subtle pen in a rich Yiddish, in a small, close-knit handwriting, a stark contrast to the mighty things expressed therein.

The first excerpt from his diary: "Every train car is waiting. Guards, their guns cocked, make sure that no one escapes. The open cars stand and wait, ready at moment's notice. Sounds of moaning fill the station. People lying strewn about on the floor, are being trampled underfoot. Many, already beaten to death, lie on the tracks, flung under the train. A Jew stands apart, in the distance, wearing a tallis, saying Hallel. A woman watches nearby, holding onto two children. It is so congested that she cannot enter the car, and she must throw her children out. The Nazis shoot randomly into the car. People are compressed like herrings, climbing over one another, some falling back and being shot.

"The station attendant, the one authorized to send the trains off, is missing. The Germans decide to leave without his permission. The trains pull out: the first, second, third, fourth. The voices linger on in the air, even after the trains have gone. Later, the station attendant is discovered in his room, spreadeagled on the floor. The goyim barely catch words which they cannot understand, "Shema Yis-

Yated Ne'eman, English-language edition

Nr 17, 9 Ijar 5753 / 30. April 1993 — DIE JÜDISCHE ZEITUNG

(auch Kinderschuhe bis Gr. 35), die wir für unsere Schützlinge in unseren Heimen dringend brauchen. Da sich die Versandspesen wiederum sehr erhöht haben, appellieren wir nochmals an Sie, uns nur saubere und gute Ware zu bringen, damit sich die Arbeit, die Spesen und der Versand auch lohnen. Wir danken Ihnen schon jetzt für Ihr Verständnis.

Zu den Schloschim von L. Jeselsohn, New York sl.

Selten hat die Ptira eines Privatmannes so viele Menschen innerlich berührt. Es war nicht nur sein Einsatz für die Allgemeinheit und die Art seiner Z'daka, welche die Achtung der Mitmenschen errang. Es war etwas viel Subtileres: Hinter den grosszügigen Abzweigungen grosser Summen für wichtige und gute Zwecke spürte man das Herz des Mannes, die persönliche Anteilnahme an Werk und Person. Die Dinge geschahen ohne Aufhebens, in äusserster Heimlichkeit, ja Anonymität - von Boston bis Jeruschalaim. In seinem weltweiten Unternehmen bemühte er sich nach Möglichkeit, junge Jehudim, von New York bis Zürich, zu fördern, schuf ihnen eine Infra-struktur, um im Geschäftsleben Jehudim zu sein, etwa durch Schiurim und Minjanim in den Räumen des Grossunternehmens. Ein nicht zur Schau gestelltes, tief innerliches Jirat Schomajim liess ihn das Bet Knesset, das er noch an seinem letzten Tag aufsuchte, lieben. Dieses Jirat Schomajim liess ihn auch vor Laschon Hora konsequent zurückschrecken, immer wieder den Chafez Chajim als sein Ideal hervorhebend. Ludwig Jesselsohn blieb immer jung, begeisterungs- und erlebnisfähig. Unbekümmert durchschritt er in Jeruschalajim den arabischen Schuk, um die Erew Schabbosatmosphäre an der Kotel einzufangen. Es war diese Jungenhaftigkeit, die die anderen so mitriss, die Kombination von Stärke mit entwaffnender Bescheidenheit - das schlug uns in seinen Bann. Ein Mensch, der auf der hohen Sprosse der sozialen Leiter vorbildlich in seiner Selbstdisziplin war. Treu und loyal zu Freund und - Gegner. Sich ständig bildend, sich Rechenschaft abgebend, sich erziehend bis zum letzten Atemzug. Seine Ptiro traf seine Familie plötzlich, ihn selbst gut vorbereitet. TNZBH

B.

Moische Spiegel (6000 Lewajes und 10 Auslandreisen im Jahr). Es wurde eine eigentliche Expedition eingeleitet. Moische erwies sich als allergrösster Glücksfall. Gewandt, zielstrebig, erfahren, mit den richtigen Beziehungen, russisch sprechend, voller Humor und trotzdem feinfühlig. Sein Gehilfe, Boruch Goldberg (Har-Sahav) hat eine 25-jährige Armee-Chewre-Kadische-Erfahrung. Moische veranlasste die notwendigen Vorabklärungen, behördlichen Bewilligungen usw..

Am Sonntag, 18. April 1993 um 10.30 fliege ich mit meinen Söhnen Chaim-Jitzchok und Nafti nach Warschau. Am Flughafen werden wir vom Chauffeur Jankel Czac erwartet. Wir steigen im Hotel Mercure, in der Nähe des jüdischen Viertels, ab. Dann besuchen wir den riesigen Friedhof, wo wegen den Feierlichkeiten zum 50.Jahrestag des Ghetto-Aufstandes viel Betrieb herrscht. Der grösste Teil des Friedhofes ist in einem desolaten Zustand, mit den hohen Bäumen und den zerfallenden Grabsteinen wirkt alles sehr gespenstisch. Ein alter Mann, Awrohom Prajs aus Gura-Calvaria (Ger), anerbietet sich, uns dorthin an die Keworim von einigen Zaddikim zu führen. Wir sagen einige Kapitel Tehillim an den Keworim vom Chiduschei-Ho'rim und S'fas-Emes.

In Warschau zurück sehen wir den berüchtigten Umschlagplatz und andere jüdische Sehenswürdigkeiten. Vom Ghetto ist nichts mehr übrig, die ganze Gegend ist neu. Nur einige

Suche nach ermordeten Jehudim in Polen

VON F. WOLGELERNTER, Zürich

Im Juni 1944, am 1. Tamus 5704 wurde mein Vater Chaim-Jitzchok, sein jüngster Bruder Meir, meine Grossmutter mütterlichseits, Jachet Platkiewicz, ihre Tochter Zena und Schwiegersohn Mordechai Zwi Erlich, die beiden Kinder Esther und Awrohom Reuven sowie der jüdische Partisan Berel Jakubowitz in ihrem Versteck im winzigen Dorf Dembowiec bei Dzialoszyce von polnischen Partisanen ermordet. Der mittlere Bruder meines Vaters, Onkel David und der ältere Sohn der Erlichs, mein Cousin Feiwel, waren zu dieser Zeit auf der Suche nach einem neuen Versteck und blieben verschont.

Seit seiner Kindheit träumt mein jüngster Sohn Nafti davon, mehr über die Umstände dieser Tragödie zu erfahren. Vor ca. 4 Jahren beschloss er das zu tun, was ich eigentlich schon viel früher hätte tun sollen, nämlich die umfangreichen Schriften meines Vaters szl. herauszugeben. Nafti ging mit viel Elan an die Sache, engagierte vier Personen, welche die schwer zu entziffernden Originale in eine leserliche Handschrift übertrugen. Es ist zu hoffen, dass das Buch demnächst erscheinen wird. Im Zuge seiner Nachforschungen besuchte Nafti auch eine Jahres-Versammlung von in Israel lebenden, ehemaligen Dzialoszycer-Juden, wo er als Urenkel von Jachet Platkiewitz und Enkel von Chaim-Itzchok Wolgelernter herzlich begrüsst wurde. Von meinem Cousin Feiwel Erlich, der mit meinem Onkel David als einziger überlebt hat, erfuhr er vom ehemaligen jüdischen Partisanen Awrohom Fuhrmann (Pelon), der mit der Gruppe in

Die Synagoge von Dzialoszyce

ihrem Versteck oft zusammengekommen war. Am Rosch Chodesch Nissan 5753 sprach Nafti mit Fuhrmann. Dieser behauptete, er und auch andere wüssten ganz genau, wo die Gruppe begraben sei. Nafti fand einen Experten aus Bne-Brak für das Auffinden und Überführen von Niftorim aus Osteuropa nach Israel,

Strassennamen erinnern daran, dass einst hunderttausend Juden hier gelebt haben.

Am Montag früh fahren wir kurz nach 6 Uhr Richtung Krakau ab, Moische und Boruch in einem grauen Ford-Van der Foreign Graves Goverment Office mit dem zuverlässigen und sympathischen Adam (Patrik) Neuschewski

11

FAMILY REUNION IN DEMBOWIEC

*F*elix (Feivel) Wolgelernter was born in Dzialoszyce, Poland, during World War II, in 1941. He and his mother survived the Nazi onslaught by passing as Aryans in a small village near Lodz. His father, Reb Chaim Yitzchok Wolgelernter, his maternal grandmother, Yachet Platkiewicz, along with other family members, and Berel Jakubovicz, a Jewish partisan, had been hiding in the tiny village of Dembowiec, near Dzialoszyce. In June 1944, Rosh Chodesh Tamuz 5704, they were murdered by Polish partisans. Reb Chaim Yitzchok's younger brother, David, and his cousin Feivel were away looking at a new hiding place, and survived. Fortunately, David had Reb Chaim Yitzchok's writings with him, which he presented to Felix on his wedding day.

*W*ho killed these Jews? Who buried them? Could their remains be recovered and brought to *kever Yisroel—the* dignity of a final resting place amongst other Jews, ideally in the Holy Land?

*F*elix Wolgelernter, who lives in Zurich, Switzerland, shares with the readers of The Jewish Observer *his struggle to resolve these questions.*

The Jewish Observer

ESTABLISHING CONTACT WITH OUR PAST

Since his childhood, my son Nafti has been eager to find out more about our family's tragedy. Four years ago he decided to publish my father's writings. During the year and a half that he was in hiding, my father kept a diary with his reports and philosophical views on the events and the war. He also composed poems in Hebrew eulogizing his murdered parents and other members of our family, as well as his famous poem on his teacher, the Ostrowzer Rebbe, הי״ד. We hope to publish the book in the near future, first in Yiddish and then in English.

While researching for this project, Nafti attended a meeting of Dzialoszyce Jews in Israel, where he was warmly welcomed as the great-grandson of Yachet Platkiewicz and the grandson of Chaim Yitzchok Wolgelernter. Nafti met with a Jewish partisan, Avrohom Fuhrman (Pelon), who had often visited my family in their hiding place, and knew exactly where our family was buried. That meant that we could finally bring our martyred elders to *kever Yisroel.* Nafti contacted Moshe Spiegel from Bnei Brak, an expert in finding *niftorim* in Eastern Europe and transporting their remains to Israel. Moshe proved to be the right man for the job—competent, fluent in Russian, with the right contacts, very sensitive. His assistant, Boruch Goldberg (Har Zahav), has 25 years of experience in the Army *Chevra Kadisha.* Moshe made the preliminary arrangements in Poland, got the necessary government permits, and the expedition was under way. The following are our notes, recorded as we progressed.

ON THE ROAD TO DEMBOWIEC

On Sunday, April 18, 1993, I board the plane to Warsaw with my sons, Chaim Yitzchok and Nafti. In Warsaw, we visit the huge cemetery, where a large crowd is gathered to mark the 50th anniver-

Feivel Wolgelernter, an electronics engineer, is a member of the Board of the Judische Gemeinde Agudas Achim, in Zürich.

Le site dans la forêt de Dembovitz.

la Choa et eut cet héritier à l'âge de 48 ans.

Le rabbi Yissakhar Dov a épousé la fille du rabbi de Wiznitz, mais pendant de longues années, ils n'ont pas eu d'enfants ; lorsque le fils tant attendu naquit enfin, il fut bien sûr élevé avec un soin tout particulier mais en même temps, son père tint à ce que l'héritier étudie... avec les autres enfants de son âge et ne s'enorgueillisse pas outre mesure de sa filiation. C'est donc ce "dauphin" qui vient d'épouser une jeune fille issue d'une famille rabbinique.

Comme le disait l'un des organisateurs : «Cette grande fête représente pour la 'hassidouth Belz la meilleure réponse à ceux qui ont voulu la détruire, elle et le peuple juif tout entier : nous vivons, et perpétuons notre tradition jusqu'à la venue du Messie !»

HUIT RAPATRIEMENTS-POSTHUMES REUSSIS : La normalisation des relations avec les anciens pays communistes a permis le dénouement heureux, si l'on peut dire, de certains drames qui ont duré presque 50 ans.

C'est ainsi que huit membres de la famille Wohlgelernter, assassinés pendant la Seconde Guerre mondiale, ont enfin eu droit à une sépulture juive en Terre promise. Originaire de Dzalovitz, en Pologne, la famille Wohlgelernter, composée de neuf personnes, trouva refuge dans une autre petite localité du nom de Dembovitz ; mais en fin de compte, ils furent tous assassinés par le paysan qui les avait cachés, quelque part dans la forêt, non loin du village. Durant 49 ans, un petit-fils, reb Feivel, a gardé l'espoir chimérique de retrouver ces corps jetés en pleine nature, et de les enterrer dans un cimetière juif. Il y a quelques années, il a rencontré un témoin qui avait vu ces malheureux avant leur cachette avant d'être massacrés, et depuis il s'est consacré corps et âme à son projet, pour tenter l'impossible. Récemment, le voyage en Pologne a eu lieu, et après maintes péripéties, huit des corps ont été retrouvés, et ensuite rapatriés et enterrés en Erets Israël, le 2 Iyar de cette année.

LES PROJETS AVORTES AUTOUR DE RABBI 'HAI TAIEB : Par contre, cela fait quelque temps déjà que le rav Guets, rav du Kotel, prépare l'opération de rapatriement du corps de rabbi 'Haï Taïeb *lo meth*, qu'il souhaitait

French-language *Kountrass* magazine

APPENDICES

Compilation of chapters not enumerated in the
diarist's handwritten table of contents

APPENDIX A
The *Judenrat*

I FIND IT NECESSARY *to call attention to two "gems" that we inherited in the wake of this dreadful war: the Jewish council, referred to as the Judenrat, which was comprised of a group of our own townspeople, and the Ordnungsdienst, or Jewish police. The latter, formed at the initiative of the Gestapo, was tasked with maintaining order among the Jews, such as enforcing curfew and supervising hygiene. Even before its true face was revealed, this new entity elicited mistrust in the streets of our town, since its members were low-class people and outcasts.*

In no time, the Ordnungsdienst developed into an unchecked authority conducting a reign of terror. Its men pandered to their German masters and distinguished themselves by implementing every decree and ordinance with the sort of cruelty exhibited by newly trained Gestapo officers. Indeed, during the Dzialoszyce expulsion raid, they did not sit with folded hands.

If ever there will arise a Jewish historian who will record the events of these days, his face will turn red with shame when he reaches the disgraceful chapter of the Ordnungsdienst. If the Germans dug the grave of the Jewish

nation, the men of the Ordnungsdienst, without a doubt, were the ones who sealed it.[1]

><

There is feverish commotion upstairs in the *Judenrat* building. The place is like a beehive. Every division of the *Judenrat* is present in its entirety — *Ordnungsdienst, Sanitärdienst,* and all other appointed personnel, along with their children, grandchildren, brothers, sisters, brothers-in-law, sisters-in-law, cousins, nephews, nieces, and anyone else affiliated with Kruk-Kolatacz and company. Parasites at the expense of the downtrodden Jewish masses, they have fortified themselves in the Council citadel, the castle of the Jewish ruling class.

On this terrible Day of Judgment for Dzialoszyce Jewry, they are gathered in their holiday finery, with red letters embroidered on their new armbands and corresponding identity cards in their pockets. They await further instructions. All they need now is the official stamp of Beyerlein, district chief of the Miechow SD, certifying that they will be permitted to remain in town.

Our "competent" Jewish police is almost entirely comprised of men from outside Dzialoszyce, who are supposedly former Zionist activists. They have just received an order from their commander Hampel, the erstwhile councilman of the Bedzin (*Bendin*) branch of Poalei Zion; a more suitable place for him would be a sanatorium for the mentally ill. Their assignment is virtually the same as that of the Gestapo: "Hand in hand with the German authorities, you are to carry out a collection of Jewish money and valuables, without sentiment for brother or sister. In return, you and your wives and children will be exempt from the deportation."

---

1. Ed. Note: The introductory paragraphs are translated from the Hebrew-language letter addressed to the author's brother in Canada.

That is all the men of the *Ordnungsdienst* need to hear. Swaggering down the street, they terrorize the already frightened townspeople who are moving forward in long lines to give away their last groschen — the community's final effort to purportedly save Dzialoszyce from the impending expulsion raid.

Lewkowicz, the professional communal activist noted for his smooth flattery, calms people's anxious emotions. "Don't worry; nothing will happen!" he assures everyone. To the question of whether the townspeople should run for their lives, he replies with an unequivocal "no."

Waga, the brain of the *Judenrat*, sits in a corner of the office, once more examining the identity cards of his half-dozen daughters. He is so disoriented he cannot be certain he hasn't misplaced any.

Grosswald, the self-hating Jew who serves as the chief of the Labor division of the *Judenrat*, runs to and fro in a sweat, disgorging a stream of obscenities. "Aha!" he exclaims. "When the Council needed money, all the Jews were poor. Suddenly they have money — when their lives are at stake! Ha, ha, ha! What a shame!"

Indeed, people are contributing such great quantities that the drawers of the *Judenrat* office are bursting with cash and valuables. A hunched old woman entreats the officials to take the gold bracelet she inherited from her great-grandmother. An elderly man carrying a bolt of white linen, set aside years ago for his burial shrouds, thrusts it into the hands of the *Judenrat*.

All in the name of "saving the town from deportation."

The officials grow tired. They begin to accept donations without counting and recording the amounts. After all, they are only human and they haven't had a bite to eat since their midday meal. Their thirst and craving for beer is intolerable, what with the thick cloud of cigarette smoke filling the room, parching their throats. They send for goose meat sandwiches and a couple of beer bottles.

Hurling an expletive in the direction of the line of Jews, one of the *Judenrat* men calls out, "They couldn't manage to come until now? They always wait for the last minute!"

In Chairman Kruk's private chamber, a closed-door meeting is in progress. In attendance, aside from the powerful, ruthless chairman himself, are the Kolatacz brothers. Common murderers in kid gloves, they were born to torment Jews.

Also present is Henoch Herzberg, brother-in-law of Pesach Szternberg's son-in-law. His official position in the *Judenrat* is not even worthy of note, but his aptitude for squeezing money out of Jews is certainly extraordinary; he has a knack for taking advantage of communal misfortune to fill up the Council's coffers. His profession as a waiter in Lodz serving enticing cakes and beverages helped him win the good graces of the Kehillah bigshots. Eventually, he was granted special privileges and admitted to the inner circle of the Kruk-Kolatacz clique.

On the agenda now is the question of how to extort even more money from the community.

"Come to think of it," exclaims Herzberg, "what do we need more money for? If we tell them we need diamonds and gold, that's what they'll bring! It can't hurt and will certainly come in handy…"

"Yes, what a great idea indeed!" Herzberg gloats, his potbelly protruding and blubbery eyes beaming.

Even the permanently ill-tempered countenance of Chairman Kruk breaks into a smile. Avremel, the younger of the Kolatacz brothers, dances around the room and rubs his hands together gleefully. "Henoch, my boy," he cries, "you deserve a round of drinks!"

Two bottles of excellent brandy and a mouthwatering cheesecake are promptly extracted from the locked cabinet that ostensibly serves as the medicine chest. And with that, they alleviate their concern for the plight of their co-religionists.

Moments later, hushed whispers can be heard in the *Judenrat* office. The Kolatacz brothers, looking around to be certain that others overhear, murmur with mock sorrow, "There is still hope of averting the deportation order. There will be a heavy price to pay, not in money but in gold and diamonds. If only we could come up with the required amount — but the Jews are sleeping! They must be alerted."

Word spreads through Dzialoszyce with lightning speed: "The Council may be able to ransom the town if we contribute our most prized valuables!"

The Jews hurry to bring precious metals for the *Judenrat's* Golden Calf. *Better than to be deported and lose it all anyway!* they reason.

In truth, the people did not have much confidence in their "protectors." On more than one occasion, the *Judenrat* took advantage of an opportunity to help the town by extorting money for their own purposes.

It hasn't been all that long since the incident with Gorniak, the drunken Ukrainian overseer of the Krakow *Arbeitsamt*.

Gorniak's assignment was to round up young Jewish men for forced labor in the Krakow-area work camps, but he could be bought off for a pittance. A number of towns successfully bribed him not to conscript their youth. It was rumored that Grosswald, too, would bribe Gorniak on behalf of the youth of Dzialoszyce. He hadn't yet come up with the money, but after all, wasn't that his job? Neither were the Kolatacz brothers' hands tied!

Just at that time, Chairman Kruk was preparing for his daughter's wedding. The list of guests expected to attend was impressive. It was time to take care of the thick debit ledger at Epsztajn's Restaurant for the various functions and private parties held by the *Judenrat* several times a day. It would not do for the chairman to be put to shame.

"Where will we get the money from?" Grosswald pondered. "Our 80,000-zloty monthly budget barely covers the salaries of our officials. Let's launch a large-scale campaign, stating that we are raising funds to bribe Gorniak. Jews will surely donate to save their children from forced labor in the malaria-ridden swamps around Krakow. We will use that money to pay up the chairman's debts, and if the accursed Gorniak rounds up some laborers, we'll be none the worse. The rich will pay — for money there are ways to get an exemption — and the poor will be happy to work for a few groschen and a free meal. If anything, the market square will be less crowded. Our young men, who are prohibited from engaging in business, loaf around with nothing to do anyway. And if Dzialoszyce will have a shortage of laborers to fill its daily quota at the local workshops, that's too bad."

As in all such matters, Chairman Kruk concurred with Grosswald.

Indeed, people donated tens of thousands of zlotys to the Council pocket. It was a while before anyone realized what was going on, but eventually there were consequences. A couple of bigmouths informed Gorniak that the Dzialoszyce *Judenrat* had conducted a collection without remitting the proceeds. The drunken boor was so incensed, he retaliated by rounding up three hundred of the town's young men for forced labor. On top of that, he carted away suitcases and crates full of cash and valuables that the Jews had brought to the Council office with their own hands.

The *Judenrat* gang made light of the whole episode.

The average person has a short memory, albeit this type of thing has been happening quite often. In any case, what alternative is there? To fall into the hands of the Jewish police is not an enviable position to be in. People would almost rather deal with the "proper" Germans. It is beyond comprehension how the men of the

Ordnungsdienst learned their trade so well. They give beatings like authentic prison guards.

A drowning man grabs at straws. Once again, the townspeople bring whatever valuables they can find. *Who knows? Perhaps this time,* they hope.

The *Judenrat* is delighted with the results. Their latest campaign is a success! Now they wait impatiently for Beyerlein, who is supposed to arrive any minute. As soon as he stamps their identity cards, exempting them from deportation, they will be safe.

"Let the people pray at the cemetery. On the contrary, if G-d helps, we surely don't mind. But their prayers are in vain, for the deportation order is already sealed. There is nothing we could have done about it. But we better not tell or our campaign will be ruined."

This was the outlook of our public servants at the *Judenrat,* while the *Yidden* of Dzialoszyce cried out to Hashem with all their might in a desperate effort to save their lives.

APPENDIX B

Righteous Gentiles

Mrs. Marta Stepanowa[1]

[Letter from Chaim Yitzchok Wolgelernter, hiding in Debowiec, to Mrs. Stepanowa in Jedlnia]

> Honorable Mrs. Stepanowa!
>
> Although the proper time has not yet arrived to evaluate your exalted act in saving my dear wife, my only child, and my niece, as I write my "Book of Tears" chronicling the memories of my family, I feel obligated to ensure that a rightful place be given to your heroism, pure conscience, and humane attitude towards a hunted and tormented people.
>
> I enclose herewith a fragment of my work that will serve as a provisional token of appreciation from an innocent, bereft, and heartbroken man.
>
> With great esteem, Henryk

---

1. Ed. Note: Apparently, the author was not aware that Mrs. Stepanowa's motives were less than altruistic; alternatively, he may have wanted to flatter her in the hope that she would continue to shelter his wife and child. Although gentiles who aided Jews for financial gain are not eligible for the "Righteous Among the Nations" designation, many Jews who survived in hiding by paying large monthly fees were, nevertheless, filled with gratitude to their hosts for saving their lives and considered them to be Righteous Gentiles.

LET THE NAMES of those few pure, uncorrupted Polish souls who were appalled at the extermination campaign implemented against Polish Jewry by Hitler's beastly murderers be inscribed with gilded lettering on the blood-soaked pages of Jewish history.

Let it be known to the world at large, and in particular to our surviving brethren overseas, that during this terrible pogrom in which twentieth-century idolatrous, cannibalistic Germans dug a mass grave for millions of innocent men, women, and children — an act unequaled in any martyrology — there were to be found in Poland lone individuals whose hearts were aglow with compassion and humanity.

Simple, noble folk they were, not politicians aiming to capitalize on their actions or careerists seeking compensation for their deeds but religious Catholics whose consciences were shocked by the barbarism perpetrated against defenseless Jews. With clear perception and open minds, these people did not allow themselves to become blinded by the daily storm of fanatical, Jew-hating propaganda printed in the tabloids. Of staunch and fearless character, they were not disconcerted by the pervasive terror that hung like the sword of Damocles over the Polish nation, with severe reprisal threatened upon any person extending aid to an unfortunate, hapless Jew.

Still fresh in my mind's eye is the dreadful scene of the first Dzialoszyce *Aussiedlung* on September 2, 1942. The streets swarmed with brown-shirted Gestapo vermin, the ostensible saviors of European civilization. Deep, wide pits were dug in the rough terrain at the edge of town, where 1500 Jewish victims were sadistically mowed down with automatic pistols, filling the pits to the top. This concluded the first act of the bloody drama.

It was followed by an even more horrifying finale: a train of hundreds of sealed wagons, innocent little children thrown aboard in paper sacks, a traveling grave of the living carrying its occupants

to an unknown destination where they found relief through a macabre death in the form of poisonous gases.

We were among the few fortunate individuals who escaped, trying desperately to save ourselves like drowning men in a raging sea clinging to a plank of their sunken ship. It was then that my dear wife, my niece, and my one remaining precious little child found a refuge, a fertile oasis in a barren wilderness, in the tranquil Jedlnia home of an idealistic and aristocratic woman, Mrs. Marta Stepanowa. The noble blood flowing through her veins was aroused by the sight of three total strangers condemned to death, who were seeking shelter under her wing. Her pure religious soul was stirred by the anguish and suffering of thousands of years of Jewish martyrdom reflected in the innocent blue eyes of little Felusz. *What wrong have I done? Why won't they let me live, along with my dear Mammeshe? Why did they snatch away my three-year-old sister? In which unknown place is my Tatteshe wandering?*

This is my opportunity to demonstrate the truth, thought Mrs. Stepanowa, *by rescuing innocent people from spiritually blind non-believers who are supposedly our cultural redeemers. The time has come to show that not everyone is poisoned with this illogical hatred towards the Jew, the helpless creature that is said to be the cause of all our woes. No, it is impossible that these decent, quiet people are warmongers. Felusz most certainly did not conduct an anti-Hitler propaganda campaign, Marisia certainly does not aspire to dominate the Aryan race, and I could swear that Helena is no international, Communist spy.*

With her rich intellectual past and broad horizons, this discerning woman would not allow baseless arguments to affect the clarity of her thoughts. Mrs. Stepanowa was proud of the moral mission Providence had sent her way. It was not for naught that the local intelligentsia and upper class held her in high esteem and paid heed to her every word. Her influence extended to all those around her and she inculcated her morals and love of

humanity into the members of her family.[2] Thus, when Marisia's sister Helenka was alone and overwhelmed, seeking refuge in the tumultuous city of Warsaw, Mrs. Stepanowa's educated daughter Krystyna appeared before her like a heavenly angel. Employed as a secretary for a German-run international firm, Krystyna used her connections to arrange a position in the company for the Jewish girl. The eight of us in hiding were able to endure our confinement thanks to Helenka who visited us often, bringing us money and other necessities. And so, if Mrs. Stepanowa directly saved the lives of my wife, son, and niece, her daughter Krystyna indirectly effected the hitherto survival of eight people.

In this murky twilight that transformed humankind into a disfigured caricature that considers base murder to be cultured civilization, these shining figures will be immortalized in the annals of our family, taking the front row in our memories alongside our dearest relatives.

Now that the clock of world events is about to strike twelve and the day of retribution approaches with giant strides, justice will be visited upon the barbaric directors of this bloody drama, the igniters of this worldwide conflagration, the hangmen of a millenia-old nation that bequeathed the Bible to the world. The mark of Cain will be carved into the foreheads of all those who joined this savage demon-dance.

And at the solemn memorial ceremony that will be held for the victims of the swastika-guillotine, tribute will be paid to the few heroic Polish individuals who came to the rescue of Jews, for they are the true followers of Casimir the Great.[3]

---

2. Ed. Note: Ironically, Chayele later harbored a vague suspicion that Mrs. Stepanowa's grandson may have been an accomplice in the murder of her family members in hiding, since he was aware that she was sending money to Debowiec.

3. Fourteenth-century king of Poland who protected the Jews; the relative prosperity and freedom enjoyed during his reign encouraged the migration of Jews from other parts of Europe to Poland.

Engineer Szeliga

BEGINNING OF SUMMER 1942: The air is thick with an explosive charge. Oppressive legislation advances like a firestorm upon the already beleaguered Jews. Gorniak, the crude Ukrainian overseer of the Krakow *Arbeitsamt*, has been stationed in Dzialoszyce for the last few days, conducting registration of all men and women between the ages of twelve and sixty. Several transports of young men have already departed for the Kostrze slave labor camp.

The first reports are appalling. A dilapidated old fortress houses the inmates. Rivulets of water run down the damp stone walls all year round. A thin layer of moldy, insect-infested straw serves as bedding. Rats and mice have free rein of the place. This dismal dungeon is where the slave laborers spend the night after a twelve-hour day working knee-deep in the malarian swamps of Kostrze, during which time they are rewarded with two hundred grams of half-baked black bread, a bit of lukewarm dark liquid, and a bowl of putrid cabbage soup at noon. Some twenty workers lie spread out on the straw in each of the dingy, stuffy rooms of the fortress. The stifling heat and the never-ending battle against the loathsome little creatures make sleep impossible.

All the letters sent home by the laborers contain the same message: "Father, if you have any hope of seeing me alive, rescue me from here even if it means selling everything you own!"

Emotions reach a boiling point in town. Mothers storm the Council building. "After all the challenges of raising our children, shall we bury them alive in the fields of Kostrze? Take everything we own and give us back our children!"

In the interim, there is a widespread rumor that women, too, will soon be sent to work, possibly even to Germany. Our household is in a state of panic. Most of us are young and able-bodied — my brother-in-law Hershel, his two sons, and two of his daughters; my

brother-in-law Yisroel; my sister-in-law Reizele; my wife. Our family alone is nearly enough to fill a transport of laborers.

Consumed with worry, we try to think of a way out. Hershel's oldest daughter Chayele is the only one who seems unruffled. The ever-charming smile on her youthful face does not fade. But her blithe attitude during these grave, uncertain circumstances incurs the wrath of the others.

"Don't you care about the trouble we *Yidden* are in?" her father chides her. "And today I noticed you talking once again to a young man in eyeglasses. What is that about?"

"Don't worry, *Tatteshe*," she replies, still smiling. "You'll see..."

Later that day, Chayele comes running in breathlessly. "Straighten up the apartment — we're having company! Engineer Szeliga, the supervisor of the Nieszkow work site, is coming to pay us a visit. He is a very decent, refined person and he might be willing to help us."

Indeed, soon seated before us was a quiet, contemplative man who measured his every word. In the course of his visit, he assigned Chayele to an office job and registered the rest of us as laborers at the sewer construction project. Naturally, these jobs were fictitious; we did not report for work.

The young man with the glasses whom Hershel had seen talking to Chayele had been Engineer Szeliga. The lighthearted Chayele had accomplished more with her youthful smile than the rest of us sitting day after day with anxious faces.

It was through the benevolence of Engineer Szeliga that our family was not sent to the Kostrze slave labor camp.

Wednesday evening, September 2, 1942: *Junacy* hooligans besiege the town of Dzialoszyce. People run madly to and fro, looking for a place to hide. The cries and wails of the ill-fated *Yidden* fill the air as the grim specter of deportation becomes reality.

Some of us had left town moments earlier. But as we trek through the furrowed fields towards the countryside, my nieces Chayele and Esther'l are still in Dzialoszyce searching for a way to break through the chain of *Junacy*.

Removing their Jewish armbands, they hurry to the outskirts of town. A *Junak*, taking them for Polish girls, allows them through. "*Zydkes!*" they hear someone call after them, as they break into a run towards the village of Nieszkow to seek help from Engineer Szeliga.

Arriving in Nieszkow, Chayele and Esther'l find the village in turmoil; the sound of gunfire can be heard in the background. The engineer is not home. He is due back from Miechow that night. The local peasants bolt the doors of their cottages and refuse to shelter the girls, explaining that the *Junacy* have come to Nieszkow because of the Jewish work site there.

As the two girls wander through wet fields, they hear the cries of the Jewish laborers a few meters away, pleading with the carousing Polish hooligans not to harm them. The situation seems hopeless. Prepared for all eventualities, they lie down beneath the big chestnut tree in Mrs. Zbyszewska's garden. With their faculties intent on detecting the slightest rustle, they do not even feel the cold evening dew saturating their thin summer garments.

In the dark of night, as they await the worst, they suddenly make out a human form. "This is it! We're done for...these are our last moments," they whisper to each other with pounding hearts. The crunch of footsteps on the fallen twigs lying about the garden floor pierces through them, as the figure comes nearer and nearer.

What's that...? I hear my name being called! Chayele realizes.

"*Baruch Hashem*! It's Engineer Szeliga!" The exhausted girls fall upon him as if he were their beloved father. "Save us!" they cry.

The aristocratic bearing of the reserved gentleman gives way and he bursts into tears. "I just got back," Engineer Szeliga explains,

wringing his hands. "Mrs. Zbyszewska told me you were here. Unfortunately, I did not yet finish arranging your Aryan documents, and now my plan to send you to my friend in Warsaw is spoiled. Without identity cards, how will you leave the village? And with the situation the way it is now, what are we to do?"

Despite his distress, the engineer does not lose heart. He brings the girls to the home of an acquaintance in another village.

I must save these children — and not only for their sake. For if they can move about freely as non-Jews, they will be able to help their family members who have taken refuge in the countryside. An opportunity has come my way to exemplify the principle of humanitarian love preached for thousands of years, the cornerstone of entire religions and cultures, which has unfortunately been caricaturized by those delusional racial theories. Yes, I will save them!

After writing a letter to his friend in Warsaw, the engineer summoned the foreman of the Nieszkow work site, handed him the letter, and ordered him to accompany the girls. With the foreman's typical Aryan features, no one would suspect that the girls traveling with him were Jewish.

By the next day, Chayele and Esther'l were on the train. From afar, they could see two genuine tears of compassion roll down from under Engineer Szeliga's eyeglasses.

They arrived at their destination and were saved.

The fifteenth of December 1942 finds me in Szyszczyce together with several family members. Fierce raids have been carried out in the surrounding area, triggering fear among the local farmers. Rumor has it that any village harboring Jews will be burned down.

Our Polish hosts begin suggesting to their Jewish guests that it is time to go. Some more bluntly inform the Jews that they must leave immediately. We cannot even entertain the thought of returning to Dzialoszyce. All the Jewish apartments there have either been sold

or rented out. A number of Jews leave for Krakow, but many are seized on the way.

Thankfully, as a result of Engineer Szeliga having arranged refuge for Chayele and Esther'l in Warsaw, my wife and child found a haven and settled down safely with Hashem's help. Still, I am extremely distraught. My concern for the fate of my parents and siblings in Kazimierz leaves me no rest. It is already several weeks since the *Aussiedlung* there and I haven't heard any news of them. And here in Szyszczyce, the bottom is sliding out from under us. Where will we all go if they drive us out of the village?

A friend and I decide to dig a cave where a group of us can hide in the event we are forced to leave the village. We are in the midst of working when a young blonde woman by the name of Magda Kaziel approaches me. She hands me a letter from my brothers.

I learn that my beloved parents and sister were murdered and that my two brokenhearted brothers miraculously managed to escape and had set out on a risky journey to search for me. Remembering that Yitta's Polish friend Magda lived in Skalbmierz, they had made their way there. After welcoming them with motherly love, Magda resolved to save them and to find me, their brother. One day, while she was riding the *kolejka*, the topic of discussion was the Jews. Kindhearted Magda spoke up in defense of the downtrodden nation. And when one of the passengers extolled the Germans' murderous actions — clearly, this Pole had been entrusted with a fortune of Jewish property for safekeeping — Magda retorted, "I am hard-pressed for money, yet if I would know where the Platkiewicz family is hiding I would even go there by foot to pay the debt I owe them. For who knows if they even have a piece of bread to eat. That is the way any devout Christian should behave."

In the corner of the railcar sat an intelligent-looking young man reading a book, appearing indifferent to the conversation around him, albeit nervously smoking a cigarette. Upon hearing the

Platkiewicz name, he rose from his seat, elbowed his way through the throng and tapped Magda on the foot. Magda got off the train and waited for him. On the side of the platform, the man told her where she could find the Platkiewicz family, adding that she must act with utmost secrecy if she had their best interests in mind. For that reason, he would not reveal his name.

And so it came to be that my brother-in-law Hershel, his wife and two sons, my mother-in-law, and I joined my brothers in Magda's house and were saved with Hashem's help, through the young man who told Magda where to find us.

The man was Engineer Szeliga.[4]

---

4. After the war, Helenka (Chayele Erlich) Dresner tried to track down Engineer Szeliga but could not find a trace of him.

APPENDIX C

Memories of Ostrovtze (Ostrowiec)

AT THE AGE OF SIXTEEN, after spending my best years in the *yeshivos* of Krakow acquiring a considerable amount of knowledge of Gemara, *Tosafos* and *mefarshim*, my soul began to thirst for more. My life in Galicia suddenly felt boring, monotonous and narrow. I needed a force that would sweep me up, catapult me to broader and loftier spiritual horizons, and resolve the various questions that gnawed at my mind. I decided to travel to Ostrowiec.

My *rebbi* in Krakow, Rav Yudel Levin, a disciple of the first Ostrovtzer Rebbe, had given me a taste of the *pilpul* method of Gemara learning in which one precise, brilliant flash of insight, sometimes derived through mathematical calculations, elucidates a broad gamut of complex, seemingly disparate Talmudic sections and cryptic sayings of the Sages. This approach to Torah study, coupled with the unusual path of serving G-d through fasting and self-denial, formed the Ostrovtze *derech*, which was shrouded in a veil of legend and captivated me so.

My elderly grandfather, Rav Yechiel Issamar Wolgelernter, who was living alone in a small, two-room apartment in Ostrowiec, invited me to board with him.[1] Food was not a concern since the Beis Meir yeshivah served meals for the *bachurim*.

And so, on the day before Shemini Atzeres 5689/1928, I stepped over the threshold of the chamber of the renowned Rebbe of Ostrowiec, Rav Yechezkel Halstuk, the only son and successor of the saintly Rav Meir Yechiel *zt"l*. To this day I cannot understand how I, an insignificant earthly being, found myself standing in the presence of the powerful light radiating from the pillar of fire that personified the Ostrovtzer Rebbe. As to whether I felt its effect on me — of that I am certain.

The rebbe welcomed me and invited me to join him for Yom Tov along with all the arriving chassidim.

The *hakafos*; the *tish* on the night of Shemini Atzeres; the *davening* in the morning, particularly the *tefillah* of *Nishmas* when the rebbe's soul expressed its yearning to cleave to Hashem — all combined to make a profound impression on me that I will never forget. You could literally visualize the pain and suffering of the Jewish people being poured out before Hashem by their great *shliach tzibbur*, as he cried out in a sea of tears: "*Heiliger Tatte*, have pity on the *Yidden* for they will do *teshuvah* and return to You!"

I felt that every bone and limb in my body was undergoing purification in a fiery crucible until my entire being was cleansed. Oblivious to everything around me, I soared higher and higher toward the infinite loftiness of the Heavenly spheres. All day long, I experienced an inner warmth and satisfaction, an exhilarating sense of spiritual elevation. The atmosphere at the *tish*, the Torah learning...it was otherworldly, a piece of the Divine, disconnected from the mundane, its purpose to lift this world to a higher realm.

---

1. His wife Leah, Chaim Yitzchok's grandmother, had passed away earlier that year.

After the *tish*, when the *talmidim* plumbed the depths of the rebbe's discourse, I was swept away by the interweaving of brilliant new concepts that touched the deepest recesses of my soul as if directed at me, resolving my doubts and slaking the thirst of my spirit. In that one day, questions that had plagued me for years were answered.

I was beginning to understand the great charismatic power for which the Ostrovtzer Rebbe was renowned.

~~~

While giving an incisive *shiur* one day, the rebbe noticed me with a pen in hand, taking notes. After *davening*, he called me into his chamber. Overawed and apprehensive, I entered the room, expecting to receive a scolding.

There was an indescribable atmosphere of respect and silence during the Ostrovtzer Rebbe's *shiur*. The power and brilliance of his delivery enraptured the *talmidim* and transported them to a lofty, ethereal sphere. While straining to comprehend the depth of a *chiddush*, one was no longer cognizant of the existence of the physical world. And here I was caught scribbling in a notebook, which could be taken as an indication that I did not grasp the complexity of the subject at hand.

To make things worse, on the previous day I had told the rebbe that I desired to study Halachah for the purpose of *horaah* — which could further imply that I was not overly interested in *pilpul*, the cornerstone of the rebbe's approach to Torah learning.

Without any preliminaries, the rebbe asked me what I had been doing in the middle of the *shiur*. Hanging my head in shame, I timidly handed over the notebook. As the rebbe perused my notes, I trembled in fear, as before a difficult exam that could jeopardize one's career. I sensed that this moment would have a critical influence on my future path.

Immersed in thought, the rebbe leaned back in his chair. Then, with my notes still on his desk, he turned towards me and began to speak.

"Listen, my *talmid*: Everything in existence is a composite of *chomer* (substance) and *tzurah* (form), known in Kabbalah as *guf* (body) and *neshamah* (soul). In Man, the crown of creation, the physical body is simply a garment for the soul, which is a segment of the Divine Source.

"The mitzvos are the spiritual sustenance and pleasure of the *neshamah*. Hence, the more mitzvos one performs, the nearer the person draws to his Divine Source, thereby bringing delight to Hashem. This is the ultimate fulfillment of Man. Moshe Rabbeinu attained the pinnacle of closeness to Hashem, speaking directly to Him.

"Elevation of the soul was the intention of every great leader who initiated a path in the service of G-d. The Baal Shem Tov founded the movement of *Chassidus*, which injected an element of passion and vitality in *avodas Hashem*, inspiring even the simple, unlearned Yid by showing him that his *neshamah*, too, could achieve its *tikkun*.

"My saintly father," continued the rebbe, "forged a path of serving Hashem through fasting and self-denial. He maintained that by rejecting the material aspects of life, man's physicality is weakened. As a result, his spiritual self is brought to the fore, and his *neshamah* rises to an ever-higher sphere. In the same vein, he understood '*yissurim shel ahavah*' as afflictions arising out of Hashem's love for the person, since the resultant elevation of the *neshamah* becomes a source of pleasure to G-d. In contrast, the Sages state that if one is stricken with *tzaraas*, his suffering is not *yissurim shel ahavah*, since the skin eruption stems from a spirit of impurity, which contaminates the soul.

"My father's innovative method of *pilpul* shared the same aim. Through hairsplitting analysis of the distinctions of the text, the

core of Man's intellect penetrates the nucleus of Torah, thereby bonding the *neshamah* to the inner light of the Torah and to Hashem, actualizing the principle of '*Oraisa, Kudsha Brich Hu, V'Yisrael chad hu* — The Torah, the Holy One, and Israel are One.'

"Your style of writing appeals to me very much," concluded the rebbe, "albeit a few points need correction. However, now that I gave you this introduction, I believe you will understand how to continue writing. In fact, I would like you to transcribe my daily *shiur* and show me your notes after each one.

"But there is something else. Yesterday you told me that you wanted to learn Halachah. Know that Halachah is a fence designed to curb the cravings of the heart. Thus, it is an expression of *yirah*, fear of G-d, while *pilpul* is an expression of *ahavah*, love of G-d. By learning both, you will be merging your heart and your intellect — *yirah* and *ahavah* — and that is the ultimate perfection of a person. Go forward, and may you succeed!"

Leaving the rebbe's chamber, I felt renewed vigor course through me. I had touched upon truth, the integration of Torah and *yirah*. My goal was beginning to materialize sooner than I had imagined: my father's dream of seeing me ordained as a *rav* was about to become a reality. All that was needed was for me to harness my youthful passion, energy, and diligence under the influence of the holy Ostrovtzer Rebbe.

It was my last Shabbos in Ostrowiec, two weeks before my wedding. On Motza'ei Shabbos, with an hour left to say goodbye to my friends and acquaintances before catching the train, I approached the rebbe at the traditional *melaveh malkah* meal to bid him farewell.

Clothed in his Shabbos attire, his face radiating a holy glow, the rebbe escorted me outside. Clasping my hand in both his hands, he whispered a silent plea. Then he spoke.

"My beloved *talmid*, you are about to leave an environment in which you toiled mightily in Torah learning. You do not know if you will be able to continue involving yourself in Torah study with the same intensity. Remember one thing: Just as the soul of a person is clothed in the body, which is akin to a garment shielding its wearer from harm and hurt, so too must one's Torah learning, the soul, the source of life, be encased in a garment. That garment is good *middos*.

"In light of this, the Sages said: *An unclothed person is forbidden to hold a Torah scroll.* In a figurative sense, the 'unclothed person' refers to one who lacks good character traits. The same idea is expressed in the dictum, *A Torah scholar who goes out with a grease stain on his clothing is deserving of death.* Figuratively, this refers to a Torah scholar who exhibits disgraceful character traits.

"In the same vein, the Sages said: *One who toils in Torah and acts kindly toward others, what will people say about him? Praiseworthy is she who bore him.* Conversely, if a Torah scholar is inconsiderate, people will say, *His mother should have buried him.* For if a *talmid chacham's* behavior and character are not in harmony with his Torah learning, he deserves to die.

"Similarly, when Rivkah told Yaakov to go and receive his father Yitzchak's blessings, *the dew of the heaven and the fatness of the land,* the verse reads: *Rivkah took her older son Eisav's finest garments, which were in her keeping in the house* — a metaphor for the *middah* of respect which Eisav demonstrated in his parents' home — *and she put them on Yaakov, her younger son* — encasing Yaakov's Torah learning in the garment of good *middos*.

"My dear *talmid*," continued the rebbe, "now that you are going out of the tent of Torah to receive the *dew of the heaven and the fatness of the land,* you must don the garment of fine character traits and good deeds.

"May the Almighty bless you, make you fruitful and numerous… And may He bestow on you the blessing of Avraham. And may your ancestor, the holy Chozeh of Lublin, safeguard you from distress so that you may serve Hashem with *ahavah* and *yirah."*

※

Ultimately, the rebbe's *tefillos* were not able to annul the Heavenly decree, sealed beyond a fortress of Divine Justice. The pillar of fire could no longer illuminate the shroud of darkness that enveloped the Jewish people. And as millions of *Yidden* were offered on the altar of *kiddush Hashem*, could their great *shliach tzibbur* not be in their midst?

When European Jewry was annihilated, their temples laid waste, their sanctuaries desecrated, there was no place for the Ark of the saintly Ostrovtzer Rebbe, and so the *Luchos* were shattered.

Kinah for the Ostrovtzer Rebbe,
Rav Yechezkel Halevi Halstuk *Hy"d*

Immersed in mourning over the loss of my father, mother, and sister,
Who were plucked during the harvest of blood,
Enshrouded alone in a twofold bereavement, my heart torn to pieces,
I sit hidden in the loft of a cowshed, my soul weeping,
When suddenly, I am startled by the news
Of the appalling murder of my rebbe and his seven sons.
And so I dedicate these lines to his sainted memory.

With the book of Zohar before him, the rebbe sits, submerged in thought,
Wearing his tefillin, wrapped in his tallis,
Mortifying his body, fasting three days in succession,
Searching in Kabbalah for a resolution to the questions that torment him
Regarding the Torah commandment:
Do not slaughter an animal and its offspring on the same day.

Thoughts and reflections wrestle within the mind of this tzaddik,
What is my purpose? What have I achieved in life?
Were all my struggles in vain?
But to us, his disciples, enfolded by his powerful influence,
His life and deeds served as a shining example and a beacon of light.

The only son of the saintly Rav Meir Yechiel of Ostrowiec,
He showed signs of superior ability
And extraordinary diligence at an early age.

His father taught him Gemara, Halachah, and the secrets of Kabbalah,
Sharpening his mind with the intricacies of Talmudic dialectics;

As the youngster eagerly drew from the sea of the Talmud, extracting its
   treasures,
His fame quickly spread in the world of Torah and among the rabbinate.
Even before he reached the age of eighteen,
The foremost rabbinical leaders of the land referred to him as a gaon and
   gadol.

After his father married him off to the daughter of the Melitzer Rebbe,
He found a suitable environment in Mielec for his holy work,
Learning Torah and serving Hashem with purity and asceticism,
Delving into the depths of Halachah without respite or sleep;
Soon he was crowned as rav in the town of Inowlodz.

The pure Ostrovtze ideology that suffused the rebbe
Enthralled all those who sought him out,
And his public sermons moved the hearts of their listeners;
After a time at his post in Inowlodz,
He was elected rav and leader of the city of Nasielsk.

When his father, Rav Meir Yechiel, returned his soul to his Maker
On 19 Adar 5688/1928,
Rav Yechezkel succeeded him as leader of the flock,
Establishing Yeshivah Beis Meir in his father's memory,
And transforming Ostrowiec into a spiritual center.
Crowned with the title of Admor and Rabbeinu,
He brought many back from their sinful ways.

When standing in prayer and supplication,
The rebbe's devotion was unequaled.
Divested of mundanity, his spirit would ascend with fiery ardor,

Cleaving to the Eternal One.
"Heiliger Tatte! Merciful Father…!" he would cry out,
With tears flowing freely and a heart filled with yearning;
Listening to him, even a heart of stone
Could not help but be broken and moved to repentance.

Our rebbe transmitted to us his father's method of pilpul:
To penetrate the core with a crystal-clear view.
With sharp-witted analysis, he clarified the intricacies of the subject
matter,
Settling innumerable questions of Halachah
And developing novel insights in Torah.
Indeed, as his students testified,
There was nary a question presented to the rebbe,
Which he could not resolve at once.

Sacrifice, humility, self-effacement,
Love for the most ordinary Jew, simplicity and modesty
Were the qualities he ingrained
In the hearts of his students and all those who flocked to him.
New insights on plain and mystical meanings of the text
Were a source of great pleasure to him.
I remember when the rebbe granted me heter horaah —
I was seventeen at the time —
He asked me to sort and transcribe his novellae.
Handing me the key to the case of his manuscripts, he said,
"Take this, Chaim Yitzchok, and guard it carefully,
For this is my only reward for all my endeavors."

In his final days, the persecutions, deportations, killings, and atrocities,
The calamity of our people, the destruction of the Jewish nation,

Saddened his spirit and his soul.
Withdrawn into seclusion, he hovered in the lofty spiritual worlds,
Searching for answers in the esoteric wisdom of Kabbalah,
When suddenly, alas!
The enemy burst in, and the rebbe was murdered,
Along with two of his sons.[2]
The incongruity of: Do not slaughter a sheep and its offspring on the same
day...
As well as the age-old question: "Is this the reward for Torah learning?"
Have not been resolved to this day.

In memory of Harav Hakadosh
Rabbeinu Yechezkel Halevi Hy"d, son of Admor Hakadosh
Rabbeinu Meir Yechiel Halstuk of Ostrowiec zt"l

Chaim Yitzchok Wolgelernter
Shevat 5703
In the loft[3]

---

2. According to later accounts by survivors, including the author's *chavrusa* Aharon Rappaport, the rebbe and two of his sons evaded the first expulsion of the Ostrowiec ghetto on October 11 and 12, 1942. They eventually hid in the Sandomierz (*Tsuzmir*) ghetto where the rebbe was murdered in cold blood by Gestapo Chief Braun in Teves/December of 1942. Three of the rebbe's sons were deported to Treblinka less than a month later. Within a short period of time, his entire family had perished — his wife Baila Mirel, seven sons, and one daughter. [For further details, see *Eileh Ezkerah: Osef Toldos Kedoshei 5700-5705 — These I Will Remember: Biographies of Leaders of Religious Jewry in Europe Who Perished During the Years 1939-1945*, Vol. IV, edited by Yitzchok Levin, New York, 1961, and *Sefer Ostrovtze L'zikaron Ule'edut*, Tel Aviv, 1971 — *Ostrowiec: A Monument on the Ruins of an Annihilated Jewish Community*, www.jewishgen.org.]

3. The acrostic *kinah* composed by Chaim Yitzchok Wolgelernter in memory of the Ostrovtzer Rebbe has previously been published in its original form in several *sefarim* pertaining to the Ostrovtze legacy: *Meir Einei Chachamim: Kadshei Yechezkel*, Reuven Mandelbaum, 1950; *Rabbi Meir Yechiel Me'Ostrovtze*, Isser Frenkel, 1953; *Sefer Ostrovtze L'zikaron Ule'edut* [ibid.]; *Mishmeres Kehunah*, Yechiel Fishel Cohen, 1997; and *Beis Meir HaTorah*, Yehuda Leib Halstuk, 2009.

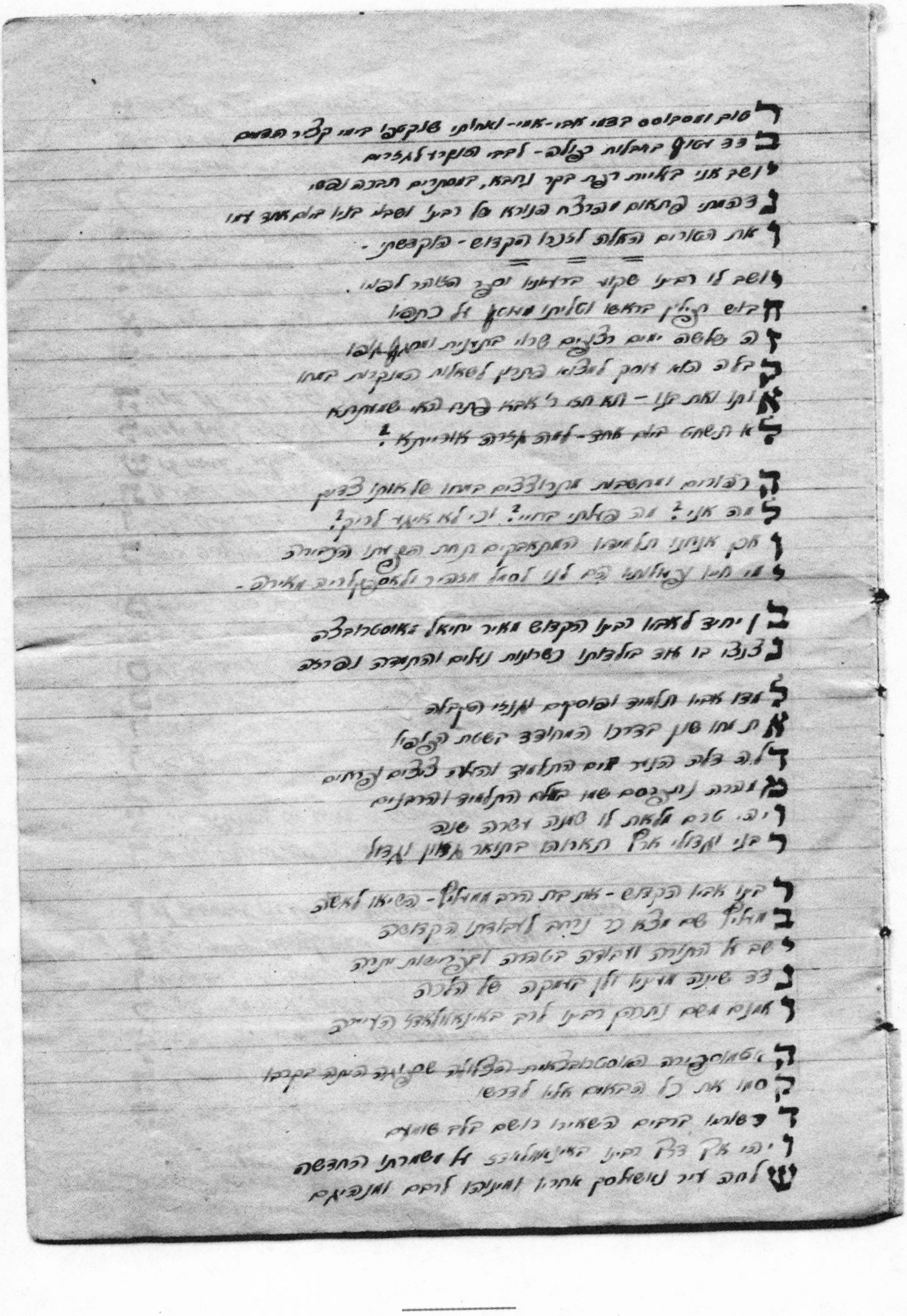

ADDENDUM

Torah and Talmudic Correspondence and Writings of
R' Chaim Yitzchok Wolgelernter Hy"d

שאלות   צפנת פענח   ותשובות   קמא

(עמוד ימני)

וקופה של צדקה ועי' ב"ב ד' ט' גבי
עני המחזיר על הפתחים, ע"ש בתוס'
ורש"י ועי' מדרים ד' מ"ה פ"ב וכבת
קל"א פ"ב אהדורי אפיתחא וכו' ועי'
שבועות כ"ה ע"א ותוס' מדרים ד' ח'
ע"ש הגירסא ורק דאז מגבין בפמחות
מפרוטה כ"מ מהרמב"ס ז"ל.

[אם מותר להדליק עלעקטרי ביום טוב]

ע"ד האלעקטרי בודאי אסור ביום טוב
להדליק ואכמ"ל, כי זה מוליד
אור.
יוסף ראזין

סימן קעד

יום ב' י"א טבת תרפ"ט דוינסק.

[לר' חיים יצחק וואלגעלערנטער
מסאזימיעזש וויעלקא]

[נדבר חולה שיש בו סכנה דקיימא לן
דמאכילין אותו הקל הקל, וכסתפקתי
היכא דאין לחולה שיב"ס רק דבר איסור
ולהבירו יש דבר היתר, אם חבירו מחויב
לתת לו את ההיתר שלו, להצילו מפיקוח
כפש, כיון דלחולה עצמו אין דבר היתר
רק דבר איסור לבד והוי כאין לו כלום
ומחויב הוא להצילו, או דילמא כיון דלחולה
שיב"ס הותר כל דבר איסור אם אין לו
היתר, ממילא אין לו לחבירו להצילו
בדבר היתר שלו.]

מ"ש בנדר אם מועל חיוב, הנה עי'
בהך מחלוקת ביומא שם גבי
טבל ותרומה יע"ש ואף דתרומה יש
גזל כהן ומתנת כהונה, משא"כ בטבל
וים בזה אריכות גדול יע"' בתום' ד'
כ"ה פ"ב, ובכ"מ בזה, גבי הנאה של
כילוי, ובאמת למה לא מוקי הגמ' שם
דמיירי בכהן דלאחר הפרשה יכול לאכול
הכל רק משום הספרשה, ובירושלמי שם
ותוספתא גבי חלה וערלה ואף דערלה
אינה ממון שום אדם כמ"ש הרמב"ס
בפמ' ערלה פ"ב דלזך א"ל להריס

(עמוד שמאלי)

חזין דמ"מ איסור קל עדיף אף שים
בו גדר גזל יע"ש [ד' פ"ג ע"כ] גבי
קפתח את הרועה, ובירושלמי שם בהך
דוד דאכל שתי לה"ש משתי בכמות
ובמנמות ד' ל"ה ע"ב, על"פ חזין דזה
חיוב על הביהנים וליכא בזה גזל השבט,
ומאוד יש להאריך בזה דבאמת זה גרע
עי' ב"ק ד' ס' ע"ב גבי מציל כו' ע"ש
בתום', והגדר דטיכא דמחיב לשלם לא
איכפת לן אבל היכא דפטור מלשלם גרע
יע"ש ב"ק ד' פ"א גבי תנאי יהושע גבי
מפסג ע"ש בזה ואכמ"ל.
יוסף ראזין

סימן קעה
להנ"ל

א) **מ"ש** גבי כוונה, הנה באמת מלימ
כה"ג בהך דמגינה ד' י"ט
ע"ב גבי טבל ועלה יע"ש בתום' הגירסא
וטודעו לא דמסני מחזיק עצמו, ולך בהך
דיבמות ד' מ"ו ע"א גבי הך דמנמין
עבדו דר"א בהדי דלי ראשו הניחו לו
זולמא דטינא משום דאף אמ"כ כי"יכול
לומר לשם בן חורין ולכך עשו בו תיקף
עבדות ט"ש אך מ"מ גבי טהרה לא
מהני זה ורק במעלה דרכנן כמו במגינה
הנ"ל.

ב) **מ"ש** מנימין דף ב' ל' גבי סתם כו'
התם הוי גדר רוב מצוין מומחין
כי בכל הדברים אמרינן זה כמו בעירכין
ותום' מנחות ד' מ"ב פ"ב ע"ש פ"ב ד"ה
ואין וכ"ל כר"ן כ"ג בקידושין בזה ועי'
בכורות ד' כ' ע"ב בזה, לכן כיון
דהם כתבו אדרבה רמ"י מוז דהם
בקיאים משא"כ שם לא שייך זה, יע'
ב"ב דף ל"ג ע"א ע"ש ע"ש בתום' גבי
כולהו ואכמ"ל.
יוסף ראזין רב דפה הנ"ל

אם ירצה לשאול ימחול לשלוח מכתב
כפול כדת. הנ"ל.

Sefer Tzafnas Paneach by Rav Yosef Rosen, the Rogatchover Gaon;
responsa to R' Chaim Yitzchok Wolgelernter, 1928

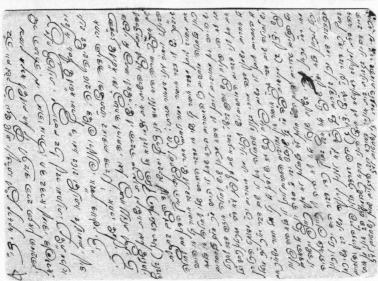

Postcard containing the corresponding Talmudical queries sent by Chaim Yitzchok
Wolgelernter to the Rogatchover Gaon in 1928. Great-grandson Sruli (Yisroel
Mordechai) Wolgelernter's interest in family history led to his discovery of the
existence of this postcard in the Yeshiva University library.
Credit: Mendel Gottesman Library, Yeshiva University, Ms. 1142

המון דלבת שכתבו תוס׳. ודוקא בקטנה מאורסה אבל בקטנה נשואה הרי אינה נפסדת כלום שגם תוספת כבר יש לה כי אנוסה היא. וכאמור. ותו ל"מ. וזה כפתור ופרח אלא שחסר ביאור בדברי המהרש"א ז"ל שסתם הרבה כפי"ז כמובן ומ"מ יש מקום לדבריו. וידוע שדבריו עמוקים בכל מקום וסומך על המעיין ומבין:

סימן סו.

להתלמיד הותיק. די באורייתא עסיק, חו"ב מתון ומסיק. שקיל וטרי תני ופסיק, חדת מלא עתיק. כר חיים יצחק וואלגילערענטער נ"י. יושב בשבת תחכמוני בישיבת קראקא יע"א:

א) מה שתמה על הריטב"א מכות שכתב דלקרבן עונשין מן הדין מהתוספתא דפ"ג דשבועות וז"ל שמע מפי אחרים מפי עצמו מנין ת"ל כי תחטא לרבות את השומע מפי עצמו כשומע מפי אחרים דברי ר"ש ריבב"א א"צ ק"ו ומה אם נדרים שאמפי"א חייבין עליהם מפי עצמן שבועה שחייב עליה מפי"א א׳ד שחייב מפיע"צ. א"ר נחמי לפני ריב"ב וכי עונשין מה"ד עכ"ל. יפה העיר:

והנה אני כעת מחוס"פ בעוה"ר מזמן השרפה ויש לעיין בכנה"ג (ובכללי הי"ג מדות מבעל כנה"ג שנדפסו בסוף מס׳ ברכות בכללי הק"ו מביא דברי הריטב"א ז"ל הנ"ל). ואפשר בספר כנה"ג העיר בזה. וכן יש לעיין במלהר"ע. וגם בכללי הגמ׳ למהריק"א ז"ל שבהליכות עולם וביבין שמועה. ובשד"ח במערכת ע׳ בזה וכל אלה אין בידי. והנלענ"ד לפום ריהטא בזה דסברת הריטב"א ז"ל דקרבן שהוא משום כפרה בשוגג ולא משום עונש לא שייך אין עונשין מן הדין. אבל קרבן שבועת העדות שמביא גם על המזיד. ונהי דגם על השוגג חייב ובלבד שידע שאסור. אבל שוגג גמור פטור. ע׳ שבועות (ל׳.) א"כ אין זה קרבן של כפרה. דהא אין קרבן מכפר על מזיד אלא עונש. ע"כ שפיר אין עונשין מה"ד. וע׳ רמב"ם רפי"ב מה׳ שבועות דאין מתכפר לו ענין השבועה בקרבן. ודו"ק. ונכון בס"ד:

ב) מה שהביא מספר פענח רזא שכתב בהא דאם ל"י אסון ענוש יענש דמי ולדות ודילמא נפל הוא ותי׳ דאזלינן ב"ר. והקשה מר דהא א"ה בממון אחר הרוב. עכ"ד. הנה הא ל"ק לי. רק בהיפך. דמה זו קושיא שמא נפל מ"מ התורה חייבה לשלם מה שהזיק ואומדין את האשה כמה היא שוה עם הולדות היינו שיקח איש אותה על הספק שכשתלד יהיו הולדות שלו. ע׳ סמ"ע סי׳ תכ"ג. וע׳ ב"ק (מ"ט.) וכיון שאדם קונה. ומשלם על הספק. הרי הזיק כך לבעל הולדות. וכמו שחייבין עדים זוממין לשלם מה שרצו להפסיד לבעל זכות הכתובה או לאשה. ע׳ מכות פ"ק דפליגי אם שמין באיש או באשה וברש"י ותוס׳ שם. ואיך שיהא כשהעידו שנתגרשה ולא שילם לה בעל הכתובה והוזמו למה ישלמו והרי הוי רק ספק שמא תמות ולא תבא לידי גביית כתובה לעולם או שמא ימות ויתחייב כל הכתובה. ומ"מ משלם כזה או כזה. משום דאומדין כמה אדם רוצה ליתן בכך על הספק. ודו"ק. וא"כ מה הקשה הפענח רזא. אכן י"ל דמ"מ לולי דרוב ולדות ב"ק לא היתה תורה מחייבת אעפ"י שיש בזה שיווי שאדם קונה כך. ודו"ק:

וע׳ רמב"ן עה"ת פסוק כאשר ישית עליו שפי׳ דר"ל אעפ"י שאין בולדות הללו דין תשלומי ממון כי מי יודע אם יצליחו אעפי"כ נשים עליו עונש והוא כמו קנס כר׳ עכ"ד ע"ש. ואין ר"ל שהוא קנס ולא שיווי ממון כמו שלשים שקלים דעבד אעפ"י שאינו שוה כלום וכיר"ב קנס קצוב כמאה סלע של מוצש"ר שאין חילוק בין גדולה שבכהונה למחותה שבישראל. שהרי שמין אותה כמה היא שוה ואינו קנס קצוב. אלא ר"ל שהתורה קנסה אעפ"י שאפשר לא יהיו בני קיימא. ואין זה בשום דאזלי׳ בתר רוב ולדות שהן בני קיימא.

8 10

שהרי באמת אפי׳ בקים לן שכלו חדשיו דאז בבן יום א׳ כלומר שיצא לאויר העולם נהרגין עליו ע׳ נדה מ"ד. מ"מ בעודו במעי אמו לאו נפש מקרי ואין נהרגין עליו אעפ"י דרוב ולדות ב"ק וגם ידוע שכלו חדשיו וע׳ בר"ן יומא (דף רכ"ד:) בשם רמב"ן ז"ל. ובסדרי טהרות על אהלות (דף קי"ז:) בשם הרמ"ה ז"ל ובסמ"ע סי׳ תכ"ה סק"ח. דמדמשלם דמי ולדות ש"מ שאין נהרגין עליו דאל"כ קלב"מ. וע׳ נוב"ת חו"מ סי׳ נ"ט בזה. וכ"ש דלא משו"ה משלם ד"ו אפי׳ בלא ידוע שכל"ת. אלא כדאמרן דהתורה חייבה משום שהזיק שהרי נמכרת בשוק עם הולדות ביותר ממה שנמכרת בלא ולדות. וכדאמרן. ומ"מ ס"ל להפענ"ר דאם היו בחזקת נפלים לא היתה תורה מחייבת. כי גם זה שנמכרת בשוק בשיווי בעבור הולדות היא ג"כ משום דרוב ולדות ב"ק וע"כ קונים כך בנ"א על הספק הקרוב להיות ודאי. ודו"ק. ואפ"ל עוד כיון דהוי רוב מעליא אזלינן בתריה גם לממון ע׳ תוס׳ סנהדרין (ג׳:) ד"ה ד"מ. אך ע׳ בנחלת צבי יו"ד סי׳ ש"ה סכ"ג דלפי דבריו שם יהא מוכח דרוב ולדות ב"ק אינו רוב מעליא דא"כ יהא עדיף גם מכ׳ החזקות ע"ש ודו"ק. עוי"ל כיון דרוב זה מהני לשאר דברים גם לממון מהני כמ"ש בהפלאה כתובות ובמנ"ח סוף מצוה מ"ט דהא בלא"ה מנ"ל דאביו הוא לשלם לו דמי ולדות ואי משום רוב בעילות אחהב"ע הרי אהבמאחה"ר. וכתב כן משם ההפלאה ושאר אחרונים כיון דהוחזק הרוב לשאר ענינים גם בממון הולכין אחריו. ואין להאריך יותר:

סימן סז.

בעה"י ג׳ לך תרפ"ט לאקאטש.

לכבוד התלמיד ותיק בישיבת מור. מר ישראל צבי האלפערין נ"י:

א) אשר שאל לפימ"ש תוס׳ סנהדרין (ע"ג:) ד"ה במפותה לחד תי׳ דמפותה שאומרת בפירוש שאינה מוחלת יש לה קנס ע"ש. א"כ מאי פריך ש"ס בכתובות (מ"ב.) לאביה נמי פשיטא מדיהיב מפתה. והא משכח"ל באומרת שאינה מוחלת עכ"ד. ויפה דיקדק:

ונלע"ד לתרץ. דאקרא פריך ש"ס דהא קים לתז"ל ואנן סהדי דמפותה מוחלת. ורק שאם אינה רוצה לינשא לו אז אפשר אינה מוחלת וכשאומרת שאינה מוחלת היינו שאינה מתרצית לינשא לו, שהרי אם מהר ימהרנה לו לאשה ליכא קנסא. וא"כ קרא דכסף ישקל אם מאן ימאן אביה לתתה לו לא מיירי בזה שבפירוש אינה מוחלת דא"כ היינו שא"ר לינשא לו דאם אינה מוחה הרי מהר ימהרנה כתיב וליכא קנס אע"כ דקרא מיירי בסתם וסתם מפותה מוחלת ואפ"ה אם מאן ימאן אביה לתתה לו כסף ישקול. וכ"ת דנוקי לקרא כשאמרה בפירוש בתנאי זה שאם יעכב אביה אינה מוחלת ונאמר שבקיה לקרא דדחיק ומוקי אנפשיה (פסחים נ"ט; ובכמ"ד) י"א דמסברא אם היא והוא אין מעכבין א"כ מצדה אנן סהדי דמוחלת. ולא כל כמיניה דאב לחייבו באם העכבה מצדו. אע"כ דהקנס בעצם לא לה רק לאביה. ודו"ק:

ב) מה שהקשה בתוס׳ יבמות פ"ק. שכתבו דהא דילפינן מכלאים בציצית דעדל"ת ולא פרכינן מה לכלאים שכן הותרו מכללן בבגדי כהונה. דלאו מטעם הותרו אלא דעשה דבג"כ דחי הל"ת. עכ"ד. א"כ בכתובות (ל"ב.) דקאמר ואי ממונא לקולא מה לחובל בחברו שכן הותר מכללו בב"ד. מאי פריך נימא דלא הותר רק שנדחה מפני העשה דעונש ב"ד עכ"ד:

לק"מ. דהכא ביבמות שפיר כתבו תוס׳ דליכא למיפרך הכי דנימא דלא הותרו כלאים רק עדל"ת והרי זהו מה שרצינו ללמוד דעדל"ת. אבל התם נהי דלא הותר רק עדל"ת מ"מ הוי שפיר פירכא מה לחובל שכן הותר עכ"פ ע״י

Sefer Meishiv Shalom by Rav Shalom Yosef Feigenbaum, Rav of Lokacze; responsum to Chaim Yitzchok Wolgelernter, 1928

Cover of spring 1938 issue of the Torah journal *Habe'er*

ד"ה ד"ח צדיקים עצמן לא כש"כ ומכל
זה נראה לפענ"ד דצריך לקדש פ"ש
ע"כ :
ישעי' פלאמן רב אבדפה"ק
הנ"ל.

סימן יח.

ב"ה דזיאלאשיק.

בפסחים ס"ג במתני' השוחט את הפסח
על החמץ עובר בלא תעשה
וכו' ר"ש אומר השוחט בי"ד וכו' חייב,
ודקדקו המפר'. למה נקט התק"ק עובר בלא
תעשי ור"ש נקט חייב דמשמע מחייב מלקות ונ"ל
דהנה השאא"א הק' האיך אפשר לחייב מלקות
על שחיטת פסח על החמץ דילמא ביטל
החמץ, ותי' המפור' דמשכחת בקנה חמץ
לאחר זמן איסורו דלא מהני ביטול, ואפי'
לר"ש דסובר דחמץ לפני זמנו אינו עובר
בלא כלום אפי"ה איכא עשה דתשביתו עי'
בתוס' פסחים כ"ח, והנה הרי"ן בע"ז פ' כל
הצלמים בסוגיא דהמוצא כלים כ' דהא
דמהני קנין בחמץ בפסח, וכן הא דישראל
מצי לקנות ע"ז של נכרי אע"ג דאין זכי'
לאיסורי הנאה, משום דקודם שזכה הישראל
החמץ מהנכרי שקנה ממנו וכן ע"ז הי'
להם היתר לאחר זמן דחמץ של נכרי לאחר
הפסח מותר וכן ע"ז של נכרי מועיל בימול
עיי"ש בר"ן, ולפי"ז לא מהני קנין בחמץ
בפסח רק לר"ש דסובר דחמץ של נכרי
לאחר הפסח מותר לגמרי, וממילא מיושב
שפיר קושיית המפור' הנ"ל דדוקא לר"ש
חייב מלקות בשוחט פסח על החמץ כשקנה
החמץ מהנכרי לאחר זמן איסורו דלא
מהני ביטול ולכן נקט ר"ש חייב ודו"ק :
בזבחים ב' דרמי רבא וכו' תנן כל
הזבחים שנזבחו שלא לשמן
וכו' הא סתמא עלו לבעלים ורמינהו נמי
פסול וכו' וסתמא בזבחים כשר מנלן

סימן יט.

בעזה"ית ראוויא מאז.

בנימין נ"ה אמר עולא דבר תורה בין
נודע בין לא נודע אינה מכפרת
ולמה אמרו לא נודע מכפרת שלא יהיו
כהנים עצבים ופירש"י שלא יהיו כהנים
עצבים שאכלו חולין שנשחטו בעזרה ופירושו
מוכרח מדברי הגמרא שם ע"ב בשלמא
לעולא היינו דקתני חטאת משום דאיכא
אכילת כהנים עיי"ש והק' המפרשים למה
וקא עצבים משום אכילת חולין בעזרה ולא

אולימא וכו' בגט נמי נימא דסתמא כשר
דלא כתיב שלא נכתב לשם אשה פסול
דמשמע דסתמא פסול ומשני אלא מהכא
עיי"ש וקשה לי לפי התוס' עירובין י"ג
ע"א ד"ה אבל שהקשו שם אהא דמגילת
סוטה מוחקין מה"ת אע"ג דסוטה בעי
כתיבה לשמה וספר תורה הוי נכתבה סתמא,
מהא דגבי גט גם כה"ג פסול. ותי' שם
בתו' דגבי גט פסול מדרבנן וגבי סוטה
לא שייך לפסול מדרבנן עיי"ש, והאחרונים
הסבירו דבדרבנן ל"ש פסול דהוי רק איסור
גרידא ול"ש פסול בעצם, ולפ"ז מאי מדחי
הגמ' דבגט ג"כ סתמא כשר דלא כתיב
שלא נכתב לשם אשה פסול, דו"א דנ"ל
דגם בגט פסול סתמא והא דלא כתיב שלא
נכתב לשם אשה פסול דלא מצי למיכתב
כך דמשמע דבעצם פסול וזה אינו פסול
רק מדרבנן, ונ"ל דרבא לשיטתו דס"ל
בסוטה י"ז ע"ב דמגילת .סוטה שנכתבה
בלילה פסולה, א"כ מגילת סוטה אסור
למחוק מה"ת דשמא נכתבה בלילה והוא
ס"ל ספיקא דאורייתא לחומרא (עי' שב
שמעתתא) וא"כ י"ל דגם סתמא בגט פסול
מדאו' דהא השתא ל"ק קו' התוס' עירובין דסוטה
ושפיר מדחה הגמ' דהו"ל שלא נכתב לשם
אשה פסול דמשמע דגם סתמא פסול
ודו"ק :

חיים יצחק וואהלגעלערנטער.

Halachic discourse contributed by Chaim Yitzchok Wolgelernter, *Habe'er*, 1938

עש"ו   עמ"י

חודש כסלו-טבת   שנת תרצ"ו

קובץ תלמודי־פלפולי

בית־מאיר

בו יתועדו חידושים וביאורים מגאוני וחכמי זמננו שליט"א
ומגאוני קדמאי זצ"ל, ונלוה אליו מדור מיוחד לתלמידי
כ"ק מרן אדמו"ר, שליט"א מאסטרובצה ובעד שאר בחורי
חמד הי"ו.

———❦———

העורך והמסדר

חיים יצחק וואהלגעלערנטער

בהרר"י שליט"א מקזימירזה-גדולה,

תלמיד כ"ק מרן אדמו"ר שליט"א

עומד תחת בקורת של

הרב ר' משה אהרן רויך שליט"א מווייסלייך.

○ ○ ○

חוברת ג'   מחירו

פיעטרקוב, בדפוס ר' חנוך העניך נ"י בהרה"ג ר' ישעי' זאב זצ"ל פאלמאן.

„Bajs Majer" Komentarze na Talmud, Ostrowiec-Kielecki w Styczniu 1936,
Red. odp.' i wyd. CH. I. Wolgelernter Ostrowiec-Kiel.

Kislev-Teves 1936 edition of the *Beis Meir* Torah journal
edited by Chaim Yitzchok Wolgelernter

כ. בית   סימן יד   מאיר

סימן יד

ב"ה קזימירזה–גדולה.

בחולין י"א בהא דיליף כנמ' דאולין בתר רוב מפסח דכתיב ועלס לא תשברו. בו ולולמא ניקב קרוס של מוח, אלא לאו משום דאולין בתר רובא, ודחי דלמא בדיק לי' ע"י נומרתא דהשורף בעצמות אין בו משום שבירם עלס, ונודע, קו' הנרשמ"א ז"ל מהא דמבואר בפסחים פ"ד ע"ב דע"י נומרתא נמי אסור משום דהוי הפסד קדשים ולא שלא ישרוף מטע מהמוות פיי"ג, וני"ל דהנה כנאלין בעל כלי חמדה בט' פ' בא מביא בשם מ' מוהריים להנאון מבריסק וז"ל לה' אהא דהקן כנרט"א האיך יליף כנמ' מפסח דאולין בתר רוב, והרי אמירה לעכו"ם מהא ויש עלס לשבור העלס ע"י עכו"ס ולבדוק הקרוס, ותי' דהנה הרא" הוא מפסח מאריס ובפסח מאריס כתב הפני' פ' בא דהי' לכם דין בן נח, וב"צ לב"צ יש שליחות אפי' לדבר עבירה כמבואר בתמני מצאת במינן הונא בש"ך ק' שלוחין, ושפיר אשכ

...

לשבור עלס אפי' ע"י עכו"ס, ושפיר מוכח מכאן דאולין בתר רובא עי"ם, והנה בחמי'ם איורי"ד סי' רל"ח מבואר דפסח מאריס לא הוי שום קרבן רק כוי הולין דלא הי' כזריקה לשם קרבן רק לאות וכן לא הי' הקטרת חלבים והמלבים אבלו כמו שאר בשר, ומס"פ הי' מותר ליקח עלס מן המלריים ולעשות מהן פסח, והרי המלריים עכבו לנאון ונעבד אסור לנבוס אפילו לאחר שנ'טולו, וע"כ דלא הוי כלל קרבן נבוס עי"ם, ולפי"ז מיושב לנכון קו' הנרשמ"א הנ"ל דהי' אסור ע"י נומרתא דהוי הפסד קדשים, כיון דכל הרהי הא מפסח מלריס דלא הי' אסור לשבור העלס ע"י עכו"ס כנ"ל שפיר רמי כנמ' דאפשר ע"י נומרתא דלא הוי כזה הפסד קדשים. כיון דלאז לי"ה כפסם שום קרבן לנבוס רק הולין לנד ליכא שום איסור ודוק.

חיים יצחק וואהלגעלערנטער.

סימן טו

ב"ה אסטראוורצא.

בסוכה דלי"ו דלאמרוג של תרומה לא יטול מפני שמפסידו [ופירש"י דהמשמוט היד ממאסון] ועי' בזרע אברהם דהקן מהא דהלוקח לולב מחבירו בשביעית וכו' הרי מפו' דמותר ליטול אתברוג מפירות שביעית, והלא גס פירות שביעית אסור להפסיד דכ' לאכלה ולא להפסד וני"ל דהא דאסור להפסיד תרומה כוח משום דכ' משמרת תרומתי ע"י ברמ"י סוכה שם, וכיון דלא כ' כהו אכילה סוי האיסור אפי' בכ"ש, עי' בי"ל חו"ם ה' נט"י, אבל בפירות שביעית דאיסור הפסד כוח מהקרא דלאכלה הוי האיסור רק בכזית דאכילה בכזית, והנה כא דמפסי' ע"י משמוט היד הקליפה במקום שנגע ודאי אין בו כזית דיכול לקלוף קלוסת דקה שלא יהי' כזית, וממי' מיושב קו' הנ"ל, דדוקא בתרומה דאסור בכ"ש דלי' אכילה אסור ליטול אבל בשביעית מותר וכן.

אלעזר הלוי בלכ"ק אאמו"ר מרן שליט"א.

סימן טז

ב"ה שעננא.

בחולין י"ז אמרי בשר נחירה שהכניסו ישראל וכו' תיקו, ובירושלמי פ"ב דעגלה מבואר דבמשה בכנכנסו ישראל לארץ אפי' חטים פנטלי' נאסרו, וויק' נאמאי נבי חרם פשיטא לי' לביררשלמי שנאסרו, וכנמ' כוח איבעי' דלא ליפשטא נבי אברי בשר נחירה, וני"ל עפי"מ שהק' ני' ישועוה מלכו פ"ג ב"ב מהל' קים בלאכרי שחיטה הוי לי' להנמ' נאיבעי' כיון דמקולין הי' מותר בשר מחירה לא מקרי בר זביחה כמו שחיטה עכו"ס, ועפי' כיון דנגילה הי' אסור במרבך רק נחירה אמרי' מחירין זו שחיטהן ומקרי בר זביחה, עכ"ס, וממי' מיושב קושיית רנני חרס כואיל ונמחרש המלוה שפיר מבואר בירושלמי דאסור. אבל לפני' בשר מחירה דהי

ר' כת מז"ט

אנו מברכים לידידנו הנעל...ה, הב' ה...'ב ומוסמך להוראה, איש האשכולות מר חיים
יצחק וואהלגעלערנטער נ"י עורך ירחוננו "בית־מאיר" לנשואיו, ולאביו ידידינו
הרב החסיד מוה"ר ישעי' שליט"א שקיימי'ה זה־גדולה, אנו מברכים שיזכה לראות אצלו,
ואצל כל יוצאי חלציו יחי' רוב טוב ואושר.
המערכת.

ב"ה

לרעי אהובי חיים יצחק נ"י לנשואיו,

ברכת מז"ט שלוחה,

תאיר לך ההצלחה את פני,

רעך יחיאל ברוך אלטמאן,

חתן הגאון אבד"ק גאסטנין זצ"ל.

אסטרובצה.

ב"ה

ברכת מז"ט וגדא טבא לכבוד ידידי אהובי
הב' החריף, מושלם במעלות ובמדות
תרומיות, סופר מהיר מר חיים יצחק
וואהלגעלערנטער יחי', עורך ירחוננו
"בית־מאיר".

יהא צעדך זה בחיים מעותר בהצלחה.

ידידך הנאמן
משה אהרן רויך.

ווייסליץ.

ב"ה

לכלילת אפריונו של אהוביגו החביב מר
חיים יצחק יחי', ברכותיגו החמות, ואחולינו
הלבביים, הנודפים מעמקי רגשותינו, אליו
שלוחים, עלה על מרום מסגת התורה־וגדולה,
האחים שמואל ויהודא סילמאן
בני הגאון אבד"ק גאסטנין זצ"ל
נכדי כ"ק מרן רשבכה"ג זצלה"ה.
אסטרובצה.

ב"ה

הנני מביע מעומק לבי ברכת מז"ט חמה
ונלבבה לכבוד ידי"נ הב' החתן החו"ב
בחדר"ת, מושלם במעלות ומדות טובות, וכו'
כש"ת חיים יצחק וואהלגעלערנטער
שליט"א, עורך ירחוננו "בית־מאיר".

ידידך
יעקב יוסף גרייטס.

קראקא.

ב"ה

ידידי חיים יצחק נ"י קבל נא
גם ממני ברכת גדא טבא לשמחתך,
תורה וגדולה תהיינה צמודות
אצלך, והגריך ירוו נחת ממך,
דובעריל לייבושעוויטש,
סליפיא־חדשה.

ב"ה

ג"א מברך לידידי יקירי החתן המופלא והמושלם, מפורסם
לשבח לתהלה, מר חיים יצחק יחי', ברכת מלא וגדא
טבא ליום בואו בברית הנשואין, יה"ר שצעדך בחיים
יהא מלווה בעושר ואושר, ולשני שלחנות תזכה כל ימיך.
ידידך המסור לך בלו"נ אהרן ראפאפורט.
אסטרובצה.

ברכת מז"ט לידידנו החסיד, הרב התו"ב
בחדר"ת, צמ"ס מוה"ר יעקב שארפזאהן
נ"י משידלדאוצא לאירוסי בנו התו"ב מר
אלימלך שיחי', יזכה לראות אצלו רוב ענג.
המערכת.

Wedding wishes to Chaim Yitzchok Wolgelernter, *Beis Meir*, Adar 1936

Glossary

G = German; P = Polish

A"h – acronym for *alav/aleha hashalom*, peace be unto him/her, said in reference to a deceased person

Achtung (G) – attention

Admor – title referring to a chassidic rebbe

Afikoman – portion of matzah eaten after the Seder meal on Pesach; some have a custom of keeping a leftover piece all year as a protective omen

Aggadah – homiletic passages or narratives in the Talmud or Midrash

Agunah – a woman who cannot remarry according to Jewish law due to lack of a valid divorce or certain knowledge of her husband's death

Ahavas Yisrael – love of a fellow Jew

Akeidah – binding; usually referring to *Akeidas Yitzchak*, when G-d commanded Avraham to sacrifice his son Yitzchak

Al kiddush Hashem – for the sanctification of G-d's Name

Aliyah – lit., going up, ascent; referring to immigration to the Land of Israel

Aron hakodesh – the ark that holds the Torah scrolls in the synagogue

Atarah – the silver adornment on a *tallis*

Avel – mourner adhering to specific laws of *aveilus* for a halachically prescribed period

Avodah – lit., work; referring to serving G-d, especially through prayer or sacrificial offerings; also referring to the main service of the *kohen gadol* on Yom Kippur

Avodas Hashem – service of G-d

Baal bitachon – one who trusts implicitly in G-d

Baal darshan – a lecturer

Baal Mussaf – one who leads the Mussaf prayer service

Baal tefillah – one who leads the prayer services

Babbeshe – Grandma

Bachur (pl. bachurim) – unmarried young man; usually referring to a yeshivah student

Baruch Dayan ha'emes – blessed is the true Judge; blessing recited upon hearing bad news

Baruch Hashem – Thank G-d

Bein hametzarim – the three-week period between Shivah Asar B'Tammuz and Tishah B'Av

Bein hazmanim – intersession; break between semesters in a yeshivah

Beis din – rabbinical court

Beis medrash – Torah-study hall, often attached to or serving as a synagogue

Beis olam – cemetery

Bekeshe – long coat of satin or silk, worn by chassidim

Ben bayis – lit., household member; referring to a person, often a friend or student, who is a regular visitor in one's home

Ben Torah (pl. bnei Torah) – referring to one who devotes himself to Torah study and observance

Bimah – platform; a reference to the table on which the Torah is read

Bitachon – trust; referring to trust in Hashem

Brachah (pl. brachos) – blessing

Bris – lit., covenant; referring to a bris milah, ritual circumcision

Chaburah – group, especially a group learning together

Chalat – an informal, lightweight robe worn by chassidim

Chalilah – G-d forbid

Chametz – leavened food, such as bread, prohibited on Passover

Chassan – bridegroom

Chatzos – halachic midday or midnight

Chavrusa – study partner

Chazzan – cantor; leader of synagogue prayer

Cheder – lit., room; traditional Jewish school for young boys

Chessed – loving-kindness

Chevlei Mashiach – birth pangs of Mashiach, referring to the suffering preceding the arrival of the Redemption

Chevra kaddisha – Jewish burial society

Chiddush (pl. chiddushim) – innovation or novel interpretation in Torah study

Chumash (pl. Chumashim) – volume of the Pentateuch

Chuppah – marriage canopy

Churban – destruction; term used for the Destruction of the Temple and now also used to refer to the Holocaust [Churban Europa]

Daven – pray

Davening – *v.* praying; *n.* prayer service

Derech – path, approach

Derech halimud – an approach to Torah learning; method of study

Din v'cheshbon – final reckoning

Drashah (pl. drashos) – Torah lecture

Dvar Torah (pl. divrei Torah) – Torah lesson or commentary

Ehrlich – devout

Eichah – Book of Lamentations by the prophet Yirmiyahu mourning the destruction of the Holy Temple; recited on Tishah B'Av

Eileh Ezkerah – prayer on Yom Kippur recalling the Ten Martyrs

Emunah – belief in G-d

Fluden – Eastern European pastry made of layers of dough with a jam-based filling

Frum – religious

Fuehrer – leader, most commonly referring to Adolf Hitler

Gabbai – one who assists a rebbe or conducts the proceedings in the synagogue

Gadol (pl. gedolim) – great man; outstanding Torah scholar; leader

Galus – exile

Gaon – brilliant Torah scholar; genius

Gartel – sash used by chassidim predominantly during prayer

Gemilus chessed – acts of loving-kindness

Gut yahr – greeting wishing one a "good year"

Haftorah – portion of the Prophets that is read after the Torah reading

Hakafos – ceremony in which the congregants circle the *bimah* while carrying the Torah scrolls, marking the completion on Simchas Torah of the weekly Torah readings

Hashem Yisbarach – G-d, may His Name be blessed

Hashgachah pratis – Divine providence

Heilig – holy

Hesped – eulogy

Hester panim – a time in which G-d hides His face, as it were, making it difficult for man to see His active involvement in natural events

Heter horaah – Rabbinical ordination

Hoshanos – supplications said on the seventh day of Sukkos

Hy"d – acronym for *Hashem yinkom damo/damah*; may G-d avenge his/her blood

Iber yahr – leap year, when an extra month of Adar is added

Im yirtzeh Hashem – G-d willing

Juden (G) – Jews

Judenfrage (G) – the Jewish Question

Judenrein (G) – free of Jews

Judenstädt(e) (G) – Jewish state(s)

Kabbalah – certification allowing one to become a *shochet*

Kadosh – *adj.* holy; *n.* holy man

Kapparah – atonement

Kareis – lit., cutting off; referring to Divine punishment by premature death

Kavod hameis – respect for the dead

Kedoshim – holy ones; referring to those who died as Jewish martyrs

Kedushah – holiness

Kehillah (pl. kehillos) – the elected local communal Jewish structure in Central and Eastern Europe; congregation; community

Kever (pl. kevarim) – grave

Kever achim – lit., grave of brothers; communal grave

Kever Yisrael – Jewish burial

Kichlech – cookies or crackers

Kiddush Hashem – sanctification of G-d's Name

Kiddush Levanah – the blessing recited for the waxing moon

Kinah (pl. kinos) – lamentation

Kinderlech – children

Kisei Hakavod – the Throne of G-d

Kittel – white robe which serves as a burial shroud for male Jews, also worn on Yom Kippur and at the Seder on Pesach eve

Klei shareis – tools of service; holy vessels used in the Beis Hamikdash

Klezmer – musical tradition of the Ashkenazi Jews of Eastern Europe

Kohen gadol – high priest in Judaism

Kol Nidrei – solemn prayer recited at the commencement of Yom Kippur

Korban (pl. korbanos) – sacrifice or offering

Korban Chatas – a sin offering

Kriah – the rending of a garment by a mourner

Kvitlech – notes with a petition or request given to a holy person or placed at a holy site

Lapanka (P) – a roundup of civilians for slave labor

Levayah – funeral

Lieber Bashefer – beloved G-d

Luchos – the tablets of stone which Moshe Rabbeinu brought from Mt. Sinai, on which were etched the Ten Commandments

Macher – busybody

Malach (pl. malachim) – angel

Malach Hamaves – the Angel of Death

Mamme lashon – mother tongue

Mamusia / Mammeshe – Polish-Yiddish for Mother

Maskil (pl. maskilim) – adherent of the Haskalah (Jewish "Enlightenment") movement

Mechutan – parent of one's in-law children

Mefarshim – commentaries; commentators

GLOSSARY

Megillah (pl. Megillos) – scroll; referring to the parchment *Scroll of Esther*

Melamed – teacher of young boys

Melaveh malkah – lit., escorting the queen; referring to the meal on Motza'ei Shabbos

Meshulach (pl. meshulachim) – fundraiser

Mezuzah (pl. mezuzos) – parchment scroll affixed to the doorpost of a Jewish home

Middah (pl. middos) – character trait

Mikveh – ritual bath

Minhag – custom

Minyan – quorum of ten men required for communal prayer

Mispallelim – congregants in prayer

Mohel – one who performs a ritual circumcision

Motza'ei Shabbos – the end of Shabbos; Saturday night

Mussar – rebuke

Nachas – pleasure, pride, especially in one's children

Navi – prophet

Ne'ilah – the last prayer on Yom Kippur

Neshamah (pl. neshamos) – soul

Niggun – tune

Nisayon – a test or trial in life

Nishmas – prayer of praise in the Shacharis service on Shabbos and Yom Tov

Nussach – style and melody of prayer service

Ohel – lit., tent; referring to the structure over a grave or burial place

Parnassah – livelihood

Paroches – the curtain that covers the ark in the synagogue

Parshah – weekly Torah portion

Peyos – sidelocks

Pikuach nefesh – preservation of human life; principle in Jewish law which mandates overriding Torah commandments (with specific exceptions) in life-threatening situations

Pilpul – method of studying the Talmud through intense textual analysis

Pirchei kehunah – young *kohanim*

Piyut (pl. piyutim) – liturgical poem sung or intoned during the prayer service

Poritz – landowner; nobleman

Rabbanim – rabbis

Rabbanus – rabbinate

Rabbeinu – lit., our rabbi; honorific title for a great *rav* or chassidic rebbe

Rav – rabbi or mentor

Rebbetzin – wife of a rabbi

Rebbi – Torah teacher

Rei'ach nicho'ach – pleasing aroma; usually associated with G-d's acceptance of an animal sacrifice

Retzuos – straps of phylacteries

Ribono shel Olam — lit., Master of the Universe; G-d

Rosh yeshivah (pl. roshei yeshivah) — dean of a yeshivah

Sandek — one who holds the baby during a circumcision ceremony

Seder — tractate

Sefer (pl. sefarim) — Jewish book

Sefer Torah — Torah scroll

Selichos — penitential poems and prayers, especially those said in the period leading up to the High Holidays

Seudah — meal, especially one that is festive

Shabbos Nachamu — lit., Shabbos of comfort; referring to the Shabbos after Tishah B'Av

Shadchan — matchmaker

Shamash — sexton of the synagogue

Shas — an acronym for *"shishah sidrei"* — referring to the six sections of the Talmud

Shechinah — the Divine Presence

Shechitah — ritual slaughter

Shecht — *v.* slaughter

Shehecheyanu — lit., "Who has given us life"; blessing of thanks

Sheitel — wig

Shemoneh Esrei — silent prayer recited in the morning, afternoon and evening services

Shidduch (pl. shidduchim) — marital match

Shiur (pl. shiurim) — Torah class

Shivah — the seven-day Jewish mourning period

Shlag kapparos — performing the traditional ritual before Yom Kippur in which one circles a chicken over his head

Shliach tzibbur — lit., emissary of the congregation; one who leads the prayer services

Shochet — traditional ritual slaughterer

Shtetl — small town with a significant Jewish population

Shtiebel (pl. shtieblech) — lit., little house or little room; small informal synagogue or place of communal prayer

Shtreimel — fur hat worn by chassidim

Shvitz — traditional Eastern European steam bath

Simchah — joy; joyous occasion

Sitra Achra — lit., the other side; a Kabbalistic reference to the force of impurity in the world

Siyum — lit., completion; referring to the completion of a major section of Torah learning

Skrytka (P) — concealed place, often a pit dug under a stable as a makeshift bunker

Sofer — scribe

Taharah — 1. preparing the body for its final rest; one of the most important elements of a proper Jewish burial, 2. purity

Taharas Yisrael — laws of ritual purity

Tallis (pl. talleisim) — prayer shawl

Talmid (pl. talmidim) – student or disciple

Talmid chacham – Torah scholar

Tattenyu – affectionate form of Tatte, Father

Tatteshe – Polish-Yiddish for Father

Techinos – supplications traditionally recited by Jewish women

Tefillah (pl. tefillos) – prayer

Tefillin – phylacteries which Jewish men don each morning during prayers

Tekiah (pl. tekios) – shofar blast

Teshuvah – repentance

Tikkun – spiritual rectification process

Tish – lit., table; gathering of chassidim by their rebbe

Tish chalat – a robe worn by chassidim at the Shabbos table

Tosafos – medieval commentaries on the Talmud

Treif – non-kosher; in the case of kosher mammals, this refers to lesions around the lungs or injury discovered after the slaughter, which renders the animal unkosher

Tumah – impurity

Tzaddekes – a righteous woman

Tzaraas – a skin disease commonly referred to as leprosy

Tzarah (pl. tzaros) – tragedy

Tzedakah – charity

Tzitzis – fringes worn on four-cornered garments by Jewish males

Verfluchte Juden (G) – cursed Jews

Yamim Nora'im – High Holy Days

Yerei Shamayim – one who fears G-d

Yeshuah – salvation

Yidden – Jews

Yiras Shamayim – lit., fear of heaven; fear of G-d

Yizkor – a special memorial prayer for the departed

Z"l – acronym for *zichrono livrachah*; may his memory be for a blessing

Zechus (pl. zechusim) – merit or privilege

Zeide – Grandfather

Zohar – the foundational work in the literature of Jewish mystical thought known as Kabbalah

Zt"l – acronym for *zecher tzaddik livrachah*; may the memory of the tzaddik be for a blessing

Zyd (P) – Jew

Index of Names

Names of family members listed on p. 68–69 and their immediate relatives have not been included in the Index.

Page numbers in *italics* indicate photos.

Index of Places

Page numbers in *italics* indicate photos.